A volume of a series in religion, edited by LUTHER A. WEIGLE, DEAN EMERITUS OF THE YALE UNIVERSITY DIVINITY SCHOOL, *and* CLARENCE P. SHEDD, STEPHEN MERRELL CLEMENT PROFESSOR OF CHRISTIAN METHODS, YALE UNIVERSITY DIVINITY SCHOOL

WAYS OF FAITH

An Introduction to Religion

By

JOHN A. HUTCHISON

Cluett Professor of Religion
Williams College

JAMES ALFRED MARTIN, Jr.

Professor of Religion
Amherst College

THE RONALD PRESS COMPANY • NEW YORK

Library of Congress Catalog Card Number: 53–5707
PRINTED IN THE UNITED STATES OF AMERICA

PREFACE

IN the past few decades there has been a steadily increasing interest in religion among thoughtful people. Academic attention is reflected by expanded religious curricula, and by the expression of faculty and student concern. Beyond the colleges and universities, certain recent developments in the arts, frequent discussion of religious problems in public forums and private groups, and a significant increase in church membership are but a few indications of a reawakened interest in the ways of faith.

But many who wish to examine intelligently the major religious traditions are either at a loss to find a single comprehensive guide or are bewildered by the variety of approaches followed in the books now available. Should one begin with the study of religious literature or of religious history? Should one concentrate on contemporary institutions or proceed chronologically through the development of institutions in the past? Should one limit one's self to Western faiths, or should one study the religions of the East as well? How far can one profitably go in the exploration of some of the basic problems of religious philosophy? The authors of this volume have wrestled with such questions both in and out of the classroom for a number of years, and this book has grown out of their efforts to provide thoughtful contemporaries with a basic and balanced introduction to religion.

The approach employed here is both historical and philosophical. A philosophical approach demands rigorous and comprehensive analysis and evaluation, carried on within the broadest possible context; it also involves the examination of some basic religious beliefs in various traditions. But philosophical speculation about religion should be based on

iii

an adequate factual knowledge of religious history. Thus we have included in this volume a history of the chief beliefs and practices of the major religious traditions. While the principal Eastern religions—Confucianism, Hinduism, and Buddhism—are examined in detail, the emphasis is on those religions of the West having a common biblical background.

Portions of this book have been used successfully with adult community-study groups. The authors have had in mind during the preparation, not only the students with whom they have worked, but all other thoughtful people for whom a pertinent understanding of religion is a matter of increasingly relevant concern in the formulation of an intelligent faith today. It is our hope that we have thus provided some basic facts and ideas which may aid the reader in finding or charting more clearly his own way of faith.

The Bible quotations in this publication are from the Revised Standard Version of The Holy Bible, copyrighted 1952 by The Division of Christian Education of The National Council of The Churches of Christ in the United States of America, and are used by permission.

John A. Hutchison

James A. Martin, Jr.

January, 1953

CONTENTS

WAYS OF FAITH

Chapter 1

WHAT IS RELIGION?

FOR many reasons the task of defining religion is fraught with difficulty. For one thing, the term "religion" is often very loosely used. Again, religion is a complex phenomenon in which it is all too easy to mistake the part for the whole—like the blind men who inspected the elephant, each mistaking the part he encountered for the whole beast. But the greatest difficulty has to do with the relation in which we stand to the term to be defined. In some fields of endeavor, as, for example, the natural sciences, it is possible for the student to stand apart in detachment from his subject matter. However, in the case of any of the deep-rooted human concerns—in any case where important human values are at stake—it is highly doubtful whether such an attitude is either possible or desirable. This means that in such an inquiry the problem of bias is enormously more difficult to handle than it is, let us say, in physics. It is worth noting, also, that bias can afflict the critic of religion as well as its adherent. It functions on many different levels. Bias, overcome in its cruder manifestations, may continue to operate in more subtle ways, covertly influencing the selection of facts or coloring the interpretation of them.

It is safe to say that no one ever rises completely above some sort of bias or partiality in the study of religion, for the simple reason that students of religion are existing human beings and not incarnations of pure reason. Therefore one factor in controlling bias is to take into account the full breadth and depth of our propensity to it. Let us be as fair-minded as we can, recognizing that at best there is doubt-

3

less more partiality in our minds than we are aware of. A completely impartial definition of religion is impossible.

In view of such problems as these, any definition offered here will be tentative and preliminary in nature. It will serve only to mark off the field to be investigated and to turn the spotlight upon certain facts in that field which may be worth further scrutiny. There may be errors or inadequacies in the definition but if so they may be corrected by the student in the course of the inquiry. In a sense this whole study is an essay in definition.

Some Current Definitions

Before a new definition is offered, it may be instructive to look briefly at some other definitions of religion. In several of the definitions which follow, there are examples of some of the problems alluded to in the preceding paragraph. For example, some definitions show obvious personal bias. Thus Solomon Reinach begins his study of religion with the following statement: "I propose to define religion as: a sum of scruples which impede the free exercise of our faculties." Another kind of partiality mistakes the part for the whole. So Whitehead's well-known definition speaks of religion as "what the individual does with his solitariness." Still another kind of definition undertakes to define religion in terms of some faculty or aspect of personality, usually an aspect of personality which the writer regards as most important. For Kant the "practical reason," or morality, is basic so it is natural for him to say, "Religion is (subjectively regarded) the recognition of all duties as divine commands." Schleiermacher wrote in a similar vein: "The common element in all expressions of religion, no matter how different, whereby they are distinguished from all other feelings, the permanent identical essence of religion, is that we are conscious of ourselves as absolutely dependent." And again Hegel defined religion as a symbolic or mythological statement of truths to which philosophy subsequently gave adequate rational expression.

Often a definition indicates the nature of a writer's interest in the subject matter. What in effect he says is this: "From where I stand, this is what I see." So William James defined religion as the "acts, feelings, and experiences of individual men in their solitude so far as they apprehend themselves to stand in relation to whatever they may consider divine." John Dewey speaks from the viewpoint of instrumental Humanism when he says: "The religious attitude is a sense of the possibilities of existence and a devotion to the cause of these possibilities." More recently he has written that "whatever introduces genuine perspective is religious . . ." Regarding the concept of value as essential, E. S. Brightman has defined religion as follows: "Religion is concern about experiences which are regarded as of supreme value; devotion toward a power or powers believed to originate, increase and conserve these values, and some suitable expression of this concern and devotion, whether through symbolic rites or through other individual and social conduct." [1] Another facet of meaning is emphasized by J. B. Noss: "All religions say in one way or another that man does not, and cannot stand alone. He is vitally related with and even dependent on powers external to himself. Dimly or clearly, he knows that he is not an independent center of force in the world, a creature divorced from Nature or the Force or forces producing it." [2] Still other aspects of religion are emphasized in V. T. A. Ferm's definition: "To be religious is to effect in some way and in some measure a vital adjustment (however tentative and incomplete) to w(W)hatever is reacted to or regarded implicitly or explicitly as worthy of serious and ulterior concern." [3] This sampling will perhaps suffice to show us how numerous and how various are the definitions of religion. One book on the subject devotes seventy-one pages to sample definitions! It is preferable for the reader to formulate his own definition and revise it as he proceeds in the light of the facts he encounters.

[1] E. S. Brightman, *Philosophy of Religion* (New York: Prentice-Hall, Inc., 1940), p. 17.
[2] J. B. Noss, *Man's Religions* (New York: The Macmillan Co., 1949), p. 3.
[3] V. T. A. Ferm, *First Chapters in Religious Philosophy* (New York: Chas. Scribner's Sons, 1936), p. 61.

Human Traits Conducive to Religion

Religion seems to be distinctive to the human species. The general agreement is that no nonhuman species exhibit religious behavior, and attempts to discover it among animal species have failed. There also seems to be general agreement that all human cultures show some behavior that can fairly be called religious. The writings of anthropologists as divergent in viewpoint as Bronislaw Malinowski and Ruth Benedict agree on this point. Thus if we may discover the way in which human consciousness differs from that of the animals we may be able to locate the source of religion. There is obviously a great deal of continuity between human and animal consciousness; there are many identities and resemblances. With the simplest forms of life man shares responsiveness to stimuli. With the more complex forms of animal life he shares awareness of objects. But man possesses a further kind of awareness. He is not only aware of objects; he is aware of himself as subject. To be sure, some of the higher animals seem on occasion to exhibit self-consciousness. But such instances may be viewed as borderline phenomena which seem only to anticipate what in men is clearly achieved and highly developed.

Now self-awareness as it occurs in man has some traits that deserve attention. In the first place, it is by no means a simple endowment which all men have in equal degree. Rather it is a kind of indefinite potentiality which grows gradually and sometimes sporadically throughout a person's lifetime, and which develops quite unequally in different human individuals. Is it not a fact that of all kinds of knowledge, self-knowledge is the most difficult to attain? And is not attainment of it a lifelong task?

Self-awareness has another property which may be termed a dimension of depth. This may best be shown by a simple experiment in introspection which the reader may perform right now. Self-awareness means the imaginative capacity to stand off and look at one's self. But one can immediately follow this act of introspection by standing off and looking at the point of view which in the immediately preceding moment one occupied. The process can then be repeated. Thus is seen what Reinhold Niebuhr means by the "capacity for self-transcendence in infinite regression." We see what is meant by the "descent into the self," or what Augustine meant when he said that the self is "a great deep." The point is that this aspect of human self-awareness is essential to an understanding of many common human phenomena.

For example, it is for man alone among the living creatures that death seems to be a basic problem. Indeed, only for man does the question "To be or not to be?" seem urgent or compelling. Such a human phenomenon as this follows from the fact that man, by virtue of his self-awareness, is able to stand clear of himself and envisage his own non-existence. It is this capacity of his imagination which makes death a problem.

Among the further traits often mentioned as distinctively human is technological capacity. Man is the tool-using animal. Some simple tools are observable among the higher animal species, but the range and complexity of human tools and machines are enormously greater. This human trait seems to follow from man's ability to stand clear of himself, to distinguish means from ends, and so deliberately to concentrate his attention on means.

Again, man is the creature of language, the *animal symbolicum*. There are, of course, real similarities between the signals observable in animal behavior and human symbols. But there is a real difference as well. A symbol is a signal which is explicitly recognized to be such. It is a signal whose communicative function is clearly recognized. This recognition enables men to organize or systematize their symbols. And it is this fact of formal organization, or syntax, which chiefly differentiates human language from animal signals. From what has just been said it may be seen how the difference follows from the clear distinction between *ego* and *alter* which is given in human consciousness.

Still again, man is educable to a degree and in a sense not true of animals. By education is meant the acquired modification of behavior. The capacity for such modification is present in many animal species. But between animal training and human education there seem to be some real differences in range and extent. Many of the activities which even among the more complex animal species are guided by instinct are among men completely dependent upon learned or acquired behavior. The extent of modification seems also to be enormously greater in the human species. Such differences as these seem to follow from the ability of man to stand off and look at himself, and thus to make the process of modification the object of deliberate activity. But there is still another way in which human education differs from anything observable in animal species. Man can distinguish means from ends, and so deliberately alter the means to achieve a given end. Though this trait is observable to some degree among some of the more complex animal species, it seems uniformly true that the ends of behavior are, for other animals, given by nature. This is not true of man. Rather the ends of behavior are for him freely imagined objects of deliberate choice or decision. Now most men include in their objects of choice some of the same necessities, such as food and sexual expression, given to animal life by instinctive activity. Nevertheless it is formally possible to deny some of or all these necessities, as the facts of asceticism and suicide show. And what is more important, the manner in which biological drives are satisfied in human life is vastly altered by the context of cultural behavior in which they are placed. And this capacity of man to choose his ends as well as his means signifies something further. A man's ends or goals define what we sometimes call his character, his personality. If he is free, within limits, to choose his ends, man is free to alter himself, to remake his world. It is this trait for which the term "morality" stands. Man is the creature who gives deliberate attention to the ends of action. And once more, it is obvious that this capacity, as well as those previously mentioned, springs from man's ability to stand clear and look at himself.

Religion Is Intimate and Ultimate Concern

Our chief interest in the human capacity for self-awareness is its relation to the search for a definition of religion. Man can stand clear of himself, and indeed of any given structure of reality. He is never, if he is a man at all, simply a piece of his environment. Human freedom means basically that the human self can stand over against the world. Now it is this aspect of man's situation, his self-transcendence and world-transcendence, which evokes from man the final questions: What is it all about? What is the meaning of it all? To what am I finally related? Why, finally, should I live or die? These are expressions of the essentially religious question. And the answer which any individual or any group gives to this question constitutes his or their religion. More formally, *religion is intimate and ultimate concern—convictions and activities dealing with the ultimate meaning of existence.* Such a concern is intimate in the sense of being inward, of having to do with one's inmost self. It is ultimate in the sense of providing the final ground for the justification or validation of one's other interests or values. It is that which provides the answers one gives to the questions Whence, Whither, and Why.

Some Implications of the Definition

1. What is here defined is not so much "religion" as the religious attitude, not the noun or substantive but the adjective. Indeed if the term "will" may be used not to signify a faculty of man but the active or functioning unity of the whole person, then it is fair to say that religion is defined here as an attitude of the human will. It is done so deliberately in the conviction that the religious attitude is the raw material of which religions are made. The adjective is in this sense more basic than the noun. Various writers (notably Dewey and Ferm) have dwelt upon this distinction between "religious" and "religion." Often, they argue, religious institutions contain other attitudes than the religious

as here defined. And, conversely, many religious attitudes find expression, especially in a society like our own, in other than explicitly religious forms. These are important and timely truths, and we may be grateful to these writers for pointing them out. It must, however, be added that the relation between attitude and institution is more complex than they seem to suppose. Some sort of religious institution, however imperfect, is essential if the religious attitude is to be effective in human society. Further, the vices of institutionalism, while extensively illustrated in religion, are by no means limited to religion.

2. Religion deals with the ultimate or the absolute, with "ultimate concern." These terms are used as they are employed in everyday speech, as, for example, when we say a man is "absolutely" honest, and mean unconditionally honest. The category "unconditional" has been given explicit and detailed philosophic treatment by Tillich, who writes as follows: "The unconditional is a quality not a being. It characterizes that which is our ultimate and consequently unconditional concern, whether we call it God . . . or whether we give it any other name. It would be a complete mistake to understand the unconditional as a being the existence of which can be discussed. . . . Unconditional is a quality which we experience in encountering reality, for instance, in the unconditional character of the voice of conscience, the logical as well as the moral. . . ." [4]

Similarly this use of the term "absolute" is to be sharply distinguished from the usage of certain types of philosophic idealism where the term designates a being, either unqualified by any relations or invested by an infinite totality of relations—a conception which has been aptly characterized by Morris Cohen as "either a fathomless depth in which no distinctions are visible" or "a fullness of being which exceeds our human comprehension." [5]

[4] Paul Tillich, The Protestant Era (Chicago: University of Chicago Press, 1948), p. 32.
[5] Morris R. Cohen, Reason and Nature (New York: Harcourt, Brace & Co., Inc., 1931), p. 146.

Rather, it is contended that the absolute is to be discovered by digging into the structure of interests or allegiances which make up human personality. If this structure of interests is examined carefully somewhere will be found an interest or a value which is characterized by just this absoluteness or finality. This character is shown by the fact that in contrast to the other interests of the same personality, this interest constitutes the final ground of validation or choice for the others. It is that value which guides human choice, and to which "in a pinch" every other one would be sacrificed. Practically speaking, religious values are those values for which men are willing to die. Any such values take on religious significance.

It may be questioned whether the interests or values which a given person holds are actually thus hierarchically organized under one supreme value. Is not the relation rather one of mutual accommodation between many values, no one of which has priority over others? There is a measure of truth in this widely held view. Actually speaking, it is true that many persons, especially in a multifarious and disorganized culture, have no single ultimate principle or interest, but rather many interests or values to which partial commitment is given. This is the psychological state represented by the religious phenomenon of polytheism. But it means that such persons must be confused when they are faced by choices between their cherished values. Furthermore, there is for such persons no principle of integration (or unification) for personality, which presumably has for all men some underlying unity. And finally, the exclusive "either-or" nature of basic human choices or decisions forces the category of the absolute upon them. There are times when men must make decisions which, whether they like it or not, whether they admit it or not, are total, final, or absolute in their character.

Again, it may be questioned whether it is not possible to stand clear of all interests or values. For the theoretical reason this may be a possibility, but for the practical reason it never is. Decision is never escaped, even though it may be the decision to suspend or defer decision. And decision is always in terms of some value judgments; we decide always in terms of some value. It is a "valuecentric predicament."

This means that it is ultimately impossible to avoid religion of some sort. If as existing men we never avoid values or concerns, and if in any human structure of such concerns or values we may always somewhere discover an ultimate concern, then religion will always manifest itself in some way in human existence. It seems thus to be an inevitable part of human existence.

This conclusion will be criticized from two viewpoints. First there are those whose object of attack is a particular religious tradition or system of religious behavior. But if what has been said is at all true, it is possible to criticize or deny a religion only from the viewpoint of another religion. The very standing ground from which the criticism proceeds thus becomes tacitly or overtly a religion. Again, there are those who make all religion the object of skeptical denial. This is a possible attitude for the theoretical reason, but for the practical reason—for action—it is not. Thus, as the skeptic turns from contemplation to action, the structure of interests of the skeptic's personality may be examined and an authentic religious response discovered. Indeed, many of the great religious reformers were denounced as atheists and blasphemers by their contemporaries, precisely because their religious insights were so deep they could not tolerate the superficial or stultifying expressions of religion in the religious institutions of their cultures!

3. When it is said that religion is "intimate and ultimate concern," it should be pointed out also that the religious concern of an individual or a group frequently appears to those involved to be evoked by a power or powers beyond control. They are not so much logically led, step by step, to a religious commitment as they are grasped by it. Religion appears to be fundamentally a response to something given in man's situation rather than something which man deliberately constructs.

4. Again, religion as it is defined here has been and continues to be associated with an endless variety of objects. Indeed there seems to be no object of human experience so common or so bizarre as to have escaped identification with religious concern by some one in some culture. This bewildering variety of religious objects, beliefs, and institutions drives many scholars to the conclusion that there is simply no such thing as religion in general. Yet the existence of the word indicates some underlying common characteristic among the multitudes of beliefs and practices which men ordinarily describe as religious. The common element in otherwise disparate religious practices is the fact that they deal with ways in which the ultimate meaning of life is expressed.

5. This last reflection recalls the word "intimate" in the definition. The concern which is religious is not only the most inclusive and decisive of human concerns, it is also that which lies deepest within the individual or group. A man's real religious faith is frequently the last thing that his closest friend can discover about him—or indeed, that he can discover about himself. Frequently only a crisis like marriage, vocational decision, parenthood, or impending death can bring out an individual's final commitments. Of course, for less civilized men the distinction between that which is intimately personal and that which is simply a part of the social structure is perhaps never clearly drawn. But in so far as men become responsibly self-conscious they develop complex depths of intimate concern. It is this fact which Whitehead and James had in mind in their otherwise deficient definitions of religion as "what one does with his solitariness" and "the acts, feelings, and experiences of individual men in their solitude . . ."

6. On the other hand, man is basically a social animal, and no matter how far developed his self-conscious individuality as over against his cultural group may be, he is never completely divorced from cultural conditioning and cultural expression. Even the genius and the prophet are conditioned by the society which produces them to rise above

and criticize it. While many recent students of religion may have overemphasized the social character of religious phenomena, it is true that all significant ways of faith have been nurtured by groups and maintained in institutions with definite patterns of group behavior.

7. When religion is spoken of as "concern," included in that word is the psychological quality of a distinctive type of human response. Schleiermacher defined religion in terms of a "feeling" of "absolute dependence," and though this definition is one-sidedly psychological, it does communicate something significant. The German word translated "feeling" actually means more than the emotional response associated with that word in everyday English. It suggests a complete response of the total personality, both intellectually and emotionally. And "absolute dependence" suggests something of the biblical sense of "the fear of the Lord," where fear means much more than animal fear, fright, or cringing. Perhaps "awe" or "wonder" is a less loaded term. Or again, religious feeling has been called "creature-feeling"—the awareness of creatureliness, of finitude, of the significance of the insignificance of the human self as measured against the vastness of reality. Such feelings come to all men at various times under various conditions. For some they are inspired chiefly by natural beauty or grandeur; for others they are evoked by masterpieces of human achievement or art which seem to point beyond themselves to the ultimate or absolute reference. Others experience them in relation to a compelling loyalty to an institution or cause. "Two things fill my soul with awe," said Immanuel Kant; "the starry heavens above, and the moral law within."

8. From all this it follows that not all religion is necessarily good or even concerned with goodness. Indeed, many men and some groups are not intimately and ultimately concerned about moral values at all. This fact is difficult for a student brought up in Western traditions to grasp, because in the Hebrew-Christian tradition holiness is primarily associated with moral righteousness. Thus Matthew Arnold could restrict religion to "morality touched with emotion."

But even in the West there have been men whose primary allegiance was to truth or beauty rather than to goodness, or who finally defined goodness in terms of truth or beauty. And in much Eastern religion, morality as the West knows it has been subordinated to aesthetic considerations in men's intimate and ultimate concerns.

Again, even in the West many powerful religious movements have been evoked by moral ideals at sharp variance with those of the Hebrew-Christian tradition as these are traditionally understood. The power of National Socialism in Germany derived in part from its conscious attempt to recover German pagan religion with its cult of blood and soil, even if it had to do so in some circles in the name of "German Christianity." It seems that men will worship something, and if they can find nothing worthy in traditional religious institutions they will turn to political or other secular concerns in search of an ideal to which they can give themselves unreservedly.

The disavowal of an otherwise good religion because of bad elements in it frequently results in the unconscious formulation of a worse religion as a substitute. In any event, the religious power of political totalitarianism is a frequently mentioned but seldom understood phenomenon. Contemporary communism, for instance, has most of the characteristics of an institutional religion—dogma, creed, hierarchy, symbols, and church. But the heart of its religious character lies in the absolute quality of the allegiance which it elicits from its adherents—the total commitment of intellect, emotion, and will of the faithful Communist to the party and its line. It is absolute in extent—embracing all aspects of life—and in intensity, involving life-and-death risk and decision. And communism is a Western religion in the sense that its final goal is a morally perfect society achieved by scientific, economic, and political theory and action. Whether its goal and techniques are fundamentally opposed to the historic Hebrew-Christian tradition, or are heretical in the sense that they derive from it while distorting it, is a question which cannot be entered here. The important point for the present discussion is that religion in the normative sense of our definition does not simply disappear from a society which theoretically challenges or denies it. In one form or another it is a universal aspect of human experience.

Some Sciences of Religion and the Significance of Their Findings

Many readers will already have expressed an objection to the preceding characterization of religion. It is, they will say, too abstract and speculative; in short, it is not scientific. And of course they are right. The preceding discussion began with the suggestion that no finally adequate characterization of religion can restrict itself to the relatively objective approach appropriate to various scientific investigations of religious phenomena. Religion embraces, among other things, the basis for the scientist's commitment to objectivity. His dedication to the search for truth is an expression of his most inward and final concern. But those who identify religion with specific religious institutions or with certain familiar religious beliefs typical of special traditions and cultures will feel that the general characterization of religion given here is too broad and indefinite, just as those whose approach to religion is highly colored by the special interests and methods of certain sciences will feel that the definition given here is too heavily philosophical and speculative.

Perhaps such objections spring from the difference between scientific and philosophical approaches to any subject, including religion. The scientist, on the one hand, must restrict himself to the selective interests and methods of his specific science. The philosopher, on the other hand, must attempt to bring all the available pertinent facts together in some critical but more inclusive whole. What, then, are some of the facts about religion which recent scientific investigations have disclosed? What are the methods employed in sciences of religion? And what is the philosophical significance of their findings?

Anthropology and the Nature of Primitive Religion

THE NATURE OF ANTHROPOLOGY. Anthropology is, as the name suggests, the science of man. Anthropologists are interested in applying to man as a distinctive kind of animal the same methods of study other scientists use in the investigation of lower forms of animal life—in so far as the nature of man renders these methods possible and appropriate. The aim is to stand apart from individuals and social groups and to analyze them as objectively and measure their various components as accurately as possible. Though the primary aim is thus to arrive at a more accurate description of human beings, anthropologists feel that such knowledge of what men actually are and have been is fundamental to any meaningful generalizations concerning what men might or should be.

But when a scientist turns to phenomena as complex as the facts of human living, the application of scientific method in the analysis of such facts becomes increasingly difficult. It is a fairly simple matter to construct apparatus for the relatively precise measurement of basic physical phenomena, and the results of such measurement may be stated in clear mathematical language. But how does one go about measuring social relations, love, hate, patriotism, and all the other independent variables of human living? Serious consideration of this question has led some anthropologists who desire to keep the methods and procedures of their science as close as possible to those employed in natural sciences like physics, chemistry, and biology to restrict their interests to physical anthropology. Physical anthropologists are interested in measuring and describing the evolution and development of the human *body* against the background of varying geographical, climatic, and cultural factors. They are interested in the science of man as a physiological entity complexly related to varying environmental conditions. Many physical anthropologists feel that the attempt to grasp more than such basic physical phenomena stretches the field beyond the limits of truly scientific methods.

Other anthropologists, however, maintain that the basic patterns of scientific investigation—i.e., careful selection of data, controlled conditions of observation, accurate measurement and analysis, and tentative conclusions subject to further testing under carefully stipulated conditions—may legitimately be applied to nonphysical aspects of human life. Simple social institutions as well as skulls and spinal columns may be measured and described with scientific accuracy, they say. Such anthropologists are frequently called cultural anthropologists, or scientific investigators of human culture. Cultural anthropologists in turn make use of the findings of physical anthropologists and other natural scientists, and also of the findings of psychologists, sociologists, economists, and other social scientists.

Now the difficulties involved in going beyond the merely physical facts in the science of man may be reduced somewhat if the investigator begins with the simplest forms of human society. He may soon learn that apparently simple societies are vastly complex in reality, but if he can deal with nonliterate peoples he at least will not have to deal with the complications introduced by written languages. Therefore cultural anthropologists turn first to so-called primitive cultures. Obviously they can discover very little about cultures which are primitive in the sense of being chronologically earliest—though the analysis of artifacts from such cultures provided by archeologists furnishes much valuable information. So they must turn to currently existing cultures which have been geographically or otherwise isolated from most of the complex developments of civilization—the cultures of South Sea Islanders, Australian aborigines, American Indians, Eskimos, and others. The fact that it is becoming increasingly difficult for even such cultures to maintain their primitive structures in the modern world of rapid communication and technological interdependence lends a certain urgency to the task of studying the unspoiled peoples.

SOME CHARACTERISTICS OF PRIMITIVE RELIGION. Two generalizations about primitive peoples seem reasonably well established by cultural anthropologists: their apparently simple and uncomplicated social institutions and practices appear, under closer scrutiny, to be very complex and delicately balanced; and there is a definite continuity between the basic needs and activities of primitive peoples and those of their more civilized brothers. There is a fundamental sense in which it is true to say that all men are alike. The apparently limitless variations in social customs and institutions are in a large measure variations on certain common themes of human living. The needs for food, sexual expression, security, and the need to celebrate and dramatize the crucial experiences of life and death are, among others, universal human needs. It is with the basic religious need of all men to relate themselves meaningfully to an ultimate that we are concerned. And this need is universally apparent in the behavior patterns of primitive cultures.

It appears that this religious need is expressed among primitive peoples primarily in feeling and in action, and only secondarily in concepts and beliefs. Man, it has been said, dances his religion before he thinks about it. He attempts to come to grips with the mystery of life first of all through gestures and acts; the concepts and beliefs which explain or rationalize the gestures and acts emerge later. Ritual, in other words, produces myth, rather than vice versa. But what is the basic or original form of religious action? Different anthropologists have given different answers to this question; and the dominant contemporary view seems to be that it is actually unanswerable. The complexity of relations between behavior patterns in specific cultures, and the variations of patterns from one culture to another, make it impossible to isolate one particular form of human behavior and say: this is universally the basic or original religious act. One must take each culture as a unit and attempt, as patiently and as sympathetically as one can, to discover which beliefs and practices in that specific culture may justifiably be termed religious as compared with other beliefs and practices in the same culture. That which for one culture is sacred may be secular for other cultures.

Totemism. Earlier anthropologists sometimes claimed that
specific practices and beliefs were universally original. Thus,
Emile Durkheim observed that the primitive peoples with
whom he was familiar all exhibited behavior associated with
an identification of the group with selected plants or animals.[6]
The Algonquins called such a tribal symbol a "totem" and
totem-poles are familiar to most people as typical objects of
primitive societies. But what is the purpose and function
of this claim of blood-relationship between a primitive human
group and totem-plants or animals? Perhaps it simply expresses the primitive human sense of continuity and solidarity
with the rest of nature. Perhaps it expresses the discovery
by a certain group of the dangers to life and limb associated
with specific plants and animals. Perhaps it represents an
attempt on the part of the group to gain for itself the powerful or otherwise desirable characteristics of the totem-animal.
In any case, the totem seems to be a symbol of some sort
of power to which the group wishes to be meaningfully related. Durkheim, working under the influence of Auguste
Comte's positivistic philosophy, was sure that the totem
symbolizes both cosmic power and the power of the group
itself—the power of group relationships. These, to primitive
men, are tangible and living things. Indeed, said Durkheim,
for primitive men cosmic power and the power of the group
are one and the same thing—and this one cosmic-social power
is the earliest and fundamental object of intimate and ultimate concern. It is ultimately society itself to which man is
related in religious belief and behavior. Originally—and for
Durkheim, finally—human society is God. In rites and ceremonies centering around totems primitive men are giving
expression to the awe of the individual for the group symbolized in the totem-animal, and, more basically, to the
dimly realized sense of absolute dependence of the human
individual upon society for the very fabric of human living.

It seems true that the distinction between "I" and "we"
is at best vague among primitive peoples. And it is obvi-

<hr>

[6] Emile Durkheim, *The Elementary Forms of the Religious Life* (London:
G. Allen & Unwin, Ltd., 1926).

ous that even the simplest human societies are so complex that the individual member is radically dependent on other members for the fulfilment of all basic human needs. Furthermore, it is the group rather than the individual that develops customs, laws, rites, and ceremonies which make life meaningful for the individual. In thus calling attention to the "we-consciousness" of primitive man and its significance for even the most highly individualistic of civilized cultures, Durkheim made a contribution to the understanding of man that other anthropologists have freely used and built upon. But it soon became apparent to other investigators that Durkheim's claim that totemism is the basic form of primitive religious life is itself a reflection of his own philosophical presuppositions.

Magic. Certain questions concerning the specific purposes of totemic rites remain. Does primitive man hope by totemic dances, sacrifices, and other rituals to control the powerful forces represented by the totem for his own ends? Or are there totemic rites which have no apparent utilitarian purpose, which are done simply for their own sake? It was to such questions that Sir James George Frazer addressed himself in his monumental study of primitive religion.[7] As a result of this study Frazer concluded that totemic and other practices of primitive peoples may have either of two fairly distinct general aims: the bending of cosmic and social powers to the will of the individual or group, or the bending of the will of the individual or group to the powers recognized to be superior. The former type of activity should properly be labeled magical, while only the latter type is distinctively religious, said Frazer.

Magical practices are aimed at the control or exploitation of natural and social forces for individual and social ends. The attitude of the magician is relatively impersonal and self-sufficient. He is actually operating on the basis of a primitive apprehension of laws of cause and effect. Black magic is an attempt to influence nature or society in a man-

[7] Sir James George Frazer, *The Golden Bough: a Study in Magic and Religion* (abridged ed.; New York: The Macmillan Co., 1923).

ner detrimental to one's enemies; white magic is the attempt
to influence nature or society in a manner favorable to one's
self. In most magic it is the individual rather than the group
who prospers or suffers as a result of the practices, but group
magic is also possible. There are many variations in magical
techniques, depending on the particular understanding—or
misunderstanding—of causal law involved. Primitive men
tend to believe that things which are alike or similar are
actually identical; thus an image of an enemy may be destroyed in the belief that the enemy himself is thereby
affected—and if the enemy also believes in magic and learns
of what has happened he usually is affected. Or again, primitive men tend to believe that persons or objects closely associated in space transfer some of their characteristics to each
other. Thus a bit of clothing taken from an enemy may be
damaged to the hurt of the enemy; or a bit of clothing worn
by a chief has some of the powers of chiefhood associated
with it and must be treated accordingly. Again, primitive
men tend to assume that events which once happen in a
given sequence will always happen in that sequence. Thus,
if it once rained after the medicine man, *shaman*, or other
magician performed a certain act, then repetition of that act
in the future should again induce rain to fall. Or perhaps
an imitation of gathering clouds, lightning and thunder, and
falling rain will have sympathetic influence on the elements
involved. These and other beliefs and practices characterize
the infinitely complex world of magic and give meaning to
various attitudes towards persons and objects in primitive
societies.

Fetish and taboo. The magical instrument becomes a
fetish, to be used for good or ill. Regulations for its use and
control become increasingly complicated and must be entrusted to those learned in the ways of magic—the magicians,
shamans, medicine men, and so on. For those who do not
understand the necessary formulae and precautions it is
taboo, not to be handled. Taboo in turn becomes associated
with group practices and customs like marriage and food

regulations which are designed to safeguard the welfare of the individual or group.

Sacrifice. The more distinctively religious approach to ultimate forces, Frazer claimed, involves a much more personal and submissive attitude. The powers to be dealt with are themselves personified, and the techniques employed in dealing with them are those appropriate for communication between persons rather than for the control of impersonal objects by persons. Thus prayers of all forms may be employed. Or sacrifices may be offered; indeed, sacrifice is one of the most universal and significant of all religious acts. This practice may stem from the early totemic sense of blood-identity between men and totems, and the belief that totem-objects or, later, gods themselves, need food just as men do. In that case, the sacrifice is an offering to the god of the very means for continued existence. In this common sharing of food, however, there is the experience of tangible communion between the devotee and his god. The basic motive for the sacrificial communion may be simply adoration of the god —the giving of the best of one's substance to that which is of ultimate concern. Such motivation would perhaps be the most purely religious as distinct from magical, in Frazer's terms. But the adoration itself might be a form of thanksgiving for benefits received from the deity, or a form of supplication to the deity to perform some desired act. Or again, it might be a form of atonement for the violation of some taboo. Or, more magically, it might be a personalized form of coercion designed to persuade the deity to do the will of the worshiper.

This last idea suggests the difficulty in Frazer's otherwise helpful distinction between the religious and the magical. How is an observer to know what the specific aims of a primitive religious act are? Indeed, are such aims clearly visualized and defined in the minds of those participating in the acts? May not primitive men, like their civilized brothers, participate in many acts whose outward form may suggest adoration while their inner intent is that of magical compulsion—and

vice versa? And, even if the intent of acts could be known,
is it not true that the same act might mean different things
for different groups, or even different things for the same
group at different times? These and similar questions have
led most modern anthropologists to conclude that, while
Frazer's distinction may be useful as a normative or theoretical distinction between two basic patterns of human behavior, in practice it is of very little use as a means of clas-
sifying specific forms of primitive religious activity.

Animism. Other anthropologists have questioned Durkheim's conclusion that the most primitive object of intimate
and ultimate concern is the power of the group. E. B. Tylor,
for instance, noticed that belief in spirits and activity associated with such belief are at least as universal as totemic
practices and are indeed presupposed in such practices.[8] In
order for groups to identify themselves with totem-animals
there must be a prior ability to think of both the human self
and the animal self as something other than the literal physical being of either. And closer investigation of primitive
cultures reveals that most primitive peoples do live in a world
of intangible spirits which serve, as someone said of the Greek
gods, to "naturalize man and humanize nature"—to bridge
the gap between the human and the nonhuman, the animate
and the inanimate in primitive thinking. Tylor called this
belief in spirits and the behavior associated with it animism,
from the Latin word *anima*, usually translated "soul."

The origins of animism are themselves obscure. It has
been suggested that the whole idea of a spirit-centered reality
constitutes a primitive world view in terms of which a number of disparate but individually baffling mysteries could be
clarified. For instance, the word *anima* itself suggests breath
or wind as well as soul. Similarly, Greek, Hebrew, and other
words relating to soul also have their origins in words meaning breath or wind. Now the mysterious forces of wind—

[8] Sir Edward Bennett Tylor, *Primitive Culture* (7th ed.; New York: Brentano's, 1924).

invisible, unpredictable, but terrifyingly devastating—would be a natural object of ultimate concern for primitive peoples. The Japanese, some readers will recall, could think of no more honorific title to give to their suicide pilots in World War II than their word for the hurricanes which have figured so largely in Japanese history—*kamikaze* or "divine wind."

But equally mysterious is the wind which seems basically related to life itself—the breath of life which moves in and out of the body. The mystery of wind and breath thus becomes identical with the mystery of life and death. And death, as we noted at the outset, is a basic matter of ultimate concern for man, the only mortal animal who knows he is mortal and must come to grips with his mortality.

To primitive men animistic phenomena would seem to suggest that the breath of life is not limited to living bodies, but that it is rather pervasively present in all nature, that the world itself is alive. But why, then, should primitive men also assume that it is personal? Some have suggested that the answer to this question lies in another mystery—the mystery of sleep and dreams, and the whole realm of imagination opened up by that mystery. Primitive men are aware that they live in many worlds at once. There is the "normal" world of waking routine, where things have a certain familiar temporal and spacial order and sequence; and there are the "other" worlds of dream and reverie, in which literally anything can happen. The individual who, in the order of one world, is asleep at a given place in space and time, suddenly finds himself hunting in a distant forest, seeing people of a neighboring tribe, and so on. Then suddenly he is back again in the waking world. Such experience can only suggest that there are, as it were, two selves involved—the self of this world and the self of the other world which is unrestricted by the regularities of wakeful reality. Furthermore, there are states of half-waking reverie in which the worlds seem to intermingle, and the distinction between the two worlds would be no more clear to primitive man than the distinction between himself and his tribe.

Again, some men seem more adept at moving back and forth between the two worlds than others—and some seem to live in the dream world of imagination most of the time. These are the *seers*, those who see what more prosaic souls cannot. For a price they may see what the enemy is doing, or where the spear was lost. Or they may *foresee* some future event. Or, more significantly, they may recall those from whom the breath of life has passed. For, once again, returning to the mystery of death, it is noted that in dreams and reverie those who have died reappear. For most men such reappearances are fitful and unpredictable; but the seer may claim to manage them at will. In any case, the continuous appearance of the deceased in dream and fancy is proof enough for many primitive peoples that physical death—the departure of the breath of life—is not the end of men. Indeed, once they have entered the spirit world they become more powerful, more to be dreaded and revered. Thus emerge all the paraphernalia of the cults of the dead. In brief, animism provides a basis for a wide variety of religious or magical practices and beliefs. The beliefs emerge and become more complex as stories are told to express and explain the ways of the spirits and men. Cult produces myth, and myth produces, finally, the arts and sciences, philosophy, and theology.

Indeed, the interpretation of animism presented above is itself the product of a relatively sophisticated level of scientific and philosophical development. It is one way in which modern man seeks to understand more primitive men. But modern man must always remember that in such attempts he is imposing on complex phenomena rational patterns which are not themselves part of the consciousness of the peoples who produce the phenomena. It is not to be supposed that primitive peoples consciously develop animistic theory in the step-by-step sequence suggested above. Indeed, anthropologists warn that the actual significance of animism and the practices associated with it varies radically from culture to culture. In brief, the perils of oversimplification must be kept in mind.

Mana. Some anthropologists have themselves been interested in pursuing the question, "Is animism the basic primitive world view in terms of which original religious practices take shape?" Thus R. R. Marett has maintained that animism is itself too sophisticated, too much dependent on ideas, plausibly to be considered the root-response of primitive man to his environment.[9] The most primitive response would more likely be even more vague and more closely related to feeling as distinct from thought. And Marett and others have found supporting evidence for this theory in the Polynesian word *mana* and the activities associated with it. Other peoples seem also to have words or feelings corresponding to that which the Polynesians call *mana*. And what is mana? The fact that it is primarily emotional in its reference—sublinguistic, as it were, makes it almost impossible to say. Mana seems to cover any and every thing that produces a total response of the total person—a response of awe or wonder. And awe is not simply fear as that word is ordinarily used. Any object, person, or event which is completely startling or incomprehensible may produce awe in primitive men. The Polynesians seem to use the word mana for the whole awe-experience. The distinction between subject and object is not too clear; thus the object is mana, the person experiencing it is mana, and the experiencing of the object is itself mana. In so far as the nature of that which elicits mana-response may be put into more definite conceptual terms, it would seem to be fundamentally power. That which is most powerful in the broadest sense of that term is mana and produces the most powerful mana-experience. Thus the divine wind of animism is mana, but as mana it is not yet personified. The totem is mana, too. All the paraphernalia of magic and of religious sacrifice are mana. Persons, things, events, institutions—if their relation to the individual or group is such as to call forth their deepest response as they confront the literally awe-ful power—all may be mana.

[9] Robert R. Marett, *The Threshold of Religion* (London: Methuen & Co., Ltd., 1929).

This means, of course, that mana is not an ethical concept; to say that something or someone is mana is not to say
that it or he is good or bad in an ethical sense. The concept
of power, it might be said, is prior to the concept of righteousness. That which is mana is to be desired in so far as its
power might thus be appropriated by an individual or group
for magical purposes—it is good in that sense. On the other
hand, it is to be more literally feared in so far as its power
may injure or destroy the individual or group unable to
approach it correctly. Thus mana gives a more basic meaning to taboo than that suggested in Durkheim's totemic
theory. Taboo is, in its broadest terms, simply the negative
side of mana. That which is mana is also taboo—dangerous,
forbidden, to be approached only with utmost caution by
those who are themselves mana and know the mana-formulae
or, in the case of customs and social institutions, to be dis-
regarded only with the risk of gravest peril. The development of complexly varying applications of this basic experience of taboo will be observed as the negative expression
of mana.

If the idea of mana seems intolerably vague to the modern
reader, it may be best to leave it thus. For, according to
many anthropologists, only vagueness could approach accuracy in communicating to civilized man the primitive sense
of mana. However, many may find helpful Rudolph Otto's
more philosophical expression of what seems to be the same
phenomenon. Otto maintains that the basic religious category is the numinous—that which lies behind the phenomenal
or the directly experienced.[10] Thus mana-objects are, in
Otto's terminology, numinous or holy. The holy is, in turn,
mysterium tremendum et fascinans—supreme and fascinating
mystery. Thus that which is mana is awe-inspiring in its
mysterious power, whether it be animistic, totemistic, or
beyond these classifications. But it is at the same time
fascinating; it attracts even as it repels. Beneath attraction
and repulsion, however, lies the truly religious dimension—

[10] Rudolph Otto, *The Idea of the Holy* (New York: Oxford University
Press, 1926).

the dimension which evokes simple awe or worship. The awe may develop along Frazer's religious lines of personal submission, or it may develop along the magical lines of control. But the root-experience is prior to all of this. Thus Otto reasons that the root-category holy is prior to and at the same time more inclusive than any of the ways in which the fascination which is an ingredient of the primal awe may be expressed. In any case, holiness is the one distinctively religious category, and worship is the one distinctively religious act. Religion in its developed forms may associate holiness and worship with physical power, with ethical goodness, with aesthetic beauty, with intellectual truth, or with any other human concern. But, to return to the original definition, the distinctively religious is simply that which is of intimate and ultimate concern and which therefore evokes awe and wonder—a sense of the holy. Thus this brief summary of anthropological views of religion leads back to our philosophical analysis and to the definition with which we began. What is the significance of the anthropological approach?

The Significance of the Anthropological Approach and Its Data

A superficial acquaintance with the findings of anthropologists concerning religious institutions and beliefs may well suggest a chastened humility on the part of any student of the field. At the simplest levels of human society, religious and other human institutions are so complex and so richly meaningful to those who nurture them that easy or condescending generalizations about religion as such are unsound as well as unwise. The foregoing attempt to summarize some anthropological findings in terms of broad philosophical categories is itself a partial falsification of the complex facts involved. Fully to appreciate the intricate and delicate balance of primitive religious phenomena would require an independent volume; hence the necessary brevity of the treatment here. But the reader is urged to read for himself some of the extensive and fascinating materials provided by cultural anthropologists today. If he can gain thereby a more humble appreciation of the rich complexity of all things human he will have increased both his factual knowledge and his philosophical wisdom.

Curiously enough, however, many modern students whose knowledge of anthropological findings does not go beyond the superficial level derive a certain smug pride from their knowledge that religious institutions had such relatively simple origins. Such students cultivate a comfortable disdain for or disparagement of "the poor primitive," whether they find him in a primitive culture or among depressed classes of more civilized cultures. Behind such thinking lies a widespread modern assumption: namely, that the latest is the best and the more complex is the more worth while. This is an assumption, and as such needs to be examined as objectively as possible. Examination of the same data and acquaintance with the same primitives might lead others who make different assumptions to a deeper sense of the continuity of human life and of what some religions call the brotherhood of man.

THE GENETIC FALLACY. Many persons make a different but related assumption when they attempt to assess the significance of anthropology or any other science which interests itself in the question of origin(s): namely, the assumption that origins determine values. In more technical language this assumption is sometimes called the genetic fallacy—the fallacy of assuming without sufficient grounds that an understanding of the genesis, the origins and development of things, produces an understanding of the true nature or significance of the phenomena investigated. According to this assumption, all things are really what they were in their earliest forms. Now of course one may use such a definition of real and such a norm of what things truly are if he wishes. But he should then be consistent in applying it, and usually those who apply the genetic fallacy in one or two areas refuse to apply it in all. For instance, some might say that since more sophisticated contemporary expressions of religious faith go back to crude animistic or totemistic beliefs and practices, therefore all religion is nothing but an emotional expression of prescientific or unscientific fears. Those who hold this view should then also say that, since science itself aims at precise knowledge of the world for purposes of prediction and control, science goes back to the mistaken causal thinking of primitive magic and therefore science is nothing but primitive magic brought up to date. Both statements would contain an element of truth, but to say that they contain the whole truth about either science or religion is to move beyond the facts to dogmatic theory.

Indeed, the facts themselves are uncertain; anthropologists are increasingly suspicious of claims that this or that belief or practice is the original magical or religious behavior. The facts are too complex, and any statement which derives from a summary of any facts phrases containing the words "nothing but . . ." is likely to be dangerously deceptive.

The genetic "nothing but" fallacy is indeed a form of a more general type of fallacious thinking technically called *reductionism*. Various forms of reductionism seek to reduce complex facts and values to some simplest, lowest common denominator. While such reduction is legitimate and necessary for the purposes of various sciences and philosophical disciplines, it may be deceptively misleading when applied to the sum total of human experience. It is in any case a distortion and therefore to some degree a falsification of the whole.

The various forms of primitive religion may be identified as they appear in the development of all the great historical ways of faith. They are present in varying forms in all religions; sometimes they are most obviously present in the earliest stages of historical development, but in many cases they operate subtly at more sophisticated levels. They may appear in a more intellectual guise, or they may simply exist alongside sophisticated practices as the actual religion of the masses, particularly in depressed classes or cultures. Totemism, animism, magic of all sorts, fetishes and taboos, sacrifices, and various ways of expressing and understanding mana or the holy—all these are encountered in the history of all major religious groups, even as they are encountered in current religious practice. It will be helpful to be able to identify them, although the nonspecialist should never forget his technical incompetence and should therefore make his identifications tentatively and cautiously, and should draw conclusions from his identifications only after careful and critical thought based on extensive study.

The History of Religions

The modern Western ideas of history as a meaningful developmental process, moving from simpler to more complex and significant stages, and of historical writing as an objective account of this process, are not as commonly assumed among the peoples of the world as most Westerners suppose. Indeed, the latter notion of a scientific account of historical events related to an objectively determined theme has been operative in the West for only a few centuries, and reached full expression only in the nineteenth century. Yet most Western students today assume that it is both possible and desirable to achieve an objective, dispassionate account of human events from the time of man's earliest civilizations to the present.

THE ROLE OF THE RELIGIOUS HISTORIAN. The historian is expected to do for the whole range of human cultural development what the anthropologist does for selected primitive cultures. Not all historians believe this is possible. Not only is the range of materials too broad for scientific analysis, they say, but the very involvement of the historian himself in history makes it inevitable that his discipline will be more of an art than a science. In any case, modern historians recognize the obligation to be as scientific as possible in the gathering of all pertinent facts, and to be as objective as possible in interpreting them.

But the range of facts included in history in general is so vast that historians must limit their field of investigation in some manner. They may do this in a number of ways. For instance, a historian may limit himself to a particular geographical area and seek to present and interpret all facts pertinent to an understanding of it. Or he may limit himself to a political entity like a nation and try to write a national history. Again, he may limit himself within geographical and political areas to certain kinds of human institutions. Thus a great deal of Western historiography has concentrated on political institutions and has sought to tell the story of nations in terms of political events, including the events of war and diplomacy. More recently there has been increasing recognition of the broader context of social and cultural factors in history and a decreasing emphasis upon the strictly political character of human events.

The historian of religion usually limits himself to the description and interpretation of religious institutions in the broadest sense of that term, with such attention to religious ideas and the relation of religious institutions to other facets of society as he thinks necessary to make the broader picture of religion in society intelligible. Of course some historians may believe that ideas produce institutions and may thus concentrate on the history of religious ideas and beliefs. Others may feel that certain creative persons are most important in the production of ideas and may thus concentrate on biographical data as the key to the understanding of ideas and institutions. In so far as chief attention is given to religious institutions—and this term means more than organized "churches"—the historian of religion moves into an area sometimes called sociology of religion, the study of religion as a social phenomenon complexly related to other social phenomena.

In any case, the historian of religion is expected to present and interpret his data as human phenomena, using only natural and human laws in his categories of explanation. As historian he is not concerned with the possible theological explanation or the theological significance of his data. Of course if he is himself otherwise committed to a theological system or religious institution his commitments will inevitably have some bearing on his final interpretation of his data. And even if he is not related to a system of ideas or social institution ordinarily called religious in his culture, his intimate and ultimate concern will necessarily have some bearing on his selection and interpretation of facts. Objectivity is, for the historian of religion, an ideal to be kept in the foreground as a basis for discipline and criticism, but it is only partially achievable.

Nevertheless, the contemporary historian of religion is usually not interested in what was once called "comparative religion." It was the fashion of a few years ago to present presumably objective accounts of the major beliefs and practices of various religions in terms of the good and bad points of each, for the purpose of comparing one with another. Sometimes it was assumed that such a comparison could provide the basis for the development of a synthetic personal faith which could combine all the good points of the various faiths and exclude all the bad points. Or, if the comparison was made by a missionary representative of a particular faith, it would demonstrate the superiority of his faith over all others. The whole idea of comparative religion is pretty much discredited among contemporary historians of religion. The complexity of the data involved, the difficulty in seeing a particular faith from the inside and thus judging it as it would be judged by one committed to it—the impossibility, in short, of jumping out of one's skin to achieve a purely rational detachment in describing, interpreting, and finally evaluating matters of religious commitment—these and other considerations lead modern historians of religion to espouse more modest aims.

Most historians of religion today would seek simply (and the matter is by no means simple) to describe as accurately as they can the external manifestations of religious systems in cults, rituals, organizations, scriptures, and other phenomena; and to describe as sympathetically as possible what the systems mean to those committed to them, as expressed by their own spokesmen. Some comparison will inevitably enter into the selection and interpretation of the data involved, but the historian is at least striving to leave the matter of comparison and final evaluation to others.

SOME HISTORICAL CLASSIFICATIONS. The historian of religion must also block out and limit his field of investigation in some manner. He cannot simply recount all the facts related to all the religions man has ever known. He may, therefore, concentrate on ideas, personalities, or institutions as suggested above. Or he may seek to relate all these in terms of some other scheme of classification. Thus he may divide religions into tribal, national, cultural, and universal religions, with reference to the actual geographical extent of their influence, or to the extent of their claims to validity. Anthropologists deal mainly with tribal religions, and a historian may use some anthropological data as a first chapter in his enterprise. Or he may be concerned with religions which have influenced and claimed special validity for specific national groups, like the ancient Egyptian religion and the state cult of modern Japanese Shinto.

Historians of religion have also found useful further schemes of classification which cut across the area classifications described above. Thus some historians have made much of the distinction between priestly and prophetic religions. Though this distinction relates primarily to philosophical and theological problems, it is relevant to the history of religion in so far as priestly religion is primarily interested in conserving and celebrating the achieved values of a group, while prophetic religion is interested in criticizing achieved values in the light of some higher ideal. Therefore, priestly religion would, in general, tend to restrict a given way of faith to the peoples among whom it originated and to its classical forms of expression, while prophetic religion moves towards broader social frames of reference and more flexible expression. The one is, in general, socially conservative, and the other socially radical.

Again, historians have noted that most religions incorporate a number of basic modes of expression, the relative significance of each varying from one faith to another. For instance, all religions include some system of devotional practices—some cultic and ritual activities designed to celebrate the intimate and ultimate concerns of that particular faith. Furthermore, all religions include some system of beliefs—some doctrines and dogmas designed to give intellectual expression to the commitment celebrated in its ritual. And all religions include some system of ethical obligations or code of conduct and social practices designed to relate them to the broader areas of political, economic, and social life.

Among the major religions Confucianism has stressed code of conduct above doctrine and ritual. Hinduism, on the other hand, has given formal recognition to the threefold character of religion in its three basic "ways of salvation": *karma-marga*, the "way of works"; *bhakti-marga*, the "way of devotion"; and *jnana-marga*, the "way of study and meditation." Buddhism also, though it began with a primary emphasis on a way of knowledge, has come to incorporate all three emphases in its complex systems. Judaism, like Confucianism, has stressed the ethical and the social aspects of faith; but its Bible and Talmud are concerned also with the intellectual bases of action, and its carefully nurtured devotional practices have kept it alive for centuries in alien and frequently hostile cultures. Christianity, like Hinduism and Buddhism, has stressed one or another of the three facets of faith at various times and in various sects, but Christianity as a whole embodies all three as interrelated essentials.

THE PERILS OF REDUCTIONISM. It may be appropriate to add a final note about the perils of reductionism in historical studies. The historian of religion may be tempted to reduce *all* historical phenomena to religious categories. Or, if his own interest lies primarily in the field of ideas, or of social institutions, or of some other aspect of the whole, he is likely to emphasize these aspects to the distortion of the whole. Again, if the historian of religion is trained primarily in economic or political history, then he is likely to explain all religious phenomena as "nothing but" expressions of various economic or political forces. The perils of "nothing but" are as great in the field of history as in any other field of inquiry. Recognizing the perils may help to avoid or at least to minimize them.

Psychology of Religion

The systematic analysis of religious consciousness has concerned representatives of the great religions of the world for centuries. Hindu sages a thousand years before Christ began to plumb the depths of the experiences of prayer and devotion in an effort to reach the basic religious reality. Gautama Buddha based his reforming religious doctrines on a subtle and profound analysis of the nature and needs of the human soul. In his *Confessions* Augustine shows how he discovered the self in his search for God as revealed in Christianity. The great classics of religious devotion have all been concerned, in a sense, with the psychology of religion.

But the contemporary emphasis upon the psychological approach to religion stems from a twofold development of late-nineteenth-century thought. Within religious circles, Protestant thinkers especially were attracted to the view of Schleiermacher, whose definition of religion was quoted earlier. Schleiermacher was convinced that religious doctrines could be defended as intellectual expressions of basic religious experience, just as scientific laws are intellectual expressions of controlled scientific experience. Thus, later, especially in America, a number of thinkers appeared who attempted to show that theology and philosophy of religion are in a meaningful sense "empirical sciences." This focused a new interest on the psychology of religious experience as such.

The Nature of Psychology

In the late nineteenth century psychology itself was gaining stature as an independent science. The first scientific psychological laboratory was established in Leipzig in 1879 by Wilhelm Wundt. Wundt and others were convinced that the whole range of human experience could be studied with the same basic methods employed in the natural sciences, and that from such study would emerge a new understanding of human consciousness. But the advocates of the young science were confronted at the outset with the necessity for defining their subject matter. What is the psyche which psychology would study scientifically? Psyche is mind, said some of the early psychologists. And what is mind? "Mind is the sum total of the states of consciousness experienced by an individual in his lifetime." By such circular definitions some of the early psychologists managed to set aside the philosophical issues implied in their inquiries and proceeded with the inquiries themselves.

The definitions, however, suggested that subjective consciousness as well as external behavior must be investigated by the psychologist. Therefore, while Wundt and others gave much attention to the accurate measurement and description of sense organs and other physiological functions, some of them also attempted to arrive at an accurate description of subjective states of consciousness as reported by observers employing the method of introspection, by "looking in upon" simple human experiences and reporting verbally what they are like. In this vein Wundt's student, Titchener, who established the first department of psychology in an American university, at Cornell, sought to arrive at an accurate description of the structure of consciousness. Following the lead of the atomic science of their day, the structuralists concluded that consciousness is made up of certain basic component parts labeled sensation, perception, memory-image, and affection or feeling.

While much valuable spadework was done by these early psychologists, it soon became apparent that their reliance on verbal descriptions of states of consciousness introduced so many independent variables into their calculations that their enterprise could hardly be called scientific in the sense of other enterprises which dealt solely with objectively measurable data. To meet this criticism many psychologists turned their attention increasingly to those facets of human experience which can be measured objectively, namely physiological processes and external behavior. The most radical of these, John B. Watson, affirmed that consciousness is actually nothing but the complex of physiological processes manifested in measurable behavior. Advocates of his behavioristic psychology also adopted a radical environmentalism and maintained that the development of an individual is solely determined by the measurable forces of his environment.

Meanwhile Sigmund Freud, Carl Jung, and Alfred Adler were affirming the significance, not merely of the basic ingredients of consciousness described by the structuralists, but of subconscious or unconscious forces, as determinative components of both normal and abnormal human behavior. Their new science of psychoanalysis was thus making an even more radical use of the techniques of introspection, and psychoanalysts were deriving from such internal analysis of their patients' experiences complex systems of explanation. In the beginning the claims of the psychoanalysts were discounted or ignored by both the medical profession, with which many early analysts were associated, and by the psychologists, who were turning more and more to physiological and behavioristic accounts of human experience.

But the extremist views of the pioneer psychologists and psychoanalysts proved to be natural expressions of the immaturity and overenthusiasm of a comparatively young science. In the past few decades psychologists have given more attention to the precise definition of their field and the development of accurate techniques of investigation. As a result most psychologists today make less sweeping philosophical claims concerning the implications of their findings, and tend to recognize the significance and limited relevance of *all* methods of approach exclusively advocated by early workers in the field. As psychology matures, in other words, psychologists become increasingly aware of the perils of reductionism.

TYPES OF RELIGIOUS PSYCHOLOGY. The various shifts of emphasis in the understanding of psychology as such are reflected in the development of psychology of religion. The earliest classic in the field is William James's *The Varieties of Religious Experience*, a volume containing his Gifford Lectures of 1901 and 1902.[11] In this work James followed

11 William James, *The Varieties of Religious Experience* (London: Longmans, Green, & Co., 1902).

the lead of early theological and philosophical investigations
of the religious life and of the introspectionist psychologists.
In his opening chapters he exposes what he considers to be
the fallacy of "medical materialism," which would reduce
dramatic religious experiences to abnormal physiological
states on the basis of similarity between such experiences and
conditions artificially induced through drugs or hypnosis.
All experiences involve physiological states, and the description of such states does not necessarily determine the logical,
social, or religious validity of the total experiences, he says.
Furthermore, basic religious experiences have lasting effects
on the total personality of the experient which do not follow
from otherwise similar medical experiences.

Rather, says James, religious experiences must be analyzed
and evaluated as independently significant phenomena. But
how is one to get at the nature of such experiences? Just as
Titchener turned to the verbal reports of trained observers of
simple sensory experiences, so James turned to the written
reports of dramatic religious experiences contained in religious
classics. He was particularly interested in mystical experiences as reported by some of the great mystics, and from his
analysis he drew certain conclusions concerning the ineffabil-
ity (not fully communicable in words), knowledge-value,
transiency, and passivity of the mystic state. In other chapters he drew certain basic distinctions between "once-born"
and "twice-born" souls, or those individuals whose religious
life develops with a more or less even continuity from relatively naïve to more mature levels, and those who experience
sudden and dramatic conversions at some stage of their lives.

Other psychologists carried forward James's interest in
the psychology of mysticism and conversion. They felt, however, that James's reliance on classical religious literature was
unscientific. So they sought to devise questionnaires which
could be answered by representative cross sections of contemporary religious groups, and also used personal interviews
after the manner of the introspectionists. Thus E. D. Star-
buck was interested primarily in the psychology of religious
conversion and concluded from his studies that conversions

can be broadly classified as positive, or freely willed; negative,
or self-surrendering; and spontaneous, or unpremeditated.
G. A. Coe was interested in the relation of personal temperament and social conditioning to conversion experiences.
G. M. Stratton, following James, maintained that deep personal conflicts lie behind most conversions. These and other
psychologists of religion also found some correlation between
the occurrence of profound religious experience and the stages
of physiological, including sexual, development. James H.
Leuba went further with the medical materialism denounced
by William James, showing the similarity between mystical
religious states and those artificially induced by the use of
drugs.

At the same time leaders of organized religion were making increasing use of the general findings of psychology in
revising the techniques of religious education. In this work
they had the precedent of such earlier students of the religious
life as Jonathan Edwards of the eighteenth- and Horace
Bushnell of the nineteenth-century American Protestant religious scenes. In general they followed the lead of Bushnell
and James in cultivating the once-born type of religious development and in seeking to effect a continuity between
religious growth and the total growth of personality. Within
the field of psychology as such, interest in the psychology of
religion waned as the complexity of the subject became more
apparent.

But a deep conflict had developed between some schools
of psychoanalysis and representatives of organized religion.
Freud's clinical experience had led him to develop a complex
theory of human behavior as motivated in part by the suppressed desires of the subconscious. The strongest of these
desires, he said, are sexual in origin and are distorted by the
family patterns imposed by modern culture. Significantly for
students of religion, he found the quasi-religious terminology
of certain Greek myths most useful in expressing the basic
structures of human behavior as he interpreted them. The
dominating myths in his system are tragic myths, and Freud
felt that modern man's situation is tragic in so far as the

cultural patterns which he must accept if he is to have the material and other benefits of civilization inevitably thwart certain natural drives and longings. In coming to grips with a fundamentally hostile environment, men are frequently driven to the comforts of certain illusions which serve to soften somewhat the full tragedy of human existence. The most important of these illusions are provided by religion. In one of his books, Freud maintained that religion tends to personalize an otherwise impersonal and hostile natural world and provides supernatural sanctions for otherwise intolerable social regulations and mores.[12] It thus provides a helpful crutch for those who cannot face the facts of life squarely and courageously. But true freedom for man will come only when he faces his true situation, makes such changes in social structures as may be demanded by both the desire for the goods of civilization and the fundamental sexual character of human drives, and bravely makes the most of his situation without the aid of religious illusions.

Jung and Adler seemed to find a more constructive place for religion within their systems. Jung sought to understand the varieties of religious experience in terms of his basic classifications of men into extroverts (outgoing and active) and introverts (introspective and passive). All men are influenced by the collective experience of the race, stored in a racial subconscious, he said. It is the function of religion dramatically to preserve this racial heritage and to channel it into socially constructive outlets. Adler, on the other hand, found a drive toward superiority and power at the heart of human activities, and made his classifications in terms of superiority-inferiority status and complexes. Religion may play either a negative or a positive role in helping men come to grips with their difficulties thus interpreted, he said.

PSYCHOLOGY AND RELIGION. Many representatives of organized religion felt that they were confronted by rival faiths

[12] Sigmund Freud, translated by W. D. Robinson-Scott, *The Future of an Illusion* (London: The Hogarth Press, & The Institute of Psychoanalysis, 1924).

rather than by therapeutically useful psychoanalytic theories in these systems. Thus there was a new and bitter round in the warfare between science and religion. Representatives of organized religion frequently denounced psychoanalysis in toto as a satanic theology, while zealous students of psychoanalytic theory frequently espoused the world view implied in their theories as a religious faith, with all the enthusiasm and narrowness of religious fanatics. Within the past few decades, however, there has been a distinct mellowing on both sides. Clergymen have found that certain therapeutic techniques employed in "depth psychology" may be used constructively in pastoral counseling. Pastors, like psychotherapists, they realize, have always been interested in the cure of souls. Similarly, theologians have discovered in the mythological world views of some schools of psychoanalysis a kindred search for the depths of that reality in terms of which human behavior is to be finally understood, and have concluded that psychoanalytic theory and theology may fruitfully learn from each other. Again, many contemporary psychotherapists seek to avoid some of the extreme theoretical conclusions of the pioneers and to maintain an open attitude towards any type of inquiry which shows promise of shedding light on the human situation. Many are calling attention to the fundamentally religious aims of the pioneer psychologists themselves, as they sought to chart a new course leading to a greater realization of human good. Thus many therapists today maintain that, just as some people in some circumstances may turn to religion for psychologically crippling aid and comfort, so others may find in dynamic and constructive religious faith the most valuable aid to mental health.[13] In many circles, psychoanalysts and psychotherapists are figuratively and literally sitting down with theologians and pastors for constructive discussion of ways in which the two fields may work together for common aims.

[13] Cf. Erich Fromm, *Psychoanalysis and Religion* (New Haven: Yale University Press, 1950).

Philosophy of Religion and Theology

What is philosophy? This is a question with which philosophers have concerned themselves from the earliest times. In its Greek derivation the word "philosophy" means simply "love of wisdom." But what is wisdom—and what kind of love of wisdom is truly philosophical? Speaking in the broadest terms, it may be said that the classical Greek philosophers defined wisdom as knowledge of the basic structure of reality, and conduct based on such knowledge. Ancient philosophy grew out of ancient mythology and theology, and to some extent it maintained a fundamentally religious aim, namely knowledge of ultimates and of the nature of the good life. It generally assumed that there is a definable, intelligible structure of reality, a *logos*, and that some men can know it and live accordingly. It aimed, in other words, at seeing life steadily and seeing it whole.

With the development of modern science and the complexities of modern civilization philosophers have become less certain about the possibility or desirability of seeing life whole—the difficulties involved in seeing it steadily are great enough in themselves. Thus more recent philosophers have been less concerned with the grand view and broad sweep of classical philosophers and more concerned with the modest task of criticism. Many modern philosophers seem to feel that philosophy is related to the various fields of human inquiry and human concern as literary criticism, for instance, is related to the special field of literature. The general field of philosophy is broken down into various specialized fields concerned with the criticism of knowledge (logic, philosophy of science, epistemology or theory of knowledge, and so on), criticism of morals (ethics), and criticism of the arts (aesthetics). Some philosophers maintain that philosophy may be further concerned with critically relating the data of these various fields to some objectively determined and tentatively held view of the whole, and thus, they are concerned also with metaphysics and ontology (the theory of being or reality).

In brief, it may be said that philosophy, in either the broader classical or more restricted modern sense, aims at the achievement of critical perspective. It is critical in a positive sense, as it seeks the most rational, logically consistent, universally communicable critique or rationale of a given area of human inquiry and concern. It seeks perspective in so far as it would rise above the particular limitations and presuppositions of a given type of inquiry in order to assess its significance objectively and relate it meaningfully to other areas of inquiry and experience. In any case, the philosopher is obliged to be as dispassionate, open, and objective as his particular finite limitations allow.

In terms of this view of philosophy in general, *the philosophy of religion is concerned with the achievement of critical perspective in matters of religious faith—that is, in matters of intimate and ultimate concern.* For this purpose the philosopher of religion must familiarize himself with as much information provided by anthropologists, historians, psychologists, and other investigators of the field as possible. The data furnished by these and related disciplines are the facts with which he works. But he will not be interested merely in collecting facts. He will be interested in knowing something of the techniques by which the facts are gathered and of the presuppositions which lie behind the employment of these techniques and thus modify the conclusions. He will be a constructive critic, in other words, of the various methods employed in gathering facts about religion. And he will attempt to relate the facts gathered by a given discipline to those gathered in other disciplines in order to get as broad a perspective on the whole field as possible. Like other philosophers, the philosopher of religion is obligated to maintain a view of his subject matter as dispassionate, open, and objective as he can.

As a philosopher he will be especially interested in the intellectual aspects of religion—that is, in religious ideas and beliefs. And, like other students of his field, he will find it necessary to devise certain broad schemes of classification in order to make his analysis of various kinds of belief manageable and intelligible. For instance, the classification of primitive religious beliefs as totemistic, animistic, and manistic is fundamentally a philosophical classification. Similarly, philosophers have traditionally classified progressively complex successors to these primitive beliefs in terms of various forms of theism. Theism is the explanation or expression of ultimate reality in terms of *theos*, deity, or God. But there are various broad types of theism expressing different views of the nature of deity and of the relation of deity to the rest of reality.

For instance, belief in *many gods* responsible for the various functions of nature and society is labeled *polytheism*. Belief in the supreme reality or significance of one god for a specific social group, which does not exclude recognition by that group of the existence of other gods for other groups, is termed *henotheism*. Belief in the sole reality of one God conceived as the creator, sustainer, and perhaps judge and redeemer of the world but not identical with the world is called *monotheism*. And belief in the divine character of all reality as such, identifying God with the world, is called *pantheism*.

Now a philosopher of religion may himself be a theist of some sort—that is, he may employ some concept of deity as the final principle of explanation and evaluation in his philosophical system; or his philosophy may be nontheistic. In either case it is his task to examine as critically and intelligently as he can the cases for the various forms of theism presented by various groups, and to defend his own conclusions with as much rational acumen as he can employ. Theoretically the philosopher of religion is committed to no presuppositions except those of rational inquiry as such. He seeks to understand religious phenomena in terms of the same systematic scheme he employs in understanding all other types of phenomena. He would relate religion, finally, to the broad sweep of a rationally coherent philosophical system.

Theology presupposes the existence of some form of deity, and seeks to draw out the rational implications of such belief for the broader range of human experience. A theologian is usually committed to some form of philosophical theism at the outset. In any case, he seeks to view the world in terms of the assumptions of a specific religious group. His aims are philosophical only in so far as he must communicate with philosophers and establish the philosophical integrity of his position. But his primary concern is to communicate with those in a given religious group who share belief in a specific kind of deity, and to enable them more intelligently and accurately to understand and celebrate their faith. The theologian is interested in religious devotion as well as philosophical speculation; he is concerned with the practical as well as with the theoretical aspects of his commitment. Therefore, his language may be more poetic and dramatic than that of most philosophers. Nevertheless, the competent theologian recognizes an obligation to strive for logical consistency and technical accuracy in the development and employment of his terms. He recognizes an obligation to be as objective and dispassionate in exploring the implications and expression of his fundamental commitment as he is capable of being. But he recognizes the fact that he cannot be objective in the same sense about his commitment as such. His fundamental premises are articles of faith rather than rational conclusions.

Now some philosophers would maintain that theology so conceived is actually a more dramatic and emotional but theoretically immature type of philosophy. Inasmuch as theologians speak about ethical, aesthetic, and metaphysical matters in the name of theology, they have the same obligation as other philosophers to justify their systems on the basis of objective rational inquiry. The appeal to faith simply represents a point of philosophical weakness, and the anthropomorphic language of religious devotion makes the philosophical thought of the theologian ambiguous and confusing. Theologies, such philosophers would say, are to be judged finally at the bar of philosophical reason.

But many theologians would claim that all philosophies of religion, despite their claims to objectivity and openness, are actually theologies in disguise. God, say such theologians, stands for that to which one is ultimately committed. Therefore, philosophers who disparage belief in the gods of specific theologies actually do so because of their previous commitment to the "reasonable" God of their own covert theology. There are some things about which even philosophers cannot be objective and dispassionate—and these things are the concern of theology. Furthermore, the language of philosophy is not as pure technically as the philosophers would like to imagine. All language is anthropomorphic in so far as it is the language of men talking about a world which they experience only indirectly, through human media. Some of the sciences, and particularly mathematics, may approach an unambiguous literal language. But when men talk about the richer dimensions of life—love, hate, and such matters of life and death as religious convictions—it is quite appropriate for them to speak poetically rather than prosaically, symbolically rather than literally. Theological language, some theologians say, is therefore superior to the bloodless talk of the metaphysicians and logicians.

Is the issue then either philosophy of religion or theology? Thinkers of various religious groups have given different answers to this question as they have faced it in different crises. Hindu thinkers finally synthesized theologically oriented thought about ultimate reality (*vishitadvaita vedanta*) and philosophically oriented thought (*advaita vedanta*) in one great system. It is a matter of individual preference and temperament, say the Vedantists, whether one thinks of the ultimately real in terms of gods one or many, or in terms of nontheistic metaphysical concepts which finally point beyond themselves to the unspeakable and unthinkable. Within the Christian tradition there are several basic answers to the problem of the relation of faith to reason. Some Christian thinkers have held, in effect, that faith excludes reason; some have held that faith includes reason and reason implies faith, and that the two can never be finally separated. Others, as in the classical Thomistic tradition, have maintained that reason alone can establish the validity of certain religious beliefs, but that faith may legitimately carry men on into further truths of revelation.

Those who hold the latter view have termed the purely philosophical approach to religious truth "natural theology," and the more frankly faith-centered approach "revealed" or "dogmatic" theology. One who prefers this scheme of classification would therefore object to the characterization of philosophy of religion as contrasted with theology given above. Actually the notion of a philosophy of religion more independent and universal than natural theology first emerged in nineteenth-century Western philosophy, notably in the philosophy of Hegel. At the present time the terms "philosophy of religion" and "theology" are loosely used in many philosophical and religious circles to the confusion of contemporary discussion. If philosophy of religion is "the search for critical perspective in matters of religious faith," it is hoped that this book will be philosophical and historical.

SUGGESTIONS FOR FURTHER READING

General Reference Books on Religion

The Encyclopedia of Religion and Ethics. New York: Chas. Scribner's Sons, 1908.

The Schaff-Herzog Encyclopedia. New York: Funk & Wagnalls Co., 1908.

The Catholic Encyclopaedia. New York: Appleton-Century-Crofts, Inc., 1907.

The Jewish Encyclopedia. New York: Funk & Wagnalls Co., 1930.

Encyclopaedia of the Social Sciences. New York: The Macmillan Co., 1930.

An Encyclopedia of Religion. New York: Philosophical Library, Inc., 1945.

ATTWATER, DONALD (ed.). A Catholic Dictionary. New York: The Macmillan Co., 1949.

BALLOU, ROBERT O. (ed.). The Bible of the World. New York: The Viking Press, 1939.

BROWNE, LEWIS (ed.). The World's Great Scriptures. New York: The Macmillan Co., 1946.

MUELLER, MAX (ed.). The Sacred Books of the East. New York: Chas. Scribner's Sons, 1897-1903.

Books Relating to Chapter 1

ALLPORT, GORDON W. The Individual and His Religion. New York: The Macmillan Co., 1950.

ARCHER, JOHN C. Faiths Men Live By. New York: The Ronald Press Co., 1934.

BAILLIE, JOHN. *The Interpretation of Religion.* New York: Chas. Scribner's Sons, 1928.

BENEDICT, RUTH. *Patterns of Culture.* Boston: Houghton Mifflin Co., 1934.

BOUQUET, ARTHUR. *Comparative Religion.* Harmondsworth, England: Penguin Books, Ltd., 1950.

BRADEN, CHARLES. *The World's Religions.* Nashville: Abingdon-Cokesbury Press, 1939.

CLEMEN, CARL (ed.). *Religions of the World.* New York: Harcourt, Brace & Co., Inc., 1931.

DEWEY, JOHN. *A Common Faith.* New Haven: Yale University Press, 1934.

DURKHEIM, EMILE. *The Elementary Forms of Religious Life.* New York: The Macmillan Co., 1915.

FRANKFORT, WILSON, and JACOBSEN. *Before Philosophy.* Harmondsworth, England: Penguin Books, Ltd., 1949.

FRAZER, JAMES G. *The Golden Bough.* Abridged Ed. New York: The Macmillan Co., 1923.

FROMM, ERICH. *Psychoanalysis and Religion.* New Haven: Yale University Press, 1950.

HUME, ROBERT E. *The World's Living Religions.* New York: Chas. Scribner's Sons, 1934.

JAMES, WILLIAM. *The Varieties of Religious Experience.* New York: Longmans, Green & Co., Inc., 1902.

LEUBA, JAMES H. *The Psychology of Religious Mysticism.* New York: Harcourt, Brace & Co., Inc., 1925.

LOWIE, ROBERT. *Primitive Religion.* New York: Liveright Publishing Corp., 1909.

MALINOWSKI, BRONISLAW. *The Foundations of Faith and Morals.* London: Oxford University Press, 1936.

MARETT, ROBERT R. *The Threshold of Religion.* London: Methuen & Co., Ltd., 1909.

MOORE, CHARLES A. *Philosophy—East and West.* Princeton: The Princeton University Press, 1946.

MOORE, GEORGE F. *History of Religions.* New York: Chas. Scribner's Sons, 1946.

NORTHROP, F. S. C. *The Meeting of East and West.* New York: The Macmillan Co., 1946.

NOSS, JOHN B. *Man's Religions.* New York: The Macmillan Co., 1949.

PRATT, JAMES B. *The Religious Consciousness.* New York: The Macmillan Co., 1920.

REINACH, SOLOMON. *Orpheus.* Paris: B. Picard, 1909.

ROBERTS, DAVID E. *Psychotherapy and a Christian View of Man.* New York: Chas. Scribner's Sons, 1950.

TYLOR, EDWARD B. *Primitive Culture.* New York: Brentano's, 1924.

VAN DER LEEUW, GERARDUS. *Religion in Essence and Manifestation.* London: George Allen & Unwin, Ltd., 1938.

WACH, JOACHIM. *Sociology of Religion.* Chicago: University of Chicago Press, 1944.

WHITEHEAD, ALFRED N. *Religion in the Making.* New York: The Macmillan Co., 1926.

Chapter 2

CLASSICAL WAYS OF CHINA

WHY BEGIN WITH CHINA?

THIS survey begins with the Orient for several good reasons. Here are chapters in human history of which no educated person ought to be ignorant. And it is a sad fact that many if not most Occidentals know very little of the Orient. To them it is still "the mysterious East." When they think of it, they think of a strange, inscrutable people, quite unlike themselves. They think of the mystic in his mountain retreat, of the Indian fakir at the fair, of the Yogi squatting on his haunches, of idols in grotesque shapes and guises.

What makes this lack of understanding so tragic is that the East and West have met and have been thrown together in the one world created by modern communication. Belatedly the West has waked up to the importance of the mysterious East.

There are two kinds of mysteries—those one does not understand, and those he cannot understand. Most Western attitudes toward the mysteries of the Orient are happily within the former class. It is therefore possible to look forward to increasing understanding between East and West at every level of communication. It is only within the past century and a half that there have been wide-scale efforts on the part of Western thinkers to familiarize themselves with the vast field of Oriental life and cultures. There have been many reasons for this: lack of communication; the provincial assumption that neither had anything to learn from the other; preoccupation with more pressing matters closer to home.

But efforts at mutual understanding are now so well under way that a good future may be predicted for them. As these enterprises proceed underlying similarities are found beneath the variety and differences. As Westerners become familiar with Eastern philosophy they find within it examples of many of the ideals and ideas of Western thought. An American scholar, who recently spent a year visiting Oriental universities interviewing cross sections of students about the life patterns or philosophies of life they preferred, discovered great variety within countries and cultures hitherto supposed to be dominated by a single philosophy or faith.[1] Apparently Oriental students differ among themselves as much as do their American cousins. Here perhaps is some empirical verification for the supposition that people the world over fall into a relatively small number of similar types which have emerged in man's long quest for meaningful existence.

It is important to emphasize the breadth and inclusiveness of many Oriental ways, for in the brief chapters which follow the reader may get a false impression of homogeneity or uniformity. That is not the case. Each of the major traditions of the East has found room in its faith and practice for all sorts and conditions of men. Furthermore, unlike the West, there is little exclusiveness in Oriental religions. In China, for instance, it is not unusual for a person to be a Confucianist, Buddhist, and Taoist at the same time, in different areas of his life. Sometimes, as in the case of Hinduism or Mahayana Buddhism, enormous variety has been comprehended within the very elastic limits of a single tradition.

Another important reason for studying the religions of the Orient is that it will serve as an excellent backdrop for a more detailed study of the West. Probably not many readers of this book will entertain the serious possibility of becoming Buddhists, Confucians, or Hindus, though the real influence

[1] Charles Morris, "Comparative Strength of Life-Ideals in Eastern and Western Cultures," in *Essays in East-West Philosophy: an Attempt at World Philosophical Synthesis* (Honolulu: University of Hawaii Press, 1951), pp. 353-70.

of Oriental faith and thought upon such Westerners as
Gerald Heard, Aldous Huxley, John Van Druten, and many
others must be pointed out. The range of serious religious
choice, however, for most Westerners lies in the four ways of
Judaism, Roman Catholicism, Protestantism, or Humanism.
But the Westerner will be better able to understand his own
faith, whatever it may be, after a look at the Orient.

The Way of Confucius

We turn first to the way of Confucius because it is safe to
say that it is the Oriental way most easily grasped by the
average Westerner. In general, it seems clear that most
Westerners, or at least most Americans, immediately think
of doing something when they think of religion. For them
religion is primarily ethical and active—in its simplest childish
forms it is a matter of being good little boys and girls. It
has primarily to do with their relations to their fellows: their
family, their state, or perhaps even "Humanity." This is
so much the case that one of the familiar definitions of religion proposed by a Western scholar has it that religion is
simply "morality touched with emotion." But this understanding of religion is not exclusively Western; there are those
in the East also who find the "good life," and hope even to
find salvation, through relating their behavior rationally to
that of their fellows in accord with some moral code based
on an accepted view of the world. This is uniquely true
in the case of those who follow the teachings of "Master
Kung," Kung-Fu-tse, or Confucius.

The Life and Times of Confucius

The culture of China was already very old, by Western
standards, when Confucius lived (551?-479 B.C.). Language
and the arts were highly developed, and for centuries there
had been a measure of social stability in a carefully graded
feudal society. Religion had found its place largely as a
social expression of men's sense of dependence on the earth,
society, and the broader universe (Heaven, Earth, and Man).

Various magical devices and systems had been developed in the attempt to understand and control nature, the art of divination having reached a semimathematical stage similar to the Pythagorean schools of ancient Greece. More significant for our present purposes is the fact that the sense of man's indebtedness to his family and racial heritage had also found elaborate expression in what is sometimes called "ancestor-worship." In China as elsewhere the fact of death had posed one of the basic religious problems, and there was broad speculation regarding the fate of the dead and the nature and extent of their influence over the living. Animistic beliefs in good and evil spirits (*shen* and *kwei*) associated with the dead were widespread, and elaborate funeral ceremonies and memorial offering rites had been developed. There seems to have been among the Chinese from very early times an unusually strong sense of family ties with both the living and the dead. The locus of this respect for the "elders," living and dead, was the natural biological and social unit of the immediate family. But ideally it extended also to the empire as a whole conceived as an inclusive family, with the emperor as "Son of Heaven" standing in the same fatherly relation to noblemen, and through them, to lower orders of society, as heads of the smaller family units stood to their members.

In Confucius' time, however, this simple and hitherto effective religious-social structure was threatened by invasions from the northwest and by increasing restlessness and rebellion within the realm. Confusion and discontent were growing, and new religious and political ideas were attracting the attention of many who sought a way out of the increasing uncertainty and instability. Confucius felt the effect of these stirrings in his own life. He was born into an aristocratic family of the state of Sung which had moved to the state of Lu on the Shantung Peninsula. There his family had fallen into economic difficulties. Apparently his father died when Confucius was young, but his mother was determined that he was to have the education of a gentleman and that he should find a place for himself in the councils of Lu. Her son proved a devoted and apt scholar, and in his teens he occupied a minor civil service post in his native state. At the same time he applied himself assiduously to the study of the literary and cultural heritage of his people. The more he understood of this heritage, the more concerned he became about its apparent neglect in his own day, and the more alarmed he became at the falling away from the traditional virtues of the traditional political and social patterns. Gradually he became convinced that the only thing that could save his people from utter chaos was a complete and wholehearted return to the teachings of the ancients, accompanied by a reform of the political order in the direction of a perfected and rational feudal system like that which had made peace and harmony possible in the past. Such a reform should work from the top down: the emperor, heads of states, and lesser officials should begin the reform by setting proper examples in their own conduct. Then dishonesty and other political vices would be exposed and rooted out.

In his late teens he accepted the minor post of collector of grain and live stock due as taxes to the Duke of Lu. But it was as a teacher that Master Kung had his real and lasting influence. He gathered boys about himself, instructing them in the "Six Disciplines:" history, poetry, government, propriety, music, and divination. He sent his students into government service. And in his fifties he entered government officialdom himself, only to fall victim to a plot in which he "lost face" and resigned. For many years he wandered from state to state seeking a ruler who would successfully implement his reforms in a local government, but always sooner or later these experiments broke down. Undiscouraged by these failures as a reformer, Confucius devoted more and more time to teaching. He was not the first teacher in China, but he appears to have been the first to accept large numbers of disciples from various strata of society. These men were to make his ideas the most potent intellectual and ethical force in subsequent Chinese history. Not long before his death, Confucius was invited to return to his native state, where he died in peace and with some recognition of the significance of his life of tireless devotion to those ideals and practices which he believed would save not only his own people but all men.

The Classics

What are these ideals and practices? Only a few of those which seem fundamental in his system can be mentioned. In general, Confucius looked to the past for guidance; and the wisdom of the past, he believed, was to be found in the Chinese Classics. Therefore it was important that men should know and appreciate the Classics. In later Confucian literature these are referred to as being six, or later five, in number: (1) The *I-Ching*, or Book of Changes, concerning the art of divination; (2) The *Shu-Ching*, or Book of History, containing history and legends of dynasties of the past; (3) The *Shi-Ching*, or the poetic Book of Odes; (4) The *Li-Chi*, or Book of Rites, an important book for later Confucianism containing regulations for religious ritual and rules of etiquette for personal conduct; (5) The *Yueh-Ching*, or Book of Music, not included as an independent book in later lists; (6) The *Chun Chiu*, or Spring and Autumn Annals, a chronicle of the state of Lu from 722-479 B.C. The exact nature of Confucius' relation to the authorship of these books is a matter of debate among the scholars. Some have held that he is responsible for much of if not all the material found in them; others have held that he merely edited and passed on what he found; and others have held that most of the material came from antiquity, but that in editing it Confucius added the imprint of his own ideas. The *Spring and Autumn Annals* is almost entirely the product of his own labor.

To the five (or six) basic Classics later Confucianists added *The Four Books*: (1) *The Analects*, a compendium of teachings attributed to the Master; (2) *The Great Learning*, (3) *The Doctrine of the Mean*, a further elaboration of the teachings of Confucius by later disciples; and (4) *The Mencius Book*, containing teachings attributed to one of the most significant of Confucius' successors in the school. The Classics and the Books, in turn, became the basis of Chinese education and government in future generations, because China was to adopt through most of her history prior to the Revolution of 1912 Confucius' view that government should be in the hands of the *ju* or literati. Primary in the Confucian way then, is careful study of the traditions and culture of the past, wherein may be found guidance toward stability in the changing present and uncertain future.

The Rectification of Names

Careful study of the Classics by the leaders and the extension of education in so far as possible to all members of society, according to needs and abilities, should lead, said Confucius, to The Rectification of Names and a lessening of the intellectual confusion which breeds moral chaos. To rectify names means to have words universally understood and precisely used. It means dependable communication in all matters of social importance. There can be no peace when different men mean different things when they use the same words—(witness the international debates of our own day). So careful attention must be given to language, and its usage must be reformed so that meanings of words will be clearly understood. If this occurs, Confucius said, men will act harmoniously, according to their station in society. If the emperor, for instance, really understands the meaning of the word "emperor," and sees what it has meant when applied to the good emperors of the past, then he will act like an emperor and not like a tyrant. If a father really understands the meaning of fatherhood, then he will behave with dignity as he sets an example for his family, and not like an irresponsible young bachelor. Each person must dependably act his part through the entire network of natural and social functions. Lest this hope of Confucius seem naïvely sanguine, the widespread interest and sometimes faith in semantics, or the science of words, among some contemporary thinkers, may be noted. It should also be noted that Confucius' interest in The Rectification of Names was an expression of more basic convictions about the nature of men and ethical behavior. He assumed that there are stable elements in nature and society.

Mutuality

The foundation of all ethical behavior, said Confucius, is to be found in *Jen*. This word has been variously translated by various expositors. Perhaps the most suggestive translations are those which begin with the fact that the Chinese character for *Jen* is the character for "man" combined with the character for "two." The character thus suggests a deep sense of the fact that each man is basically related to every other man, so that what concerns one ultimately concerns all. This deep sense of relatedness, or mutuality, in turn is reflected in an attitude of man-to-manness, sympathy, compassion, human-heartedness, or love. Thus *Jen* appears to be primarily a matter of attitude, determining the motive of ethical conduct. Conduct which springs from a sense of one's relatedness to others and of men's mutual dependence on each other is good; conduct otherwise motivated is bad. The most famous expression of *Jen* in Confucius' teaching reads as follows: "Tzu-Kung asked, saying, 'Is there a word which may serve as a rule of practice for all one's life?' The master said 'Is not Reciprocity (*shu*) such a word? What you do not want done to yourself, do not do to others.' " [2] We recognize here, of course, a "negative" expression of "the Golden Rule." But the negative form of its expression is a linguistic accident, and it seems clear from a study of other things that Confucius says about *Jen* that his concept of its results embraces both positive (*shu*) and negative (*chung*) actions. To be motivated by *Jen* means both to do those things which are mutually beneficial to self and neighbor and to refrain from doing those things which are not mutually beneficial.

Duty

If one is motivated in his behavior by a sense of *Jen*, his actions will always be governed by the requirements of duty or righteousness in each situation, rather than by personal

[2] Charles A. Wong, *The Analects of Confucius* (China, no imp. n. d.), p. 413, as reprinted in John B. Noss, *Man's Religions* (New York: The Macmillan Co., 1949), p. 353.

preference or desire. He will always ask, not "What would I *like* to do?" but "What *ought* I to do in the light of my inter-dependent relatedness to all men?" In other words, the good man, said Confucius, never asks "What is there in this for me?" Rather he does that which is right simply because it is right—he is good for nothing—nothing ulterior to goodness. It should be noted that Confucius apparently lived his own life with a deep sense of duty and mission. Knowing that his reform programs had little if any chance of adoption, he nevertheless was not deterred by apparent defeat but con-tinued in his mission simply because he was convinced that it was his duty to do so. Encountering opposition on one occasion he is reported to have said, "Heaven begot the power that is in me. What have I to fear from such a one as Huan T'uei?" [3]

Propriety

For one to hold that all activities should be motivated by a sense of compassion or sympathy and performed solely be-cause of duty is to provide only formal principles for ethical conduct. Such principles in themselves say nothing about one's specific duty in a specific situation. Thus more than a good motive and recognition of the imperative of duty is needed if men are to have a sufficient guide to conduct. What is needed, said Confucius, is an understanding and implementation of *Li*. What is *Li*? Confucius uses the term perhaps more frequently than any other in his ethical discus-sions, and yet it is difficult to express; indeed, its expression varies with the concrete situations in which men find them-selves. In general, it might be called a sense of propriety—a discriminating sensitivity to and appreciation of that which is fitting and proper in social relationships. It involves an imagi-native understanding of the feelings of others, a deep sense of humility, and a realistic awareness of the possibilities and limi-tations inherent in each social situation. To act according to *Li*, in other words, is to behave as a gentleman in every cir-

[3] Arthur Waley, *The Analects of Confucius* (London: G. Allen & Unwin, Ltd., 1938), p. 127.

cumstance with kindness and social grace, so as to cause a
minimum of unpleasantness and a maximum of dignified
harmony. *Li* is thus something which requires careful cultivation and broad experience. It may begin as sheer imitation
of the ways of the mature and wise and the blind following
of the precepts set forth in the *Li Chi*. But through practice,
if motive and intent are sound, it will become spontaneous,
second nature, for the morally whole man—the gentleman.
This means, of course, that the expression in *Li* of *Jen* and *Yi*
will not be the same in all circumstances, but rather that the
expression will be adapted with an appropriate sense of form
to the specific relations involved in each circumstance. Thus
to live the good life is truly an art, and the good man is an
artist in social relations. Indeed, it has been suggested that
Confucius' entire ethical system is modeled on the ideals of
art or aesthetics. The good life, like the beautiful work of art,
is characterized by order, harmony, balance, and the appropriate adaptation of form to material and intent. And this
means that the good man, or superior man, as Confucius
called him, will have a proper and lively appreciation of ritual
and ceremony as well as of music and letters, because ritual
and ceremony dignify human relations and provide ordered
and beautiful expression for basic human emotions of love,
joy, anxiety, sorrow, bereavement, and the like. There is
appropriate ceremony and appropriate behavior for each of
the basic social relations.

The Five Relations

These basic social relations, according to Confucius, are as
follows: the relations of (1) emperor to subject; (2) father to
son; (3) husband to wife; (4) elder brother to younger brothers; and (5) elders in general to juniors in general. *Li* for the
emperor means sensitivity to the needs of the subjects and behavior appropriate to his office as one who sets an example for
the empire, while *Li* for subjects means grateful emulation of
and obedience to the emperor. *Li* for the husband involves
sensitivity to the needs of the wife and to his responsibilities as
her provider and protector; *Li* for the wife means grateful serv-

ice and obedience. *Li* for the father means setting the proper example for the son; *Li* for the son means respect for the father—engaging in conduct which will honor him, and cherishing his memory after death through the proper ritual. *Li* for elders in general means conduct and demeanor worthy of emulation, while *Li* for juniors in general means proper respect for and emulation of the elders. Of all these relations, however, Confucius treats the relation of father to son and son to father at greatest length. "Filial piety" is fundamental in the whole scheme of social relations. If fathers could only be good fathers and sons could only be good sons, then other social relations would fall into place. Nor does Confucius leave one groping around for specific examples of what is meant by "filial piety"—concrete case after case is cited in the Classics, and specific patterns of conduct are described in meticulous detail. Proper observance of periods of mourning, for instance, is regarded as especially important.

Implied in the doctrine of *Li*, then, is the notion that one is not to treat all men alike, even though one may have a sense of mutuality in social relations. It is natural and good that we are bound more closely to some persons by biological ties than we are to others. Therefore the expression of *Jen* in the *Li* of family relationship is different from the expression of *Jen* in the *Li* of biologically more distant relationships. Ideally, perhaps, one should love all men as one loves the members of one's own family, but actually one does not—perhaps cannot. Therefore, perhaps one should not try. Or perhaps it would be better to say that it is more fruitful to begin the practice of *Jen-Li* where it has the best natural chance of success, i.e., in the family. Only when it is first perfected there should one go on to extend its bounds. Confucius seemed to think, in other words, that charity (*Jen*) begins at home. Furthermore he held that it is unwise to say that *Jen* means the same *Li* for good men as for bad, for the just as for the unjust. Rather one should return good for good and justice for evil. The good man is to be treated with goodness; the bad man is to be treated with justice. In all instances, therefore, the good man, motivated by a sense of *Jen* and acting according to *Yi*, will carefully discriminate so that specific actions are correctly graded by *Li*.

Faith and Conduct

How is this code of conduct related to religious belief? To answer this question, we must ask again "What is religion?" If by religion one means belief in supernatural powers and conduct based on such belief, then it may be pointed out that Confucius stressed the need for proper and careful observance of the traditional rites and ceremonies of his people. Sacrifices and prayers should be made in stated ways on stated occasions, he said, and the "superior" man will not neglect the niceties of religious worship. However, it seems that much of his concern for such matters is based on a belief in the social utility of the rites: they function as celebrations of family and state unity and serve to remind men of their dependence on their heritage and on each other as well as on the forces of "Heaven and Earth."

Again, Confucius seemed to be impressed by the aesthetic value of ceremony—the order, balance, and symmetry are beautiful and therefore valuable. As noted above, it has been suggested that aesthetic and ethical values are never separated in Confucius' mind: the good life and the good state, like the beautiful creations of the arts, are characterized principally by order, balance, and harmony. Thus one of Confucius' successors, Hsün-tzu (289-238 B.C.), could give a purely naturalistic and humanistic explanation of and justification for religious rites as affording an ordered outlet for natural emotions and a magnification of social values. It is probable that the intellectual Confucian has traditionally shared Hsün-tzu's views on these matters.

However, evidence from Confucius' life as a whole suggests that his concern for religious rites went deeper. Like Socrates, he spoke often of a sense of divine mission in his work. On occasions when it appeared evident that his reform programs had little chance of success, he declared that his obligation to work for them was not dependent on their earthly success or failure. The issues of his life, and the issues of all life, he felt, are in the last analysis expressions of *Ming*. Now *Ming* is sometimes translated "fate," but in Confucius' day it seems to have had a more personally religious meaning —"The Will of Heaven." It suggests a cosmic moral purpose running through the course of human events—a purpose or a will to which the good man must give himself without reservation and which finally underlies his good works. A sense of dedication to cosmic purpose pervades the traditional accounts of Confucius' life and much of his teaching. But like many other persons whose fundamental concern is ethics, Confucius was at times critical of supernaturalism as a distraction from urgent human and social concerns. Asked about duties to the dead, he replied, "Before we are able to do our duty by the living, how can we do it by the spirits of the dead?" [4] For himself he appears to have believed that when a man acts morally, he does the will of Heaven.

The Fate of Confucianism

In later Confucianism, Confucius himself was exalted to become an object of worship, and his teachings took on an aura of divinity for many of the common people. Various commentators on the Classics arose to produce different schools of interpretation and practice as the social and political situation in China changed through the ages. It is regrettable that we cannot examine some of these schools here, because some of them are more suggestive and comprehensive than what is generally regarded as the original school of the Master himself. Until recent times a reformulation and adaptation of his tradition known as Neo-Confucianism,—a movement itself containing various conflicting groups—dominated Chinese thought. At the same time the traditional family and state ceremonies approved by Confucius were repeated generation after generation in nearly every family and village as well as in the ancient imperial capital at Peking, whose magnificent Temple of Heaven, surrounded by a stately park, was the religious center of the empire. A state cult of Confucius flourished at various times in Chinese history prior

[4] Quoted in John B. Noss, *op. cit.*, p. 365.

to the revolution of 1912, and there was a brief revival under the Kuomintang in the 1930's. The future of Confucianism in China is, to say the least, uncertain. In general, it seems that the Master's teachings are now looked upon as too conservative for a revolutionary age.

THE WAY OF THE TAO

Yang-Yin Dualism

Confucius was reported to have been extremely reluctant to speak much about metaphysical and theological matters. His way was pre-eminently a way of works, a system of ethical action, and he was interested in speculations about the ultimate nature of man and the universe—and Heaven—only in so far as these affected, usually adversely, he thought, the practical concerns of men and governments. But we have also seen that the masses of the Chinese people, like the masses of people everywhere, needed more than a commonsense guide to action for the rich complexity of their daily lives. They needed also to worship, to enter into communion with the personified forces of nature and society, and to celebrate the great occasions of life with religious ritual and pageantry.

But from the earliest times there had been those in China who wondered what lay behind the nature and society in which action occurred, and what lay behind the spirits and gods who were worshiped. At approximately the time when Indian thinkers were attacking these questions and producing the speculations of the *Upanishads,* and when early Greek nature-philosophers were raising some of the same questions in the West, unknown Chinese sages were making their own speculative ventures. Like the others, they were first impressed by the fact of regularity in the doings of nature. Once they progressed beyond primitive awe and fear in the face of nature's power, and once the social order had become stable enough to permit more leisurely reflection, it could be observed that through the cataclysms and the more peaceful workings of nature there seems to be some sort of pattern—

some recurrences like the cycle of the seasons, some order like the orderly course of the heavenly bodies. Predicting the course of these latter had been a chief concern for those who turned to the mysterious heavens for magical powers, but as the predictions become more successful, some thinkers crossed the thin line which separates magical curiosity from scientific speculation. Thus early Chinese inquirers were profoundly impressed by the harmony of nature.

But this harmony is obviously not a static balance of forces. Nature is an ongoing affair, full of conflict and contrast, force and opposing force. Perhaps, therefore, unitary harmony is actually a balance of positive and negative forces in constant interaction—positive and negative forces whose presence can be detected in the structure of all that exists, animate and inanimate. Yes, said these early Chinese speculators, there are two such basic forces in the world: the *Yang* and the *Yin*. To the *Yang* belongs all that is masculine, active, productive, hot, dry, bright, assertive, positive; to the *Yin* belongs all that is female, passive, receptive, cool, moist, shadowy, negative. By extending the pairs of contrasts it is possible to describe all things as combinations and balances of the two basic positive and negative forces. Thus elaborate books of divinations and descriptions of all manner of things and events resulted from the application of this primitive yet arrestingly contemporary theory.

Most significantly, a "numbers school" developed which stressed the fact that all that can be counted can be counted in terms of odd and even numbers; all numbers are combinations, then, of mathematical Yang-Yin, and all that is real is thus countable. Here, then, was a touchstone by which the secret of the universe could be known:

> Man is the product of the attributes of heaven and earth, by the interaction of the dual forces of nature . . . The five elements are distributed through the four seasons, and it is by their harmonious action that the moon is produced, which therefore keeps waxing for fifteen days and waning for fifteen. . . . The five flavors, with the six condiments, and the twelve articles of diet, come each one, in their revolutions in the course of a year,

to give its character to the food. . . . Thus it was that when
the sages would make rules for men they felt it necessary . . .
to make the two forces of nature the commencement of all.[5]

From this point of departure Chinese science and nature
philosophy were to undergo remarkable development. And,
as the last sentence of the quotation above suggests, those
who, like Confucius, were interested in making rules for men,
felt it necessary to know and pattern their rules after the
Yang-Yin nature of the universe.

Beyond Yang and Yin, the Tao

There were those who could not rest content with Yang-
Yin dualism, no matter how complexly developed and how
successful in the control of nature and society it might be.
These men were haunted by the perennial question, "What
is beyond or behind the conflicting forces whose balance constitutes the world?" Is there, beyond and prior to duality,
unity—behind the two, One? Such were the men who produced the literature of Chinese mysticism as found in a
movement called *Taoism*. It was traditionally supposed that
Taoism was founded by a man called Lao-tse who gave to it
its basic teachings. The tradition is obscure, however, as to
when, where, and how this man lived. Some scholars believe
that there were at least two formative figures in the movement. Some say Lao-tse lived around 604 B.C., others that he
was much later. It is perhaps appropriate that the founding
of Taoism should be historically obscure. Standard legends
have it, however, that Lao-tse (literally "the Old Boy") was
born with a white beard, signifying his lifelong wisdom; that
he was for a time a librarian in the court of the state of Chou;
that he became disillusioned with the activistic attempts of
men in the spirit of Confucianism to reform governments and

[5] From *The Li Ki*, in *The Portable World Bible* (New York: The Viking
Press, 1944), pp. 492-93. *The Portable World Bible* and *The Bible of the
World* (New York: The Viking Press, 1939), from which several passages
in this volume are taken, are compilations of other and earlier sources reprinted by The Viking Press with the permission of the original publishers.

force upon others an active code of conduct; and that he
accordingly forsook his position and the world in middle age
and rode off on a black ox into the Western Hills, there to
spend his life in meditation and quest for the One. Before he
passed the borders of the kingdom, however, he thoughtfully
paused long enough to toss off a collection of cryptic sayings
which constitute the basic scripture of Taoism, the *Tao Te
Ching*.

The Tao Te Ching

It is the *Tao Te Ching*, "The Book of The Tao and Its
Activity," which is of primary importance for the understanding of Taoism. And perhaps the typical Western student has
already impatiently asked "What *is* this *Tao* whose '-ism' constitutes China's indigenous mysticism, the book of whose 'activity' is so important?" Well, the Taoist would reply that the
very asking of such a question betrays a Western prejudice
and presupposition which the Westerner would do well critically to examine. Westerners, they would say, take it for
granted that anything true, real, or significant can be defined
—can be put into words which are parts of a logically ordered
system of language. What is real, Westerners feel, can be
pointed to, if only with a word. But just at this point the
Taoist and those like him part company with the West. The
most important thing that can be said about the *Tao*, he
would say, is that nothing positive can be said about it—not
even that it is an *it*. When we *de-fine* things, make them
finite, we separate them from other things by labeling them.
Indeed, there have been those in the West who have maintained that things and names are identical, and that names,
like things, are irreducibly plural. Names which refer to
classes of names are merely "breathings." Other Westerners
have felt that universals as well as particulars can be named,
and that they too accordingly "exist." But that there is
something more important than the nameable which is basic
to all names is not an intelligible notion to most Westerners.
Yet the Taoist says:

The Tao that can be expressed is not the eternal Tao;
The name that can be defined is not the unchanging name.[6]

If that which lies beyond the Yang and Yin, the concrete and the nameable, is unnameable and inexpressible, then that would seem to be the end of the matter, the typical Westerner thinks. If the most profound statement is silence, then so be it. But the Taoist is not content to leave the matter there. What he means, he says, is that the nature and meaning of the *Tao* are not exhaustively expressed in words, though words can be used to point to it and, negatively, to bring one to an awareness of it. Thus the *Tao Te Ching* goes on to point out that the world of names, the world of Yin and Yang, is the world of existence—of coming into being and passing away—of change and flux. That which lies beyond and behind this world then, the nameless, is nonexistence, which never comes into being and never passes away, but is eternal and unchanging:

> Non-existence is called the antecedent of heaven and earth;
> Existence is the mother of all things.
> From eternal non-existence, therefore, we serenely observe the mysterious beginning of the universe. . . .
> This sameness is called profundity. Infinite profundity is the gate whence comes the beginning of all parts of the universe.[7]

There is, in other words, a logical priority of nonbeing (*wu-ming*) over being (*yu-ming*), just as there is a mathematical priority of the one over the many: without unity, duality is impossible—without the *Tao*, nothing is.

Is the *Tao* then active, since it is the source of all activity? No, it is beyond action:

> The Tao is ever inactive, yet there is nothing that it does not do.[8]

Being inactive, it is unchanging, or invariable—are not the laws of change themselves unchanging? And do not all ap-

---

[6] From the *Tao Te Ching* in *The World Bible, op. cit.*, p. 542.
[7] *Ibid.*, p. 542.
[8] *Ibid.*, p. 548.

parent oppositions eventually resolve into harmony? Do not all extremes pass over into their apparent opposites—if anything is pushed too far, does it not change into something else?

> I call it Tao, and I name it as supreme.
> Supreme means going on;
> Going on means far;
> Going far means returning.
> Therefore Tao is supreme; heaven is supreme; earth is supreme;
> And man also is supreme. . . .
> Man follows the laws of the earth;
> Earth follows the laws of heaven;
> Heaven follows the laws of Tao;
> Tao follows the laws of its intrinsic nature.[9]

The *Tao*, then, is the All, even though, strictly speaking, it is No-thing. The word "Tao" means literally "The Way" —the way things are, the way of things, the way of being.

It should be noted, however, that those who were chiefly concerned with knowing and identifying themselves with the *Tao* also derived from their concern a code of conduct—or rather, codeless conduct. As suggested in the legend, Lao-tse is said to have become convinced that the chief trouble with men is their busy-ness. In their eagerness to control nature and society they forget that nature and society are themselves controlled by *Tao*. If only men would pay attention to the natural ways of doing things—the way of *Tao*—and stop trying to create, reform, bend, and construct, then all would be well. The wisest course of action is really inaction; the best way of doing is doing what comes naturally. Men, as children of *Tao*, are naturally good, as *Tao* is naturally good. Indeed, it is from the *Tao* that we get our notion of good, or the way things should be as contrasted with the way they are. If men were left alone, then all would be well. Laws and governments are confessions of evil and failure; rules of ethics are indications of departure from the *Tao*. Thus:

[9] *Ibid.*, p. 547.

Not exalting the worthy keeps the people from emulation.
Not valuing rare things keeps them from theft . . . Therefore
    the sage rules
By emptying their hearts,
Filling their stomachs,
Weakening their ambitions
And strengthening their bones.
He always keeps them from knowing what is evil and desiring
    what is good . . .
He governs by non-action; consequently there is nothing un-
    governed.[10]

The highest goodness is like water. Water is beneficent to all
    things but does not contend. It stays in places which
    others despise. Therefore it is near Tao. . . .

Do away with learning, and grief will not be known.
Do away with sageness and eject wisdom, and the people will
    benefit a hundred times . . .
The weakest things in the world can overmatch the strongest
    things in the world . . .
The weak can overcome the strong and the yielding can over-
    come the hard . . .

(Therefore)

Return love for hatred.
Otherwise, when a great hatred is reconciled, some of it will
    surely remain . . .
The Tao of heaven shows no partiality; it abides always with
    good men.[11]

Such is the direction of the life of one who knows the *Tao*.

Later Development of Taoism

It should not be surprising to learn that Taoism, which began with such strange philosophical doctrines, would make
its greatest impact upon the Chinese people in a much more
this-worldly fashion. The attainment of salvation through

[10] *The World Bible, op. cit.,* p. 543.
[11] *Ibid.,* pp. 543-52.

knowledge of the *Tao* is a difficult matter indeed, despite the Taoist's protestations of its simplicity and spontaneity. Yet the goal it offers is an attractive one—namely, unity with the central power of the universe and the consequent appropriation of that power in one's own life. What is more, it had been shown that the *Tao* is eternal; thus if one could really know the *Tao*, become immersed in it, he too would be eternal. For the Taoists spoke of knowing the *Tao* in terms which suggested that he who truly knows it becomes it and lives in its eternal power. And so it came about that men less competent philosophically than the compilers of the *Tao Te Ching* began to look for more tangible short-cuts to the immortal power of the *Tao*.

Now the Chinese, like other peoples, had long been interested in alchemy and the production of edible gold. The belief had arisen that if one could produce edible gold and eat it he would possess limitless power. Was this not also the limitless power of the *Tao?* Then perhaps those who could not reach the *Tao* through understanding could drink it in an elixir of immortality or swallow it in a pill of eternal life. Soon there were many magicians and priests operating in the name of Taoism who offered just this sort of salvation. Legends sprang up of Magic Mountains and Heavenly Islands where the immortal dwelt and from which magic potions had been stolen—potions obtainable from qualified doctors of the soul for a suitable fee. It is said that many Chinese met their death by drinking elixirs of immortality. Yet it was as a magical and erotic cult that Taoism became popular in China around the turn of the first century A.D., and to this day "lower Taoism" is identified with magic and superstition.

Finally, Taoism underwent a third transformtion and became, for multitudes of people, the chief vehicle of Chinese devotional practices, present'·· to be described. This occurred when Buddhism entered China in the seventh century A.D., and began to fill the need of the Chinese people for a religious life more richly emotional than Confucianism, more respectable intellectually than lower Taoism, and more easily understandable than higher or philosophical Taoism. Already a formal Taoist priesthood had been established and a sort of Taoist papacy installed on Dragon-Tiger Mountain in Kiang-si province. Now, aided and abetted by certain emperors who needed religious sanctions to bolster political prestige, the ancient Chinese gods and goddesses, spirits, and demons were revived under the Taoist banner to provide a native Chinese alternative to the Buddhist Bhoddisatvas and ceremonies. Lao-tse was deified to supply a man-god, and the whole gamut of traditional Chinese ceremonies described below was fostered by the Taoists. In this guise Taoism was, from time to time, the official state religion; but in this guise it has recently lost prestige rapidly.

But the Lao-tse of the *Tao Te Ching* has had his followers; there has been continuous interest in the provocative statements contained in that book. The most famous of the traditional Lao-tse's successors was Chuang-tze, who lived in the fourth century B.C. and is one of China's most important and suggestive philosophers. His teachings, preserved in the *Chuang-tze Book*, rank along with those ascribed to Lao-tse in the literature of higher Taoism. He carried the cosmological speculations of the *Tao Te Ching* to deeper speculative levels and described in much greater detail the ecstasy which comes to one who truly attains knowledge of and union with the *Tao*. In describing the *Tao* itself he made the suggestive statement that "it has functions without form." [12] It is perhaps appropriate to conclude this brief description of Taoism with two of the most famous stories from the *Chuang-tze Book*:

THREE IN THE MORNING

. . . To wear out one's intellect in an obstinate adherence to the individuality of things, not recognizing the fact that all things are one—this is called *Three In The Morning*.

"What is *Three In The Morning*?" asked Tze Yu.

"A keeper of monkeys," replied Tze Chi, "said with regard to their rations of chestnuts that each monkey was to have three

[12] From *The Works of Chuang-tze*, in *The World Bible, op. cit.*, p. 553.

in the morning and four at night. But at this the monkeys were angry, so the keeper said they might have four in the morning and three at night, with which arrangement they were all well pleased." [13]

THE DREAM AND THE DREAMER

Once upon a time I, Chuang-tze, dreamt I was a butterfly, flitting hither and thither, to all intents and purposes a butterfly. I was conscious only of following my fancies as a butterfly, and was unconscious of my individuality as a man. Suddenly I awoke, and there I lay, myself again. Now I do not know whether I was then a man dreaming I was a butterfly, or whether I am now a butterfly dreaming I am a man.[14]

CHINESE WAYS OF WORSHIP

Confucius, though he was primarily interested in social problems and a code of conduct which would lead men to a peaceful and harmonious social life, nevertheless recognized the social value of many traditional Chinese religious ceremonies and customs. Many such customs were deeply imbedded in Chinese life long before the time of the Sage, and Confucius knew that they were expressions of fundamental human needs. Therefore, though he himself said little about the gods, he said much about reverence for the powers of nature and the social bonds of the family, especially as the latter is expressed in gratitude for and honor to one's elders, living and dead. It is these two forces, nature and society, which from earliest times elicited devotional response from the Chinese people.

Reverence for Nature

Like other peoples, the ancient Chinese early distinguished between two basic mysteries in the total mystery of nature's power—the mystery of heaven, or the heavens, and the mystery of earth. The great overarching sky with its heavenly

[13] *Ibid.*, p. 554.
[14] *Ibid.*, pp. 556-57.

bodies, whence come the sunshine and the rain, the lightning and thunder, the hail and snow, the wind and all that seems to be inseparably bound up with the conditions of life in all its precariousness, has elicited a worshipful response from peoples ranging from the most primitive savages to the philosopher Kant who confessed that "two things filled his soul with awe and wonder: the starry sky above, and the moral law within." For primitive peoples there is probably no distinction between the sky-god or gods and the sky itself, and so for ancient Chinese *T'ien* probably signified simply the great inverted bowl of the heavens in its wonder and awesomeness. As time passed the concept became more abstract, and it was possible to distinguish between the heavens themselves and Heaven, the mysterious power which lay behind them and their operations. Thus *T'ien* as Heaven became a widely used term to denote the impersonal, ordered power of the heavens and, later, of earth as well. Confucius spoke frequently of Heaven in this sense, apparently meaning by it simply the powers that be.

Others, however, needed a more concrete and more personal reference for their sense of the powers that be. Thus in Shang times a deity called *Ti* or *Shang Ti*, "the ruler above" was worshiped. *Shang Ti* was to the heavens what the emperor was to the earth. It was he who directed the course of the sun and the stars, the wind and the rain. Like earthly emperors, he could be influenced for good or ill by those who knew the way to his favor. And finally, as in Greece, India, and elsewhere, the Chinese became conscious of the semi-independent powers of individual heavenly bodies like the sun and moon and began to think of them as spirits or gods in their own right. Elesewhere, one or the other of these heavenly beings, like the sun-goddess *Amaterasu* in Japanese Shinto, would emerge as the supreme power of heaven and earth in the thinking of the people. In China, however, it appears that *T'ien* or, at times, *Shang Ti*, remained supreme over the lesser individual heavenly bodies and powers.

"The good earth," however, is too obviously bound up with the forces of life not to receive independent worship.

The rain and the sun are important, but their powers would be wasted if Mother Earth were not there to receive them, nurture them, and transform them into the powers of fertility. Early Chinese nature-philosophers began to talk of a dual basis for the power and structure of the universe, Yang and Yin, expressed in the duality of Heaven and Earth. For others, however, earth was simply the mother of all existence, teeming with warmth and power, sometimes sustaining and sometimes forsaking her children, a mother who must be reverenced, adored, and propitiated. Hence in early Chinese fields there appeared small mounds of earth, *she*, symbolizing the fertility of the soil. To the *she* at the time of planting or harvest could be brought sacrificial offerings, and around the *she* ritual dances and other ceremonies could be performed, in gratitude for the bounty of the earth, or in an attempt to aid or force the earth's fertile powers. Eventually each village as well as each farm had its *she*, and in imperial times there were central *shes* in the imperial city, Peking, where the emperor could worship for all the people at the Great Altar of the Gods.

But just as the total power of the heavens must be broken up into the particular and more comprehensible powers of the various heavenly bodies, so the total power of the earth must be divided, in the minds of many folk, into multitudes of mysterious spirits. Spirits were in the mountains, the valleys, the forests, the streams, the rocks, the roads, and the fields—they were found wherever the powers of earth manifested themselves in special ways. Some of these spirits were benevolent and concerned with human well-being; these were the *shen*. Others were malevolent, evil, destructive, concerned with the destruction of all that men consider valuable; these were the *kwei*. It became very important, therefore, properly to please and incur the favor of the *shen* and properly to ward off and control the fury of the *kwei*. Thus arose the whole gamut of Chinese magical practices and beliefs, later to become identified with the religious movement of Taoism and still very much a part of the lives of millions of Chinese.

Personified *kwei* lived in popular imagination as demons about whom countless stories and legends sprang up. Their evil powers could be overcome in dragon dances (the dragon as such is not necessarily evil); by smearing blood over vulnerable spots—particularly the blood of the cock, who seems to be in close communion with the sun—by offering food, particularly rice, to appease the hunger of the demons (the rice offered at wedding festivals, for example); by shooting off firecrackers to scare them away (on occasions such as the Fourth of July or its equivalent); by parading peach blossoms, whose spring blooming is symbolic of triumph over the evil spirits of winter and darkness; or by using articles made of peachwood with mottoes from the sages inscribed on them; or even by hanging up pieces of red paper cut like peach blossoms or other good things, having inscribed upon them magic words and proverbs. In such ways men could have commerce with the *shen* and the *kwei*.

Reverence for Society

The Chinese have always had a profound sense of the solidarity of human society and the dependence of each individual, first and most vividly upon his own family, past and present; secondly upon the imperial family of the nation as a whole; and thirdly and more vaguely upon the family of men everywhere. It is said that as early as Shun times in the twenty-third century B.C. Chinese worship was directed toward a trinity of Heaven, Earth, and Man. Man, the human family, has never been missing from the Chinese sense of the intimate and the ultimate. The Chinese have always known that men are dependent upon nature for their being, but they have also known that individual men are dependent upon other men, living and dead, for the richness of their being. Thus there has been among the Chinese an unusually strong sense of family solidarity and dependence, expressed in what is often called ancestor worship.

In its primitive forms ancestor worship was probably associated with primitive fear and awe in the presence of death, expressed in a lively belief that the dead lingered on indefinitely as invisible but powerful spirits, for good or for ill. Hence, many of the acts involved in ancestor-rites reflected a nature and intent similar to that described in the treatment of Animism in Chapter 1. Through sacrifices the dead could be provided with food and other essentials, even if these reached them only in smoke and even if the articles offered were only paper imitations of the real things. But these would be of little avail if the dead had not been ushered into the land of the dead with proper ceremony. Rules and regulations for funeral observances thus became very complex, and the etiquette of mourning became elaborate and detailed. Confucius is said to have been especially concerned with the proper carrying out of funeral and mourning requirements both by others and by himself. In early times physical necessities and luxuries, and perhaps even human servants, were buried with the dead to aid them in the life beyond. Later it was felt to be enough if paper or other images of the offerings were substituted. Burial places themselves were places of deep emotional attachment and had to be properly cared for. Each family burying ground had its temple in which memorial tablets for the deceased were placed and to which the living came with sacrifices, for meditation, or to report important events in the life of the family such as weddings or important business or other plans. In spring and fall special pilgrimages were made to the burial places.

In each home, too, there was a shrine or shrine-room where memorial tablets were kept, or memorial papers hung, preserving the memory of at least five generations. Flowers were placed and incense burned before these each day while the family performed the "three kneelings" and "nine knockings" of the forehead against the ground—the kow-tow. Thus the sense of indebtedness to the past was kept alive. Many Chinese who followed the ancient family customs no longer believed literally in spirits of the dead, but they did believe in the importance and power of preserving a lively sense of one's heritage. There are those, particularly among modern Chinese reformers, who feel that this reverence for the past and its attendant "dead weight of convention" have been major obstacles in the way of Chinese progress, and there is at present a widespread revolt against the entire family system with its emphasis upon, respect for, and control by the elders. It may be that experience will show that Confucian restraint is wisest in reform also.

To conclude, a brief description of a few typical traditional ceremonies designed to celebrate significant occasions in the life of the individual and nation may serve to vivify in more concrete detail the actual operation of this Chinese way of devotion. In traditional Chinese home life Confucian ethics with its emphasis upon *Li* has been central in the regulation of conduct. A book of ceremonial etiquette was to be found in every well-ordered house, usually in the custody of the grandmother or grandfather. Before a child entered the family, proper ceremonies were performed to assure an auspicious birth, and, after the birth, announcements were sent to friends and relatives on red paper, symbolic of good luck. In response to congratulatory gifts which came to the parents, eggs dyed red were sent in return—an odd number for a boy and an even number for a girl.[15] The naming ceremony took place only after consultation with astrologers, and perhaps the real name was not given for some time, the children being called rather by their mathematical order of appearance. Special offerings of thanksgiving were made each year on the child's birthday until he had reached the age of sixteen.

Adulthood meant marriage, which traditionally was arranged by match-makers in bargaining consultation with the parents of prospective brides and grooms. On the day of the ceremony a procession as elaborate as could be afforded proceeded from the bridegroom's home to call for the bride, who brought with her a suitable dowry. The wedding ceremony, performed at the groom's home, included drinking from cups bound with a red cord while vows were exchanged.

[15] For further descriptions of these and other ceremonies, with appropriate illustrative photographs, see Florence Mary Fitch, *Their Search for God, Ways of Worship in the Orient* (New York: Lothrop, Lee & Shepard Co., 1947), pp. 53-85.

At the conclusion of the ceremony the bride joined her husband in bowing before the household shrines of Heaven and Earth and the family ancestral tablets. By this act the bride renounced her ties to her own family and became subject to the family of the groom; in the case of his death it was the responsibility of his family to care for her, and her responsibility to serve his family. But man and wife were expected to treat each other with mutual respect, and frequently, in practice, the wife became the dominant figure of the household. Traditionally, however, the position of the woman in China has been definitely subordinate to that of the man.

Family life was enlivened with many seasonal and family festivals, New Year's Eve being the chief time for family reunion with the living and the dead. Then appropriate gifts—peach stones, pieces of ivory, pomegranates—were placed upon the family altar, incense was burned, and the significant events of the family's year were reported to those who had gone before. Messages from the children to the previous five generations of ancestors were burned in a special urn, and finally holiday feasts were spread, first for the dead, and then for the living. The latter was the occasion of boisterous merriment. Other festivals marked the coming of spring, "The Double Fifth" or summer solstice, harvest time, and the winter solstice. The latter included such Yuletide customs as the preparation of special goodies and the exchange of gifts. A moving spirit in the New Year's activities was *Chang* or *Tsao Shen*, the fat god of the hearth. He, with a bit of fire from the hearth, was the last to leave a house when a family moved and the first to enter a new house. He presided over and reported on the affairs of the family to the powers above—especially the affairs and conduct of the younger members of the family. Thus at the end of each year a special ceremony was held in which *Chang* was regaled with presents and sweets, which he thoughtfully shared with the children. After he had thus been put into a happy frame of mind he was sent in smoke to Heaven, where, it was hoped, he would give a good report of his wards. On the fourth day of the new year a new image or portrait would be back in its place at the hearth to remind the family of the abiding presence of the spirit of good family living.

Other familiar and beloved figures in the typical Chinese household were "The Eight Immortals." In actuality these happy folk lived in mountains or isles of the blessed, but their humanly happy life among the blessed was represented by figures showing four of them seated under a pine tree and two sipping wine heated by another, while still another provided musical entertainment on a flute. Sometimes the figures were presented singly and with some variations. Frequently there would be *Ho Haien Ku*, who, by living on a diet of mother-of-pearl, became the Maiden Immortal. She, like the others, was a member of a fairy kingdom presided over by a fairy queen who saw to it that her subjects performed all the functions of their kind recorded in the tales of many cultures.

In each town was a village temple in which were housed appropriate ancestral tablets and an image of *Cheng Huang*, the city god. His function was to preside over and report on the moral life of the town, as *Chang* presided over and reported on the moral life of individual homes. Thus moral law was celebrated and enforced in both social units. But the great national festivals of thanksgiving, penitence, and aspiration occurred at midsummer and midwinter in the magnificent Temple of Heaven at Peking. The emperor, as father of the nation and "Son of Heaven," offered the "Great Sacrifice" on the massive, marble Altar of the Gods—perhaps a single calf, perhaps many animals of different kinds—and then led a colorful procession to the Temple of Heaven where imperial reports to imperial predecessors were made and national resolutions were proclaimed. The emperor made the journey from the Altar to the Temple across holy ground on foot—the only time imperial feet touched the ground. With the end of the Manchu dynasty in 1912 the elaborate apparatus of state worship was abandoned, and in the recent past the great park in the northern suburb of Peking, which is the site of the imperial temple and altar, has been a public park and playground.

The abandonment of the Temple of Heaven and of most of the Confucian temples and many of the city temples is symbolic, of course, of the great cultural revolution now sweeping China. There are those who say that it will eventually sweep away all remnants of the traditional Chinese ways of faith, as the new Marxist faith develops its own heroes and its own shrines. Many Chinese feel that this is best. Therefore the traditional devotional beliefs and practices are described here in the past tense. It may be, however, that the rich culture of China, with its roots in remote antiquity and its centuries of experience in adopting, absorbing, and eventually naturalizing foreign ideologies, will eventually find a new place for, and new meanings in, the colorful devotional practices by which Chinese have for many ages expressed their reverence for Heaven, Earth, and Man.

SUGGESTIONS FOR FURTHER READING

ARCHER, JOHN C. *Faiths Men Live By.* New York: The Ronald Press Co., 1934, chaps. iii-v.

BOUQUET, ARTHUR. *Comparative Religion.* Harmondsworth, England: Penguin Books, Ltd., 1950, chap. viii.

CLEMEN, CARL. *Religions of the World.* New York: Harcourt, Brace & Co., Inc., 1931, III, 3.

FITCH, FLORENCE M. *Their Search for God.* New York: Lothrop, Lee & Shepard Co., Inc., 1947.

FUNG, YU L. *A History of Chinese Philosophy.* Peking: Henry Vetch, 1937.

GILES, H. A. *Chuang Tzu—Mystic, Moralist, and Social Reformer.* Shanghai: Kelly & Walsh, 1926.

GOODRICH, L. C. *A Short History of the Chinese People.* New York: Harper & Bros., 1943.

HUGHES, E. R. *Chinese Philosophy in Classical Times.* London: Everyman, J. M. Dent & Sons, 1941.

JURJI, EDWARD. *The Great Religions of the Modern World.* Princeton: Princeton University Press, 1946.

LATOURETTE, KENNETH S. *The Chinese, Their History and Culture.* New York: The Macmillan Co., 1934.

LIN YU TANG (ed.). *The Wisdom of Confucius.* New York: Modern Library, Random House, Inc., 1938.

MOORE, CHARLES A. *Philosophy—East and West.* Princeton: Princeton University Press, 1944.

82 WAYS OF FAITH

MOORE, GEORGE F. *History of Religions.* New York: Chas. Scribner's Sons, 1946, chaps. i-iv.
NOSS, JOHN B. *Man's Religions.* New York: The Macmillan Co., 1949.
WALEY, ARTHUR (trans.). *The Book of Songs.* London: George Allen & Unwin, Ltd., 1937.
————. *The Analects of Confucius.* London: George Allen & Unwin, Ltd., 1938.

Chapter 3

THE WAYS OF HINDUISM

"HINDUISM" is the over-all term for an incredibly vast range of rites, codes, myths, and philosophies which have accumulated in the long course of history on the subcontinent of India. The one unifying factor is the ethnic or national factor. But even the term "national" is too narrow and constricting if it is understood in a Western sense. Only in recent times and as a response to Western influences has India developed national feeling. India and her faiths must be understood in their own terms.

THE ORIGINS OF HINDUISM

Orthodox Hinduism divides the ways of faith into ways of works, devotion, and knowledge. This, coupled with the fact that all three paths are recognized as equally valid by the orthodox Hindu, suggests the remarkable diversity and breadth of Hinduism. Indeed, it is sometimes questioned whether Hinduism is one religion or many. In its broadest term "Hinduism" seems to be simply a word applied to the ways of rite and conduct practiced by those inhabitants of the Indian subcontinent who are not formally attached to one of the more clearly defined sectarian faiths which have sprung from Hinduism or have entered India from the outside world. Some of the people and some of the ideas which, over a period of two thousand years of ferment, assimilation, and structuring gradually produced the cultural phenomenon now called Hinduism, came to India from the outside world. The Aryans who invaded India from the Northwest sometime prior to 1,000 B.C. were tall, active, light-skinned cousins of West Europeans—an offshoot of the Indo-European parent family whose earliest home anthropologists, philologists, and historians have been diligently seeking to locate. The social story of India is the story of conquest and amalgamation. Thus the reader should not be surprised to find in the story many words, ideas, and practices similar to those encountered in Western cultural history.

But the Indo-Aryans found in India a culture which was already old, made up of dark-skinned Dravidians in the south and Mongolians in the north. Most of the practices of these natives were primitive by religious as well as other standards, and they preserved evidence of a still older and more advanced culture along the Indus river. It was on the upper Indus that the Indo-Aryans first settled, and several hundreds of years were required for them to make the transition from a nomadic folk to a village and agricultural folk. Their general outlook on life seems to have been practical and optimistic, and their chief occupations were hunting and tilling, fighting when necessary, and enjoying the simple but lusty pleasures of an uncomplicated society—such as the intoxicating pleasures of the fruits of the *soma* plant. As in China, the family was the basic social unit, with the father exercising all the rights and privileges of the head of the household, including the function of family priest. A crude form of filial piety was enforced, though the women seem to have enjoyed more freedom than in early Chinese culture. But, as social groups grew larger, class divisions within society became more important: the warriors claimed special privileges for themselves by virtue of their peculiar service, and the rulers drew farther apart from the masses as government became more complex and more centralized. Always there was the problem of the status of the increasing numbers of conquered Dravidians. Finally those who claimed to control the relation of the whole of society to the whole of the universe—the priests—began to claim special rights and privileges for themselves. Out of the internal and external conflicts thus engendered came the bases of many legends and epics later to be incorporated in

Hindu literature, such as "The Adventures of Rama" (*Ramayana*) and "The Great Bharata War" (*Mahabharata*). And out of this situation grew also the most distinctive Indian social phenomenon—the caste system.

THE HINDU WAY OF WORKS

The Vedic Code

With the developing epics and folk-tales came formulas for magical ritual guides, prayer-hymns, and naïve but charming theological speculations. The more important and popular of these were preserved and handed down orally from generation to generation. Gradually they took on the status of Classics—guides to the ways of the ancients—and it was felt that they contained the basic knowledge by which men should live. They were called *Vedas,* the plural of a root-word meaning "knowledge," whose European offshoots are seen in such words as "wit" and "wisdom." They are the world's oldest religious literature. Since they are concerned mainly with praise of the various deities then worshiped, they will be considered in greater detail with the Hindu devotional practices. But it should be noted here that the *Vedas* embody also a relatively exalted if homely conception of those works through which one may find himself in the favor of gods and men. Simple justice and fair play in the ordinary affairs of society are enjoined. Personal integrity and careful consideration of the duties as well as the privileges of one's station are stressed in a manner similar to that found in the Chinese ethical Classics or, indeed, in the commonsense books of moral practice native to most cultures. Typical hymns ask forgiveness for cheating in either work or play and enjoin the practice of liberality upon the believer.

> The riches of the liberal never waste away, while he who will not give finds none to comfort him. . . . The man with food in store who, when the needy comes begging for bread to eat, hardens his heart against him . . . finds not one to comfort him.[1]

[1] *The World Bible* (New York: The Viking Press, 1944), pp. 34-35.

Through poetic proverbs like these the *Vedas* suggest that from the earliest times the Hindus considered ethical activity essential to the life of devotion and knowledge which these early hymns extol.

The Development of the Caste System

The Vedic literature reveals a growing complexity in the rites and ceremonies developed by the Indo-Aryans. Prescriptions for sacrifices and designations of deities to whom various sacrifices should be offered for various purposes became so complicated that gradually a specialized priesthood emerged with specially trained men to perform the necessary ceremonies in the name of the community or for private needs. Since the religious rites constituted the accepted way of relating the individual and society to nature and of controlling the latter for personal and social ends, the power of the priests steadily increased. Already there had emerged a sharp social distinction between the lighter-skinned Aryans and those of darker complexion, with the blacker Dravidians forced to the bottom of the social scale and permitted only the most menial of occupations. It is interesting to note that the Hindu word for caste is *varna*, meaning "color." But the rising power of the priesthood accentuated another element in the caste system as it finally took shape—the element of vocation. We have seen that earlier Indo-Aryan society had centered around heads of families. Later some of these patriarchs and their families gained control over others, and more powerful rajahs emerged to control some clans by hereditary right. At the same time the military men claimed their share of social benefit and prestige by virtue of their crucial contributions to society and their power, at times, to control society by force. Thus conflict developed between rulers, warriors, priests, and the common people who made up the bulk of society—mostly farmers and artisans. This conflict in turn was further complicated by the color-conflict already prevailing. As a result, the question of what conduct one should perform to live the good life came to be answered increasingly in terms of the

special duties and privileges of the social group into which
one was born.

For a period the *Kshatriyas* or nobles were generally recognized to be superior to all other groups and to enjoy special
privileges of conduct. Next to them in prestige came the
Brahmins or priests, and under them the *Vaisyas* or Aryan
common people. These three groups, in turn, held themselves
increasingly apart from the darker *Shudras*. Each group had
its rules and customs, and each tended to inbreed as marriages across class, and especially across color, lines, were
proscribed. Eventually the Brahmins or priests gained the
upper hand in the struggle for prestige—after all, the Kshatriyas were dependent upon them for the religious bases of
social stability, and the Vaisyas came to feel that the forces
of nature and art upon which the life of the farmer and
the artisan depend were completely under the control of the
Brahmins. This belief had been further strengthened by the
writing down, beginning around 700 B.C., of a voluminous
collection of complicated and detailed descriptions of and
prescriptions for rites and ceremonies called the *Brahmanas*.
It was the duty of the Brahmins to study and follow these,
and the ability to read and write was generally restricted to
their circles. Thus another element entered into the classical
caste-system—the distinction between the literate and illi-
terate, the educated and the uneducated, and the control of
the former over the latter.

So far it would appear that the caste system grew out of
social forces and distinctions common to nearly all societies
in one form or another. Such, indeed, is the case. But in
order to understand its deeper roots in India and the relative
lack of fluidity in its subsequent operations, we must turn
to two philosophical concepts which were to become essential
parts of the Hindu philosophical scheme. These are: (1)
belief in the transmigration and reincarnation of souls (*samsara*), and (2) belief in an inexorable law of cause and effect
operating across and determining the direction of successive
incarnations (the law of *Karma*).

Samsara and Karma

The early Hindus shared with most primitive peoples the belief that the essential and vitalizing principle in man is not inextricably bound up with the physical body; rather the body is the temporal form in which that which is essential expresses itself during a given lifetime. This belief in the ultimate reality of "soul" as the seat of life and intelligence has taken many forms among various peoples. Peoples have differed, too, in their answers to the question of the destiny of the soul after death of the physical body. The early Greeks and Hebrews envisioned a shadowy underworld of dark memory for all souls. Later Hebrews and Christians, like followers of the Greek mystery religions, proclaimed a full and joyous existence beyond death for those souls in proper communion with deity. It is probable that the early Indo-Aryans shared the beliefs of their contemporary Greek cousins. But by the time of Plato in Greece and by the time of the *Upanishads*, a momentous collection of Indian philosophical poems dating from 800-400 B.C., the Indo-Aryans and Greeks were asserting that souls persist indefinitely through a series of births and rebirths, in many forms and many bodies, until they are somehow delivered from the cycle. This belief may have been held by the pre-Aryan Dravidians and other native Indians. But it appears in Hindu literature for the first time in the *Upanishads*, to which more detailed attention will be given later. Once it was accepted, it became a basic ingredient in the classical Hindu view of life and affected all phases of Hindu doctrine. It involves, of course, a distinctive view of time. Rather than conceiving time for the individual as having a beginning and an end within a given lifetime, with the consequent life-or-death seriousness of this-worldly choices and the impelling possibility of this-worldly progress, *samsara* teaches that time for the individual has neither a beginning nor an end. The individual is caught in a cycle of births and rebirths which can end only when he escapes from time itself through absorption into the timeless or eternal. A metaphor which may not be completely valid, but which is frequently used to illustrate the contrast between this view of time and that to which most Westerners are accustomed, asserts that *samsara* views time as being like the ripples on the surface of the motionless pool of eternity while the typical Western view likens time to an arrow in flight, coming from and going to definable points. In order to show the effect of belief in *samsara* upon the development of caste and the Hindu way of works the doctrine of *karma* must be investigated further.

Karma, stated in its simplest form, holds that "as ye sow, so shall ye reap." As such it is a basic observation of the universal course of human experience and appears in the wisdom of most peoples. In Hinduism, and later in Buddhism, however, the principle is enunciated in the context of belief in *samsara* and thus takes on cosmic significance. What one is and can become, it asserts, depends on what one has been and has done previously, either in this life or some other. Likewise, what one will be in the future, in this life or another, depends on what one does here and now. The law of *karma* is thus an inexorable law of cause and effect, binding character to previous conduct and future conduct to present character. It is viewed by Hindus as a law in the strictest sense of the term, as impersonal with no exceptions in its operation. What one is, is the result of what one has been; what one shall be is the result of what one is. From one point of view this implies an impersonal and hopeless fatalism. From another point of view, however, it implies a hopeful optimism, because it asserts that if one accepts the lot which previous action has given him and follows diligently one or all of the three paths to salvation, in some future existence one may achieve deliverance from the whole cycle of *samsara* and from the power of *karma* which is supreme in the realm of *samsara*. If the series of incarnations which constitute *samsara* is likened to a wheel turning endlessly through indefinite revolutions of birth and rebirth, *karma* could be likened to the power which turns the wheel. To escape from the wheel is to escape from the power; but as long as one is bound to the wheel of time, the power of *karma* in determining his life is inescapable.

Now the relation of *samsara-karma* to the development of caste should be obvious. Society had crystallized into four major and many minor divisions. If one then asked why he was born a Shudra rather than a Brahmin, the answer was clear: it was because the *karma* of a previous existence determined it. The course of wisdom, then, lay in accepting rather than rebelling against the inescapable *karma*. If one wished to improve his lot he could do so by living to the best of his ability the life of the caste into which he was born, accepting its limitations and fulfilling faithfully its requirements. Then, perhaps in a future incarnation one might reappear in a more desirable station. On the other hand, if one rebelled against his fate or lived immorally in his station, he would certainly reappear in a worse state in the future—perhaps not even in a human state, but as an animal or vegetable, because all living things are souls. Or, perhaps one would not immediately reappear in an earthly existence at all. Perhaps he would go for an indefinite period of time to a joyous heaven to reap the rewards of his good life; or perhaps he would go for a period of purging into a miserable hell—and Hindu imagination has been as fertile as that of other peoples in picturing the fantastic horrors of places of punishment. In any event, existence will go on and on until, through faithful pursuit of a way of salvation, deliverance—*moksha*—comes.

Caste is written into the very texture of reality, and one's only hope is to make the most of it. Thus we see that, while many of the forces making for the development of the caste system are found also in other cultures—differences in social function, color, education, and the like—in India the whole complex was given religious and metaphysical sanction. We should hasten to add that later Hindu reformers have found within the same doctrines which traditionally supported the caste system, bases for attacks on its evils. But through most of Hindu history *samsara, karma,* and caste have been viewed as three necessary facets of a single and consistent world view. Traditionally, if one sought deliverance through the way of works, then, he must do well that which the duties of his caste demanded and aspire to no more than that in a given lifetime.

The Laws of Manu

Around 200 B.C., a group of lawyer-priests compiled a list of rules of conduct called the *Laws of Manu* which was to become especially authoritative in the later development of Indian legal codes. These laws deal in great detail with religious rites and ceremonies, but they also prescribe social conduct expected in various stations of life. Like the Chinese Classics, they center on the basic relations of the sexes to each other, of the ruler to the ruled, and so on. For instance, women are assigned a definitely inferior status as compared with men; as daughters they are subject to fathers and as wives they are subject to husbands. So completely dependent is the wife upon the husband for status and support according to this code that the practice of *suttee,* or the self-immolation of widows, was widespread for centuries. In any event widows were declared to be subject to sons, and wives were required literally to forsake their own families and become subject to the family of the husband. Marriages were based on family considerations and contracted at a very early age. But men were also enjoined to respect and support their wives and to take seriously the duties as well as the privileges of their station. And in the course of time many women were to rise to positions of social prominence as the concrete experience of daily life produced many variations in the application of the classical rules in this and other areas of social concern.

The Ashramas

In the *Laws of Manu* there appeared also a more concrete program which members of the Brahmin caste could follow if they wished so seek final deliverance from the wheel of *karma* within a given lifetime. This program nicely combines elements of the three Hindu ways of faith—works, devotion, and knowledge. And, though in the *Laws of Manu* the pro-

gram appears to be open only to qualified Brahmins, Hinduism has traditionally held that any male member of any of
the three upper castes may embark upon it and thus seek
deliverance from the roots of caste, even while observing caste
distinctions. As the three upper castes drew increasingly
apart from the Shudras and the "outcastes," they began to
speak of themselves as the "twice-born," or those for whom
salvation in a single lifetime is a theoretical possibility. As a
symbol of their status they were invested with a scarlet thread
in special rites during childhood. The program thus opened
to the twice-born has thus become an important ingredient
in and modification of the caste-system as a whole, and has
greatly affected the whole Hindu way of works.

Briefly, the program envisions four stages or *ashramas*
in the life of the twice-born man seeking salvation within a
given lifetime.

1. After the appropriate rites of childhood, according to
the program of *ashramas,* the young man seeking salvation
should devote himself to study of the religious classics, especially the *Vedas,* under the guidance of a competent teacher
and spiritual adviser or *guru.* This period of study should last
until student and guru feel that the young man is ready to
go on to further obligations, usually in his mid-twenties.

2. Next comes a period of indefinite duration more obviously devoted to the way of works,—the period of the
"householder." The aspirant should marry and establish a
family and prove himself capable of living worthily through
normal social responsibilities, and at the same time make a
concrete economic contribution to the life of society. It is
very important to note well this requirement, because it
means that in classical Hinduism the ways of devotion or
knowledge were never considered sufficient in themselves.
The most ascetic holy man is assumed to have fulfilled, at
some time, his duties as father and citizen; if he has not, his
piety is a delusion and of no avail. The decision as to
whether one is ready to pass from one *ashrama* to another
is a very serious and a very difficult one. If one errs he pays
for it by beginning in another life at the point where he made

his mistake. Naturally then, many of the twice-born who embark on the program of *ashramas* never advance beyond the second stage, devoted to the way of works. Aspiration fails, or they become too much attached to family and vocation, or the rigors of the next stages deter them. In other words, for the average Hindu, including the twice-born, life involves essentially the same obligations and occupations found among people of similar status in other cultures. To do well one's duty to one's family, in one's business or profession, and in one's citizenship is as much as may be expected or normally required.

3. If, however, one feels sincerely called and ready to go beyond the normal way of works, usually in later life, though sometimes in middle age or earlier, he may forsake the world and retire to the forest or elsewhere to live as a hermit, V*anapastra*, or "forest-dweller." He may go alone, or, in some cases, accompanied by his wife as a servant. Here, cut off from the world, he must begin to cultivate a complete indifference towards all that he had previously cherished as a student and householder. He must penetrate to the spiritual significance of all things and activities—even those religious acts which had formerly been his duty—so that he may worship completely without external aids. His studies will be concentrated on the philosophical classics, and his aim will be to become completely spiritual in every aspect of his being. When he has reached this stage of apparent indifference to all things, even his wife must leave him as he continues on to the final stages alone.

4. In the final stage he will live as a *Sannyasin* or holy man. He may leave his hermitage and mingle in the society of the world, but as one not of the world. Food and drink will come from those who consider his mere presence among them a blessing and the lowliest service to him a spiritual privilege. In some cases he may go without clothing, in complete disregard of all fleshly requirements. He may subject himself to rigorous physical and mental discipline through *yoga* practices in a final supreme effort to free himself from the bonds of finitude. It is believed that some blessed souls thus achieve

in this life the goal of *samadhi* and are beyond good and evil
and all other finite considerations.

The Way of Works in the *Bhagavadgita*

We have now glanced at some phases of the development
of the Hindu way of works through the Vedic, Brahmanic,
and Upanishadic periods, culminating in the *Laws of Manu*,
the complex development of the caste system, and the program of *ashramas* for the twice-born. We must now give
special attention to the discussion of this way in the most beloved and influential of all Hindu classics, the *Bhagavadgita*.
This book has been called the New Testament of Hinduism
and is of such worth in the eyes of the devout that it is commonly believed that merely to hear it recited in a public
prayer-meeting is to acquire great spiritual merit. Actually it
is a part of the long and rambling epic of the Great Bharata
War mentioned previously, *The Mahabharata*.

Literally translated "The Lord's Song," the *Gita* relates
an incident in the war between the family of Pandu (Pan-
davas) and the family of Dhritarashtra, relatives of the Pan-
davas who had illegally deprived the latter of some property
rights. The war was thus, by ordinary standards, a just war.
But Arjuna, a son of Pandu, pauses on the verge of leading
his forces into battle to ponder the morality of fighting even
a just war. Ranged against him he sees his kinsmen—uncles
and cousins who are men like himself and who love life as
much as he does. Could it be right to kill these men? Thus
Arjuna raises the profound question of the moral ambiguity
of all action, particularly violent action. If one acts, no matter how just his cause, someone will somehow suffer as a
result of his action. A morally pure act is impossible. Arjuna's situation dramatizes the dilemma most forcibly. Can
the way of works lead to salvation, after all?

Fortunately for Arjuna he is able to put his question to his
charioteer, who is actually the god *Krishna* in disguise. Indeed, the chief historical significance of the *Gita* lies in the
fact that it extolls personal communion with a personal God,
the way of devotion, as a valid way of salvation. More im-

portant for present purposes is the answer which Arjuna receives on divine authority to his question about the way of
works. "The Blessed Lord" begins by reproaching him for his
dejection over the apparent futility and moral ambiguity of
the course of action open to him:

> Whence has come to thee this stain (this dejection) of spirit
> in this hour of crisis? It is unknown to men of noble mind;
> . . . it does not lead to heaven; on earth it causes disgrace.[2]

Next he reminds Arjuna that he has forgotten a basic
truth—the truth of *samsara*. He is concerned over killing,
while the truth is that nothing essential can be destroyed.

> Know thou that that by which all this is pervaded is inde-
> structible. Of this immutable being, no one can bring about
> destruction. . . .
>
> He who thinks that this slays and he who thinks that this is
> slain; both of them fail to perceive the truth; this one neither
> slays nor is slain. . . . He is not slain when the body is slain.
> . . . Just as a person casts off worn-out garments and puts on
> others that are new, even so does the embodied soul cast off
> worn-out bodies and take on others that are new . . . Even if
> thou thinkest that the self is perpetually born and perpetually
> dies, even then . . . thou shouldst not grieve. . . . For to the
> one that is born death is certain and certain is birth for the one
> that has died. Therefore for what is unavoidable, thou shouldst
> not grieve.[3]

The right and wrong of action, then, cannot be determined by
considering its results in terms of purely accidental and superficial questions of living or dying, killing or being killed.

One basic test can be applied to the question of action,
however, and that is the test of duty. Compare Confucius'
remarks about *Yi* with "the Blessed Lord's" statement concerning Arjuna's duty in his concrete situation:

> Further, having regard for duty, thou shouldst not falter, for
> there exists no greater good for a Kshatriya than a war enjoined

[2] S. Radhakrishnan (trans.), *The Bhagavadgita* (New York: Harper &
Bros., 1948; London: George Allen & Unwin, Ltd., 1947), p. 99.
[3] *Ibid.*, pp. 106-10.

> by duty . . . Happy are the Kshatriyas, for whom such a war comes of its own accord as an open door to heaven.[4]

In other words, caste obligations come before all else in the quest for salvation. And there is never a real choice between action and inaction, because inaction itself has the consequences of action for others.

> Not by abstention from work does a man attain freedom from action; not by mere renunciation does he attain to his perfection. . . . For no man can remain a moment without doing work; every one is made to act helplessly by the impulses born of nature.[5]

The choice, then, is not between action and inaction, but between action in accord with duty and shirking one's duty for selfish reasons mistakenly clothed in moral and religious terms:

> Verily the renunciation of any duty that ought to be done is not right. . . .

> He who gives up a duty because it is painful or from fear of physical suffering, performs only the relinquishment of the "passionate" kind and does not gain the reward of the relinquishment. . . .

> The wise man, who renounces, whose doubts are dispelled, whose nature is of goodness, has no aversion to disagreeable action and no attachment to agreeable action.[6]

But these passages suggest also that even one's duty must not be performed for selfish reasons, and this is a theme which is further developed in the *Gita*, as it delves into the complex question of the relation of motive to act. Action is inescapable, it says; and duty rather than pleasure or pain, life or death, is of permanent concern. But if a dutiful act is done for selfish motives, for the sake of reward of any kind—if the doer of the act is concerned over its consequences and fruits

[4] *Ibid.*, p. 112.
[5] *Ibid.*, p. 133.
[6] *Ibid.*, p. 353-54.

—then the act is not a truly good act. Duty is its own reward; the good act is done for its own sake, in detached attachment:

> To action alone hast thou a right and never at all to its fruits; let not the fruits of action be thy motive; neither let there be in thee any attachment to inaction.[7]

This famous passage suggests that the way of works cannot be finally divorced from the way of knowledge through which alone one can achieve the detachment necessary for truly fruitful action, or from the way of devotion through which alone that singleness of purpose can be achieved which makes detached action possible. The important point, however, is that in the Hindu way of works as expressed in the most important of Hindu scriptures, action—even violent action—is viewed as a necessity. Its value is judged in terms of duty and motive rather than in terms of its physical and social results. And, properly performed in intelligent devotion, it can lead to deliverance of the soul.

Ahimsa and Modern Hindu Social Movements

Doubtless many readers are puzzled by the fact that the most popular Hindu classic has here been presented as teaching the necessity of violent action, when it had been their impression that Hindus are traditionally pacifists and exponents of nonviolent resistance. Did not Gandhi successfully advocate the use of "soul-force" rather than arms in throwing off British rule? Of course traditional Hinduism has, as a matter of fact, made much of the doctrine of nonviolence (*Ahimsa*), and Hindu history records many victories of Hindu tolerance over conflicting ideologies. It is logical that many Hindus should hold that, if all men are composed ultimately of the same soul-stuff, then it is wrong for one man to injure another in any way. Some have extended this belief to include all living things, and Jainism, an offshoot of Hinduism, includes followers who will not tread on an insect and who wear cloths before their faces for fear of inhaling insect life. *Ahimsa* is also one factor in orthodox Hindu vegetarianism,

---

[7] *Ibid.*, p. 119.

though the famous cow-worship springs from early economic dependence upon the cow for milk, fertilizer, and other necessities.

Furthermore, the higher stages of life of the twice-born, to which all Hindus aspire, are obviously peaceful and nonviolent, but they are also detached from ordinary social responsibility. Even so, many Hindu commentators have maintained that the warfare in question in the *Gita* is not to be taken literally but allegorically, and that in fact heroic resistance to evil through peaceful means rather than actual fighting is really advocated. Traditionally, it appears, most Hindus have believed in *Ahimsa* as an ideal for most duties of a relatively private and personal type. But concerning its relevance for social conflict there has been division and difference of opinion. Some would hold that Gandhi was actually the first to make nonviolent resistance an organized method of social conflict. And many even of Gandhi's followers maintain that the *Mahatma* (Saint) did not enjoin the method as a rule-of-thumb practice for all conceivable social situations. They point out that *Ahimsa* is derived from *Abhaya*, which means, not "without violence," but "without fear." As the *Gita* seems to say, it is the intent and quality of the act rather than its physical result which is of supreme ethical importance, and there may be situations in which refusal to kill is personally and socially more deplorable than killing. Gandhi himself is reported to have said that if the choice is between cowardice and violence, violence is preferable; but if there is a real choice between violence and nonviolence, then nonviolence is obviously preferable.

Thus Gandhi's successors in the leadership of modern India have not committed the new nation to nonviolence in international relations. Like Gandhi, they uphold *Ahimsa* as the ideal in terms of which all actions must be judged. But, following the *Gita*, which, along with the New Testament, appears to have been Gandhi's chief inspiration, they hold themselves ready to fight when such a choice seems the lesser evil in the morally ambiguous world in which all action occurs. In many other ways, too, modern Indian leaders are finding impelling reasons for democratic social reform in reinterpreted Hindu beliefs about the way of works. The doctrine of *karma*, for instance, is interpreted with an emphasis upon its socially positive implications. Not only is it true that men and societies are what they are because of past decisions and actions, but it is also true that courageous social action today can make a better society possible tomorrow. And, while traditional Hinduism has sought final escape from this world, modern Hindus point out that this world is the scene of redemption and is thus very important even though it may not be supremely important.

Similarly, while traditional Hinduism has focused attention upon the soul rather than the body, modern Hindus point out that the destiny of the soul cannot be divorced from the socially determined bodily conditions of its this-worldly existence. Finally, even the age-old caste system is now subject to re-examination and reinterpretation. Many Hindu social philosophers maintain that it developed as a protective device to "freeze" Hindu culture and thus preserve it through centuries of invasion and attack by foreign powers and ideas. Ideally, they say, it is nothing more than a recognition of the role of classes in any society; and, by conceiving this division of social functions in organic terms, a revised caste—or class-system—may prove to be a significant Indian contribution to present social thought. Among the revisions necessary are the abolition of the untouchability of the outcastes, finding for them a wholesome place within society. Accordingly, the present Indian government has outlawed all forms of discrimination against former outcastes and has also taken steps to assure more fluidity of movement within the existing class-structure, with social opportunity based more on ability and less on heredity.

Thus the classical Hindu way of works is very much alive in contemporary Indian society. Its reinterpretation and application to present problems undoubtedly reflect the impact of non-Hindu ideas upon the Indian scene—Mohammedan, Christian, Marxist, and others—and there have been various movements and organizations designed to bring classical

Hindu ideas into active association with others from the West and elsewhere for purposes of political and social reform. It is enough to suggest that the millennia of thought and experience which have gone into the development of the Hindu view of the way of works have produced ideas and attitudes to which the non-Hindu world may well give serious attention in the socially difficult days of the present era.

VEDANTA, THE HINDU WAY OF KNOWLEDGE

The Upanishads

The earliest Hindu scriptures, the *Vedas*, take their name from a word meaning "wisdom" or "knowledge." The naïve but moving prayers and speculations embodied in these ancient scriptures point beyond the simple polytheism and nature-worship of the earliest Indo-Aryan times to a quest for a more subtle and basic understanding of reality. This quest took the form of highly elaborated ritual prescriptions in the *Brahmanas* and led to the rich development of the Hindu way of devotion. But the program of *ashramas* outlined in the *Code of Manu* suggested that the period of works should be followed by a period of quiet withdrawal and meditation. Thus over a period of time extending perhaps from the eighth to the fourth centuries B.C. more philosophical appendages were added to the growing body of Hindu scripture. These latter took the form of loose-knit philosophical dialogues and monologues, obviously designed for memorizing, and came to be called the *Upanishads*, a name derived from a word meaning "sitting close by"—that which is learned at the feet of the teacher, the secret doctrine which finally dispels all ignorance. Eventually over two hundred texts were to claim the title *Upanishad*, but only a few over a hundred are now accepted as canonical by orthodox Hindus. Of these, ten or twelve are principally used, and two of them, the *Bradhankya* or Great Forest Book and the *Chandogya*, are by far the most popular. In common Hindu usage the term *Veda* is applied to the entire body of Hindu scripture: the four classical *Vedas*, the

Brahmanas, the *Arankyas* or Forest Books, and the *Upanishads.* Philosophical systems claiming orthodox Hindu scriptural authority constitute Vedanta, or knowledge derived
from that which is *sruti* or revealed in V*eda.*

Generally speaking, there are three criteria by which a
Hindu philosophical system is judged orthodox: (1) scriptural
authority—the authority of the V*edas* in the broad sense just
described; (2) reason—or demonstration that the system is not
mere mechanical dogmatism derived from a literalistic or
magical view of scripture; and (3) personal experience, the acid
test for all Hinduism—inner experimental evidence of the
saving power of the system. A way of knowledge which successfully meets these three criteria in the opinion of scholars
over a period of years is accepted as Vedanta, or approved
Hindu philosophy, even though there be wide divergence of
viewpoints within and among the systems so accepted.

The Search for the Real in Vedanta

The *Upanishads* are a loose-knit and frequently repetitious
collection of philosophical speculations. Furthermore, there
is no uniform doctrine taught in them. Even individual
Upanishads contain within themselves apparently conflicting
views. It is interesting to note that the speakers in the dialogues include members of castes other than the Brahmin
and even number several wise women among them. But,
though there is no uniformity of doctrine, there is singleness
of purpose in all the Upanishadic discussion: it is to lay bare
the nature of ultimate reality, that which is really real, unconditioned, absolute—that upon which all else depends. Thus
the central question of the dialogues is "What is that which,
when known, brings understanding of all that can be known?"
The basic quest of the *Upanishads,* in other words, is similar
to, if not identical with, the basic quest of the Taoist sages—
the quest for salvation through knowledge of the real.

The *Upanishads* give no uniform answer to the basic question with which they are concerned. But through the centuries two major schools of interpretation have found two
major answers. One school, the Qualified Non-Dualistic

School (*Vishitadvaita Vedanta*), whose great master is a twelfth-century (A.D.) thinker named Ramanuja, maintains that the One Reality to which Upanishadic teaching points is a concrete and personal deity. The other school, the Unqualified Non-Dualistic School (*Advaita Vedanta*), whose great master is a ninth-century (A.D.) thinker named Shankara, holds that the One Reality is beyond all qualifying attributes, even personal attributes, and is ultimately indescribable. Members of the latter school appear to be in the majority among contemporary Hindu thinkers, so we may, for purposes of exposition, follow their analysis of Upanishadic teaching. One advantage which they hold over the Vishitadvaita Vedantists is that they do not deny that the *Upanishads* teach, at one level, a personal and describable ultimate, which is perhaps the form in which many people must conceive the Real. But they maintain that there is also a deeper level of understanding for those desirous or capable of going beyond the notion of a personal deity or absolute.

According to a typical Advaita exposition [8] of Upanishadic doctrine, the twofold view of ultimate reality in the *Upanishads* parallels a twofold view of knowledge. There is, first of all, a broad realm of lower knowledge (*aparavidya*) which includes all forms of cognition which most people, including nearly all Westerners, would recognize as valid. All knowledge derived from sense-data, for instance, is included in this category—also all knowledge based on ordinary reasoning processes or ordinary emotional experiences. All knowledge of all concrete objects or subjects in space and time—including knowledge of a personal God or gods—is included. Even Advaita Vedanta, it should be noted, does not deny the reality and significance of such knowledge and its objects. It accepts and is interested in all forms of scientific, ethical, and aesthetic inquiry which have proved fruitful, and does not look upon such forms of inquiry as unimportant.

But beyond this realm of "lower" or "cultured" knowledge, *aparavidya*, lies *paravidya*, pure or "higher" knowledge. Pure

[8] Swami Nikhilananda, "Discussion of Brahman or the First Principle in the Upanishads," in *Essays in East-West Philosophy*, *op. cit.*, pp. 234-48.

knowledge is direct rather than indirect, intuitional rather than perceptional, existential rather than theoretical. It cuts through and goes beyond the distinction between knower and known, subject and object, relative and absolute. It is knowledge from the inside rather than knowledge from the outside. It is pure and unalloyed direct cognition of the Real in its innermost essence—knowledge *of* rather than knowledge *about*. Such knowledge is not easily achieved, and claims to it are subject to much misunderstanding and abuse, both from those who speciously claim to have attained it, and from those whose presuppositions about knowledge rule out the possibility of *paravidya* as the *Upanishads* describe it.

Higher knowledge is the result of a long and arduous process of preparation and experimentation, say the Vedantists. The term generally used to describe the process and the various techniques which have been developed for it is *yoga*. This term, much abused and misunderstood in the West, simply means "a yoking"—a way of binding oneself to or yoking oneself with the Real ("Take my yoke upon you. . . ."). Many yoga systems have been developed by various seers and schools, and there is not space here to describe any of them in detail. A brief account of the major emphases in one of the most ancient and popular systems, *Raja-yoga* or "royal path," will perhaps indicate the general character of yoga practice.

In *Raja-yoga* there are eight parts or "limbs." The first two "limbs," *yama* and *niyama*, are concerned with ethical preparation for saving knowledge. It is very important for Westerners to note that most yoga systems insist upon strict moral discipline and ethical purity as a prerequisite for any further advance in *yoga*. The tricks and stunts of the *fakir* are at best secondary parts of the entire yoga discipline. For most men an entire lifetime is required for significant progress in ethical preparation, which includes the cultivation of absolute personal integrity, compassion toward others, and the like. Only when this has been achieved can the physical and intellectual stages of *yoga* be fruitful. As a Sanskrit proverb puts it, "To feed a cobra milk without first removing its fangs is merely to increase its supply of venom!" The wisdom of these moral prerequisites in *yoga* should be apparent to a West now debating the moral presuppositions and implications of scientific inquiry.

The third and fourth "limbs" of Royal *yoga* involve those physical exercises which most Westerners associate with *yoga* as a whole. The third deals with posture. In general, the body must be relaxed, any posture which makes this possible being satisfactory. However, those classical postures which make it possible to hold the spinal column erect and the arms and legs at rest have proved most effective. The fourth "limb" deals with breath-control. Until the breath is so carefully regulated that the breather is unaware of it even in absolute rest and silence, the body is not completely relaxed and under control. The aim of the physical stages of *yoga* is simply to bring the body completely under the control of the mind, in order that thought may be undistracted.

In the fifth stage the efforts of the seeker are concentrated on detaching the mind from concern with all sense-objects, all particulars. This may be done by concentrating it upon one sense-object or quality such as a color. It may be aided by allowing the mind to roam freely through all its distracting imaginings until it has played itself out. Eventually it must be brought completely under control. When it is thus under control, attention and awareness must be sharply focused and concentrated, in the sixth stage of the process. This effect may be aided by fixing attention on a single part of the body until that object is in consciousness and all else has faded out. Then, and only then, one is ready for meditation proper. If the preparation has been successful the thoughts which flow through the mind in such meditation are characterized by hitherto-unknown clarity and fluidity; particular cognitions and universal connections are known and understood at a level of understanding hitherto unimagined. Finally, after an indefinite period of time—perhaps a lifetime, or many lifetimes—of preparation, there comes *samadhi* or bliss—that absolute and pure knowledge which can be described in no terms short of its own fullness and which is the goal of all seeking. In this final stage the knower pierces the distinction between the knower and the known, the relative and the absolute, and enjoys direct and full awareness of the Real.

The Nature of the Real in the Upanishads

The name usually given to the Real as known through either lower or higher knowledge in the *Upanishads* is *Brahma*, or *Brahman* (not to be confused with Brahm*in*). The word apparently comes from a root *brh* which in Vedic times meant prayer. Its derivation perhaps suggests an early feeling that the basic power of the universe is somehow identical with the power experienced in prayer. Later the root came to mean "to burst forth and grow," and *Brahman* would thus suggest "that from which all grows." As such it includes all forms of reality which Westerners would describe as objective—all objects in space and time known through various forms of *aparavidya*; and also all forms of reality considered subjective in Western terms—thoughts, emotions, attitudes, universals, and abstractions, including all that is usually meant by the term "soul." It is from the word for soul (or also "breath"); [9] *atman*, that the subjective aspect of *Brahman* derives its name. *Brahman* as such embraces both subjective and objective experience and reality and is beyond subjective-objective distinctions. Thus the basic insight of the *Upanishads* is the realization *tat tvam asi:* "That art Thou." All that appears particular and separate, such as the individuality of the self over against other selves or the subjectivity of the self over against the objectivity of that which in lower knowledge seems outside the self, is ultimately One in *Brahman*. *Brahman* is all and in all; the source and the totality of being. To know this truth is to be saved—saved from the ignorance which, according to Vedanta, is the root of all evil.

But can any more be said about the nature of this One? The *Upanishads* describe *Brahman* in two different ways. Sometimes *Brahman* is *Saguna Brahman*, or *Brahman* with attributes; at other times *Brahman* is *Nirguna Brahman*, or

[9] Cf. the dual meaning of the Greek *pneuma*, the Latin *anima*, and the Hebrew *ruach*.

Brahman without attributes. *Saguna Brahman* is spoken of with personal pronouns, not as it but as "He"; or, a frequent word for him is "Self":

> Verily the Self is to be seen, to be heard, to be perceived, to be marked. . . . When we see, hear, perceive, and know the Self, then all this is known. . . . Whosoever looks for anything elsewhere than in the Self, was abandoned by everything. This Brahman-caste, this Kshatriya-caste, these worlds, these Devas, these creatures, this everything, is all that Self.
>
> As all waters find their center in the sea, all touches in the skin, all tastes in the tongue, all smells in the nose, all colours in the eyes, all sounds in the ear, all percepts in the mind, all knowledge in the heart, all actions in the hands, all movements in the feet, and all the Vedas in speech;
>
> As a lump of salt, when thrown into the water, becomes dissolved into water, and could not be taken out again, but wherever we taste (the water) it is salt—thus verily . . . does this great Being, endless, unlimited, consisting of nothing but knowledge, rise from out these elements, and vanish again into them. When he has departed, there is no more knowledge.[10]

Or, in Vishitadvaita, *Saguna Brahman* may be conceived as a personal God—perhaps in the classical trinity of *Vishnu-Shiva-Rama* as Creator, Preserver, Destroyer. It is in this form that *Brahman* is approached and understood in the way of devotion. Those who stress Upanishadic passages which speak of *Brahman* as ultimately personal maintain that to know Him thus is *paravidya,* the highest knowledge. Some of these would not deny that He may also be known as impersonal and distinctionless, but would maintain that the deepest and richest knowledge of Him takes the form of personal communion. The goal of Vedanta in this case, it should be noted, is personal communion with a personal Absolute, not impersonal union with an impersonal Absolute.

Advaita Vedantists, on the other hand, reverse this estimate. They maintain that *Brahman* may be known as personal, and that this form of knowing may be the most appro-

10 Robert O. Ballou and Friedrich Spiegelberg, eds., *The Bible of the World* (New York: The Viking Press, 1939), p. 43.

priate form for those who must follow primarily the way of devotion—and there are frequent suggestions that these are the spiritually and philosophically immature. But true *para-vidya* realizes Brahman as *Nirguna*, totally unconditioned and without attributes, "from whence all speech, together with the mind, turns away, unable to reach it." [11] Thus the *Up-anishads* frequently picture teachers communicating the deepest nature of *Brahman* in silence. However, words may aid in bringing one to a realization of the inexpressible *Brahman* if they are used negatively to rid the mind of all restrictive ideas. *Neti, neti* is a recurrent phrase in such use of language: "Not this, not that." In this vein it is asserted that

> He is myself within the heart, smaller than a corn or rice, smaller than a corn of barley, smaller than a mustard-seed, smaller than a canary-seed or the kernel of a canary-seed. He is myself within the heart, greater than the earth, greater than the sky, greater than heaven, greater than all these worlds.[12]
>
> Beyond the sense there are objects, beyond the objects there is the mind, beyond the mind there is the intellect, the Great Self is beyond the intellect. Beyond the Great there is the undeveloped, beyond the Undeveloped there is the Person. Beyond the Person there is nothing—this is the goal, the highest road. . . .
>
> He who has perceived that which is without sound, without touch, without form, without decay, without taste, eternal, without smell, without beginning, without end, beyond the Great, and unchangeable, is freed from the jaws of death.[13]

Timeless, spaceless, causeless, *Brahman* is nevertheless described in special terms as "existence, consciousness, and bliss." But through all these descriptions runs a sense of the insufficiency of all words to describe that which is the source and goal of language.

Of course these descriptions of *Brahman* leave unanswered the question which plagues all theories of this sort: if ultimate reality is such as is here described, how and why is it that

[11] *Taittiriya Upanishad* II v, 1, quoted in Swami Nikhilananda, *op. cit.*
[12] *Chandogya Upanishad* III xiv, 3, *ibid.*
[13] *Bible of The World, op. cit.,* p. 49.

finite beings in a pluralistic world must carry on most of the business of living and knowing in a realm far removed from the infinite? In general, Vedanta leaves the question unanswered as the basic mystery of all systems, Vedantist or otherwise. It is the mystery of creation or being. Actually there are many divisions of schools within Vedanta which take different positions on the question of the relation of the ordinary world of sense perception to the deeper realms of *Brahman*. Some of these are monistic, some dualistic, some pluralistic. One of the monistic schools, the *Charvaka*, even espouses a crude materialism in its analysis of the real world—but Charvaka is not a live option for most Indian thinkers. Similarly, there are divisions of schools over the question of how the finite world, on the one hand, and the infinite, on the other, are known. Some schools are realistic, some nonrealistic, and so on. But most are agreed that the world known through lower knowledge, the world of finite relativity, is *maya*.

Now this word *maya* is usually translated "illusion" and has suggested to many Western students the idea that Vedantists consider the ordinary world of space and time to be illusory in a psychological sense. This obviously is not the case; Vedanta considers the finite world to be as real as sense-experience and reason show it to be. Vedantists insist, however, that the finite world is not the only or the most important realm. It consists rather of appearances of that which is beyond. The realm of *maya*, then, is the realm of appearance —not unimportant, but not supremely important. Indeed, the goal of all knowledge, all worship, all activity, is to find deliverance from ignorant bondage to the world of appearance in order to experience *moksha*, salvation, with its attendant immortal bliss, *samadhi*.

BHAKTI, THE HINDU WAY OF DEVOTION

The Gods of the Vedas

The early Indo-Aryans shared with the Chinese and other men a deep sense of the awesome and mysterious powers of nature. Thus we have seen that their earliest scriptures, the

Vedas, are made up of prayers and hymns, magical rites, and incantations designed to express reverence for and fascination with the powers of heaven and earth. The oldest of the Veda collections, the Rig-Veda, consists mostly of hymns recited by priests presiding at nature-sacrifices. The Yajur-Veda contains more detailed magical formulae recited at various stages of more complex ceremonies. The Sama-Veda is made up in part of hymns sung by priests in sacrificial festivals. And the Atharva-Veda is largely a collection of magical charms and prescriptions.

Though many of the Vedas fail to identify the object of worship as a special personalized deity, others address prayers to several fairly definitely developed spirit-gods or devas associated with various natural powers and functions. Nearly a quarter of the Vedic hymns are thus addressed to Indra, a god of war and thunder who, riding upon his tawny steeds, slew the dragon Vitra, and released the rains—an event of special importance in drought-conscious India. Close to Indra in popularity is Agni the fire-god, strong, purifying, and lively. Agni is fire in all its forms: the hearth-fire which is cared for by Tsao-Shen in China as well as the fire of the sacrifices which consumes the victims and carries them to the spirits. Thus Agni is also the messenger of the gods, and he delivers their messages in lightning. Typical of hymns to Indra and Agni are the following:

I will declare the manly deeds of Indra, the first that he achieved, the thunderwielder.
He slew the dragon, then disclosed the waters, and cleft the channels of the mountain torrents.

He slew the dragon lying on the mountain: his heavenly bolt of thunder Tvashtar fashioned.
Like lowing kine in rapid flow descending the waters glided downward to the ocean.

Nothing availed him lightning, nothing thunder, hailstorm or mist which he had spread before him;
When Indra and the dragon strove in battle, Maghavan gained the victory forever.

Indra is the king of all that moves and moves not, of creatures
    tame and horned, the thunderwielder.
Over all living men he rules as sovereign, containing all as spokes
    within the felly.

Dear, ageless sacrificial drink is offered in light-discovering,
    heaven-pervading Agni.
The gods spread forth through his celestial nature, that he might
    bear the world up and sustain it.

The world was swallowed and concealed in darkness; Agni was
    born, and light became apparent.
The deities, the broad earth, and the heavens, plants, and waters
    gloried in his friendship.

How many are the fires and suns in number? What is the
    number of the dawns and waters?
Not jestingly I speak to you, O fathers. Sages, I ask you this
    for information.

As great as the fair-winged morning's presence to him who
    dwells beside us, Matarisvan!
Is what the Brahamana does when he approaches to the sacrifice
    and sits below the Hotar.[14]

Of great importance in the sacrifices is the intoxicating
juice of the *soma*-plant, the "dear, ageless sacrificial drink."
Soma has obvious powers to bring the joy and exhilaration
of the spirits into the worshipers, and eventually *Soma* as such
became a god—the god of strength, courage, healing, purging, and even immortality. His development thus suggests
the similar life-history of Dionysus in Greece and other wine-
gods elsewhere. But storm, fire, and intoxicating spirits are
subsidiary in many *Vedas* to the more remote but more majestic powers of the heavens. *Ushas* (cf. Eos, Aurora) the goddess of "rosy-fingered dawn," evoked some of the most beautiful of Vedic poems:

This light is come, amid all lights the fairest; born is the bril-
    liant, far-extending brightness.
Night, sent away for Savitar's uprising, hath yielded up a birth-
    place for the morning.

[14] *The Bible of The World, op. cit.,* pp. 5-7, 10-12.

The fair, the bright is come with her white offspring; to her the
dark one hath resigned her dwelling.
Akin, immortal, following each other, changing their colours the
heavens move onward.

Bright leader of glad sounds, our eyes behold her; splendid in
hue she hath unclosed the portals.
She, stirring up the world, hath shown us riches; Dawn hath
awakened every living creature.[15]

Then there is also the familiar god of the skies as such.
The Indo-Aryan equivalent of *T'ien*, whose very name suggests his kinship to the Greek Zeus, the Latin *deus*, and deity,
is *Dyaus*. *Dyaus* is worshiped as the total majesty of the
powers above, deep and mysterious in his awesome grandeur.
Others, however, must personalize *Dyaus*, as *T'ien* was supplanted for some Chinese by *Shang Ti*. Thus a large number
of Vedic hymns to the heavens are addressed, not to *Dyaus*,
but to *Varuna*, "king of gods and men," "the all-covering,"
he who holds heaven and earth apart and directs not only the
physical but also the moral laws of nature.

Sing forth a hymn sublime and solemn, grateful to glorious
Varuna, imperial ruler,
Who hath struck out, like one who slays the victim, earth as a
skin to spread in front of Surya.

In the treetops the air he hath extended, put milk in kine and
vigorous speed in horses,
Set intellect in hearts, fire in the waters, Surya in heaven and
Soma on earth.

None, verily, hath ever let or hindered this most wise god's
mighty deed of magic,
Whereby with all their flood, the lucid waters fill not one sea
wherein they pour their waters.

If we have sinned against the man who loves us, have ever
wronged a brother, friend, or comrade,
The neighbor ever with us, or a stranger, O Varuna, remove
from us the trespass.

[15] *Ibid.*, p. 4.

If we, as gamesters, cheat at play, have cheated, done wrong un-
wittingly or sinned of purpose
Cast all these sins away like loosened fetters, and, Varuna, let us
be thine own beloved.[16]

In remarkable hymns like these, moral and natural powers
are linked in the domain of one great god of heaven and earth.
In others the more abstract order which is the stuff of moral
and natural law is exalted as Rita, deity of "the ordered course
of things" (cf. rite and ritual), the power of fate comparable
to the Greek Moira. And in those hymns quoted above addressed to particular specialized gods, the reader has perhaps
detected a tendency to exalt each in turn into a position of
pre-eminence and to ascribe to him or her many functions
elsewhere ascribed to other deities. This development would
be natural to the worshiper who, in the frenzy of particular-
ized adoration, would progressively magnify the object of his
devotion—in part, perhaps, to flatter the deity, and in part
because of the temporary conviction that no other deity really
exists or is of any real significance. This tendency, common
to comparable stages of development in other religions, has
been called "opportunistic monotheism" and is close to "henotheism," in which one deity is exalted above others, even
though the existence of others is not denied.

But opportunistic monotheism is as close as the Vedas, or
Hinduism in general, has come to that form of theism which
has been basic to the great religions of the West. Hinduism
seems to have toyed with and then passed over the possibility
that one transcendent deity, not identical with the world,
might be the creator and preserver, the judge and redeemer
of all, in the sight of whom "all the gods of the peoples are
idols and all the nations of the earth as a drop in a bucket."
This is a very significant fact to bear in mind as we proceed
to describe the ways of the East as compared with the ways
of the West. Hinduism developed from the early crude polytheism, or belief in the coexistence of many gods, each with
a specific function, through the opportunistic monotheism

[16] Ibid., pp. 8-9.

mentioned above, into pantheism and philosophical monism, which hold that all things are expressions of and ultimately identical with deity or a neutral world-stuff. And on the basis of pantheism or monism it is impossible logically to declare that any object, any belief, or any practice is idolatrous; all are expressions of the One and are thus equally important or equally unimportant "under the aspect of eternity." Hence, Hinduism has been characterized by that broad tolerance which stretches charity to the point of indifference, with all the virtues and all the vices—of chaos and disorder—which absolute tolerance engenders.

In the *Vedas* themselves we see the beginnings of that trend toward pantheism and monism which, in the *Brahmanas* and *Upanishads*, was to form the basis of the Hindu way of knowledge. One of the best-known and most hauntingly beautiful of all Vedic hymns is the following "Hymn of Creation."

> Then was not non-existence or existent; there was no realm of
>   air, no sky beyond it.
> What covered in, and where? and what gave shelter? Was
>   water there, unfathomed depth of water?
>
> Death was not then, nor was there aught immortal: no sign was
>   there, the day's and night's divider.
> That One Thing, breathless, breathed by its own nature: apart
>   from it was nothing whatsoever.
>
> Darkness there was: at first concealed in darkness. All was un-
>   discriminated chaos.
> All that existed then was void and formless: by the great power
>   of warmth was born that unit.
>
> Thereafter rose desire in the beginning, the primal seed and
>   germ of spirit.
> Sages who searched with their heart's thought discovered the
>   existent's kinship in the non-existent.
>
> Who verily knows and who can here declare it, whence it was
>   born and whence comes this creation?
> The gods are later than the world's production. Who knows
>   then whence it first came into being?

He, the first origin of this creation, whether he formed it all or
    did not form it,
Whose eye controls this world in highest heaven, he verily
    knows it, or perhaps he knows not.[17]

In this hymn, whose origins go back perhaps a thousand years
before Christ, an ancient Hindu sage had already raised the
question which was constantly to challenge the way of devotion. To those whose sense of the ultimate mystery is expressed in the faithful affirmation "he verily knows . . ."
comes the suggestion ". . . or perhaps he knows not . . ."
for "the gods are later than the world's production."

The Devotional Epics

The six hundred years following the Vedic period produced an elaboration of cultic prescriptions, along with further hints at pantheism or monism, in the *Brahmanas* (?1000-
?700 B.C.). A great philosophical development followed in
the period of the *Upanishads* (?800-400 B.C.). But there were
spiritually hungry souls who found the rigorous way of works
developing from Brahminic control in the caste-system, and
the abstract way of knowledge developing from Upanishadic
speculation, insufficient spiritual food. The ultimate concern
of such souls could not be satisfied with practices and doctrines which seemed to them less human and less moving than
the theistic poetry of the *Vedas*. For them the Holy must be
made vivid in stories of human achievement and human love
which could bridge the gap between the human and the divine
and make the riches of grace available to those who would
accept them in grateful faith. Therefore, there grew through
the centuries a rich body of legend and folk tale designed to
dramatize basic human emotions and imaginings and to relate
these to the sources of human life. Eventually these tales
were collected in two great epics, the *Ramayana* and the
Mahabharata, and from the stories of gods and men contained
in them the classical *Bhakti* or way of devotion has taken its
multifarious forms.

[17] *Ibid.*, pp. 3-4.

THE RAMAYANA. This is the story of an ideal king, Rama, and his ideal queen, Sita. It is of enormous length, containing 500 cantos and 24,000 couplets, and it has been translated with various changes and additions into all the major dialects of India. It is said that the original was the work of a poet named Valmiki and was written in Sanskrit. But authorship and date are uncertain in all such literature, and particularly so in India where individual persons and dates have traditionally been of little interest or consequence. The most significant and popular translation is that of a sixteenth-century poet, Tulsi Das.

It seems that, in the earliest forms of the tale, Rama is an earthly prince, perhaps a northern Indian hero, who is a follower of the deity *Vishnu*. He is described as the ideal warrior-knight and later as an ideal ruler, while Sita is the epitome of Indian womanhood: faithful, intelligent, and obedient. According to the story, Rama's father, Dasartha, has three wives, each of whom bears him a son. In addition to Rama the favorite, there are Bharata and Lakshmana. Bharata's mother, unknown to Bharata, plays a trick by which she succeeds in having Dasartha banish Rama and Lakshmana from the kingdom for fourteen years, during which time Bharata takes the throne after his father's death. When Bharata discovers his mother's trickery he attempts to step down and recall Rama to his rightful rule. Rama, however, feels bound by his late father's decree, which has the power of *Rita* or fate, and insists on carrying out his banishment. In the course of it he and his faithful Sita undergo all sorts of hardships and adventures through which their courageous love emerges triumphant.

Rama, for instance, is approached by a she-demon who is attracted by his physical charms. When he repulses her she enlists the aid of a demon brother to strike back at Rama through Sita. Sita also spurns the attractive blandishments of a he-demon, but when Rama and Lakshmana are lured away on a hunt the male demon, Ravana, seizes Sita and carries her off to Ceylon. Hanuman, the monkey-god, a friend of righteousness, discovers Sita's prison through his elaborate network of treetop spies, and with a single leap bounds over to Ceylon to supervise construction of a bridge across which Rama leads his liberating forces. Sita is redeemed and proves her faithfulness through ordeals of fire. Finally the victorious Rama with his noble queen and his brother Lakshmana return to claim their kingdom and begin their triumphant rule, having proved worthy of the privilege through their sacrificial bravery.

In the early form of the story *Brahma* (or *Brahman*) appears as the greatest god, along with *Shiva* and the previously-mentioned *Vishnu* and their respective wives *Uma* (light) and *Lakshmi* (goddess of fortune). *Vishnu* is usually pictured riding upon his sacred bird, *Garuda*. In later forms *Brahma-Shiva-Vishnu* form a trinity, and Rama is declared to be an incarnation, or *avatar*, of *Vishnu*, sent to earth to defeat the evil aims of Ravana, the incarnation of evil, and to redeem men from their wickedness, details of which are elaborately described. Rama's purity and valor are extolled in sweeping praise, and it is proclaimed that by faith in him and his selfless love all the requirements for salvation may be met. Some worshipers go so far as to maintain that man by himself is worthless and absolutely incapable of salvation in his own power; only the grace of *Vishnu* incarnate in Rama can save man. Others hold that men must at least cooperate with *Vishnu* by opening themselves to his saving power. The former group, dominant in the south, are frequently referred to as the "cat school," because one of their favorite analogies likens the relation of men to *Vishnu* to that of a kitten being carried by the nape of its neck. The latter school, dominant in the north, is called the "monkey school" because it maintains that men must cooperate with *Vishnu* as the baby monkey cooperates with its mother by clinging to her as it is carried.

THE MAHABHARATA. This work is even longer than the *Ramayana*, containing 90,000 couplets. Its theme is a great war between alliances of northern-Indian tribes related by blood ties. Many of its heroes, like those of Homer, are demigods. The strife between two of them, Arjuna and Karma, furnishes a dominant theme of the rambling and often disconnected whole. The *Mahabharata* is chiefly significant, as was previously suggested, for its inclusion of The *Bhagavadgita* or "Lord's Song" as one of its episodes. Scholarly opinion is divided as to the dates and circumstances of the *Gita* and the exact nature of its relation to the *Mahabharata* as a whole. In general it is believed that the *Gita* in its modern form reflects many stages of development and a number of editings by people interested in various aspects of the problem of salvation. It is today, however, the single greatest classic of Hindu devotional literature, just as it has greatly influenced the Hindu way of works in ways previously suggested.

THE DEVOTIONAL TEACHINGS OF THE BHAGAVADGITA. In the episode described in the *Gita*, it will be recalled, Arjuna is faced at the outset with the moral problem of action which can be neither purely good nor purely evil. To this problem he receives the answer previously discussed. Discussion of the problem of action, however leads to a discussion of the whole problem of salvation, and elements of all the traditional Hindu ways are presented in turn by the charioteer who is actually an incarnation of *Vishnu* through one *Krishna Vasudeva*, an incarnation once-removed. Nevertheless his words have the full power of divinity. Thus, his teaching in the *Gita* that, along with, and perhaps even superseding the traditional ways of works and knowledge, there is the way of loving devotion to a personal Lord through whom men may be saved, is of tremendous significance. Let us therefore note in some detail a few of the crucial passages in the *Gita* which teach the way of *Bhakti* or devotion to a personal God:

> Whosoever offers to Me with devotion a leaf, a flower, a fruit, or water, that offering of love, of the pure of heart I accept.

> Whatever thou doest, whatever thou eatest, whatever thou offerest, whatever thou givest away, whatever austerities thou dost practice—do that, O Son of Kunti (Arjuna) as an offering to Me.

Thus shalt thou be freed from the good and evil results which are the bonds of action. With thy mind firmly set on the way of renunciation, thou shalt become free and attain to Me.

Even if a man of the most vile conduct worships Me with undistracted devotion, he must be reckoned as righteous for he has rightly resolved.

On Me fix thy mind; to Me be devoted; worship Me; revere Me; thus having disciplined thyself, with Me as thy goal, to Me thou shalt come.[18]

. . . .

Having thus spoken, O King, Hari, the great lord of Yoga, then revealed to Partha (Arjuna) His Supreme and Divine Form.

Of many mouths and eyes, of many visions of marvel, of many divine ornaments, of many divine uplifted weapons,

Wearing divine garlands and raiments, with divine perfumes and ornaments, made up of all wonders, resplendent, boundless, with face turned everywhere,

If the light of a thousand suns were to blaze forth all at once in the sky, that might resemble the splendour of that exalted Being.

There the Pandava (Arjuna) beheld the whole universe, with its manifold divisions gathered together into one, in the body of the God of gods.[19]

. . . .

Those who fixing their minds on Me worship Me, ever harmonized and possessed of supreme faith—them do I consider most perfect in yoga.

But those who worship the Imperishable, the Undefinable, the Unmanifested, the Omnipresent, the Unthinkable, the Unchanging and the Immobile, the Constant,

[18] S. Radhakrishnan, op. cit., pp. 248-55.
[19] Ibid., pp. 272-74.

By restraining the sense, being even minded in all conditions, rejoicing in the welfare of all creatures, they come to Me indeed (just like the others).

The difficulty of those whose thoughts are set on the Unmanifested is greater, for the goal of the Unmanifested is hard to reach by embodied beings.

But those who, laying all their actions on Me, intent on Me, worship, meditating on Me, with unswerving devotion,

These whose thoughts are set on Me, I straightway deliver from the ocean of death-bound existence. . . .

He who has no ill will to any being, who is friendly and compassionate, free from egoism, and self-sense, even-minded in pain and pleasure and patient,

The Yogi who is ever content, self-controlled, unshakable in determination, with mind and understanding given up to Me— he, my devotee, is dear to Me.

He who from whom the world does not shrink and who does not shrink from the world and who is free from joy and anger, fear and agitation, he too is dear to Me. . . .

But those who with faith, holding Me as their supreme aim, follow this immortal wisdom, those devotees are exceeding dear to Me.[20]

Here is the acme of the Hindu way of devotion—a way which does not exclude or minimize the significance of the ways of works and knowledge, but which promises to the believer who is unable or disinclined to follow them the full joy of salvation as the reward of singleminded devotion to a loving and personal Lord.

The Sects

Within the framework of the broad tolerance suggested in the *Gita* and further emphasized in the way of knowledge, devotional Hinduism has multiplied into many sects, stressing loyalty to one or another of the many personal gods or

[20] *Ibid.*, pp. 291-99.

avatars of personal gods, and emphasizing varying aspects of
the life of devotion in practice. We have already noted the
contrasting emphases of the "monkey" and "cat" schools of
devotion to Vishnu. As Vaishnavism has developed through
the years it has continued its emphasis upon the power of
Vishnu made concretely available through various partial and
discontinuous incarnations. The two most popular incarnations are Rama and Krishna. Though the latter is sometimes
identified with local tribal deities, Krishnaism has been in
turn the most popular form of Vaishnavism. Through the
years Krishna has taken on the characteristics of classical fer-
tility-gods, and Krishna worship has frequently been erotic,
sensual, and libertarian. Many other heroes including Mahatma Gandhi and King George V have also been proclaimed
avatars of Vishnu from time to time by enthusiastic groups of
devotees.

Almost equally popular with the masses has been Saivism,
the worship of Shiva, in its various forms. Saivism has, on the
whole, made much less of the idea of incarnations, treating
its saints and heroes rather as prophets of Shiva. And from
earliest times Shiva himself has been associated with the dark,
destructive, terrifying forces of life and nature. A favorite
representation shows him surrounded by leaping flames dancing the fiery dance of life—the life-force personified. Associated with him is a consort, the goddess Kali, who is even more
terrifying and sensuous in her activities, at times demanding
for her worship bloody sacrifice and sexual orgy. Nevertheless
Shiva and Kali are addressed in other guises as a loving Father
and tender Mother who have evoked from their followers
hymns of passionate devotion. Saivism has also produced its
theologians and theological-philosophical schools, some of
them far-removed from the earthy devotional practices of the
masses. Outstanding among these are the schools of Shankara and Ramanuja.

TYPICAL DEVOTIONAL PRACTICES. As in China, the birth
of a child is occasion for rejoicing—doubly if the child is a
boy—and the good news is heralded by blasts on conch shells.

Then follow a series of ceremonies designed to celebrate and clothe with religious dignity and meaning each crucial stage of the individual's life. As described and photographically illustrated by Florence Mary Fitch [21] these begin with a name-giving ceremony, carried out with proper astrological advice. It is customary to include the name of a god in the given name of the child, in order that the parents may acquire merit from repeating the god's name when addressing the child. Later there may be special ceremonies for the first giving of rice or solid food and for the cutting of the hair of the "twice-born." But most important for boys of the twice-born or three upper castes is the ceremony in which they receive the scarlet thread—earlier for Brahmins than for Vaishyas, and earlier for Vaishyas than Shudras. Then they receive their secret name from their *gurus* along with the sacred text of the prayer with which they will begin every day of their adult lives. With this ceremony the boy becomes a man and lives in men's quarters until he is married. A girl of any caste can only prepare herself for the best possible service as wife and mother. To that end she is trained in rituals of cooking, bathing, and dressing, and she prays that she may be a good wife to a good husband and give him many sons.

As in China, marriages are usually arranged by match-makers who know both families. In the twilight ceremony the veiled bride and groom are led separately into the inner courtyard of the marriage home to take their places before the sacred fire. After proper prayers have been offered by the parents, a priest joins the bride and groom with a silken scarf while repeating sacred words, and they then exchange vows as *ghee*, or melted butter, a favorite sacrificial substance, is poured into the flames. Finally the couple take seven sacred steps around the fire, exchanging promises. In some parts of the country they conclude the ceremony by eating a common meal from a single plate—the only time in their lives when they will eat together.

[21] Florence Mary Fitch, *Their Search for God* (New York: Lothrop, Lee & Shepard Co., 1947), pp. 11-53.

The Hindu year is studded with festivals to mark the cycles of nature, some joyous, some sad; some centering in temples, and some centering in homes. In general their intent is similar to that of the Chinese festivals previously described. The autumn festival for *Shiva* is typical. For days previous to the festival minstrels have sung her praises through the streets, and families have worshiped her portrayed as standing upon a lion with spear in hand, poised to slay the demon of evil. On the day of the festival a priest causes the spirit of the Great Mother to enter the image by sprinkling it with holy water representing the seven sacred rivers. Elaborate offerings are then presented to her as hymns of praise are chanted. She may be paraded through the streets for the adoration of the masses, and at the end of the day she may be ceremoniously taken to a nearby river, where she is taken out in festooned boats to be lowered into the water.

The rivers are everywhere centers of devotional practice, and of all the rivers the Ganges, "Mother Ganga," is most sacred, and Benares on her shore is the holiest of all cities. A pilgrimage to Benares is the acme of devotional aspiration. Let us therefore conclude our glance at Hindu devotional practices with a visit to Benares as described by John Clark Archer, a long-time resident of India and distinguished student of Indian religion:[22]

> Follow, if you will, a pilgrim to Benares. A young man goes at the behest of a mother too old to make the journey. She would have him go, name her name to *Ganga-Ma* (Mother Ganges), and bring her sacred water to offer to *Shiva Mahadeva*, thus making her heart lighter for the long transmigration. . . . He joins a company journeying by ox-cart and afoot. . . . They have bedding for the oxen, cotton quilts for themselves, flour and grain with vessels to cook them in, hookah pipes, and black tobacco, and jars for holy water. . . . They make slow progress, but are not impatient, so at last they reach the outskirts of the Holy City, where our young man leaves the company to go his own way. . . . He may fall in with the customary routine

[22] John Clark Archer, *Faiths Men Live By* (New York: The Ronald Press Co., 1938), pp. 181 ff.

from temple to temple, from this ghat to that, and at last complete the circuit of the sacred city, thereafter making his way
home again, empty of purse, but with his jar of precious Ganges
water and a heart full of unquestioning satisfaction in his religious heritage. . . .

Benares is a city of 200,000 souls . . . including 30,000
Brahmans. . . . It has 1500 temples and a quarter of a million
idols. . . . While it is a seat of all the gods of the Hindu pantheon, it is pre-eminently the *City of Shiva* whose followers
predominate. The Golden Temple is his; the Well of Knowl-
ledge is his; the so-called Monkey Temple is dedicated to his
wife; there are temples to his son, *Ganesha*. The sacred bull is
his, whether sculptured or alive, and wandering freely among
the temples. . . .

One should approach Benares with a sense of the Hindu's
other-worldliness and his utter subjection to symbolism. Not
otherwise may a Westerner escape offense at floors bespread
with cow-dung, and awash with holy water; at the foul odors
of decaying marigold, smouldering dung, and sizzling human
flesh (at the burning-ghat); and at the dark delapidation of
muddy walls. . . .

Benares, however, is said to combine the virtues of all other
places of pilgrimage, and if the weary pilgrim die within the
panch kosi or five *kos* road (a *kos* is a mile and a half or two)
around the city he is released immediately from the cycle of
recurrent rebirths, being transported directly to the heaven of
his devotion. His body is burned on a burning-ghat and his
ashes spread on the river. . . . Every pilgrim is expected to
make the *"panch kosi"* circuit of the city, which may cover
forty miles and occupy six days. The city, therefore, is crowded
with earnest souls occupied with ritual: reverent men in prayer
to the vivifying Sun; widows bathing carefully and devoutly;
pilgrims . . . bottling holy water; ascetics begging alms or prac-
ticing austerities; hundreds of priests, bare of breast and arms,
each sitting under his straw sun-shade and marking with the
God-sign the foreheads of any of the faithful who resort to him.

Especially serious is the group that comes for burning a body
they may have brought from a distance. The corpse bound in
cloth is carried on bamboo poles. The bearers have come
through the streets crying aloud, "Ram, Ram," "Mahadeva," or
some note of last appeal. Arrived at the burning-ghat they rest

its feet in the river, while they gather the wood—at a price—
and build the pyre. When the pyre is ready—*wealthy* mourners
may make it of sandalwood—the men nearest akin to the dead
buy from a nearby temple the necessary sparks of sacred fire.
The body is then placed on the wood and burned; what remains
is thrown into the river. A jar of water is ceremoniously broken
over the place of burning, and the mourners go their way. . . .

There have always been Hindus who question the efficacy of
the rites; perhaps they are more numerous today than ever before, even within the Holy City itself. . . . They openly condemn the primitive magic so widely current. There is no doubt,
however, that the average Hindu pilgrim is driven by a great
compulsion; the sanctity of his shrines, the power of his priests,
and the merit of his ceremonial. It is probable that our young
pilgrim will return with a sense of merit, and with merit for his
aged mother also. So preëminent is Benares, the seat of all the
gods!"

SUGGESTIONS FOR FURTHER READING

ARCHER, JOHN C. *Faiths Men Live By.* New York: The Ronald Press Co.,
1938, chaps. viii-ix.
BOUQUET, ARTHUR. *Comparative Religion.* Harmondsworth, England: Pen-
guin Books, Ltd., 1950, chap. vii.
CHATTERJEE, S. and DATTA, D. *An Introduction to Indian Philosophy.* Cal-
cutta: Calcutta University, 1931.
CLEMEN, CARL. *Religions of the World.* New York: Harcourt, Brace &
Co., Inc., 1931, III, 4.
ELIOT, SIR CHARLES. *Hinduism and Buddhism.* London: Edward Arnold
& Co., 1921.
FITCH, FLORENCE M. *Their Search for God.* New York: Lothrop, Lee &
Shepard Co., Inc., 1947.
GANDHI, MOHANDAS K. *Gandhi's Autobiography.* Washington, D. C.: Pub-
lic Affairs Press, 1948.
HUME, ROBERT E. *The Thirteen Principal Upanishads.* London: Oxford
University Press, 1921.
ISHERWOOD, CHRISTOPHER. *Vedanta for Modern Man.* Hollywood: Mar-
shall Rodd, 1945.
JURJI, EDWARD. *The Great Religions of the Modern World.* Princeton:
Princeton University Press, 1946, pp. 44-90.
MOORE, CHARLES A. *Philosophy—East and West.* Princeton: Princeton
University Press, 1944.
MOORE, GEORGE F. *History of Religions.* New York: Chas. Scribner's Sons,
1946, chaps. xi-xiv.
NEHRU, JAWAHARLAL. *Toward Freedom.* New York: John Day Co., Inc.,
1941.

Noss, John B. *Man's Religions*. New York: The Macmillan Co., 1948, chaps. iii-vii.

Pratt, James B. *India and Its Faiths*. Boston: Houghton Mifflin Co., 1915.

Radhakrishnan, Sri. *The Philosophy of the Upanishads*. London: George Allen & Unwin, Ltd., 1924.

———. *Indian Philosophy*. New York: The Macmillan Co., 1923-27.

Zimmer, Heinrich. *Myth and Symbol in Indian Art and Civilization*. New York: Pantheon Books, Inc., 1946.

Chapter 4

THE WAYS OF BUDDHISM

The Life and Teachings of the Buddha

SIDDHARTHA GAUTAMA, a son of the noble-caste clan of Sakya in Northern India, was born around 563 B.C. From his clan name comes one of the most beloved of the names used for him by his followers, particularly in China and Japan: *Sakyamuni*, or "sage of the Sakyas." For others he is *Tatagatha*, "the thus-come"; still others call him *Bhagavadth*, "the Blessed One." But the title by which he is best known to the world is simply "the Buddha," or "the Enlightened One." Thus, frequently he is called "Gautama Buddha."

Gautama as a youth lived a protected and sheltered life, as his father prepared him carefully for the duties of an aristocrat. In good Hindu fashion, he began his journey through the *ashramas* open to the twice-born, devoting much time in his youth to the study of the *Vedas* and other Hindu classics. Then, at the age of nineteen he married a princess named Yashadhara who, ten years later, bore him a son, Rahula. He was now ready for the special duties of the Kshatriya caste as a householder and ruler. But as Gautama embarked upon the way of works customary for one of his position, he found himself troubled more and more by deep spiritual unrest. Though he was always sensitive to spiritual values, his protected life had allowed him little contact with the struggling masses of men. Now he felt that he must know how other men lived, and what he learned changed the course of his life.

The Enlightenment of Gautama

According to Buddhist tradition, Gautama experienced over a period of time "Four Appearances." First, while going on a journey one day, he saw "a decrepit old man, broken-toothed, gray-haired, crooked and bent of body, leaning on a staff, and trembling." And thus he realized vividly the fact of old age and its difficulties. Later he saw "a diseased man, repulsive with running sores," and he was led to recognize the facts of disease and suffering in the world. Then he saw a corpse lying by the side of the road, and he faced the fact of death for all men. These experiences moved Gautama to the depths of his being, because he realized that he was the men he had seen—the frailty, suffering, and mortality of these men no man can escape. All the pleasure and all the glory of life must be measured in terms of these three inescapable facts, and in the balance it seemed to Gautama that life is basically tragic.

But Gautama was not to remain inactive for long in his perplexity. According to tradition, the fourth appearance was in the form of a monk, yellow-robed and calm. Here was one way of life which seemed to escape tragedy. Thus Gautama was brought at a relatively early age to the point where he felt that he must renounce his duties and privileges as a householder and ruler and pass on immediately into the third of the *ashramas*. He must withdraw from the world, become a hermit, and devote all his energies to the search for salvation from the misery he had seen. There are colorful legends of various attempts on the part of his father to detain him, entertaining him with dancing girls, and so on. But one of the most moving stories is of Gautama slipping into the room where his young wife and child were sleeping to bid them a silent farewell before departing for the forest and a life of asceticism.

It is said that many months passed while Gautama tried first the Hindu way of knowledge, immersing himself in the philosophical classics, and then turned desperately to the more extreme ways of works offered in yoga practices of self-mortification. So strenuously did he follow this traditional path of works that he nearly destroyed himself. Then, finally, just as he was despairing of finding an answer to the burning question of the meaning of life in its tragic complexity, illumination came. He was sitting, it is said, under a Bo- (fig) tree near Gaya (Patna), 150 miles east of Benares. Suddenly a man appeared before him and did him homage. Why? Gautama wondered. Then it occurred to him that his long period of search had not been fruitless, after all; at least he had gained some negative knowledge: he had learned that the traditional Hindu ways of knowledge and works could not bring him deliverance. And then he realized that he had perhaps been his own worst enemy in the fervent search; in striving too earnestly to find the way, he had gotten in his own way. His intense desire had been the root of his difficulty. Indeed, perhaps desire is at the root of all difficulties. Perhaps men are basically bundles of desires, and perhaps there can be no freedom until they know this in the depths of their being, and, through this knowledge, achieve the last and greatest freedom—freedom from self. Perhaps, strictly and ontologically speaking, there is no self, but only changing complexes of desire. Then, if there is no self in the usual sense of the term, and one can know this, selfishness may be overcome by knowledge. If men are liberated from self-centered desire, or egocentricity, then for the first time their actions can be free and spontaneous, without compulsion, and without attachment to the results of action. These, it appears, are some of the thoughts that came flooding into Gautama's mind as he sat under the Bo-tree. In thoughts like these he found Enlightenment, or bliss.

Gautama resisted the temptation to keep his precious and hard-won insight to himself. Instead he went to a group of monks who had once been his disciples but had been unable to follow him through the extremes of his asceticism, and told them what he had learned. Buddhist tradition has distilled this first and essential teaching into a discourse called "The Sermon at Benares," the Buddhist equivalent of the Christian "Sermon on the Mount." The basic direction of

the way it describes is called by Buddhists "the Middle Path."
It is necessary in all things, said Buddha, to avoid extremes.
The dangers of extreme indulgence he had learned as a youth;
the dangers of extreme asceticism he had learned as a hermit-
monk. The self-defeating character of extreme attachment to
any thing or any course of conduct he had realized in the
experience under the Bo-tree. So the first rule of ethics, he
said, is to find and follow the Middle Path, or, as Aristotle
in Greece put it, "the Golden Mean": nothing to excess
at any time.

The Fourfold Noble Truths

Gautama accepted two basic presuppositions from the
Hinduism in which he was nurtured: the doctrines of *karma*
and *samsara*. All his thinking, like the thinking of later
Buddhists, proceeded on the assumption that individuals are
caught in an indefinite cycle of finite existences propelled and
measured by an inexorable moral law of cause and effect, and
that the goal of all knowledge is salvation, or deliverance from
finitude. Thus there is no basic disagreement between Buddhists and Hindus, or between different sects within Buddhism, about the nature of man's basic religious problem.
The differences concern the more detailed analyses of the
problem, the ways of salvation offered, and, to some extent,
the nature of the state of deliverance.

ALL IS SORROW. Proceeding from the assumption of *karma*
and *samsara*, Gautama taught in his Fourfold Noble Truths
subtle and imaginative psychology and metaphysics. In his
view the one cannot be divorced from the other—true understanding of the self is impossible without insight into the
nature of the reality of which the self is a part, and true
understanding of reality must begin and end with understanding of the self which knows and acts in reality. Thus
the first of the Noble Truths asserts that all is sorrow, or
dukkha. Now it must be understood that this statement is
looked upon by Buddhists as a statement of fact, not as a
value-judgment. That is to say, there is no sentimental tear-

shedding, bitterness, or disillusionment suggested. Nor does the statement imply by the word "sorrow," *dukkha*, that all life is a matter of painful weeping and wailing. Its minimum meaning is that, as a matter of fact, we live in a world in which all is not what it should be; the times are always out of joint. *Dukkha* thus implies disharmony, commotion, turmoil, confusion. Later Buddhist scholars further subdivided *dukkha* into (a) *Dukkha-dukkha*, things which are intrinsically tormenting, such as unrelieved hunger and disease, and (b) *Vipaninama-dukkha*, things which are not intrinsically evil but are so in the context in which they are experienced, or prove to be so in the long run. An example of the latter is eating. While one is eating, the experience is good. But if one eats too much the result is evil and outweighs the good; and, even if one does not eat too much, eating will be followed, sooner or later, by hunger, which is an evil.

SORROW SPRINGS FROM DESIRE. This last point suggests the insight of the second Noble Truth—that sorrow springs from desire, thirst, or craving. It is the restless yearning of man, expressed in physical appetite, economic acquisitiveness, intellectual and spiritual drives, and the like, which leads him to seek again and again those apparent goods which always let him down. Even the highest and relatively most enduring aesthetic and intellectual pleasures are tainted by one certain fact: they will pass away. In other words, it is the temporality, the transitoriness, of all goods which makes them ultimately *dukkha*. This is a very important point to bear in mind in understanding, assessing, and comparing most Eastern views of good and evil with Western views. At the heart of Buddhism's Four Noble Truths is the conviction that time itself is evil or is the root of evil. We have encountered the same conviction expressed in the Hindu view of *maya*, and it is implied in the Taoist search for that union with the eternal which can save from temporal futility. It is this conviction which leads to the Buddhist assertion that any kind of activity aimed at personal satisfactions and finite goods is ulti-

mately *dukkha*. If the result is transitory and hence evil, then
the cause of activity in thirst or craving is a prior evil.

DESIRE MAY BE ELIMINATED. The Third Noble Truth
draws the logical conclusion that *dukkha* may cease if the
cause of *dukkha*, craving or thirst—restless desire—is eliminated. But the selfishness of the self cannot be eliminated
unless the self is understood. So Gautama agreed with Socrates and many other wise men that the first step toward
the good life is to "know thyself." What, then, is the self?
According to a typical Buddhist interpretation of Buddha's
teachings on this point, the self is an active unity of five lesser
unities or aggregates (*khandas*). These subunities within the
larger organic unity of the self include *Rupas*, physical form;
Sannas, sensation or contact of sense-organs with stimuli;
Vedanas, feelings or affections; *Sankaras*, perceptions; and
Vinnanas, conceptual thoughts. The whole is interestingly
called *Mannas*, literally "mind." The self plus the prenatal
forces of its *karma, sankhara*, is the basic metaphysical unit
in the realm of space and time.

It is *karma* which determines the nature and amount of
tanha, craving, desire, or thirst, with which a given individual
is endowed and which he must overcome if salvation is to
be achieved. *Karma* in turn is of various forms. *Kusala*
karma determines how one is born; *kanaka-karma* determines
where one is born; *potisandhi-karma* determines the nature
of the connection between previous consciousness and that
of the new life, and so on. The latter *karma*, incidentally,
suggests that one's dying thoughts are of great significance
and consequence for the future; hence the practice in some
Buddhist circles of writing one's good deeds down in a
book which is read to one on his deathbed.

But what is it that is passed from one life to another
according to the complexities of *karma?* At this point a
further disagreement between many Buddhists and Hindus
occurs. Hindus maintain that the individual self or ego
crosses over from life to life. But Buddha had shown in his
Second Noble Truth that, strictly speaking, there is no self

—there is only a bundle of cravings constantly changing and never the same. What is there then between one life and another? Simply a *gati*, a "going," Buddhists reply. If the self is a process, then that which connects process with process must itself be process. According to a favorite analogy employed by Buddhists to explain this idea, the passing is not like the passing of a bird from one nest to another; rather it is like the passing from one drop of water to another in a flowing stream. In any event, the law of *karma* in the context of *samsara* affords an adequate explanation of differences between people as well as differences in the amount of craving or thirst which each must overcome. How much better are the scientific explanations of individual differences in terms of heredity and environment, Buddhists ask? Indeed, modern Buddhists maintain that the facts of environmental and hereditary determination are simply some of the facts of *karma* put into different language for different purposes.

THE MIDDLE PATH. The Fourth Noble Truth contains an eightfold explanation of the Middle Path by which desire, and thus sorrow, may be overcome. This Eightfold Noble Path, therefore, is the basis for classical Buddhist ethics.

Buddhist Ethics: The Eightfold Noble Path

1. Basic to all right action, said Buddha, is *right belief*. If one does not understand himself and the world in which he acts, as this understanding is epitomized in the Four Noble Truths, then his action will be ultimately self-defeating.

2. But merely to understand with the intellect the nature of the self and the world is not enough. Understanding must produce and be colored by *right aspiration*. Knowledge, at least merely theoretical knowledge, is not virtue; there must be a basic emotional set of the personality toward good conduct before knowledge can result in good conduct.

3. Also basic to good conduct is clarity of thought and expression. Confused words bespeak a confused mind, and orderly conduct cannot issue from mental confusion. Therefore, *right speech* is the third aspect of the Eightfold Noble

Path. (Compare Confucius' emphasis on "The Rectification of Names.")

4. If belief, aspiration, and speech are right, then *good conduct* may follow. But what is good conduct? As expanded by a typical commentator of the Hinayana school (see below) good conduct means, among other things:

a) Not wilfully hurting any living creature. This Buddhist statement of *ahimsa* has been subject to varying interpretations and degrees of application in various sects at various times. But, in general, it seems fair to say that Buddhists have been the most consistent pacifists among the world's religious groups.

b) Not taking what is not given. This includes stealing or coveting in any form—including, as modern Buddhist social reformers point out, stealing or coveting another man's labor.

c) Avoiding overindulgence of the senses—moderation in physical appetite and activity. For Buddhist monks this means asceticism in varying degrees; for laymen it means sobriety and temperance. Intoxicating beverages, foods, or drugs are to be avoided—and also, say modern Buddhists, intoxicating ideas!

5. Good conduct of this sort in turn means that one will engage only in those occupations which are consistent with its aims and ideals. *Right livelihood* is essential. This step of the path has caused restrictions in those forms of work open to devout Buddhist laymen in various parts of the world from time to time. Sometimes it has led to a false conservatism hindering the social progress of Buddhist countries. Sometimes it has also produced a critical evaluation of what constitutes genuine progress which most Westerners might well consider.

6. Good conduct also requires constant renewal of that aspiration and effort which makes the difference between knowledge and virtue; continuous *right effort*, exertion of will, persistence in one's duty and aim, is necessary.

7. Right effort, however, may become sheer emotion unless it is accompanied by steady and deepening understanding, an understanding which transforms the basic right belief into a broader and richer constant frame of mind called *right mindfulness*.

8. Finally, if one follows faithfully the first seven steps in the Eightfold Path, he will come to that deliverance from all desire and all sorrow which is the goal of his quest: *right rapture*.

The Goal: Nirvana

What is the nature of the state of deliverence? We have seen that both Taoists and Vedantists have said that, since the state of deliverence is beyond the realm in which language is applicable, it is obviously and literally indescribable. This insight, however, has not prevented Taoist and Hindu sages from offering detailed descriptions, if only in negative and paradoxical language. Indeed, some have gone further and described the "realm of bliss" in concrete and sensuous terms.

It seems that Gautama, however, was consistently agnostic (literally, "without knowledge") concerning such questions and many others which have traditionally occupied theologians and metaphysicians. It is enough, he said, to know what man is, what is wrong with him, and how he may overcome that wrong. To fly beyond this knowledge into realms of speculation where certainty is obviously impossible adds nothing to the knowledge necessary for salvation. On the contrary, too much speculation about the nature of Heaven may deter men from the concrete business of understanding how to get there. Thus one of the most famous dialogues between Gautama and one of his disciples is the following:

Reverend Sir, these theories which the Blessed One has left unelucidated, has set aside and rejected—that the world is eternal, that the world is not eternal. . . . That the saint neither exists nor does not exist after death, if the Blessed One will elucidate them to me, in that case I will lead the religious life under the Blessed One. If the Blessed One will not elucidate

them, I will abandon religious training and return to the lower
life of a layman. . . .

The religious life, Malunkyaputta, does not depend on the
dogma that the world is eternal, nor on the dogma that the
world is not eternal. Whether the dogma obtain or not, there
still remain birth, old age, sorrow . . . and despair, for the extinction of which in this present life I am prescribing. . . .

Accordingly, Malunkyaputta, . . . I have not elucidated
. . . that the world is eternal; I have not elucidated that the
world is not eternal; . . . I have not elucidated that the
saint neither exists nor does not exist after death. And why
. . . have I not elucidated this? . . . Because . . . this profits
not, nor has to do with the fundamentals of religion, nor tends
to aversion, absence of passion, cessation . . . supreme wisdom,
and Nirvana.[1]

In this last paragraph appears the word which Buddhists
have traditionally used to designate the state of deliverance:
Nirvana. But questions as to whether Nirvana is actually a
state; whether it involves existence or nonexistence; consciousness or unconsciousness; bliss or nothingness—all these are
matters, say those Buddhists who claim to be closest to the
teaching of the Master, which "tend not to edification." The
indescribable is simply indescribable.

However, we shall see that this lofty doctrine has not
satisfied the masses. Nor has it satisfied the sages of many
Buddhist schools, particularly in northern Asia, who would
develop more concrete and elaborate pictures of countless
heavens, hells, and paradises.

The Universality of the Way

The basic way taught by Gautama is, his followers claim,
simple and practical. It is a way open to all sorts and conditions of men. Buddha himself made one of his sharpest
breaks with traditional Hinduism when he proclaimed that
in his way there is no caste. The important differences between men, he said, are differences of spiritual and moral
quality; in the light of these, differences relating to color,

[1] *The Bible of The World, op. cit.*, pp. 256-59.

vocation, or social status are accidental and superficial. So he admitted men, and later women, of all castes to his company. Anyone, anywhere, may seek to know and follow the Middle Way by understanding the Four Noble Truths and living by the Eightfold Path. It is not surprising to learn that in contemporary India some leaders of outcaste groups who observe that their status has not been magically changed overnight by the new democratic social legislation are turning once again to Buddhism as a faith which is truly universal in its scope.

Not only is the way universally open to men who will follow it, but it also teaches a way of compassion which is universal in its outreach. The enlightened man, said Buddha, loves all men equally—and therefore he loves no one in exclusive particularity. This being true, he weeps no more over the death of a parent than over the death of a stranger. He treats all men alike in what appears to be indifference—but it is an indifference, or impartiality, born of love! Compare this view with Confucius' careful gradation of social relations according to *Li*, and with the complex restrictions of the traditional Hindu caste-system. Compare also Confucius' statement that wise men must return good for good and justice for evil with the following:

"He abused me, he beat me, he defeated me, he robbed me" —in those who harbor such thoughts hatred will never cease.

"He abused me, he defeated me, he robbed me"—in those who do not harbor such thoughts hatred will cease.

For hatred does not cease by hatred at any time: hatred ceases by love—this is an old rule.[2]

THE SCOPE OF BUDDHIST INFLUENCE

The Emergence of a Missionary Faith

We have seen that Confucianism, as its name implies, has centered around the teachings of its founder as interpreted

[2] *The World Bible, op. cit.,* p. 135.

in various schools. Yet it has never been, strictly speaking, a missionary religion. Its influence has been largely limited to Chinese culture, with which it has been at times almost synonymous. Confucian ideals, to be sure, have profoundly influenced other cultures which have come under the aegis of Chinese culture, such as the Japanese and Korean. But there has been no serious and systematic attempt to extend Confucianism as a faith beyond the outreaches of Chinese culture as such.

Hinduism, on the other hand, looks to no single founder. Indeed, it considers such matters as names and dates to be of little interest, because its whole world view minimizes the significance of the particular and the historical. And Hinduism, like Confucianism, has not been a missionary faith. In the recent past some Hindu groups, influenced in part by Christian and other Western ideas, have set out to acquaint the West with the ideas and ideals of Vedanta. But traditionally Hinduism has been as indigenous to India as Confucianism has been indigenous to China.

In Buddhism however, we find a faith intimately bound up with reverence for the life and teachings of its founder which has aspired to be a geographically and spiritually universal faith. Some of the reasons for this difference are perhaps apparent from a cursory glance at some major emphases in the traditional formulations of the three faiths. Other reasons are bound up with the political and social fortunes of the cultures in which each appeared.

The Buddhist Orders

Buddha gathered around him early in his ministry a body of disciples who turned their backs on the indigenous Hinduism and constituted an order which cut across caste and cultural lines. The three classic pillars of Buddhism are *Buddha-Dharma-Sangha*—The Enlightened One—His Teaching—The Order. Gautama continued to labor for and with his company of disciples until his death at the age of seventy. And the disciples felt, as millions have felt since then, that his way is gospel—literally "good news"—too good to keep.

Thus they, like the Master, have continued to feel compelled
to share with others the secret of life as they understand it,
through preaching, teaching, and ministering to all the needs
of their fellow-men as best they could.

Though Gautama himself lived very frugally, his rule of
life for his order was relatively moderate. Each monk, he
said, was to have three robes or changes of clothing; a begging
bowl; needle and thread; and a razor. But none was to give
or receive gold or silver—a rule that has been interestingly
modified in subsequent developments. They were to live on
the generosity of others, but were to repay their benefactors
with teaching or some other kind of service. Later, as noted
above, orders for women were established. And still later
lay orders were established for those who do not feel called
to forsake the world as completely as the monks and nuns,
but wish to approximate their rules of life as closely as possible in the normal responsibilities of life. As time went on
conflicts developed within and among the orders, some becoming more strict and some more lax than the founder had
decreed. But through the ages the various Buddhist orders
have carried the main stream of Buddhist teaching and
activity in all the lands touched by the faith. The monk
usually may be recognized in all these lands by his yellow
robe, his clean-shaven head, and his alms-bowl—though the
latter may be purely symbolic. Frequently he carries books,
too, because study and teaching have been major occupations
of the orders. Indeed, it is said that a monk of ancient times,
upon hearing that he could own only what he could carry
on his back, undertook strenuous physical exercises in order
to be able to carry a sizeable library around with him.

Yet Buddhism was destined to decline in its native India
even as it prospered elsewhere. Why? India was torn by a
series of invasions during the early Buddhist centuries, and
the established Hinduism, with its protective caste-system
and its ancient roots in India's past, could withstand the
consequent social upheaval better than could the more loosely
organized and heretical Buddhism. Furthermore, Hinduism
reacted to the Buddhist challenge in a typically Hindu fashion

—it proceeded to absorb and embody within itself many significant Buddhist insights. The Buddhist challenge touched off some of the philosophical reforms which we have previously noted. On the other hand, Buddhism itself, losing many of its intellectual leaders and much of its popular appeal because of these and other factors, gradually degenerated in India until it became mainly identified with various magical and erotic cults. Thus it was dominant even in its native Bihar only until the time of the Mohammedan invasion in the twelfth century of the Christian era.

Hinayana Lands

There were Buddhist emperors of India, and one, Asoka, was a man of great spiritual as well as political stature. Buddhists are fond of pointing to his reign in the third century A.D. as a model epoch of peaceful progress and tolerance. It was largely due to his influence that Buddhism was carried to Ceylon near the middle of the third century. Within a century the faith had won nearly all that country, and the Buddhists of Ceylon began to make their own distinctive contributions to the movement, one of the most notable being the copying and preserving of the *Pali Canon*, the most ancient collection of Buddhist scriptures. Though there were times of Buddhist decline when political tensions developed between Ceylon and India, by the end of the thirteenth century Buddhism was firmly entrenched as the state religion of Ceylon. It was threatened in the sixteenth century by over-zealous Portuguese Roman Catholics, but enjoyed periods of tolerance under the Dutch and British. With the achievement of virtual independence as a member of the British Commonwealth, Ceylon has reaffirmed her devotion to Buddhist faith and culture.

Buddhism had entered Burma also by the end of the first century A.D., and by 1000 A.D. was firmly established as the religious framework of Burmese culture. From Burma it spread to Siam, where its fortunes have reflected the political fortunes of that country in a manner similar to that in Ceylon. Within recent centuries it has developed freely in all these lands, and today Buddhism is of considerable political as well as religious significance in south-east Asia. The new Marxist faith is claiming some Buddhists' allegiance, even as many Buddhists are affirming the essential incompatibility between the two faiths. In many areas Buddhist leaders have identified themselves with the various nationalistic independence movements.

The Buddhism of these southern lands has been, generally speaking, simpler and closer to what appear to be the original teachings of Gautama than has that of such northern lands as China and Japan. We shall note certain important differences in our discussion of devotional practices below. Indeed, members of the northern schools refer to the southern schools as *Hinayana* or "the lesser vehicle," and to themselves as *Mahayana* or "greater vehicle." But Buddhists of the southern schools prefer to call themselves *Therevada*—"followers of the doctrine of the elders."

As indicated above, the southern Buddhists have long cherished the ancient scriptures written in Singhalese about the time of Asoka and retranslated into Pali texts in the fifth century by the great scholar Buddhagosa. These scriptures are traditionally called the *Tripitaka* or "Three Baskets." They include the *Vinaya*, a collection of monastic rules; the *Sutta*, a collection of discourses on basic Buddhist doctrines; and the *Abidhamma*, a group of scholastic commentaries.

Members of the southern schools find in these scriptures no sanction for many of the beliefs and practices of Mahayana, particularly those bound up with belief in the divinity of Buddha or other Buddha-deities. Hinayana—or Therevada—maintains that Gautama was The Enlightened One, the Great Teacher, but not divine in a sense denied to other men. We shall note in a moment ways in which this belief is reflected in differences of devotional practice.

In the south the monks are of special importance as bearers of the tradition. It was once estimated that 8,000 of three million Buddhists in Ceylon were monks; 90,000 of eleven million in Burma; and 50,000 of nine million in Siam. The contributions of the monks to these lands have been great.

For centuries they have been the chief educators and their monasteries the chief educational centers. Also, in addition to the usual preaching and ceremonial activities, they have engaged in various forms of social service. Their teaching and preaching has stressed the classical Fourfold Truths and Eightfold Path, and the layman is expected to devote himself conscientiously to a way of life modeled on them. He hears frequent discourses on the love and compassion of Sakyamuni toward all men and aspires to emulate The Teacher. There are no *ashramas* for him to follow, but he may enter a monastery whenever he feels called or equal to it; indeed, in Siam young men are expected to spend at least three months in a monastery before undertaking the responsibilities of marriage and citizenship. The concrete political and economic results of these teachings have varied from country to country and from time to time. It is safe to say that the Buddhist leaven has always influenced positively and constructively, to some degree, the social life of Hinayana lands. There may be exaggerated enthusiasm in the claim of an intelligent and cultured contemporary Buddhist of Ceylon that, as a result of Buddhist influence, his land has never known starvation or persecution. Nevertheless, there is much for Westerners and others to learn from the traditional and contemporary social application of the Buddhist way as understood in southern Asia.

Mahayana Schools

The Buddhism which penetrated into China, Japan, and other northern Asiatic countries had already undergone many changes as a result of interplay with Hindu philosophical and devotional schools and with Syrian, Greek, and Scythian religions in the Greco-Bactrian culture of the Punjab (northwest India) in the first two centuries before Christ. As a result of this interplay it had yielded more and more to the need of common folk for concrete divinities to worship and to the need of philosophers for abstract speculative intellectual systems. Its emphasis thus was more and more upon ways of knowledge and devotion, and increasingly less upon the classical ethics, except as various devotional practices were considered good works.

Then, when Buddhism entered China in the first two or three centuries A.D., it found Confucianism already established as a comprehensive ethical system for the Chinese, and Taoism filling many, but not all, of the devotional needs. Its chief contributions to China, then, would be devotional and theological in character. China had known virtually no theology, strictly speaking, until Buddhism came. And eventually Chinese Buddhism was also to fill the needs of the masses for elaborate ceremony and ritual, particularly as these concern death and the future life. The monks were to remain more distinctly Buddhist, but Buddhism for the layman became more and more Chinese as time went on. The average layman saw no ambiguity in turning to Confucianism for his ethics, to Taoism for his meditation or magic, and to Buddhism for his theology and ceremonies for the dead. As a result of this emphasis upon devotion and theology, Chinese Buddhism developed five major and many minor sects, each stressing varying types of devotion ranging from extreme mysticism to crude magic.

In Japan Buddhism has been a more distinctive and definite faith. It entered that country in the sixth century from Korea when Japanese culture was less highly developed than Chinese culture. It appears that it was accepted not so much for its religious value as for its association with what was recognized to be a higher Indian-Chinese culture. The Japanese had already developed a way of their own in the relatively primitive *Shinto* or "Way of The Gods"—a way which stressed the basic feudal virtues of loyalty to one's superiors and to one's country, courage in the performance of one's duty, and honesty in the conduct of one's daily life. Later the Confucian way entered and further influenced the Japanese way of faith. But Buddhism offered a more spiritualized concept of deity, a more highly developed speculative philosophy, and the artistic and literary achievements of a higher culture. Thus within three hundred years of its introduction Buddhism became the official religion of the Japanese government. From that time on, with various periods of decline and resurgence, it has been the dominant religion of the Japanese people—even when the ancient Shinto was artificially revived for political and militaristic purposes in the more recent past.

In Japan the major Chinese sects established themselves and produced a few native Japanese variants. As in China, the sects are divided over and primarily concerned with theological and devotional matters. One of the most significant, the Zen sect, has disavowed theological speculation and espouses an austere and subtle mysticism or existentialism. As in China, Buddhist ethical influence has been, on the whole, indirect—although some sects have been of great political importance as a result of their identification with various rulers and political aspirants. When a recognized Japanese Buddhist writer describes Mahayana in action in Japan she speaks mainly of the religious activities of the priests, monks, and nuns; of the devotional practices of laymen; of services for the remembrance of the dead and other religious observances; and of techniques of meditation.[3] In her brief survey she has no separate treatment of Buddhist ethics because, she says, the subject is treated in the *sutras* or scriptures which she mentions and in the Five Precepts, which are an adaptation of the traditional path previously described: Not to kill any living being; not to steal; not to be unchaste; not to lie; and not to become intoxicated.[4] This would seem to indicate that the impact of Mahayana in Japan and elsewhere is largely upon individual conduct and only indirectly upon social issues. Yet it should also be pointed out that, as in Hinayana Lands, Buddhist contributions to education have been inestimable. And in the recent past there has been much organized Buddhist social service in hospitals and community centers, and in such organizations as The Young Men's Buddhist Association—whose very name suggests stimulation from non-Buddhist sources.

[3] Beatrice Lane Suzuki, *Mahayana Buddhism* (London: David Marlowe, Ltd., 1948), chap iv.
[4] *Ibid.*, p. 130.

BUDDHIST DEVOTIONAL PRACTICES

Gautama Buddha was an atheist. It has been noted that there is no mention of a deity, personal or impersonal, in what appears to be earliest and basic Buddhist gospel. When Gautama was in search of a way of deliverance he is reported to have exhausted the Hindu ways of works and knowledge current in his times, but there is no mention of his turning to *Bhakti* in any of its forms—indeed, the major types of *Bhakti* took their classical forms after his time. And there is no indication that either he or his early followers considered Gautama to be anything more than a man, a teacher, a "Ford-finder." Down through the years there have been Buddhists who have remained true to what they believe to be the original doctrine and its estimate of the role of Gautama. But, as in other traditions, the masses of worshipers needed more than an intellectual system proclaimed by a mere man, even if by following that system they could achieve the insight and bliss of the founder. Thus the needs of devotion produced legends of a miraculous birth and a wondrous life, and eventually an elaborate soteriology filled the pages of Buddhist devotional classics.[5]

Hinayana Devotional Practices

Hinayana schools claim to have remained closer to the original nontheistic teachings of Gautama than have their northern cousins. Most Hinayana scholars would maintain that there is in Hinayana lands no worship—or at least no officially sanctioned worship—of Buddha as a deity or even of personal gods as such. There are various expressions of reverence for Gautama and expressions of aspiration to emulate him, they say. And it may be that the common people find it difficult to draw the line between reverence for, and worship of, a person. Nevertheless, they insist, Hinayana Buddhism is essentially atheistic in its teaching and human-

[5] For an interesting comparison of Buddhist and Christian stories, see Joseph E. Carpenter, *Buddhism and Christianity* (London: Hodder & Stoughton, Ltd., 1923), chap. iii.

istic in its practices. At the same time it has had to accommodate itself to the thinking of the people, and it inherited in each of the Hinayana lands native religions made up of animistic and other practices common to all primitive faiths. Therefore popular Hinayana has absorbed into itself many magical and superstitious practices along with many indigenous, colorful, and socially meaningful festivals and customs, and all these together make up what is in fact the devotional life of Hinayana.

One of the most popular ways to vivify respect for the memory of a saint is to associate that respect with reverence for a relic associated with his person. Therefore, alleged relics of the Buddha—of his life and of the places he visited during his ministry—form the nucleus of extensive devotional practice, including art and architecture, in Hinayana domains. The most distinctive architectural feature of Hinayana devotion, the pagoda, has grown out of relic-reverence. It appears that the origins of pagodas are traceable to the use of the parasol in hot Hinayana lands as a symbol of royalty. When relics of the Buddha were brought in or "discovered" it was thus appropriate to place parasols over them in their resting-places, both for protection from the sun and to indicate their significance. Reverence could be indicated by stacking parasol upon parasol until there was a tier of parasols. And the tier of parasols gave to the pagoda its classical architectural style. Each pagoda houses at least one sacred relic associated with the life and teaching of the Buddha. And, since it was early understood that the erection of a pagoda as beautiful and expensive as one could afford over a relic as popular as could be found was an obvious way of achieving good *karma*, pagodas now dot the countryside of southeast Asia and form, along with the monasteries, centers of devotional life. Gleaming stately in the sun, their tinkling bells symbolizing the continuous prayers (or aspirations) of the worshipers, they are constant reminders of the role of Buddhism in the life of the people.

The monasteries are usually built around courtyards containing pagodas, lotus ponds, and relics of various sorts. Perhaps there is a footprint of the Buddha; perhaps a Bo-tree sprung from a scion of the original; perhaps a sacred tooth like the famous one at Kandy in Ceylon. The monastery may be simply constructed of mud and plaster as in Ceylon or ornately designed of carved teakwood as in Burma. In any event, it is the center of devotional instruction and practice. It may house only a handful of yellow-robed, bald-pated monks, or several hundred—typically, only a few. The chief duties of the monks, as indicated previously, are to instruct the people in the classics of Buddhism as well as in other learning, to carry out a daily round of meditation and ministration, and to preach to those who come for encouragement and spiritual nurture.

A typical worshiper comes to the monastery shrine; washes himself; places an offering of flowers before the Buddha-image (not, strictly speaking an idol, Hinayana scholars assert); repeats the classical "Refuge": "I take refuge in the Buddha, the Doctrine, and the Order"; sits for a time in silent prayer or meditation; perhaps wanders into the courtyard to hear a monk preach; and returns to his home or his occupation refreshed in mind and spirit. Except for festival days there are no regularly scheduled or formal services of worship, but in the cool of many evenings groups may gather in the courtyard for communal prayer and preaching. Special services may occur on the "moon days," the four days in each month when the moon goes through its various quarters, because the moon in its phases symbolizes the cycle of samsara. Other festivals occur at the beginning and end of the various seasons, with intent and character similar to that of those described in the sections on Chinese and Indian devotional practices. Similarly, too, there are special family services to herald the birth and life-stages of children, to remember the dead, and so on.

Intertwined with these relatively restrained and beautifully significant practices are elements of more primitive animism and astrology. The latter is of special significance in the political life of the Hinayana countries, as astrologers must be consulted about all important dates in the life of individuals, families, or nations. The governments of enlightened Hinayana countries frequently conduct the affairs of state, including inaugurations and other important events, with due respect for popular belief in the role of the heavenly bodies in human affairs. As for spirits, there are legions of both good and bad ones involved in the daily life of the masses in most Hinayana regions. To deal with them an elaborate system of charms and exorcism has developed, sometimes against the opposition and sometimes with the cooperation of Buddhist priests and monks. The Burmese *nats*, for instance, comprise an elaborate hierarchy of spirits and demons who intervene in all aspects of daily life. They include local nature-spirits, ghosts and ancestral spirits, and superior demigod spirits of local heroes and Hindu epics. Magic for dealing with them takes all the forms familiar in other primitive religions, including the exotic devil-dancing of Ceylon with which some Westerners are familiar.

The Devotional Theology of Mahayana

The northward and eastward movement of Buddhism from India brought it into contact with relatively highly developed philosophical and theological systems which had entered northern Indian in various invasions of Western groups, including Greeks and Persians, who followed the path of the earlier Indo-Aryans. Then as Buddhism took root in China, and later in Korea and Japan, it was faced with indigenous systems of thought and practice and forced to develop its own contributions in a manner which would make them supplementary and complementary. Therefore the originally simple intellectual faith of Buddhism developed in Mahayana lands into a bewildering mass of theological doctrines reflected in the devotional practices of these countries. To the earlier *Pali Canon* were added lengthy collections of new *sutras* or scriptures, beginning with the development of the influential *Diamond Sutra* in China in the fourth century A.D. This was followed in time by the *Pure Land Sutras* of the Pure Land (or Paradise) Sects, of which more will be said later; the *Lotus of the True Law*; and many others—eventually a large

library of scriptures covering all manner of theological speculations, rules of conduct, and prescriptions for devotional activities. There is not space here to examine any of these
sutras in detail. We may sample their thought, however, by
noting in summary fashion the theories of deity which eventually emerged.

In Hinayana Buddhism, it is believed that Gautama
achieved *Nirvana*, the goal of all life, and that he can inspire
by his example any who wish to undertake the Eightfold Path.
Those who seem to succeed in achieving an unusual depth
of spiritual understanding are called *arhats* or saints. Mahayana, however, developed the idea of many human beings
in various *kulpas* or eras achieving Buddhahood even as Gautama had achieved it in the present era. Such beings, called
Manushi Buddhas, are now in a position to inspire those who
seek Buddhahood and to answer their prayers. They also
inspire the pilgrim towards *Nirvana* by recalling various aspects of the life and work of earthly Buddhas. Thus many
of the familiar images of Buddhas are of the *Manushi* in
various classical poses.

The Buddha of meditation, for instance, is shown seated
in classical Yogi posture, palms upward in the lap. The earth-
witness Buddha touches the ground with the tips of the
fingers of the right hand, palm outward; this recalls Gautama's calling upon the earth to bear witness to his resistance
to the temptations of Mara, the Evil One. The teaching
Buddha holds both hands before the breast, with index finger
and thumb of the right hand touching the tip of a finger on
the left hand, ticking off the various points of essential doctrine. Dear to those in pain or danger is the fearless or protecting Buddha, with hand extended palm outward to ward
off the powers of evil. And comforting and inspiring to all
is the gracious or charitable Buddha, with right arm hanging
downward and palm extended in a posture of benign giving.
Most of these Buddhas have the traditional sacred mark on
the forehead. Most of the faces are expressionless, reflecting
the calm beyond *dukkha* which is the Buddhist goal. Frequently the Buddha is portrayed seated on a lotus blossom.

What could symbolize more aptly the fragile purity of absolute calm and tranquillity rising above the world of sorrow than the lotus blossom which rises delicately and beautifully out of murky water?

Even more significant for the devotional practices of Mahayana, however, are the *Bodhisattvas*. These are beings who vowed to achieve Buddhahood, have stored up enough good *karma* to enter upon it, but out of sheer love and compassion for struggling humanity have voluntarily postponed the enjoyment of pure bliss in order to help those who call upon them. The free grace of the Bodhisattvas thus serves as an example and compelling motive for Buddhist missionary and social service work. There are countless Bodhisattvas in Mahayana lore—indeed, some Mahayana scholars and sects maintain that each sincere Buddhist is called to be a Bodhisattva and is one, in principle, as soon as he begins his discipleship.[6] For devotional purposes, however, those Bodhisattvas are most important who have actually achieved sufficient merit to share a surplus with others. One of the most popular of these is *Maitreya* (Chinese *Wen Fu*), the "Buddha-elect" of the next age—the Messiah, as it were—he who is to come. The notion of a messianic age in the future as the goal of social progress has received relatively little stress in Buddhism, however, and it is as a gracious Bodhisattva with favors to bestow here and now that Maitreya has been most significant.

Then there is *Manjusri* (Chinese *Wen Yu*), the Bodhisattva of wisdom and the patron of scholars. He is pictured carrying a sword and a book (the power of knowledge), riding upon a lion, and is sometimes accompanied by a consort, *Samantabhadra*, patroness of kindness (the kindness that accompanies wisdom). Then there is *Avalokitesuara*, around whom in various guises many cults have formed, including the Chinese cult of *Kwan-Yin*, goddess of mercy, with her Japanese counterpart *Kwannon* and Korean sister *Koan-Eum*. This mercy-goddess is the great Madonna of the East. Pictured in tender and graceful postures, frequently holding a

[6] Cf. Beatrice Lane Suzuki, *op. cit.*, pp. 51 ff.

child, she is especially concerned with the welfare of women
in childbirth and with children in general. But she is also
invoked by millions for countless other needs which can
best be met by a tender and maternal representation of the
intimate and the ultimate.

Another popular Bodhisattva of healing, a deliverer from
suffering, is *Kshitigarbha* (Chinese *Ti-Tsang,* Japanese *Jizo*).
Beyond these there is a veritable pantheon of Bodhisattvas
associated with all sorts of natural powers and phenomena,
all manner of human emotions and needs. In the sixth century A.D. the worship of the consort-goddess *Shakti* appeared
in India, spread into Mahayana lands, and had an especially
strong influence in Bihar and Nepal and in the Lamaism of
Tibet. Shaktism frequently involves erotic and orgiastic practices. In many Mahayana temples the worshiper may find a
Buddha or Bodhisattva image vividly expressing just the
human emotion, passion, or need which is uppermost in his
mind at the time of worship.

Finally, exalted even above the Bodhisattvas are the
Dhyani Buddhas—superhuman beings who achieved and have
known the bliss of Buddhahood or *arhatship,* but have postponed entrance into *Nirvana* in order to carry on the merciful
work of the Bodhisattvas, at a higher level and with greater
power. These are the Lords of the various Paradises which
are pictured in Mahayana *sutras,* and are symbols of the all-
pervading character of the basic Buddha-nature. As in Hinduism, Mahayana reflection on the round of birth and rebirth
in *samsara* interposed a number of vividly conceived heavens
and hells as intermediary stages through which souls may pass
according to the *karma* they create. Beyond that, there were
those who said that all reality, the realm of *samsara* in its
entirety with all creations, lifespans, heavens and hells, is but
an imperfect expression of an underlying Buddha-substance,
with which to become identical is to achieve *Nirvana.* We
may merely note here the devotional influence of such Dhyani
Buddhas as *Vairocana,* descriptions of whom seem to link him
with sun-gods like Mithra and Apollo; *Bhaisajvagura,* the
Dhyani Buddha of healing (faith-healing has been a con-

tinuous feature of Mahayana Buddhist sects); and *Amitabha* (Chinese *O-Mi-To*, Japanese and Korean *Amida*), God of The Western Paradise and Lord of the Pure Land.

The Pure Land Sects and Saviors

The "Pure Land," or Paradise sects of Mahayana, notably the Chinese *Ching-t'u* and the Japanese *Jodo* and *Shin*, are of special interest to Westerners seeking to understand the devotional richness of Buddhism. The *Jodo* sect, it is said, was founded by a Japanese scholar Genku who, having despaired of finding salvation through any of the ways of works or knowledge then prevalent or known to him, read in a Chinese Amidist scripture the "good news" that all that is required for salvation is the reverent repetition of the sacred name of Amitabha. This opens the heart to Amitabha's unmerited favor or grace. Salvation, in other words, is by faith in and through the grace of Amitabha. The heart of Jodo doctrine is thus a joyous proclamation which has brought comfort to millions who find strict ethical codes repelling or difficult and philosophical or theological speculations incomprehensible. At times the gospel has degenerated into the mere magical repetition of the name of the savior by those seeking material benefits. At other times it has resulted in a happy and outgoing form of devotional service.

The *Shin* sect was founded by Genku's disciple Shinran Shonin and has become one of the most powerful Japanese sects, with a married and hereditary priesthood and an easygoing accommodation to the pleasures and policies of this world. At times it has had considerable political influence. In recent times the Pure Land sects in general have made the most of their similarity to Christian groups in doctrine and practice and have adopted many of the external paraphernalia of the latter. There is congregational worship, including Buddhist versions of familiar Christian gospel-songs, and extensive social activity on the part of laymen's, women's, and young peoples' groups.

Thus in the Mahayana doctrines of Manushi-Buddhas, Bodhisattvas, and Dhyani-Buddhas generally, and in Amida-

Buddhism in particular, one encounters beliefs and practices startingly similar to many he had perhaps previously considered uniquely Christian. What is to be made of the appearance of incarnate avatars and their attendant doctrines and practices in Hindu Bhakti, and of their Mahayana Buddhist counterparts just described? In what ways are the beliefs associated with these Hindu and Buddhist savior-gods identical with those espoused in Christianity? And in what respects, if any, is Christianity unique after all? These are questions which the reader may profitably keep in mind as he goes on to study the roots of Western religious traditions.

One conclusion which he may provisionally draw is that there appears to be among all peoples a need for a way of devotion in their quest for the ultimate, and that in the way of devotion there appears to be a further need for bridging the gap between God and man, eternity and time, perfection and finitude, in a fashion comprehensible to the humblest trusting souls. Beyond that one may consider the suggestions of A. C. Bouquet, a British Christian scholar, on the matter:

. . . . . (The idea of a savior-god) is clearly present in the popular religion (of Hinduism) of about the second century B.C., and it is significant that it appears, just about the same time, as a vital element in . . . Mahayana Buddhism. The conjecture has been made that the idea of a discontinuous descent of a Divine Being in human form to help and save mankind originated somewhere outside India, perhaps in the north-east of Iran, and that it became diffused eastward and westward from this area. Certainly there is a scripture called the Bahram Yasht which has a list of incarnate appearances of an Iranian divinity called Verethragna, most of which are sub-human, though one is human. Verethragna can hardly be the same as Vishnu, though in India Vishnu has a number of *avatars* of which the first five are sub-human, the sixth a human figure, Rama with the axe. Yet Verethragna is apparently the same as Vrittrahan, "the victorious one", which is an epithet applied to another Vedic god, Indra, and since the Vedic gods gradually become fused and interchangeable, and may in any case be addressed with similar adjectives, it seems quite likely that we have here in Iran an earlier example of the *avatar* idea. Again, Mahayana Buddhism develops the idea of a succession of incarnations or *bodhisattvas* of the Cosmic Buddha-Spirit, for the help of suffering mankind. Of these an important one is Amitabha, and Sir Charles Eliot gives reasons for thinking that at least this particular *Bodhisattva*, if not some others, has strong affinities with a being found in Zoroastrian beliefs.

At any rate, wherever it originated, this idea of a discontinuous incarnation is certainly as much present in India as it was in the Hellenistic world of St. Paul's day. The main differences are that in India the *avatar* is surrounded by myth and legend, whereas in Christendom, apart from the apocryphal gospels, the incarnation of Christ is strictly historical; and again, that in India the appearances of the Godhead in the flesh are not invariably human, and are certainly plural in number, while they present the form of a visionary illusion, a mere appearance rather than a fleshly reality. . . . In Christianity the incarnation is not multiple, but 'once-for-all', and is never sub-human, the Self-Expression or Logos of God reaching its peak in the life of Jesus of Nazareth, in whom alone 'dwelt all the fulness of the Godhead bodily'.[7]

SUGGESTIONS FOR FURTHER READING

ARCHER, JOHN C.   *Faiths Men Live By.*   New York: The Ronald Press Co., 1938, chap. xi.

BOUQUET, ARTHUR.   *Comparative Religion.*   Harmondsworth, England: Penguin Books, Ltd., chap. vii.

BREWSTER, E.   *The Life of Gotoma the Buddha.*   London: Kegan Paul, Trench, Trubner & Co., Ltd., 1926.

CLEMEN, CARL.   *Religions of the World.*   New York: Harcourt, Brace & Co., Inc., IV, 2, 1931.

COOMARASWAMY, A.   *Hinduism and Buddhism.*   New York: Philosophical Library, Inc., 1943.

DAVID, T. RHYS.   *A Manual of Buddhism.*   New York: The Macmillan Co., 1932.

ELIOT, SIR CHARLES.   *Hinduism and Buddhism.*   London: Edward Arnold & Co., 1921.

FITCH, FLORENCE M.   *Their Search for God.*   New York: Lothrop, Lee & Shepard Co., Inc., 1947.

HAMILTON, CLARENCE H. (ed.).   *Buddhism: A Religion of Infinite Compassion.*   New York: The Liberal Arts Press, 1952.

[7] A. C. Bouquet, *Hinduism* (London: Hutchinson's Universal Library—New York: Longman's, Green and Co., Inc., 1948), pp. 80-82.

HUMPHREYS, CHARLES. *Buddhism.* Harmondsworth, England: Penguin Books, Ltd., 1951.

KEITH, ARTHUR B. *Buddhist Philosophy in India and Ceylon.* London: Clarendon Press, 1923.

MOORE, CHARLES A. *Philosophy—East and West.* Princeton: Princeton University Press, 1944.

MOORE, GEORGE F. *History of Religions.* New York: Chas. Scribner's Sons, 1946, chaps. v, vii, xii.

NOSS, JOHN B. *Man's Religions.* New York: The Macmillan Co., 1949, chaps. v, vi.

PRATT, JAMES B. *The Pilgrimage of Buddhism.* New York: The Macmillan Co., 1928.

SOOTHILL, W. E. (trans.). *The Lotus of the Wonderful Law.* London: Clarendon Press, 1920.

SUZUKI, D. T. *Outlines of Mahayana Buddhism.* London: Luzac & Co., Ltd., 1907.

————. *Essays in Zen Buddhism.* London: Luzac & Co., Ltd., 1928-1934.

Chapter 5

THE WAY OF ISRAEL

AS WE turn from the religions of the Far East to those
which originated in the Near East, we must be prepared for
differences as well as similarities. The prophet of Israel, who
is the epitome of Israel's faith, while in some ways like the
Hindu ascetic, Buddhist monk, or Confucian sage, is in other
respects quite unlike any of them. Like the mystics he pro-
claims a God who transcends or stands above the world of
men and nations. But unlike the deity conceived by the
Orient, Israel's God is also encountered in human history
and society. God is conceived as having a will or purpose
which defines the meaning of human life. Where the Orient
uses the metaphor of seeing God (and at last being united,
"swallowed up" in him), Israel speaks more often of hearing
and doing the will of God. Moreover the God who speaks
thus is characteristically regarded as sovereign or king—as
almighty will. Man correspondingly finds his proper destiny
in a lifelong attitude of active and trusting obedience to the
divine will.

Such concepts of deity entail important consequences for
man's life. Indeed, for Israel the terms "God" and "man"
are correlative concepts; one is meaningless apart from the
other. Thus Israel's God implies a conception of man as
active, social, and historical. For man as well as God, action
or doing is the basic category. The biblical Hebrews could
say, as Aristotle could not, that the end of man is action rather
than passive contemplation.

Exploration of this fact of man's active character led in
turn to the discovery of his inner life, the secret heights and

depths hidden within the individual person. Nevertheless, while Israel came in the course of her seeking to discover the importance of the individual, the facts of community and the proper relations of man to man were for her more basic and more important. It is fair to say that, for Israel, God's first requirement of man is an attitude of brotherhood towards his fellow-man. These two aspects of man's existence imply a further aspect, namely his historical character.

We have seen some of the characteristic conceptions of time in the Orient. Under the constraint of her distinctive way of construing God and God's relation to man, Israel produced a momentously different conception of time and history. Time for Israel is recognized, not in the cycles of nature or the unreal changes or appearances of phenomena, but in the real and unique duration of human destiny. In this connection we must note how much more important a place the very concept of history plays in Hebrew religion than in Indian or Chinese religion. Not nature but history is man's environing medium for the biblical Hebrews. And it is to history rather than to nature that Israel turns for God's revelation of himself. From Israel's active conception of history has sprung the characteristically active attitude of Western culture, with its ideas of progress and amelioration.

From Israel have sprung three world religions—Judaism, Christianity, and Islam. Two of these, Judaism and Christianity, have played a role of major importance in Western culture. Their origins are contained in the Jewish Bible, the "Old Testament" of the Christian Bible. Some of the salient facts of the history, literature, and religion of Israel are reflected in this collection of documents. The facts, however, do not lie on the surface of narrative waiting to be picked up, but, like precious metals, are buried deep in sources that are sometimes obscure and difficult. As a tool, therefore, we shall use what biblical scholars call the Higher Criticism. This may be defined as the use of modern methods of literary and historical study in interpreting the Bible. This approach to the Bible, at first denounced as negative and destructive in its results, is now widely, if not unanimously, accepted. And it has yielded rich fruit in producing a richer understanding of the Bible. It is fair to say that as a result of such study, the Bible has been more carefully and more completely examined than any other book or collection of books in the world, and that we are now in a position to understand the Bible more accurately than any generation since biblical times.

THE HEBREW EPIC

The opening books of the Bible deal with historical materials in such a way that the term "Hebrew epic" is appropriate, for an epic combines fact and interpretation in a dramatic whole. Genesis, as the name suggests, is a book of origins, containing stories of the origin of the world, man, and various human institutions, as well as the beginnings of the Hebrews and neighboring peoples. Exodus tells the story of the deliverance of the Hebrews from Egyptian slavery, and of the beginnings of the nation and its faith. Joshua and Judges give varying accounts of the Hebrew invasion of Palestine. The Books of Samuel and Kings carry on the story of the Hebrew monarchy and its people. Taken together, these books give us an account of the origin and destiny of the Hebrew nation, set in the wide context of universal history and theological meaning.

This epic was not written all at once or by a single author. Many pens and many minds contributed; its origins are very ancient and extend over many centuries. Jewish and Christian tradition attributes the first five books of the Bible to Moses, but most modern scholars understand them differently. Beginning perhaps with songs of the patriarchs sung by ancient rhapsodists, other parts of the present narrative were successively incorporated. Many modern scholars believe that one of the earliest writings was the story of the founding of the kingdom now found in I and II Samuel, which dates from ca. 1000-950 B.C. To this were added other stories until the present narrative emerged.

The Creation Stories

Hebrew historical imagination looked back in time to the beginning of things. One writer, described by modern scholarship as the J writer, began his story with the garden of Eden and the fall of man (Gen. 2:3-3:24). It is enough like Babylonian creation stories to suggest a common origin. But Hebrew religious genius took common themes and materials and treated them distinctively, as a careful comparison of Babylonian and biblical creation stories will show. For here in Genesis we have, not polytheism, but a universal creator, God. The story may be taken as a celebration in the language of poetry of the dependence of all things upon the divine will.

It is followed by an account of man and the origins of his contradictory nature. To the vivid and graphic Garden of Eden story with its anthropomorphic God, its conniving Satan, its Adam and Eve, was later added the more abstract and speculative story now found in Gen. 1:1-2:2. Then other stories from the ancient past were added—stories of the flood and of Noah and his ark (Gen. 7-10); of the tower of Babel (Gen. 11); of the origin of the blood feud (Gen. 4:23-24); of the first worship of the Lord (Gen. 4:26); of the origins of music (Gen. 4:21); metalworking (Gen. 4:22), etc.

The Patriarchs

Hebrew memory sought to trace the national ancestry. Early singers and story tellers traced the origin of their own nation as well as that of neighboring peoples to a figure named Abraham, who in early days had migrated from Ur of the Chaldees to Harran—that is, from Mesopotamia northwestward to northern Syria, and from thence to Palestine. While Abraham appears before us as a shadowy, prehistoric figure, modern archeology bears out this tradition of a westward migration into Palestine.[1]

---

[1] See F. Filson and E. Wright, *Historical Atlas of the Bible* (Philadelphia: Westminster Press, 1945), p. 25.

Hebrew singers told many tales of Abraham, of his son Isaac, of his grandson Jacob, and of Jacob's twelve sons. The westward migration is given a religious interpretation: Abraham was called by God to go out to a new land (Gen. 12:1-2). In Palestine Abraham lived as a nomad and sojourner, though God met him there and promised the land to his descendants. In time of famine Abraham went down to Egypt, and did not hesitate to deceive Pharaoh about his wife's identity. But he was generous in offering his nephew, Lot, the choice of pasture lands upon their return to Palestine. Lot is depicted as the father, by incestuous union with his two daughters, of the Ammonites and Moabites (Gen. 19:34-38). Later Abraham was providentially delivered from the necessity of sacrificing his son, Isaac, as a test of his obedience to God. Then he sent back to Syria for a wife for Isaac. To Isaac and Rebecca were born twin sons, Jacob, or "Israel," the ancestor of the Jews, and Esau, the ancestor of the Edomites. In nationalist fashion, Jewish authors told how Jacob supplanted his brother Esau. Many stories were told of Jacob's fortunes in various travels and adventures. His twelve sons, the twelve patriarchs, were, according to tradition, the originators of the twelve tribes of Israel. Under one of them, Joseph, the Hebrews found their way to Egypt. The literary excellence of the Joseph stories reminds us that many of these ancient tales were remembered for their deep human interest as well as for their historical value.

The patriarchal stories show a form of life and social organization much like that of similar nomadic groups today. Life was a continual search for grasslands for the flocks of cattle and sheep on which existence depended. Wars were fought over pasturage and ever-scarce water. The tribal group was subject to the authority of the patriarch or shiekh, who was at once father, priest, judge, and king. However, a council of elders provided a measure of democracy from the earliest days. Polygamy was practiced, and the status of women, while not as inferior as in some cultures, was definitely subordinate to that of men. The tribe or group was a close-knit unity in which everyone worked for the group interest.

Within the tribal brotherhood there was, however, a deep respect for personality.

The religious customs of these nomadic Israelites are of particular interest. Natural objects such as springs, stones, wells, trees, and hills were commonly regarded as holy or even divine, for within them *els* or spirits were tho᛫ ᛫ht to dwell. The name frequently applied to such a religious pattern is *polydemonism*, which is a form of the animism previously described. But this was not the whole of Hebrew religion, even at this early date. There is evidence that some men, perhaps the leaders or chiefs, felt themselves to be in a personal relation to deity, like sons before a father or citizens in the presence of a king. In the stories of Abraham's worship there is an important element of choice or decision. God chose Abraham, commanding him to do certain things and promising certain results, and in return Abraham freely chose Jahweh as his God. How much of this covenant concept, so important throughout the long course of Israel's life and thought, was actually present in patriarchal times is impossible to say. But it is not unreasonable to find here the germ of later developments.

Moses and the Exodus

Moses was the founder of Judaism and one of the great religious figures of mankind. Out of the events of his life the Hebrew nation as well as the Hebrew faith was born. For Judaism, the events of the Egyptian deliverance and the giving of the Torah or Law at Mount Sinai stand as the center of history, the crucial disclosure of God's will for man's life, comparable to the coming of Jesus Christ for Christianity.

While the historical facts about Moses and his work are obscured by many layers of tradition, it is still possible to discern a few historical outlines. A passage of time is indicated between Genesis and Exodus, for the sojourn in Egypt had turned into bitter servitude and persecution under a Pharaoh who "knew not Joseph." The historical evidence for the time of these events is fragmentary and does not speak with a single voice, but a date soon after the beginning of the thirteenth century seems most probable—about 1290 B.C.

Moses appears as a Jew born in Egypt, reared at the royal court with all the advantages of Egyptian culture and education. Grown to manhood, he broke forcibly with his environment and identified himself with his fellow-countrymen by the murder of an Egyptian slavemaster. This act, while emphasizing Moses' lifelong passion for social justice, nevertheless was foolhardy and forced him to flee for his life. He found refuge among the Midianites, a nomadic tribe of the Sinai peninsula, where he lived as a shepherd, and where also he married the daughter of the tribal chief.

There a decisive event took place. As the Book of Exodus tells the story, Moses was standing one day on the slopes of Mount Horeb (or Sinai), when the Lord Jahweh[2] appeared to him through a burning bush, commanding him to go down to Egypt to lead his people from slavery to freedom, and promising to lead them all to a good future in Palestine (Exod. 3:1-22). While the details of this experience cannot be recovered with any absolute certainty, overlaid as it is with the interpretations and opinions of many editors, it marked a decisive turning point in the life of Moses. It may also be termed as a direct experience of God. Many readers of the Bible have called it a mystical experience, though if this term is used, some distinctively Hebraic elements must be noted

---

[2] Attention may be called at this point to some of the problems involved in the name of deity in Hebrew religion. Chief among these names in Hebrew were "Elohim," "Adonai," and "Jahweh," or "Yahweh." The first was originally the plural form of a term meaning "spirit" or "demon," but in the course of time it came to have the meaning, "deity" or "godhead." The second word is the familiar Hebrew term of address to deity, usually translated as "my lord." The last is the proper name of the Hebrew deity; it is sometimes rendered without the vowels as the tetragrammation, "JHWH"; and it was transliterated in the American Revised Bible as "Jehovah." More recent scholarship has shown that "Jahweh" was the original form of the name. However the King James and Revised Standard translations of the Bible translate the Hebrew "Jahweh" as "LORD." Aside from literary values, this translation does render in English an essential and primary meaning which Hebrew religion attributed to deity. We shall follow this usage, using "the LORD" for the Hebrew name of deity, except where the term "Jahweh" is essential to our meaning.

in it. The Lord is here represented as a God who spoke to
Moses in the context of a specific historical crisis, to whom
Moses responded in active service. He revealed himself
to Moses by setting for Moses a task of ethical significance and
promising a great historical destiny for Moses and his children.

How much historical fact and how much poetic interpretation are in the story of Moses' and Aaron's return to Egypt,
their interviews with the recalcitrant Pharaoh, the plagues,
the Passover, and the Red Sea deliverance is hard to say.
Very few precise details as to time and place are given in the
story itself. Many scholars incline to a different origin for
the Passover, regarding it as a nomadic festival celebrating the
coming of spring and the birth of lambs, here woven by pious
tradition into the narrative of the Egyptian deliverance. It
is enough to say that under the inspired leadership of Moses
the Jews made good their escape from a house of bondage.
The creation of a great nation from a group of nomadic slaves
is, after all, the great miracle of the story.

After the deliverance, they made their way to Sinai, the
mountain of the Lord. The traditional location of Mount
Sinai is in the south central part of the Sinai peninsula,
though this point has been the subject of scholarly debate.
The Book of Exodus tells of the making of the covenant between Israel and God and the giving of the Torah at the holy
mountain (Exod. 19 ff.). The important point in the narrative is not the precise accuracy of historical detail, but rather
its expression of the way in which Israel construed her relation to God—a relation which defined her national existence,
and, more important, her religious heritage. The idea of the
covenant meant that the Lord chose Israel, putting her under
command and promise, and that Israel freely chose the Lord,
committing her way to him as one to serve. Thus commitment and vocation were placed at the heart of Israel's religious experience.

The terms of Israel's service of the Lord were expressed in
the moral and religious code often called the Book of the
Covenant (Exod. 20-23). It begins with one of three versions of the Ten Commandments (Compare Exod. 20:1-17,

Exod. 34:1-26, Deut. 6:1-19), and proceeds to a series of rules covering many aspects of social life. The present version of the Book of the Covenant, reflecting as it does the conditions of an agricultural society, must come from a later period of Jewish history. But it is quite possible that the essence of these laws goes back to Moses. Socially, this code shows the marks of its time and place. Slavery is recognized, though the lot of Hebrew slaves is easier than that of foreign slaves. Women occupy a subordinate place. The law of blood revenge restrains acts of violence against persons. Property rights are defined. There is a strong sense of social responsibility, and, within narrow limits, a respect for persons. It is noteworthy that some of the laws are stated categorically, "Thou shalt . . . ," in contrast to the usual, hypothetical formulation, "If . . . then . . . ," introducing the note of absoluteness into Israel's service of her God.

Some of the laws deal directly with religious and cultic duties. The Lord is to be sought and found in the Ark of the Covenant, a box in which the tables of the Torah were placed, and in the tabernacle or tent of meeting. Feast days as well as worship by sacrifice are prescribed. The manner in which God is conceived is highly important. He is the personal sovereign who of his own free will makes and keeps covenant with Israel. The famous verse, "I am that I am" (Exod. 3:14), would, in the minds of some authorities, better be translated "He causes to be what comes into existence," [3] thus presenting us with the Creator God whom we meet so often throughout the Bible. The Lord, the sovereign and creator, is holy, standing apart from his people and demanding an exclusive worship. But he is also in the midst of their common life, demanding righteousness and promising a great destiny. Scholars disagree as to whether this notion of exclusive worship and service of God is, at this point, genuine monotheism. It is true that other deities are referred to in Mosaic religion, but for Israel there is effectively just one God whose service is the whole meaning of existence.

[3] W. F. Albright, *From Stone Age to Christianity* (Baltimore: Johns Hopkins University Press, 1946), p. 198.

The Conquest of Palestine

Following the Egyptian deliverance and the giving of the Law, Israel wandered nomadically to the south and east of Palestine. The traditional estimate of forty years for this period fits approximately with modern scholarship, for there is archeological evidence that by the middle of the thirteenth century Israel had begun to break into Palestine. The Book of Joshua describes, in an exciting fashion, a brief and victorious military conquest under the inspired leadership of Joshua. By contrast, the Book of Judges describes a gradual process of infiltration over a period of several centuries. There is probably historical foundation for both accounts. Joshua's campaign, magnified and glorified by a later writer, appears before us as a succession of victories, marred only by the initial defeat at Ai, and culminating in the complete conquest of Canaan and the division of the land at the Shechem assembly. There seems to be no good reason to doubt an initial conquest, limited largely to the south central portion of Palestine, in which Hebrew forces under Joshua won battles at Jericho, Ai, Aijalon, and other places, and secured for themselves a precarious toe-hold in the new country.

But initial success was followed by a long period of barely holding on, and also by times of defeat at the hands of more powerful antagonists, as depicted in the Book of Judges. This book, written by a later writer with a viewpoint which identified good fortune with fidelity to the Lord and misfortune with infidelity, points historically to a long period when Israel contested possession of Palestine with other, often more powerful, groups. Sometimes the Moabites appeared in control of parts of the land, and Israel rebelled against them. At another time the Hebrews under Deborah and Barak successfully threw off the yoke of the Canaanites under Sisera. The "Ode of Deborah" (Judg. 5) is at once an important source of Hebrew history, ethics, and religion. It is a great poem as well. At still another time, Gideon arose as a leader, driving off raids of marauding Midianites. It was a time of great social disunity for the Hebrews. Establishing themselves in the hill country of Palestine, but having neither central government nor military command they readily fell victim to more organized peoples.

It was also a time of religious conflict. The Hebrews came into Palestine as a closely knit nomadic community, firm in the faith of the Lord. But they found other religious customs in the new country. There was worship of the local *baals* (the word "baal" in Hebrew means "lord," "husband," or "owner"), who appear to have been at once gods of each town and also fertility gods who acted by giving good crops. There was also a high god or baal, who manifested himself chiefly in storms. The problem confronting the Hebrews was the relation of the Lord to the new scene. Should they leave the Lord and worship the new gods? Did the Lord rule the new country as he ruled the desert? It took many centuries to answer these and similar questions. But the answer finally given was a new application or extension of the already discovered sovereign authority of the Lord. This authority was extended over all of nature and over the new land.

The last and most powerful opponents of the Hebrews for the mastery of Palestine were a group of refugees from the island of Crete who made their way across Asia Minor and Syria to the borders of Egypt. Being repulsed there, they settled on the seacoast of Palestine soon after the beginning of the thirteenth century. Ironically, they gave their name to the country, for "Palestine" is a corrupted form of "Philistine." Organized in city-states, and well-armed, the Philistines made themselves virtual masters of the country, and denied the Hebrews use of iron tools. Such was the low state to which Hebrew fortune had sunk at the time of Samuel.

The Hebrew Monarchy

In such circumstances the Hebrews demanded a king who could provide effective military command and central authority. But there appears to have been opposition on the part of those who held that Jahweh alone was king of Israel. Called the "theocratic party," this group exerted age-long influence on the religion and politics of Israel. One of the two source-

narratives of Saul's reign seems to have been written by such
an author, who did not hesitate to write his anti-monarchical
prejudices into history. The Bible gives two accounts of
Saul's accession to the throne. According to one, he was
anointed by the seer and priest, Samuel; according to the
other, he was chosen by popular assembly. In any case, he
showed initiative in raising an army and successfully lifting
the siege of the Ammonites on the border city of Jabeth in
Gilead. Turning upon the Philistines, he had initial success,
in this case due largely to the courage and daring of his son,
Jonathan, who surprised and defeated the Philistine garrison
at Michmash.

But Saul was unable, for several reasons, to follow up his
successes. He appears to have alienated Samuel, who turned
his support to another aspirant for the throne, David. Saul
was plagued by a kind of melancholia (called by the biblical
writer "an evil spirit from the Lord") which robbed him of
his effectiveness as a leader and made him psychopathically
jealous of David. After much delay, the Philistines gathered
their forces and struck. At the battle of Mount Gilboa the
Hebrews were completely defeated, and both Saul and Jonathan perished.

Saul's decline was accompanied by the rise of David. Son
of a prominent Judean family, various accounts are given in
the Bible of his rise to fame. According to one account, he
was anointed by Samuel, who in this way indicated his divine
election. According to another, he was a harpist and singer
who relieved Saul's melancholy with his songs. As a member
of the royal court he married Saul's daughter, Michal. Thus
he seems to have been, at an early age, a popular and prominent figure who would naturally incur Saul's jealousy. This
jealousy led to attempts on David's life, forcing him to flee
from Saul. He gathered a group of malcontents about himself in southern Palestine, living the life of an outlaw. At
one point he took his group over into Philistine service as
mercenaries. But during all the time that Saul threatened
and pursued him, David showed a remarkable restraint, refus-
ing to strike back, and not pressing his claims to the throne.

He seems to have regarded the king as a sacred person, God's anointed.

But when Saul died, the picture changed. David was now free to assert his claims. He was king of his native Judea for seven years, while Ish-baal, son of Saul, reigned over the rest of the nation. Again, David took no action against the house of Saul. But when assassination removed Ish-baal, David quickly grasped the opportunity, becoming king of a united Israel. His reign (ca. 1000-970 B.C.) was the high point of Hebrew national existence.

Internationally, he defeated the Philistines and also subjugated the Ammonites, Moabites, and Edomites, thus extending the national boundaries farther than ever before. At home, stable government and a prosperous economy led to the flowering of art and culture. David himself was a poet and musician. The great national epics, to which we have already alluded, began to take shape under the pens of poets and historians. Hebrew language assumed the classical form. Religiously David was a Jahweh-enthusiast who inspired his people with his faith. Little wonder that the reign of David became known to later generations as Israel's golden age!

But David was not so successful in his personal life. He conducted an illicit affair with Bathsheba, the wife of one of his military men. This episode shows us the figure of the prophet Nathan, who did not hesitate to criticize David's unjust use of royal power. David was also not very successful in the management of his family. Amnon raped his half sister, Tamar, a crime for which Tamar's brother, Absalom, killed the offender. Absalom also gained dubious fame by intrigue culminating in open rebellion against his father, David. After coming perilously close to success, the rebellion was put down and Absalom killed.

And David's old age was marred by the struggle for succession to the throne, which split the court wide open. Solomon and Adonijah were the chief contenders; and when the former won, he proceeded to purge his rival and his rival's followers. Lacking both his father's military ability and his democratic sensibilities, he set up his court as an Oriental despotism. In addition to his temple, Solomon's extensive public building enterprises included a palace for himself; another for his favorite wife, the princess of Egypt; a hall of judgment; and many other buildings. He established a navy with a Red Sea base, and carried on overseas commerce, especially in such luxury goods as ivory, apes, and peacocks. His numerous menage and his expensive court were supported by heavy taxation and forced labor. His reputation as a wise and incisive judge apparently did not reflect a social conscience! There were repeated rumblings of revolt during his reign.

When Solomon died, his subjects met in popular assembly at Shechem to petition for redress of grievances. Meeting cold rebuff at the hands of Solomon's son, Rehoboam, they did not hesitate to secede from the dynasty of David, setting up their own government at Shechem (ca. 926 B.C.) under the rule of Jeroboam I, a former rebel against Solomon. This secession split the nation disastrously in half, the southern tribes of Judah and Benjamin remaining true to the house of David and possessing the capital city of Jerusalem, and the ten northern tribes claiming most of the territory, wealth, and population.

The half-century which followed the division of the kingdom was characterized by an intermittent border warfare which consumed the energies of both kingdoms. The northern kingdom, lacking a recognized dynasty, was plagued by political instability in which king followed king in rapid and often violent succession. This condition was successfully remedied by the long, prosperous, and successful reign of the house of Omri. Omri was a military man who seized the throne in 882 B.C. Once established he reigned wisely and well. He built the city of Samaria, and established it as his capital. Prosperity was made secure. Omri's foreign relations with Syria were cemented by the royal marriage of Omri's son, Ahab, and the Tyrian princess, Jezebel.

Ahab succeeded to his father's throne in 871 B.C. and reigned for nineteen eventful years. His reign was marked by the struggle of the Jahwist party against Jezebel. Jezebel was an ardent devotee of the great Tyrian baal, Melkart, whose worship she sought to introduce into Israel. In this she collided head-on with the Jahwists, a religious and political party which from the earliest days had maintained an exclusive and often fanatically fierce loyalty to Jahweh. Emerging as the leader of this group, Elijah saw the issue in uncompromising terms. Israel could worship and serve baal Melkart, or she could worship and serve Jahweh, but both she could not do. He denounced the royal policies in unsparing terms and summoned Israel to choose which god to serve. The worship of Jahweh was connected in the mind of Elijah with both national independence and social justice. When the poor man, Naboth, was framed and killed by Jezebel in order to get his land, Elijah rose to superb heights of courage to denounce the act as a violation of the Lord's law of righteous conduct. This and other stories of the great prophet were written down not long after his death, probably by a follower. They show a figure second only to Moses among the great ones of Israel. Elijah's opposition to the dynasty of Omri came to fruition after his death in the Jahwist-inspired revolt of Jehu. This revolt in 847 B.C. destroyed the house of Omri, and put Jehu on the throne. Elijah's work as a prophet of Jahweh was carried on by his successors, the great prophets of the eighth and seventh centuries.

After Elijah, the northern kingdom lasted for another century, falling victim to Assyrian invasion in 721 B.C., and disappearing from the scenes of history. The tiny southern kingdom continued to exist until 586 B.C. when Nebuchadnezzar captured Jerusalem, and led her people captive to Babylonia. But the epic story of Israel did not end with the end of her national existence. However, subsequent chapters of this great tale can be more readily told in other connections. For in the period at which we have arrived, namely the eighth century, the center of interest shifts from Israel's national existence to the rise of prophetic religion. We must therefore turn to a description of the work and writings of the prophets. But to understand the prophets we must always keep in mind that they assumed as their tradition and back-

ground the story of Israel's beginnings which we have here
briefly sketched. The God who spoke to the prophets, and
through the prophets to Israel, was the same God who had
brought Abraham out of Ur of the Chaldees and set a great
destiny before him. He was the same God who had spoken
to Moses and led Israel out of Egypt, giving them the Ten
Commandments at Sinai, and guiding their feet through the
wilderness into the Promised Land. This Lord, Jahweh, still
spoke and still acted, said the prophets. Indeed, he had new
things to say and do, to match each new moment of history.
Indeed, for the prophets, history was man's response to God's
address. In seeking, under the command of God, to reform
and purify Israel's perception of the Lord, the prophets
greatly developed Hebrew religion.

Prophetic Religion

What is a prophet? Many would answer that he is a man
gifted with prescience, a predictor of things to come. Such
figures occur in many religions. But the important fact about
Hebrew religion is that the prophet became something quite
different from this. It is true, of course, that the biblical
prophets sometimes predicted things to come. Sometimes
their predictions came true, and sometimes they did not. But
the essence of their prophetic task lay elsewhere. The prophets of the Bible were men possessed by an immediately and
powerfully perceived vocation to speak for God. The prophet
is often likened to the mystic, because of his direct, immediate awareness of God. But the Hebrew prophet contrasts
sharply with the Eastern mystic in his primary emphasis on
volition and action, and thus upon the moral and social aspects
of religion. Holding the norm of God's will as a standard
for the judgment of all human existence, prophetic religion
involves a radical criticism of every aspect of man's life and
society.

The origins of prophecy go far back in Hebrew history.
In some respects Moses was a prophet. Later, in the first days

of Israel's life in Palestine, bands or schools of prophets, Jahweh-enthusiasts, wandered the countryside, prophesying. Some individual figures, such as Samuel, Nathan, and Elijah, stand out for depth of religious conviction, and for the way in which they dared to criticize royal power. But the prophetic movement took on new significance in the eighth century B.C. when the prophets' words came to be not only uttered but written down. To the eighth-century prophetic movement we must now turn.

The eighth century B.C. has been called the Indian summer of the Hebrew nation. Jeroboam II (787-747) was on the throne of Israel, and Uzziah (785-747) on the throne of Judah. Peace and prosperity seemed to prevail. But the peace was deceptive, for Assyrian aggression, so like twentieth-century parallels, appeared on the northern horizon as a dark menace to Israel's security. Alliances of small western Syrian powers, of which Israel and Judah were but two, delayed, but were powerless to stop, the onward march of the aggressor. At home, domestic prosperity had brought to prominence a newly-rich class which lived in luxury amid the grinding poverty of the poorer classes. Religiously, the worship of baals was still popular, providing an elaborate and colorful cult, but completely lacking any morality.

Amos (ca. 750 B.C.)

The first of the writing prophets was a farmer and shepherd whose home was the Judean highland village of Tekoa. In compressed language, giving no detail, he denied professional status, but expressed the burning vocation he felt:

> Then Amos answered Amaziah, "I am no prophet, nor a prophet's son; but I am a herdsman, and a dresser of sycamore trees, and the LORD took me from following the flock, and the LORD said to me, 'Go, prophesy to my people Israel.' " (Amos 7:14-15)

To this vocation Amos brought a sharp eye for human and social realities. He saw and expressed in unforgettable words

the misery of the poor and the decadent luxury of the rich
(Amos 6:1-11; 8:4-6). He saw with equal clarity the hypoc-
risy of ritual religion that bore no relation to the daily conduct
of its adherents, and he raised his voice in denunciation, putting into the mouth of God the words,

"I hate, I despise your feasts,
    and I take no delight in your solemn assemblies.
Even though you offer me your burnt offerings and cereal offer-
        ings,
    I will not accept them,
and the peace offerings of your fatted beasts
    I will not look upon.
Take away from me the noise of your songs;
    to the melody of your harps I will not listen.
But let justice roll down like waters,
    and righteousness like an overflowing stream."

(Amos 5:21-24)

An immoral cult is a blasphemous irrelevance. Rather, justice
and righteousness are the whole content of God's will for man.

Further, unrighteous or unjust action always brings doom
as its inexorable consequence. Thus, the prevailing note of
Amos' writing became the judgment of God upon Israel's
evils. God's judgment upon evil was for Amos no capricious
or arbitrary action. It rose rather out of the structure of human existence. God has written his law of brotherhood into
human life. Thus evil is a violation of the norms of man's
life. As a wall not squarely built falls of its own weight, so a
society which breaks the law of justice must perish (Amos
7:7-8). As a destroying nemesis, God tracks down evildoers
to the end of the earth or to the depths of the sea (Amos
9:3-4).

The people of Israel looked forward with hopeful expect-
ancy to the "day of the Lord," conceived as a time of vindication when their God would give them victory over all enemies.
But Amos warned, "The day of the Lord will be darkness and
not light." History moved not toward triumph but to judgment. With brutal clarity Amos saw that injustice had so

weakened the national morale that Israel stood no chance of
resisting the Assyrian advance. She would therefore be led
away captive into exile (Amos 4:2-3).

Words like those of Amos are seldom popular. It is without surprise that we read of the prophet's quarrel with the
court chaplain, Amaziah (Amos 7:10-13). Amaziah heard
Amos' scorching words, called him subversive and told him
to go back home or be silent. Amos replied with a prediction
of doom upon Amaziah and his whole nation.

Amos clearly saw not only the justice of God but also his
universality. Indeed, if Israel had any special relation to God,
it involved special responsibilities. "You only have I known
of all the families of the earth, therefore you will I punish."
(Amos 3:2.) Amos was explicit in seeing God at work not
only in the history of the Hebrews but of other nations as
well (Amos 9:7). The divine justice, moreover, plays no
favorites. In the same way in which God judges the sins of
other nations, so he will judge Israel. Jahweh is truly the
judge of all the earth.

Hosea (ca. 740-730 B.C.)

A few years after Amos, another and different prophetic
voice, that of Hosea, was raised. A native of the northern
kingdom, his writing suggests that he was a scion of a priestly
family. He spoke with many of the same accents as Amos,
denouncing false conduct and false worship. His children
were walking sermons, bearing such names as Lo-ammi (not
my people) and Lo-ruhannah (she who has not obtained
mercy). There is the same presentiment of impending doom
regarded as the judgment of God upon human evil (Hosea
4:1-2; 2:10-12).

But immediately a difference in viewpoint between Amos
and Hosea is noted—a radical difference rooted in personal
experience. In the first three chapters of his book, Hosea re-
counts the experience which made him a prophet. The story
is obscurely told, and the text is at points so badly distorted
that we will do well to read it with the help of scholarship.
There is some difference of opinion between scholars as to

whether the story was originally intended as history or alle-
gory. Briefly, the story is this. Hosea married a wife named
Gomer who bore him two children. Then to his great chagrin
he discovered that she had been unfaithful to him. Hebrew
law decreed divorce as the just fate for such a woman. With
a sad heart Hosea undertook to put the decree into effect,
when suddenly, as a command from God, he felt constrained
to love his erring wife still, and through his love to win her
back to himself. For so, Hosea perceived, Jahweh loved the
children of Israel and through all their wanderings and back-
slidings sought to win them back to himself.

This tragic marital experience was Hosea's call to the prophetic office, and in it he found a parable for the Lord's relation to Israel. Israel is the Lord's wife, but she too has turned
in infidelity to serve the baals. This figure of speech carried
a peculiar poignancy for Hosea's bearers, for sexual promis-
cuity and religious prostitution were frequent features of baal-
ism. For her sins, Israel must be punished, yet through
punishment the Lord seeks her redemption and reconciliation.
Thus the sufferings of Israel have a redemptive purpose;
through them the Lord seeks to purge the sufferer and win
her back to himself. At least once in Hosea's book the figure
of speech changes, and the Lord becomes the loving father
and Israel the wayward son—the first time this figure appears
in the Bible (Hos. 11:1-11). No prophet declared the for-
giving and healing love of God in more lyrically beautiful
language than Hosea (Hos. 14:4-5).

Hosea's viewpoint was more inward than Amos'. Where
Amos castigated evil action, Hosea looked upon the evil affections of the heart which are the inward sources of bad action.
The lack of vision or knowledge of God is, for him, the prime
source of evil (Hos. 4:4-6). Inconstancy of the heart, which
turns from God to trivial things, is the root of wrong action.

One consequence of such false loves is idolatry, which
Hosea scorned so bitterly and mocked so skilfully (Hos.
13:2-3). The monarchy was related in Hosea's mind to idolatry, for a king so easily confused himself with God. Hosea
was a true theocrat. So he made the Lord say,

They made kings, but not through me.
>   They set up princes, but without my knowledge.
With their silver and gold they made idols
>   for their own destruction.

(Hos. 8:4)

But the Lord is always near. If Israel persists in infidelity, he declares "I am your destruction, O Israel, who can help you?" (Hos. 13:9). But he is also ready in loving-kindness to receive her back.

> "So you, by the help of your God, return,
>   hold fast to love and justice,
>   and wait continually for your God."

(Hos. 12:6)

Hosea's words were the death-knell of the northern kingdom. In 732 the Assyrians took Damascus and overran Israel, appointing a puppet king of Samaria. In 724 he rebelled, the Assyrians besieged the city, and after a long and cruel siege, took it in 721. According to the established practice of the Assyrians, many of the people of Israel were carried away captive to distant parts of the Assyrian empire, and foreigners were brought in to populate the northern kingdom. So the ten lost tribes of Israel passed from the scenes of history.

Isaiah of Jerusalem (742-697 B.C.)

While Hosea was speaking to the northern kingdom, there arose in Judah the mighty figure, Isaiah of Jerusalem. He recorded in precise detail the experience which made him a prophet (Isa. 6). In the temple of Jerusalem one day in the closing year of Uzziah's reign, he "saw the Lord." The vision produced within him a sense of sin, which gave way to forgiveness. The Lord then asked "Who will go for us?" And Isaiah replied "Here am I, send me." Thus launched upon his career, Isaiah was a man of God, statesman, preacher, and reformer in the tumultuous years which followed.

He spoke as Amos and Hosea before him about false conduct and false worship. But Isaiah introduced a new note of faith, conceived as trust in the Lord. Man's true source of strength was not, as many contended, arrogant self-trust; nor, as others contended, did it consist in dalliance with weak and fickle Egypt. Rather it was to be found in quiet and constant trust in the Lord alone. In a famous scene Isaiah met King Ahaz as the king went out to Jerusalem to inspect the city's water supply in anticipation of war and siege (Isa. 7:1-9). The prophet bade the king not to fear, warning him, "If you will not believe, surely you shall not be established" (Isa. 7:9). In the face of the king's incredulity he declared a sign. A child would be born, named Immanuel, meaning God-with-us. In the length of time necessary for him to grow to knowledge of good and evil, the king's enemies would be brought to naught (Isa. 7:10-16). But what Isaiah really wished to impress on the king was the fact that above all kings and warriors, God rules history.

This conviction led to some of Isaiah's profoundest words. The Lord uses men and nations as the instruments of his purposes, he said. He could even use the hated Assyrians as the rod of his anger to punish the perverse Hebrews. But it is also significant to note that in this case the prophet changed his mind. When the Assyrians invaded Judea, and Isaiah saw their wanton cruelty at first hand, he cried out, "Shall the axe boast itself against him that wields it?" (Isa. 10:5-19). Surely the Lord would cast off so evil an instrument of his purpose. Proud self-sufficiency must be condemned, whether in Israel or in her enemies.

As Isaiah scanned the horizon he saw doom and judgment in the immediate future. But he could look beyond this darkness to a better time which would come. He declared that a remnant of Israel would persist through the impending exile as an expression of God's persisting purpose. His son bore the symbolic name, Shearjashub—"a remnant shall return." He spoke of Israel as a tree cut down, from whose stump new growth would presently come. God spoke not only in judgment but in redemption as well.

Moreover, this purpose of God in Israel's history would someday come to fulfilment. The prophet did not give historical details, but he described the ideal king who would establish his rule in justice and peace over all the earth (Isa. 9:2-9; 11:1-9). The golden age of the future would especially be a time when swords would be beaten into plowshares and men would learn war no more (Isa. 2:2-4). In such ways Isaiah probed and depicted the ways of the Lord in history.

Micah (ca. 725-700 B.C.)

Besides the towering figure of Isaiah, Micah seems small. But he had an authentic message from Jahweh to speak to unready contemporaries. A countryman, he cried out in anger against the injustice and evils of the city, predicting inevitable doom as the result of urban life and policies.

> All this is for the transgression of Jacob
>   and for the sins of the house of Israel.
> What is the transgression of Jacob?
>   Is it not Samaria?
> And what is the sin of the house of Judah?
>   Is it not Jerusalem?
> Therefore I will make Samaria a heap in the open country,
>   a place for planting vineyards;
> and I will pour down her stones into the valley,
>   and uncover her foundations.
>
> (Mic. 1:5-6)

But such angry denunciation was moderated in later utterances such as Micah's classic summary of prophetic religion.

> "With what shall I come before the LORD,
>   and bow myself before God on high?
> Shall I come before him with burnt offerings,
>   with calves a year old?
> Will the LORD be pleased with thousands of rams,
>   with ten thousands of rivers of oil?
> Shall I give my first-born for my transgression,
>   the fruit of my body for the sin of my soul?"
> He has showed you, O man, what is good;
>   and what does the LORD require of you
> but to do justice, and to love kindness,
>   and to walk humbly with your God?"
>
> (Mic. 6:6-8)

Deuteronomy (621 B.C.)

Micah's reference to human sacrifice was ominously significant, for under King Manasseh (693-639 B.C.) such rites flourished. During the long years of his reign the prophets were silent, probably being suppressed while Manasseh's combination of Canaanitish religion with the worship of the Lord held sway. Manasseh was also an Assyrian vassal; so it is more than probable that the gods and goddesses of Assyria were introduced to Israel.

But, during this time of hiding the prophetic party was not idle. It formulated its program of reform. When Manasseh's grandson, Josiah, came to the throne, their opportunity came. In 621 Josiah, a pious king, ordered long overdue repairs on the temple. The high priest reported the "finding" of a long-lost book of Mosaic Law. In the view of most modern students of the Bible the document was the program of reform composed during the reign of Manasseh. The high priest spoke of it as the law of Moses; it was surely an effort to codify the Mosaic tradition.

The word "Deuteronomy" means "second law." The book is in the form of a series of addresses by Moses. The style is distinctive; it is the hortatory, repetitive, yet eloquent style of a great preacher. Not a few of the teachings show prophetic influence. Thus, most modern students of the Bible hold that while it is in the spirit and tradition of Moses, it was actually composed by the prophetic party during the years of Manasseh's reign.

Under Josiah, the Deuteronomic reform was put into effect. The remnants of foreign cults were rooted out and destroyed. The local shrines, or high places, were closed, for they had all too often been centers of baal worship. All worship was henceforth to be centered in Jerusalem. One God implied one sanctuary, argued the Deuteronomists. The Deuteronomists did not go so far as the eighth-century prophets in their denunciation of ritual religion, but they demanded a purified ritual, purged of all evil and supplemented by an active social ethic.

The law code of Deuteronomy contained between Chapters 12 to 26, shows great similarity with the Exodus code. There is the same sense of social responsibility, a similar recognition of property rights. But there are also several new features which show prophetic influence. Every seventh year debts are to be canceled (Deut. 15:1-2). A judicial system is provided for, including a right of appeal (Deut. 16:18; 17:13). A king is recognized, but his powers are strictly limited (Deut. 17:14-20). Rules of war, including the office of chaplain, are specified. These rules are notable for the generous system of exemption from service, and the desire to make war less brutal (Deut. 20:1-20). There are laws prescribing wages and treatment of labor, and in behalf of debtors and other oppressed or neglected groups in this code of Deuteronomy (Deut. 24:6, 14, 16, etc.).

The spirit of Deuteronomy is well summed up in the famous verse, sometimes called the *Shema.*

> "Hear, O Israel, the LORD our God is one LORD, and you
> shall love the LORD your God with all your heart, and with all
> your soul, and with all your might." (Deut. 6:4-5)

There is also a pervading emphasis upon the study of God's precepts as found within the pages of the Deuteronomic code. Judaism was thus set on the way to being a religion of the Book and the Law.

Jeremiah (650-580 B.C.)

Jeremiah was born of priestly parents in the village of Anathoth, a few miles north of Jerusalem, about the middle of the seventh century. A shy, retiring man, it was nevertheless his lot to participate actively in some of Israel's most tumultuous history. In 608 the good King Josiah was tragically killed in a battle with Egypt. In the years that followed, the little land of Judah fell ever more into the orbit of Babylonia. Futile and intermittent resistance led finally to the capture of Jerusalem by Nebuchadnezzar in 597 and again in 586. The second fall of Jerusalem brought an end to

Judah's existence as an independent nation and began the
Babylonian exile. During these troubled years Jeremiah
lived, and spoke, and wrote.

He described his call to the prophetic office, speaking of
his misgivings and shyness, overridden by the divine constraint
which was laid upon him with all the force of predestination
(Jer. 1:4-10). Like his predecessors in the prophetic vocation, he spoke in criticism of church and society (Jer. 22:13-
17, etc.). His predictions of doom were so persistently dole-
ful that the word "jeremiad" has come to mean a prophecy
of disaster.

Like Isaiah before him, Jeremiah pondered the meaning
of history. Like Isaiah he believed that the Lord ruled history, and that men were instruments of the divine purpose.
But there were important differences. Where Isaiah a century before had declared Jerusalem impregnable, defying the
invading Assyrians, Jeremiah believed and taught that the
city must fall to the Babylonians. Trust in Jerusalem as if
it were God was a false trust. Therefore, resistance was futile
and foolish. In this way he seemed to see God at work beyond the boundaries of any particular nation or people. After
the first exiles from Jerusalem were led away to Babylonia in
597, he wrote them a letter, bidding them settle down in their
new homes and worship God there (Jer. 29). For worship
was not connected with any particular place or location, being
an inward, spiritual relation to the universal God. Furthermore, Jeremiah believed, contrary to the general expectation,
that the exiles would be in Babylonia a long time.

Jeremiah formulated his own unique idea of the "good
time" coming. As we have seen, most of his utterances expressed only doom for the future. But while the Babylonians
were besieging Jerusalem, his cousin, Hanamel, offered to sell
him land. It was the Hebrew custom that land for sale must
first be offered to a relative in order to keep it within the family. One would not ordinarily buy land in a doomed nation.
But strangely enough Jeremiah reversed his previous attitude
and bought the land, saying,

"For thus says the LORD of hosts, the God of Israel: Houses and fields and vineyards shall again be bought in this land." (Jer. 32:15)

His act inspired him to go on to depict the age to come. He described it as a time of "new covenant."

"Behold, the days are coming, says the LORD, when I will make a new covenant with the house of Israel and the house of Judah, not like the covenant which I made with their fathers when I took them by the hand to bring them out of the land of Egypt, my covenant which they broke, though I was their husband, says the LORD. But this is the covenant which I will make with the house of Israel after those days, says the LORD: I will put my law within them, and I will write it upon their hearts; and I will be their God, and they shall be my people. And no longer shall each man teach his neighbor and each his brother, saying, 'Know the LORD,' for they shall all know me, from the least of them to the greatest, says the LORD; for I will forgive their iniquity, and I will remember their sin no more." (Jer. 31:31-34)

This passage, notable for the description of inward and spiritual religion and for its development of the covenant idea, was destined to play an important role in both Jewish and Christian history.

Jeremiah's conception of religion was also characterized by a high degree of individualism. In a notable series of prayers in which he poured out his innermost feelings to God, religion took on a solitary and individual nature (Jer. 14:7-9; 17:9-18). It became the communion of the individual soul with God. It is a fact worth noting that it was in the presence of the Lord that Jeremiah discovered the depths of his own inner life.

When Nebuchadnezzar captured Jerusalem in 586, he left Jeremiah among the small band of survivors in the ruined city. Jeremiah sought to reconcile his fellow-countrymen to their sorry plight. But to no avail, for they assassinated the Babylonian governor and escaped to Egypt, kidnapping the great prophet and taking him along with them. The last view we get of Jeremiah is in Egypt, telling his fellow-countrymen that even there they would not be free from the avenging hand of the king of Babylon.

Deutero-Isaiah (ca. 550 B.C.)

Israel remained in exile in Babylonia from 586 until 538 when Babylon was captured by Cyrus, the Medo-Persian emperor, and a small group of Jews were permitted to return home. The prophetic movement came to its highest expression during the Exile, in the words of an unknown prophet whose writings have been preserved for us in Isa. 40-55. The marked differences in style and content, as well as specific allusions to Cyrus and other sixth-century persons and events, make it plain that these passages were not by Isaiah of Jerusalem. Careful study of the text enables us to say a few things about the author. He is regarded by many scholars as a Jew of the Babylonian exile, though some argue that he lived and wrote in Palestine. He wrote with exquisite beauty, and he wrestled with some of the profoundest problems of human existence. Living as he did during the second half of the Exile, when the advance of the Medo-Persians made it plain that Babylon's days were numbered, the prophet spoke logically of Cyrus as the "servant of the Lord," looking to him in the hope that Israel might return soon to Jerusalem. It was this hopeful expectation which caused him to burst into song.

> Comfort, comfort my people,
>   says your God.
> Speak tenderly to Jerusalem,
>   and cry to her
> that her warfare is ended,
>   that her iniquity is pardoned,
> that she has received from the LORD's
>   hand
>   double for all her sins.
>
> (Isa. 40:1-2)

History is not only judgment; it is promise and redemption as well.

The "second" Isaiah also brought the prophetic conception of God to its highest expression. The Lord is the universal sovereign and creator of all things, before whom the
nations are a drop in the bucket (Isa. 40:12-17). Before the
Lord, the gods of the nations are worthless, impotent idols.
One of Isaiah's keenest passages is a satire on the making of
idols (Isa. 44:9-20). Only the starry heavens to which man
lifts up his eyes are an adequate symbol of the God who is
their creator.

No biblical writer had a more universally human outlook,
yet Isaiah was also a loyal Jew. Between these loyalties there
was real tension. If the Lord was sovereign of all the earth,
was he in any special sense the God of Israel? Furthermore,
if he was the God of Israel, why had he permitted Israel to
suffer so much? Such questions as these burned their way
into the prophet's mind, and his answer was one of the profoundest conceptions of Hebrew religion, namely the figure
of the "suffering servant." In Isaiah's writings we encounter
a series of poems (42:1-4; 49:1-6; 50:4-5; 52:13; 53:12) which
are distinguishable from their context both by their metrical
form and by their subject matter. They deal with a figure
who is called "the servant of the Lord," and they describe his
role in history. Whom did the prophet mean by the servant?
Christians have long read these passages as a prediction of
Christ. Jews have seen in them a depiction of Israel's role in
history. Others have argued that the prophet was describing his own life. Evidence indicates that Isaiah was describing
either the nation Israel or a creative minority in it.

The important issue, however, is not the precise identity
of the servant but his meaning in Isaiah's thought. The figure of the servant was Isaiah's answer to the question of suffering, and also to the question of Israel's relation to the world.
Israel had a special relation to God, and a special vocation
from God. But the nature of this vocation was to spread the
knowledge of God to all the earth. This was Israel's special
destiny. Moreover, it was through the servant's patient and
free endurance of suffering that this mission was to be accomplished. The meaning of Israel's suffering, then, lay in this

fact; through Israel's acceptance of a cruel and tragic fate the
world would be won to Israel's God. In the last of the servant
poems, the nations speak of the servant, saying,

> But he was wounded for our transgressions,
>   he was bruised for our iniquities;
> upon him was the chastisement that made us whole,
>   and with his stripes we are healed.
> All we like sheep have gone astray;
>   we have turned every one to his own way;
> and the LORD has laid on him
>   the iniquity of us all.
>
> (Isa. 53:5-6)

POST-EXILIC JUDAISM

The Babylonian exile was the great watershed of Jewish
history, separating what scholars have come to call classical
Hebraism, the faith of the prophets, from post-Exilic Judaism.
The distinction is useful, but it has its limitations. As we
have already seen, Deutero-Isaiah, the greatest of the prophets,
came during the Exile after Ezekiel, who in many respects was
the father of Judaism. Moreover, there are continuities of
the greatest importance between the two periods. The same
conception of God as sovereign and creator and as the Lord
of history continued. But there were sharp differences as
well. Both the similarities and the differences appear in
Ezekiel.

Ezekiel (600-570 B.C.)

Among the exiles in 597 was a young Jewish noble named
Ezekiel. He became pastor of the Jewish community at Tel
Aviv on the river Chebar in Babylonia. In his book he tells
us in vivid and often labored detail, spread over three long
chapters, the experience which made him a prophet (Ezek.
1:1; 3:27). The visions here depicted reflect not only the
quality of Ezekiel's imagination, but also the symbolism of
Babylonian art. Nevertheless, they still show an essentially
prophetic conception of the relation of man to God. God

speaks to man, and man responds in obedient action. Ezekiel's life was surely that of a man under orders. He left un-
used no resource of object lesson or figure of speech to bring
the word of God home to his people.

His writing continues the great tradition of prophecy in
that it contains much criticism of false worship and false conduct (Ezek. 7, 8, 9, etc.). His prophecies concerning the
nations, Egypt, Tyre, Sidon, and others, read like a dirge upon
human pride, the pride which so inevitably goes before a fall
(Ezek. 26-32). He had, moreover, a vivid sense of divine
judgment on Jerusalem, which must fall, he said, as a punishment for her sins. He regarded the fall of 586 B.C. as a fulfilment of this presentiment, and he described the shattering
emotional impact upon him of the news of the fall (Ezek.
33:21-33).

But this event proved to be a decisive turning point in the
prophet's life and thought, for after this he became not a
prophet of doom but of the coming restoration of Jerusalem
and Israel. He painted vivid word pictures of the nation,
city, and temple as they would one day be restored. And as
he did, chasms of difference opened between him and the
prophets who had gone before. He spoke of the restoration
of the nation in the famous figure of the valley of dry bones,
revivified by the spirit of Jahweh (Ezek. 37:1-14). He went
on to speak of the reunion of Israel and Judah. This was
all very nationalistic, for in the restored kingdom no foreigners would be permitted. The land would be divided once
more between the twelve tribes.

In the restored nation the central object was to be the
reconstructed temple. Amos, with his rejection of ritual religion, must have stirred uneasily in his grave as Ezekiel lingered in loving interest over every detail of the temple, its
priesthood, its sacrifices and feast days (Ezek. 40-48).

Between Ezekiel and the fulfilment of his dreams for a
restored Israel lay the barrier of foreign domination. So he
dreamed of a great conquest, a final battle between Israel and
the nations. After a titanic struggle, the nations, led by the
mythical Gog of Magog, would be overcome and the new age

could begin (Ezek. 38-39). In this we see the germs of a new type of thinking about history, which was to prove momentously significant in days to come. It is called *apocalypse,* meaning a vision of the hidden future.

It is easy for the twentieth-century reader to criticize Ezekiel, to see a falling-off of the ethical idealism of the great prophets of previous ages, and a corresponding increase of emphasis upon ritual and national factors. Nevertheless there were good historical reasons for the change. The nation of Israel, in the centuries after the Exile, was a pitifully small, weak, and obscure race of people—literally a very small province of the vast Persian empire, fighting for its life and the life of its faith. It was inevitable, under such circumstances, that the Jews should become more conscious of nation and cult in a time when their whole faith hung in the balance. Furthermore, the lofty intellectual and ethical precepts of prophetic religion could not long exist in a vacuum. They must be nourished and dramatized in priestly celebration and carefully taught through popular education. In such attitudes as these, Ezekiel set a pattern for his successors, earning the title "Father of Judaism."

In 538 a small company of Jews set out from Babylonia to Jerusalem with official Persian permission to reoccupy Judea. What they found when they arrived was in sorry contrast to the lofty predictions of Isaiah of Babylon and Ezekiel. But they did found, or rather refound, a little community which continued the tradition of Hebrew religion, keeping the flame alive during the centuries which ensued.

As Judaism emerged in the post-Exilic community, different patterns of thought and faith made their appearance. We shall look briefly at the main ones, priestly and legal Judaism, devotional Judaism, wisdom literature, and apocalypse.

Priestly and Legal Judaism

For almost two decades after their return to Palestine, the little community of Jews eked out a miserable existence. Then there arose two prophets, Haggai and Zechariah, who pointed out that the Lord's temple was still in ruins, and that if the people would only rebuild it, all would be well. One notes the increasing preoccupation in all this with matters of ritual. Despite opposition, Haggai and Zechariah carried the day, and in 516 the new temple was dedicated. It stood as the center of Judaism until the days of Herod the Great.

The new temple was a modest building, but it was the scene of intense activity. The energies which a free people usually exert in politics went, in the case of the Jews, into ritual religion. In addition to numerous priests, the temple also housed scholars who carried forward the job of editing and re-editing the religious writings of Israel. They gathered together the previous documents of Israel's history and faith and added their own accounts in many instances, exercising the editorial prerogatives of selection and interpretation. The result was the completion of many of the books of the Bible in their present form. One of the best products of these priestly editors was the story of creation contained in Gen. 1:1-2:3, with its lofty and spiritual conception of God, and its scheme of creation in six days and rest on the seventh or sabbath day. Sabbath observance was so important to these priestly editors that they did not hesitate to write it into the scheme of creation.

The priestly editors also possessed a distinctive philosophy of history. History was divided into four great ages or epochs, each related to the origin of an important aspect of priestly religion. The first age began with creation, when the sabbath was instituted; the second began with Noah and the prohibition of the eating of blood; the third began with Abraham and the beginning of circumcision; the fourth began with Moses and the Passover. However artificial their scheme of history, these writers did have a notion of universal history and the God who speaks in and through history to men.

For priestly religion, sacrifice was all-important. Consequently, while earlier ages of Hebrew religion had practiced it, none developed it so elaborately as priestly Judaism. Every occasion, public or private, had its appropriate sacrifice. The manner in which the sacrifice was to be made was precisely and elaborately described. The Book of Leviticus sets forth much of this laborious detail, as well as many other details of cultic religion. The high point of the religious year was the Day of Atonement, Yom Kippur, when the high priest entered the holy of holies of the temple to intercede for the sins of the nation (Lev. 16). Here as elsewhere, the aim of priestly religion was to make the people ritually holy, and thus acceptable to the Lord.

Closely allied with priestly Judaism was the development of the Law or Torah. Having its origin as far back as Moses, the Law had gained impetus from the time of Deuteronomy onward. The Babylonian exile increased this interest; from this period we may date the Holiness Code (Lev. 17-26), written by an anonymous disciple of Ezekiel as a law for the coming restoration. A climax was achieved with the canonizing of the Torah under Ezra about the year 400 B.C. Ezra is an obscure and shadowy figure, about whom many questions continue to be asked. But he stands as the archetype of the scribe, the priest who was also lawyer, scholar, and teacher. He seems to have returned to Jerusalem during the latter fifth century (the precise date is much in dispute) to assume the religious leadership of the Jewish nation. In a scene described in Neh. 8-10, Ezra read the Torah of Pentateuch to a public assembly of the people, who responded by accepting it as the God-given norm or standard for all life.

This event was of great historical importance as the first canonizing, or setting apart as sacred, of a body of Jewish religious literature.[4] To the Torah, thus certified as God's word, other documents were added in the course of time until the Jewish Bible was complete. But the Torah or Law, consisting of the first five books, has always held a place of primary importance. Here Jahweh has spoken to his people. So the Law as well as the temple came to be an object of deep devotion. Judaism emerged clearly as the religion of the Torah.

[4] There had been, however, an official acceptance of the Covenant of Deuteronomy in 621 B. C.

Devotional Judaism

Several patterns of religion took shape with the years, one of them having its center in the Book of Psalms. It would not be far from the mark to call the Book of Psalms the hymn book of post-Exilic Judaism. It contains much religious poetry for musical rendition, and much of it is connected with the temple. Some psalms antedate the second temple, quite a few of them show no relation to the temple, but for many parts of the book the temple is the center of interest. There is great variety in the vast collection. There are psalms for public and for private worship, psalms for times of prosperity and for times of misfortune. Some of the psalms show high literary quality, others are doggerel. The religious and ethical level likewise varies greatly from psalm to psalm; thus Psalm 109 is a cry for vengeance, while Psalm 51 is a prayer for forgiveness.

Pervading this remarkable collection is a spirit appropriately called devotional Judaism. Amid catastrophes and afflictions past numbering, past understanding, and past all mortal solution, the heart of the faithful Jew could always turn to Jahweh and there find joy and peace which the world could not give or take away. So one psalmist cried out;

> As a hart longs
>   for flowing streams,
> so longs my soul
>   for thee, O God.
>   (Ps. 42:1)

And another could sing exultantly;

> Bless the LORD, O my soul;
>   and all that is within me, bless his holy name!
>   (Ps. 103:1)

Amid shifting fortunes and changing scenes, Israel's heart clung passionately to the Lord, and her poetry celebrated this devotion.

Wisdom Literature

Meanwhile other men concerned themselves with other themes. Some sages or wise men found expression for their minds in a type of writing called Wisdom Literature. Three examples of this type found their way into the Jewish Bible: Proverbs, Job, and Ecclesiastes; and there are many other examples, outside the Bible, in Jewish and other ancient literature. The sages spoke as old men who had seen much of the world, and out of their mature experience addressed themselves to the young men. The wisdom they offered was not the heroic faith of the prophets nor yet the legal prescriptions of the scribes. At worst it was a work-a-day, pedestrian morality, and at best it was a cosmopolitan insight into the ways of the world. The sages concerned themselves with such issues as success and misfortune, wealth, wisdom, marriage, religion, and the like. Often they spoke not as Jews but simply as men.

One theme which recurred in their writings was the relation of goodness to a good fortune. The orthodox authors of Proverbs were sure that if a man were virtuous, good fortune would automatically follow, and that conversely all misfortune was the result of some sin or misdeed. So the writers of proverbs sang their praises of a God who paid off the wages of sin and righteousness "every Saturday night," as it were, and of men who were sublimely content with these divine wages.

But once this view was questioned, other less orthodox thinkers began to explore the problem of virtue and reward. The unknown author of Job asked himself the question "If God be good, why should good men have such a bad time of it?" The question burned its way into his mind, and he wrote his conclusions in the form of a philosophic drama in which Job, the righteous man, becomes a kind of test case for his questionings. Afflicted with every sort of misfortune and evil, he is visited by orthodox and complacent friends who offer him the cold comfort of self-righteous advice. If only Job will view his afflictions as punishment for some secret sin, or as discipline from God, then all will be well. But Job stubbornly refuses to confess sins of which he is not conscious. So in his integrity he resists his friends. He even defies God in his search for an answer to his agonizing question. He gets no pat answer. But at the end of the drama, when Job has successfully resisted answers which are evidently false, God appears to him, giving him not an answer but the assurance and strength of fellowship in which he may surmount his troubles.

The author of Job clung by a slender thread to traditional faith. Other writers were not so orthodox. The author of Ecclesiastes was a skeptic who concluded that the Almighty had no concern for man or man's works; that human life is marked by no perceptible plan or purpose from above; and that blind chance rules all human events. In the end death brings extinction, canceling out whatever intimations of meaning there may have been. So amid mortal vanity, man must content himself with the simple joys of work, friendship, and marriage. For in the end, Ecclesiastes concludes,

> Vanity of vanities, says the Preacher,
> vanity of vanities! All is vanity.
>   (Eccles. 1:2)

Apocalypse

The religious thought of Israel took still another turn, that of apocalypse. We have seen its origin in such books as Ezekiel. In the centuries that followed, it grew until it became a recognized type of religion and literature. Only one example, the Book of Daniel, found its way into the canon of the Jewish Bible, but there are many other examples in Jewish and other ancient literatures. For many centuries this literature was regarded as a vast enigma, but modern biblical study has found the key and unlocked its meaning.

Apocalyptic literature grew out of prophetic thought on the problems of history. But where the prophetic writer was content to see God's hand at work in the normal processes of history, the apocalyptic seer saw all history building up to a great climax in the very near future. This climax, which was to be heralded by series of ascending woes and calamities, divided history into an old evil age, and a great new age soon to dawn. Amid the woes to come God would intervene supernaturally to defeat evil and bring in the new age. In bizarre symbols apocalypse presents us with issues basic to Hebrew thought. It was a desperate way of saying amid crisis that God still ruled history. Often it was a cry, half in faith and half in despair, of people who saw no earthly deliverance from their troubles.

The key which modern biblical scholarship has used to unlock apocalypse is that it was written about the situation in which the authors lived. Written in cryptic symbolism, which however had an intelligible meaning for the people to whom it was addressed, it was essentially a collection of cryptic tracts for bad times. Thus, the Book of Daniel has traditionally been misinterpreted as referring to some time in the distant future. Modern biblical scholarship has shown that it was written during the Maccabean revolt against the Greek tyrant, Antiochus Epiphanes (176-164 B.C.). Understood in this way, it gains enormously in historial meaning as a cry of indignation of an oppressed and rebelling people against a tyrant who suppressed their traditional worship and confused himself with God.

When Alexander the Great conquered the Near East, he substituted Greek for Persian hegemony. When he died in 321 his generals divided his farflung empire between themselves, the Ptolemies who received Egypt, and the Seleucids who acquired Syria. Despite the pressure of Greek culture, including Greek language, literature, education and religion, traditional Jewish faith held its own. The Greeks had a missionary zeal to spread their culture, but they were too wise to try to force it upon the Jews. But in 176, Antiochus IV ascended by way of assassination to the Syrian throne. He resolved to break the will of the stubborn Jews. After a series of provocative acts, in 168 he forbade the practice of the Torah and sacrifice in the temple in Jerusalem. Under the desperate but inspired leadership of Mattathias Maccabaeus and his five sons, the Jews turned upon their tormentors. As they engaged in battle with Greek power, their cause seemed well-nigh hopeless. It was during this civil war that the Book of Daniel appeared, as a morale tract for hardpressed Jews.[5] In cryptic symbols it bade the Jews to be of good courage, for the hour of vindication was near.

By 164 the Jews had gained enough success to liberate most of Jerusalem and rededicate the temple, though intermittent fighting continued for several years. An independent Jewish state under the rule of the Maccabean house was set up in Palestine. With varying fortunes it continued to rule until 64 B.C., when Palestine became a Roman province. The Maccabean period was at first one of flowering culture, prosperity, and religion. But conflict between Pharisees and Sadducees, whom we shall consider later, broke into civil war. Finally, as the Roman general, Pompey, appeared in the Near East, both sides appealed to him to bring peace to their troubled nation, a request to which he gladly responded.

SUGGESTIONS FOR FURTHER READING

ALBRIGHT, WILLIAM F. *From Stone Age to Christianity.* Baltimore: Johns Hopkins University Press, 1940.

ANDERSON, BERNHARD. *Rediscovering the Bible.* New York: Association Press, 1951.

ARCHER, JOHN C. *Faiths Men Live By.* New York: The Ronald Press Co., 1938, chap. xiv.

BARTON, GEORGE A. *Archeology and the Bible.* Philadelphia: American Sunday School Union, 1933.

BEWER, JULIUS. *Literature of the Old Testament.* New York: Columbia University Press, 1933.

BUBER, MARTIN. *The Prophetic Faith.* New York: The Macmillan Co., 1950.

DODD, CHARLES. *The Bible Today.* New York: The Macmillan Co., 1948.

FILSON, FLOYD, and WRIGHT, G. ERNEST. *Westminster Historical Atlas of the Bible.* Philadelphia: Westminster Press, 1945.

FINEGAN, JACK. *Light from the Ancient Past.* Princeton: Princeton University Press, 1946.

JAMES, FLEMING. *Personalities in the Old Testament.* New York: Chas. Scribner's Sons, 1939.

MANSON, THOMAS (ed.). *A Companion to the Bible.* Edinburgh: T. & T. Clark, 1947.

MINEAR, PAUL. *Eyes of Faith.* Philadelphia: Westminster Press, 1946.

[5] For detailed evidence, see especially Dan. 2, 7, 8, 9.

MOORE, GEORGE F. *History of Religions.* New York: Chas. Scribner's Sons, 1946, Vol. II, chaps. i-iv.

MOULD, ELMER. *Essentials of Bible History.* New York: The Ronald Press Co., 1951.

NOSS, JOHN B. *Man's Religions.* New York: The Macmillan Co., 1949, chap. xiii.

OESTERLEY, W. and ROBINSON, T. *A History of Israel.* London: Clarendon Press, 1932.

————. *Hebrew Religion.* New York: The Macmillan Co., 1937.

PEDERSEN, JOHANNES. *Israel.* London: Oxford University Press, 1946.

PFEIFFER, ROBERT. *Introduction to the Old Testament.* New York: Harper & Bros., 1941.

ROWLEY, HAROLD. *The Rediscovery of the Old Testament.* Philadelphia: Westminster Press, 1946.

WRIGHT, G. ERNEST. *The Challenge of Israel's Faith.* Chicago: University of Chicago Press, 1944.

Chapter 6

POST-BIBLICAL JUDAISM

Judaism in the Ancient World

The End of the Biblical Jewish State

THE successful rising of the Maccabees against Antiochus Epiphanes was followed by almost a century of independence. During this time, and also the time between 63 B.C. and 132 A.D. when Palestine was a Roman province, events of great importance to Judaism took place. The last chapter noted the rise, during the Maccabean age, of the two parties, the *Pharisees* and *Sadducees*. The former were spiritual descendants of the Maccabean rebels. The name "Pharisee" probably means "Separatist," i.e., one who separates himself from compromises with the world. Deeply concerned for the faith of their fathers, they believed that the Scripture was the norm of all human life, even though they had to "interpret" its provisions to make them relevant to new and changing situations. As time went on, they came more and more into opposition to the Maccabean house, a policy for which they suffered terrible persecution—though it must be added that when rulers more congenial to them came to power, they retaliated in kind. Taking their stand upon the spirit rather than the letter of Scripture, they accepted such innovations in belief as the resurrection of the dead, apocalyptic writing, and angels. Ethically, they were rigorous in their practice of the Law, at times inflexible, legalistic, and exclusive. In this respect they were not unlike the Puritans of Protestant Christianity. However, they were deeply and genuinely religious men with whom the future of Judaism lay. The traditional Christian estimate of the Pharisees as moral monsters is wide of the mark.

The Sadducees, by contrast, took a more accommodating view of the world. They tended to agree with the ruling powers and to enjoy their favor. They took a more tolerant view of Greek ways. Their attitude toward Scripture was, curiously, one of literalism. Opposing the Pharisees, they rejected apocalypse and belief in angels and resurrection of the dead. But there was a reason for this. By drawing the sharp line of literal interpretation of the Scripture, they could exclude much of human life from scriptural control or authority, in such realms being free to do as they liked. Most of them were prosperous in this life and thus had no interest in a future life determined by divine judgment.

Other sects and parties arose in Judaism during this period. Concerning the *Essenes*, little is known except that they gathered in celibate, monastic communities, living under a strict religious discipline, including a rigid sabbath observance. They wore white garments, and practiced frequent ablutions to avoid uncleanness. They espoused vegetarianism, community of property, and pacifism. They waited quietly in their communities until God should establish his kingdom.

The *Zealots*, on the other hand, did not favor so passive an attitude. Theirs was a fierce, religiously inspired, colonial nationalism, which defiantly declared, "No king but Jahweh, and no tax but to the temple." Intermittently during the first century A.D. they rose in rebellion, and Rome did not hesitate to soak the soil of Palestine with their blood. One famous rising in 6 A.D., under Judas the Galilean, led to the complete destruction of the town of Sepphoris as punishment by the Romans.

Less extreme than the Zealots, the *Herodians* were a home-rule party. When Rome ended the rule of the Herod family in Judea and administered the obstinate province by procurators, some Jews favored a return to the House of Herod. These were the Herodians. Meanwhile the people of the land, the masses of Judaism, while lacking the definite outlines of a religious party, continued to practice religion according to their lights and their circumstances, and to keep a simple faith in the God of their fathers. It is probable that Jesus' parents were of this group.

During this period the task of interpreting the Torah continued apace in temple, synagogue, and school. The rabbis set themselves the task of interpreting orally the written Torah. Bodies of interpretation accumulated in minds accustomed to memorization, for it was regarded as an offense to the Torah to write an interpretation. Two names, Shammai and Hillel, especially stand out. They lived and flourished in the last years of the first century B.C. The former was a Palestinian by birth and more conservative in his interpretations. Hillel was a native of Babylonia, at once freer than Shammai with the letter of the Law, and a genial and humane spirit. While there is no record of their carrying on competing schools, their followers in the first century A.D. placed the opinions of Shammai and Hillel against one another. At first the followers of Shammai were more numerous, but in the end Hillel's interpretations came to be regarded as normative.

During the last century B.C. and the first century A.D. changing political fortunes greatly affected Israel's religion. Rome sought at first to rule Palestine through a local king or ethnarch. An Idumaean, or Edomite, named Antipater was first chosen. His more famous son, Herod the Great, ruled from 40 to 4 B.C. He beat down opposition and maintained a restive peace. He also undertook and carried through an extensive campaign of public building which included a large and beautiful new temple. But despite this and other measures of conciliation he never succeeded in allaying the mingled contempt and hatred of his Jewish subjects. His later years were clouded by a policy of cruelty and carnage that took the lives of many of his own family as well as untold numbers of subjects. The nation rejoiced at his death. His kingdom was divided among his sons, Archelaus ruling in Judea and Samaria, Herod Antipas in Galilee, and Philip in territory north and east of Galilee. Archelaus proved so

inept that at the request of leading Jews he was removed
from office in 4 A.D. and replaced by a series of procurators
who were direct representatives of Rome. They kept peace,
cruelly suppressing uprisings, and they plundered the country. Pontius Pilate (26-36 A.D.) was among the worst as well
as the most famous of the procurators of Judea.

As the plight of the Jews worsened, messianic expectation
rose to a new intensity. A desperate people looked for their
God to send his anointed deliverer. Often this deliverance
was set forth in apocalyptic terms; in cryptic symbols and
weird pictures the coming of God's Messiah and his triumph
over all enemies were described. Sometimes the Messiah was
described as a military figure, a man on horseback, who would
lead the hosts of Israel to victory over the hated Romans.
Sometimes, more conservatively, the coming of the Messiah
was described in purely supernatural terms; the heavens would
open and he would descend to bring in the new order. But
always the sands of time were seen as running out; the old
age was soon to end, and God's new age was about to dawn.
These ideas proved to be important not only for Judaism, but
for Christianity as well. They show not only the desperation
of first-century Palestine, but also the incorrigibly historical
nature of Hebrew thought.

Hope long deferred sometimes breaks out in desperate
revolt. There were intermittent uprisings throughout the
first century A.D. But full-fledged war came finally in 67 A.D.
It was protracted and bitter, culminating in a siege of Jerusalem which lasted for many months and ended in 70 A.D.
with the slaughter of its defenders and the well-nigh complete
destruction of the city. Jerusalem ceased from that time
onward to be in any active sense the center of Judaism. Jews
wandered to places as distant as Spain and Babylonia, taking
with them their law, their faith, and their ways.

A few lived on in Palestine. By 127 A.D. they had gathered
sufficient strength for a final thrust at Roman rule. The
occasion was a series of repressive measures on the part of
the emperor, Hadrian, including his plan to rebuild Jerusa-

lem on a Roman model. Under a popular messianic aspirant, Bar-Kochbah, who was ardently supported by the celebrated Rabbi Akiba, Jewish armies hurled themselves at Rome. The war lasted three years, ending in the complete destruction of Jerusalem, the mass slaughter of her people, and a strict Roman prohibition of Jewish occupancy of the city. The one exception was the privilege, purchased once a year from the Roman sentries, of entering and standing in sorrow before a fragment of the temple wall—the "wailing wall." Hadrian renamed the city Aelia Capitolina, and on the site of the sanctuary built a temple to the Capitoline Jupiter.

The Dispersion

The "Dispersion" is the name for the age-long scattering of Israelites over the nations. It is impossible to set a definite date for its beginning. By no means had all or most of the Jews in Babylonia in 538 B.C. returned home to Jerusalem. The process of dispersion continued during the centuries of Persian rule. There were large groups of Jews in Egypt, Babylonia, and elsewhere during this time. When, in the second-half of the fourth century B.C., Alexandrian Greece displaced the empire of Persia, the process of diffusion increased. Soon colonies of Jews were to be found in cities throughout the Mediterranean world. Alexandria especially had a large and influential Jewish community. Philo wrote that two of Alexandria's five sections were exclusively Jewish, and the population of Alexandria was almost a million. These Jews of the dispersion, living as they did amid an alien culture, were much affected by their surroundings. Compared with their Palestinian brethren, they were less strict in their interpretation of the Law, and in other requirements of their faith. But the wonder of it is that they did maintain their loyalty to Judaism. They maintained their synagogues and served the Lord. They paid the tax for the support of the temple in Jerusalem, they respected the decisions of the Sanhedrin, the ecclesiastical council in Jerusalem, and when possible they made pilgrimages to Jerusalem. Their refusal to be assimilated entirely in Hellenistic culture often gained for them dislike and discrimination at the hands of non-Jews, but many Jews held positions of honor and respect in their cities.

The Jews of the Dispersion also exerted a profound influence on Judaism. An illustration of this influence was the translation of the Jewish Bible into Hellenistic Greek. This translation, made in the late third century B.C., was called the Septuagint. Pious legend has it that Ptolemy II, the Egyptian king, wanting a copy of the Bible for his Alexandrian library, secured the labors of seventy-two scholars, who, laboring separately for seventy-two days, produced identical translations. The translation was important both for its introduction of Jewish learning and literature to the Greek world and for bringing the Scriptures to many Jews in the only language they knew. The translation, however, took liberties with the biblical text, which caused the conservatively-minded rabbis to frown upon it.

Philo

The interplay of Greek and Jewish thought is also illustrated by the great figure of Philo Judaeus (20 B.C.-50 A.D.). While little is known beyond anecdotes of Philo's life, it is certain that he was one of the most honored and learned members of the Jewish community in Alexandria. Thoroughly Greek in his education and habits of mind, he was especially a lover of Plato. But he was also a loyal Jew for whom the Law of Moses was the word of God. To such a man it seemed that Moses and Plato said very similar things. The same God spoke through Greek philosophers and Hebrew prophets. Philo was able by the method of allegorizing the Scripture (which he greatly popularized) to eliminate crudities and anthropomorphisms in the Bible, and to introduce new meanings, showing the similarity of Greek philosophy and Jewish religion.

God, for Philo, was absolute spirit who surpasses all human limitation and definition. One might say that God *is*, but to say what he is imputes a quite undivine limitation or qualification to deity. For Philo, such a God combines

Hebrew monotheism with Plato's monism. A problem which resulted from such a conception is the relation of God to matter. Philo solved the problem by positing a series of intermediaries or seminal principles of reason (*logoi spermatokoi*) which inform all things, giving to matter a determinate form. These *logoi*, similar as they are to Plato's ideas, derive from the Logos or divine reason, which for Philo is the chief instrument of God's activity. Through the divine Logos the world was created. Philo suggests at one point that the Logos was begotten by God of the truly virgin wisdom. At other points in Philo's thought the Logos seems to be the intelligible structure of the world. Philo's *logoi* appear again in Christian thought.

Ethically, Philo believed that salvation consists in freeing man's good spirit from the trammels of evil flesh. But he also took much from the spirit of active justice and righteousness of the Law and the prophets. Here as elsewhere Philo's thought was a blend of Greek and Jewish elements.

Perhaps for this reason the rabbis of Judaism had little use for Philo. In the centuries immediately following his death he was better known among Greek philosophers and Christian fathers than among Jews. However, as we shall see, his influence upon medieval Jewish mysticism was great. And in modern times, as many of the problems which Philo faced have recurred, many liberal Jews have turned back to the great Alexandrian philosopher of religion.

As we have seen, events in first- and second-century Palestine greatly increased the process of dispersion. As Roman armies devastated Jerusalem and Palestine, more and more Jews sought homes abroad, in places ranging from Babylon to Rome. With the Roman defeat of Bar-Kochbah, the greatest dispersion began. Cut off from Palestine, Israel has been for nearly 2,000 years a wanderer in alien lands.

The Making of the Talmud

From the days of Ezra when the Torah first assumed its place as a sacred norm of Jewish life, it had been interpreted by scholars and teachers. These interpretations, at first oral

and then written down, were gathered into bodies of tradition. During the first century A.D. the work begun by Hillel
and Shammai went on. While Roman armies laid siege to
Jerusalem in 69 A.D., Rabbi Johannan ben Zakkai made his
way through Roman lines, and escaped to the Judean coastal
town of Jabneh, there to found a new house of studies. The
Academy at Jabneh became the intellectual center of Judaism
for the next sixty years. Johannan organized a council of
Teachers, the Beth Din, which became the authoritative voice
of Judaism. At Jabneh, following the death of Johannan,
Hillel's decisions were given precedence over Shammai's, the
canon of Hebrew Scripture was fixed, and the process of interpretation went on unceasingly. At Jabneh the famous
Rabbi Akiba lived and worked, prior to the war against Hadrian in which he was martyred.

The school at Jabneh was a casualty of this war, and
extremely repressive measures were put in force by the Romans. The mere reading of the Torah became a capital
offense. The remnants of the school of Jabneh now gathered
in the Galilean town of Usha and, despite persecution, worked
on. With the lightening of repression, schools flourished in
Galilee. Rabbi Meir, a scholar of wide learning and breadth
of spirit, assumed the leadership in the task of redaction.
He was followed, late in the second century A.D., by Rabbi
Judah who brought the *Mishnah* into being. The word
"Mishnah" means "repetition." This vast document was
composed of the opinions of one hundred and forty-eight
Tannaim or teachers, and was arranged under six main categories: "Seeds," containing mainly agricultural laws; "Feasts,"
containing rules for the observance of holidays, fast-days and
the like; "Women," containing rules of marriage, divorce, and
inheritance; "Damages," which had to do with civil and
criminal law; and "Sacred Things," which had to do with
sacrifices and ritual connected with the temple. The Mishnah spanned nearly six hundred years of Jewish history, and
reflected a great variety of social circumstances. Its compila-
tion was a milestone in Jewish history, for it became an au-

thoritative legal code. It grew in the space of another two centuries into the Palestinian Talmud.

But the real center of Jewish thought and life had shifted meanwhile from Palestine to Babylonia, where the Jewish population was well over a million. The Jewish community possessed a degree of autonomy, being organized under the Resh Galuta, or exilarch. There in Babylonia the task of interpretation of the Torah went on. At Sura an academy was established by Abba Arika, often known as Rab, who was both scholar and pastor. Other schools of learning sprang up elsewhere. But in the third century A.D. the lot of the Jews worsened when the peaceful Parthian rulers were displaced by the fierce Sassanids. The Sassanids were Zoroastrians who worshiped fire and forbade Jews the use of sabbath lights. Revering the earth, they also forbade Jews the right to bury the dead. But even amid persecution the work of scholarship went on.

Late in the fourth century, the task of committing to writing the vast body of law and lore was undertaken. The enormous undertaking was not completed until the opening of the sixth century. It was the monumental *Babylonian Talmud*, composed of the *Mishnah*, or text received from Palestine, and the Gemara, or supplementary learning. It runs in English translation to sixty-three volumes. The Babylonian Talmud was destined to eclipse completely the Palestinian Talmud.

The Talmud is a puzzling document, especially when one sees the heterogeneity of its contents. Here science and superstition, old wives' tales and the exalted visions of Israel's greatest seers lie side by side. Cursed, misunderstood, and burned by hostile men, the Talmud has been to the Jew a light for his path, second only to the Torah. Aside from its religious significance, it has been a fruitful and often unrecognized source of literature. The *Haggadah* or narrative (in contrast to the *Halakah* or law) contains stories and legends which have delighted countless generations of readers and have greatly influenced other writers.

JEWS IN THE MEDIEVAL WORLD

Judaism and Islam

The treatment of the Jews varied in the Roman empire from severe persecution to tolerance. Despite a general contempt for "superstition," the Romans inclined to tolerance toward the Jews. But the decline of Roman power and the rise of Christianity was another and a sadder story. Beginning as a sect within Judaism, worshiping a Jewish Christ, and sharing with Judaism large sections of its Bible, Christianity sought earnestly to convert Jews to the new faith. When this failed, relations between the two religions sank into bitter opposition. Had not the Jews failed to recognize Jesus as the Messiah?—indeed had they not killed him?—misguided Christians asked. Furthermore, Christianity joined itself as time went on to Greek ways of thought, which led to even more scornful rejection by the Jews. Thus when Christianity came to position of power in the empire at the beginning of the fourth century, the lot of the Jews worsened. Tolerance gave way to suspicion, discrimination, and persecution.

But as Christian Europe became more and more intolerable for the Jews, the Arabian civilization of Islam offered a new promise of life. Islam burst upon the world with the visions of an Arab camel driver named Mohammed. Born in great poverty, reared as an orphan by an uncle, Mohammed went to work early in life as a camel driver. He saw much of the Near Eastern world and its religions from the backs of camels. And much that he saw he keenly disliked. The fratricidal strife of his fellow-Arabs and their generally low standard of life and culture he deplored. He was also critical of both Christians and Jews. He married his employer, the widow Khadijah, who became his life-long helper and companion. A religious genius, he began to receive messages from God, and to proclaim them in oracles to his scornful fellow-citizens of Mecca. He was forced by opposition in Mecca to flee to Medina a few hundred miles away. Moslems reckon their calendar from the year of the Hegira, the Prophet's flight

from Mecca to Medina, 622 A.D. Successful in the latter city
as a religious, political, and military leader he eventually led
its armies to victory over Mecca. When Mohammed died
in the hour of his triumph, 632 A.D., his followers took up his
religious and military conquests and did not rest until Islam
had spread from India to Spain.

The term "Moslem" means "submitter," that is, one who
gives an absolute and unquestioning obedience to the sovereign will of Allah. Based upon this foundation of rigorous
monotheism, the teachings of Mohammed which constitute
the core of Moslem doctrine form a simple and straight-
forward structure. God or Allah is the absolutely sovereign
ruler and creator of all that is. Among the messengers or
prophets of Allah are Abraham, Moses, and Jesus. But the
last, greatest, and most decisive prophet is Mohammed. It
is significant to note that Islam has never deified the Prophet;
he is simply regarded as man at his highest and best. The
Koran, consisting of oracles of Mohammed, is regarded as
containing the absolute and authoritative will of God for
man. Also prominent among the teachings of Islam is a
very vivid belief in Last Judgment, with the promise of sensuous bliss for the saved, and infernal fires for the damned.

Followers of the Prophet pray five times daily, attend religious services at the mosque on Friday, fast during the day
in the holy month of Ramadan, give alms for the care of the
poor, and, if possible, make a pilgrimage to Mecca sometime
during their lives. The code of ethics includes a strict prohibition of gambling and the drinking of wine. While polygamy has been characteristic of Islam, the actual import of
Mohammed's teaching on this point was to limit the number
of wives and raise the status of women. While Islam has
generally practiced a "brotherhood of Arabs," Christianity
has often greatly exaggerated Moslem intolerance to non-
Moslems.

In the course of history Islam has split into almost as many
competing and often warring sects as has Christianity. The
largest minority sect are the Shi'ites, who refuse to recognize
the first three caliphs, and trace their own lineage from the

fourth caliph, Ali, the son-in-law of Mohammed. The Shi'ites
have splintered into innumerable sects, some of them committed to violence for the accomplishment of their ends.
There is also a split between the Rationalists (Mutazalites)
and the Traditionalists (Sunnis). Islam has also had a tradition of mysticism, which has ranged from the lofty writings
of Al Ghazzali (1058-1111 A.D.), the greatest philosopher of
Islam, to the ecstatic behavior of whirling dervishes.

Even from such cursory treatment of Islam as it is possible
to include here, the reader will be able to characterize it as a
theistic religion, along with Judaism and Christianity, in contrast to the monistic religions, such as Buddhism, or the
naturalistic religions such as Confucianism. Religiously
speaking there is little that is original in Islam. In fact it
may be argued that the teachings of the Prophet represent
a return to an earlier and more primitive level of religion,
which Judaism had traversed and transcended many centuries
before—but which was an advance over the crude practices
of Arabia in Mohammed's day. The real driving force of
Islam from its beginning has been the unity it has given Arabic
and some Far Eastern peoples, especially in their struggles
with the West.

Islam's relations to Judaism, however, fit no single pattern.
At first, Mohammed and his followers were receptive to the
teachings of Judaism. Were they not themselves, as Arabs,
descended through Ishmael from Abraham? So Mohammed
at first ordered his followers to fast on the Day of Atonement
and to pray toward Jerusalem. But Jewish teachers and leaders were scornful of Mohammed. He seemed to them ignorant of their Bible and their traditions. When his power in
Medina was secure, he broke with the Jews and had the
double vengeance of pillaging rich Jewish communities and
purging Islam of all Jewish influence.

But while the Prophet and his immediate followers were
intolerant, fortunes changed for the better as time went on.
After the first victorious sweep of Islam, its leaders did not
force subject peoples to accept their faith. There was some
discrimination; Jews and Christians were not permitted to

bear arms, hold office, or own Moslem slaves. But in the course of a century most of these rules became dead letters. And when in the eighth century A.D. the caliphate of Baghdad became the spiritual and intellectual center of Islam, an unparalleled degree of peace and freedom was enjoyed by the Jews. An urbane and civilized culture embracing commerce, philosophy, and science, as well as religion, flourished in Baghdad, and the Jews enjoyed a respite from the age-old persecution which has been their lot.

The Karaite Revolt

During this period the sect known as "Karaites" or "readers" came into being. Of the founder, Anan ben David, little is known. He was candidate for exilarch in 767 A.D. but, suspected of heresy, he was passed over for his more orthodox brother. However, under the protection of a friendly caliph he was permitted to spread his ideas. He and his followers denied the sole authority of the Talmud as the interpretation of Scripture. The authority of the Talmud was by this time a fixed and final thing. Against this Anan rebelled. "Back to the Torah," he taught. Moreover, it was every man's duty to study the Torah and come to his own conclusions about its meaning.

The new teaching changed some of the basic features of traditional Judaism. The dietary laws were made less stringent. No Sabbath lights were permitted. Fast days, however, were multiplied. Venison was the only meat permitted. Physicians were barred, for the Bible taught that God was his people's healer.

The Karaite heresy spread, and attained considerable strength. Opposition from orthodox leaders was bitter, and to this day orthodox Jewish Law prohibits marriage with a Karaite. The decline of the Karaites came as a result of their fragmentation into groups of quarreling sects. Today, only a few thousand of their numbers in Russia and Turkey remain. However, the Karaite revolt was a stimulus to the orthodox tradition. It had raised challenging questions. What answer would orthodoxy give to them?

Jewish Scholasticism

One of the most notable effects of Karaism was to provoke
on the part of the orthodox the need for an intellectual justification for their faith. Other influences helped to produce
the same effect. Intellectual questions were in the air. The
philosophical heritage of Greece made itself felt throughout
the Near East. Traditionally, Judaism had not been a philosophically-minded faith, but now philosophical questions began to be raised. How can God be omnipotent? How is
Satan evil? Once these questions were asked, answers were
necessary; and the answers involved philosophy. The use of
philosophy to justify religion, of reason to expound and vindicate faith, is what is meant by "scholasticism." It is a phenomenon we shall encounter in Christianity as well as in
Judaism. The first notable Jewish scholastic was Saadia ben
Joseph (888-942 A.D.). Born in Egypt, he was educated in
Greek and Moslem thought as well as in Judaism. He gained
fame as the head of the Sura Academy in Babylonia, and as
an opponent of the Karaites. A man of wide interests, he
contributed to Hebrew philosophy, as well as translating sections of the Bible into Arabic. But his real significance lay
in philosophy. A rational spirit who insisted upon the duty
of thinking about religious matters, he nevertheless found a
place for revelation. His conception of the complementary
roles of reason and revelation set the pattern not only for
Jewish but for Christian scholasticism. His philosophy also
emphasized human freedom, a future life, and a messianic
age.

What Saadia began, others carried on, in Babylonia and
later in western Europe, notably in Spain. Under Moslem
rule, the Jews found in Spain a haven from persecution and
an opportunity to develop a broad, humanistic culture.
Among the most important centers of learning was the famous Academy of Cordova, founded during the tenth century
under the patronage of Hasdai ibn Shaprut (915-970 A.D.),
physician and friend of the ruler Abd Ar Rahrman III. A
center of Talmudic study, it also produced notable work in

literature and philosophy. Spanish Jewry produced during this period such notable figures as Ibn Gabirol (1021-1058), Judah Halevi (d. 1143), and Ibn Ezra (d. 1138). Gabirol was a poet, theologian, and philosopher who celebrated faith in God in beautiful lyrics, and wrote a philosophical volume entitled *The Fountain of Life.* Halevi was also a poet whose art ranged from the love of women to the love of God. He wrote a philosophical dialogue in defense of Judaism called *The Cuzari.* His poems express a passionate love for Zion, and he actually traveled to Palestine where his last days were spent. Ibn Ezra was a penniless, itinerant scholar and poet of a skeptical turn of mind.

But the most important and most famous figure of medieval Judaism was Moses ben Maimon, or Maimonides (1135-1204). Born in Cordova, he was educated in the arts and sciences as well as in all branches of Jewish scholarship. Driven out of Cordova by persecution, he and his family wandered through Spain and North Africa to Egypt. There Maimonides took up the study of medicine, and rose at length to the position of personal physician of Saladin. His deepest interests, however, were not in medicine but in philosophy and theology. He was a learned man in an age when to be learned meant to encompass all knowledge. After a commentary on the *Mishnah*, called the *Siraj*, he toiled for more than ten years on a work called the *Mishneh Torah*, a codification in clear and systematic form of all biblical and rabbinical law.

Turning to philosophy, he produced his most important work, the *Guide of the Perplexed.* At once an honest and seeking mind and a devoted Jew, he believed that faith and reason were aspects of a single harmonious reality. As the title suggests, Maimonides sought to give intellectual support to Jewish faith. The problem of biblical anthropomorphism concerned him; and he did not hesitate to write off many biblical phrases as poetry or metaphor. He also made extensive use of allegorical interpretation.

The philosophic viewpoint of the *Guide* is Aristotelian. The being of God is thus proven by analysis of causation.

God is the first cause, existing in pure actuality above and
before all the potentialities of the world. Between God and
the material universe is a series of emanations, of which man's
active intellect is the last, though humanly speaking the
most important. Man's soul is characterized by reason,
which is its highest part. Nevertheless, prophecy is held to
be the highest use of man's mind as well as an emanation of
God. Thus did Maimonides weave faith and reason into the
orderly pattern of his philosophy.

The main tenets of his philosophy are summed up in a
concise statement from the *Mishneh Torah* which has become the most widely accepted creed of orthodox Judaism:

> I believe with perfect faith that God is; that he is one with a
> unique unity; that he is incorporeal; that he is eternal; that to
> him alone prayer is to be made; that all the words of the Prophets
> are true; that Moses is the chief of the prophets; that the Law
> given to Moses has been transmitted without alteration; that
> this law will never be changed or superseded; that God knows
> all the deeds and thoughts of men; that he rewards the obedient
> and punishes transgressors; that the Messiah will come; that
> there will be a resurrection of the dead.[1]

Medieval Jewish Mysticism

Many Jews did not follow Maimonides and his fellow scho-
lastics in their assumption that religion is expressible in philosophic, rational terms. Religion was in their view a thing
of the spirit which only mysticism can penetrate and understand. Medieval Jewish mysticism found expression through
the books of the Kabbala. The term "Kabbala" means "tradition," and in this usage referred to an esoteric tradition of
which the Kabbalists believed themselves to be the inheritors.
One of the first and most famous books of the Kabbala was
the *Zohar* (Radiance) published by Moses de Leon in 1285.
It purported to be an early Aramaic translation of the Bible
proving that the Bible was not to be taken literally. Such a
view opened the way for a wholesale allegorizing of the Bible.

[1] Quoted from G. F. Moore, *History of Religions* (New York: Chas. Scribner's Sons, 1946), Vol. II, p. 94.

Since Hebrew numbers are letters of the alphabet, it was not difficult for mystics to find esoteric significance in every name in the Bible.

The ideas of the Kabbala were largely derived from gnostic or neoplatonic sources. God is the absolute or boundless, (in Hebrew *en-soph*) of whom nothing definite may be asserted,—an idea we have already encountered in Philo of Alexandria. Between God and the world is placed a series of emanations, at the end of which lies the world and man. Man himself is the microcosm who contains within himself an epitome of the macrocosm. He is at once animal, moral, and spiritual in nature; but only as spiritual can he rise through the various spheres to oneness with God. The Kabbalists were quick to see in all human and sensible things signs or symbols for the higher, spiritual world. They raised many philosophical questions as to why a God who is perfect should make an imperfect world; why there should be evil in the world, why there should be matter, and so on. The doctrines of the Kabbala led in some cases to magic of the grossest sort, and in other instances they nourished mystical traditions in Judaism and even had their influence on Christian mystics. For several centuries, knowledge of the Kabbala was an essential part of rabbinic education.

Calculations from the Kabbala produced a crop of messianic aspirants who through several centuries invariably disappointed their followers. Isaac de Luria (d. 1572), a Palestinian student of the Kabbala, announced himself the forerunner of the Messiah and gained many adherents. Influenced by Luria's speculations was Shabbathai Zebi (d. 1626) who after a varied life embraced Islam. Jacob Frank (d. 1791), the last of such Kabbalist Messiahs, embraced Christianity.

Jews in Medieval Christian Society

While philosophers reflected and mystics dreamed, the living heart of Judaism continued to be a corporate way of life and worship, centering in the synagogue. The synagogue, following the destruction of the temple and homeland in

Palestine, became more than a house of worship. It was
school and town hall as well,—the living center of the Jewish
way of life. During late antiquity and the early Middle Ages,
its ritual assumed the form it was to have for the next millennium and a half, which strictly orthodox Judaism preserves
to this day.

Since the Jews remained unassimilated and "different,"
they became objects of suspicion throughout the Middle Ages
of Europe. From the earliest times of European history, they
had suffered discrimination and deprivation. But beginning
with the tenth and eleventh centuries, their lot greatly
worsened. Known as "Christ killers" in many parts of Europe,
they were subject to random mob violence, especially during
the Christian Holy Week. Gregory VII forbade Christian
rulers to employ Jews in any capacity, and imposed other
harsh restrictions. The Crusades, especially in Germany, developed into massacres of the infidels at home, i.e., the Jews.
In the Rhineland, in a few months' time, twelve thousand
men, women, and children perished. Innocent III extended
his heresy-hunting to include the Jews along with the Albi-
genses. The Fourth Lateran Council in 1215 ordered the
Jew-badge to be worn at all times in public by Jews as a
symbol of shame. The Talmud, especially, became the object
of grossest misrepresentation and distortion in many parts of
Europe. In Paris in 1242 it was publicly "tried" and burned.
The Jews became scapegoats for all human evils; when the
Black Death swept through Europe in the mid-fourteenth
century, the Jews were suspected of causing it and were mas-
sacred for it. Rumors were passed around of Jewish rites
where the blood of Christian children was drunk, and of
Jewish mischief, such as poisoning wells. One by one the
nations of Europe expelled them, England in 1290, France
in 1306, Germany in 1298, and Spain in 1478. The Jews
took refuge in Poland and Russia and the Middle East.

The most vivid symbol of Jewish degradation was the
ghetto, the segregation of Jews into prescribed sections of
cities, usually the most crowded and unhealthy sections.
Going back in origin in some European cities to the early

Middle Ages, by the sixteenth century the ghetto was a standard feature of European city life. Jews were forbidden to live outside the ghetto and they were locked in at night. Huddling behind the ghetto walls, the Jews managed to maintain and develop their own way of life and culture, but they were shut off from stimulating contact with European culture of the time. And this culture was deprived of stimulating Jewish influence.

Hasidism

One of the most significant and fruitful movements in Jewish history is Hasidism. The word *Hasid* (plural *Hasidim*) means "holy" or "holy one." Polish and Russian Judaism was the source of this movement, the founder of which was an itinerant teacher, preacher and faith-healer known as Israel ben Eliezer, nicknamed Baal Shem-Tob (master of the Good Name). Born about 1700 in Bukovina, he showed no inclination toward talmudic study or education, being content to wander over hills and fields, finding God in nature. After an unsuccessful first marriage, he settled down happily to a humble living with a second wife. But the spirit of God was in him; he gathered a group of disciples about him, teaching them in an informal fashion until his death in 1760.

His movement had the double aspect of a revolt against the ironclad authority of the Talmud, and a spontaneous revival of spiritual and mystical religion. Against the massive and often hair-splitting wisdom of the scribes, he set simply the immediate experience of God, seeking to revive faith in men's hearts. Informally and aphoristically he taught that God dwells in all things in nature and man. Since God is thus in all things, the good is in all things and all men. There was no asceticism in Baal's teaching. The pervasive attitude was a humble, unaffected, and generous love for all God's world. Prayer was conceived not so much as petition as cleaving to God. By the power of prayer, miracles or exorcisms might be wrought. This latter aspect of Hasidism, as the movement came to be called, was emphasized by the *Zaddikim*, or Hasidic rabbis who rose after Baal's lifetime as leaders. They often tended to degrading abuses of their master's teaching.

Hasidism made its way against the opposition of the orthodox and the intellectuals. Elijah of Vilna, spiritual leader of eastern European Jewry, excommunicated the Hasidim and forbade the orthodox all contact with them. Nevertheless, the movement grew to several hundred thousand, and still has a following in Poland and Russia. Its mysticism irrigated the dry intellectualism of talmudic Judaism and brought emotion back into Jewish piety. Its simple pietism came alive in untutored hearts for whom rabbinic study was remote and strange. It made a permanent contribution to Jewish literature, philosophy, and faith, and is persuasively represented in modern thought by Martin Buber.

JUDAISM IN THE MODERN WORLD

Modern enlightenment with its doctrines of toleration, freedom, and humanity, came late to the Jews of Europe. The Reformation brought them little relief. Luther, in his early years wrote tolerantly, but later changed his views and lashed out in bitter prejudice. The Protestants, in the main, were as intolerant as were the Catholics. There were some havens of refuge. Seventeenth-century Holland granted a measure of freedom; and under Oliver Cromwell the Jews were permitted to return to England. But progress was pitifully slow. Even the eighteenth-century enlightenment cast fitful gleams into the darkness which surrounded the Jews. And in eastern Europe where the enlightenment did not penetrate, the lot of the Jews continued to be one of separation and persecution.

Moses Mendelssohn

The change of attitude which slowly dawned in Western Europe is nowhere better illustrated than in the life of Moses Mendelssohn. Born in Dessau in 1729, the son of a scribe, a frail and humpbacked child but an avid student, he managed to make his way through the bars of discrimination into

Berlin at the age of fourteen. In Berlin he came into contact
with the new ideas of the time. A brilliant and hardworking
student, he struggled against odds for an education. By
happy chance he met the writer, Lessing, with whom he soon
became fast friends. Lessing had already begun to preach
his gospel of tolerance; and he took keen delight in assisting
Mendelssohn. Lessing's *Nathan the Wise* was in all probability created around the character of Mendelssohn. His
rise to fame was climaxed by a removal of the usual Jewish
disabilities. His own writing included a dialogue on immortality, written in Platonic style, called the *Phaedon*; a translation of the Pentateuch into good German prose; and a
little volume called *Jerusalem*, in which he pleaded the cause
of emancipation for his people. All his life, by precept and
practice, Mendelssohn worked for the right of his people to
participate freely in the life of Europe.

The French Revolution

Perhaps the most crucial event in the emancipation of
European Jewry was the French revolution. Despite Mendelssohn and others like him, old laws and old barriers remained.
But the explosion which shook everything in Europe and destroyed so many old things, destroyed the separate and un-
equal status of France's Jews. In 1789 the Declaration of the
Rights of Man made all men equal before the law. Successive
laws in 1790 and 1791 applied these principles specifically to
Jews, granting them full citizenship. In the years following,
these principles spread, despite bitter opposition, to other
European nations.

Here, as in so many other respects, Napoleon consolidated
what the revolution first achieved. No special friend of the
Jews and at times not above bitterly anti-Semitic utterances,
he sought to mobilize the Jews behind his regime. A gathering of Jewish notables met in Paris in 1806 and pledged loyalty to Napoleon and France. Napoleon suggested a permanent body modeled on the Sanhedrin of Bible times. Such
a group met once, but died for lack of interest. But there
were other, more enduring results for the Jews of Napoleon's

regime. Wherever his armies marched, ghetto walls were razed, and the discrimination of centuries gave way to full civil rights.

However, the reaction which swept Europe in the wake of Napoleon's fall threatened many of these gains. In many cities Jews were once again confronted with the choice between ghetto walls or conversion to Christianity. Many Jews joined secret revolutionary organizations and fought for democratic rights. But, finally, nineteenth-century democracy brought to Jews full admission into the life of European society.

Types of Modern Judaism

Modern ideas and practices had their impact upon Judaism. During the centuries when the life and culture of Europe had been denied to the Jews, it had been easy to maintain traditional ways of faith and life. Now it was not so easy. Demands were made to bring Judaism into line with modern thought and life. Changes were made in the synagogue ritual. Words and rites which had lost meaning were dropped. More and more of the service came to be translated from Hebrew into the language of the nation in which it took place. There were moderates and radicals among the reform party. The radicals organized the Frankfort Society of the Friends of Reform, which in 1843 issued its declaration of principles:

> First, we recognize the possibility of unlimited development in the Mosaic religion. Second, the collection of controversies and prescriptions commonly designated by the name Talmud possess for us no authority from either the doctrinal or the practical standpoint. Third, a Messiah who is to lead back the Israelites to the land of Palestine is neither expected nor desired by us; we know no fatherland but that to which we belong by birth or citizenship.[2]

This statement was roundly denounced by less radical Jews. In Germany, Abraham Geiger (1810-1874), who emerged as

[2] Quoted from Moore, op. cit., p. 103.

the leader of Reform Judaism, had to wage a long fight to take his position as rabbi of Breslau, and when finally he became chief rabbi, conservatives withdrew and formed their own congregation.

In America similar divisions arose. There had been few Jews in America in earlier days, but immigration greatly increased their numbers during the nineteenth century. The newcomers brought with them many of the ideas which were stimulating and dividing European Jews. Similar issues were also raised by problems confronted in America. As a result, three groups within Judaism have emerged, Orthodox, Conservative, and Reform. David Einhorn introduced in America the prayerbook of the German Reformed synagogues, which served as a model for the Union Prayerbook of 1905. Rabbi Isaac M. Wise (1819-1900), rabbi of a large congregation in Cincinnati, has been called the architect of American Reformed Judaism. He was responsible for the founding of the Union of American Hebrew Congregations (1873), the Hebrew Union College (1875) for the education of Reformed rabbis, and the Central Conference of American Rabbis (1889). The Pittsburgh Platform summarizes the main tenets of Reformed Judaism. Judaism, it holds, presents the "highest conception of the God-idea," as "the central religious truth for the human race." It extols the value of the Bible as the "record of consecration of the Jewish people to its mission." The moral, in contrast to the ceremonial, law is held still valid. Jews are not now a nation but a religious community, and Judaism is termed a progressive religion which seeks national cooperation with its daughter religions, Christianity and Islam, and with all who seek to establish on earth the messianic kingdom of justice and peace. Bodily resurrection is rejected as an outmoded idea, but individual immortality is valid. It is in accord with Mosaic principles to seek solution for modern social problems.[3]

Emerging in controversies between Reform and Orthodox groups, as a center party, is Conservative Judaism. Leaders

[3] Quoted from Horace Friess and Herbert Schneider, *Religion in Various Cultures* (New York: Henry Holt & Co., Inc., 1932), pp. 294-95.

in the Conservative movement in the last century were such figures as Zecharias Frankel, Isaac Lesser, and Heinrich Graetz. The Jewish Theological Seminary in New York, founded in 1876, has taught views of this group. Its congregations are joined in the United Synagogues of America, and its rabbis in the Rabbinical Assembly. Conservative Jews feel that Reform went too far in rejecting all historic worship practices, and they seek to preserve a balance between the traditional and the modern in faith and practice.

Orthodoxy, which has remained numerically the strongest group in American Judaism, was substantially reinforced by waves of immigration to America from eastern Europe in the last half of the nineteenth century. Samson Hirsch gave intellectual leadership to the movement; and in 1912 the Isaac Elchanan Yeshiva or Academy was organized in New York to train orthodox rabbis. Despite the threefold division of American Judaism it is a fact that many of America's 10,000,000 Jews do not fall clearly into one or another of these groups, their sympathies, if not their affiliation, being mixed—and many no longer feel any loyalty whatever to Judaism as a religion.

Contemporary Anti-Semitism

While American Jews were adapting themselves in different ways to the new world, things were not going so well elsewhere. For the Jews in Russia the nineteenth century was a nightmare. Policies of traditional restriction and segregation gave way to open terror, persecution, and pogroms. Moreover, anti-Semitism, both theoretical and practical, greatly increased in western Europe in the late years of the nineteenth century. The writings of Houston Chamberlain and others gave anti-semitism in some quarters an intellectual respectability it did not deserve. In Germany, Austria-Hungary, and the Balkans, it was either permitted or secretly encouraged by public officials as a diversion from other social problems. The Dreyfus case, in which a Jewish army captain was framed and condemned for treason, engaged the attention of France from 1894 to 1906. While it ended with

Dreyfus' exoneration and the discrediting of his accusers, it illustrated the hold of anti-Jewish ideas on wide sections of the public mind.

Such ideas, endemic in the European mind, became epidemic in the Hitler movement in Germany. Hitler was openly and explicitly anti-Semitic from the beginning of his career, so that it was no surprise that when he became Chancellor in 1933, all Jews were dismissed from public office. In 1935 the Nurnberg laws deprived Jews of German citizenship. In 1938 there was a nationwide pogrom with untold looting and thousands of deaths. In 1939, when World War II opened, every able-bodied Jew was conscripted into Hitler's labor corps. And as German legions spread their conquests over Europe, they took virulent anti-Semitism wherever they went. During the war, German Nazis undertook the task of literally exterminating the Jewish people. They were used as guinea pigs in Nazi experiments, and in vast numbers herded into extermination camps and killed. Of Europe's 6,500,000 Jews (excluding those in the U.S.S.R.) it is estimated that more than 4,500,000 perished during the holocaust. Never before had anti-Semitism taken so vast and terrible a toll in so short a time. Nor did the coming of peace provide a panacea. For more than 500,000 Jews it meant nothing more than the meager existence of a displaced-persons' camp. Efforts at resettlement and rehabilitation go on; but there are many problems for which, at present, no solution is in sight.

Zionism

The modern revival of anti-Semitism, together with Israel's traditional feeling for the Holy Land, has produced the Zionist movement. Throughout the centuries of wandering, Jews cherished the dream of returning to Palestine. Some even undertook to realize the dream. During the nineteenth century, schemes for the Jewish recolonization of Palestine were propounded by a number of individual Jews and Christians. But it remained for Theodore Herzl to dramatize the idea and organize the movement. Born in Budapest in 1860, he was educated for the bar and journalism. In his early life he was a literary man without any deep feeling for his people. But the spread of anti-Semitism stimulated him to publish, in 1896, a book entitled *The Jewish State*. The following year Herzl was instrumental in organizing the First Zionist Congress, held in Basel, Switzerland, where the Zionist movement was launched. At first it was opposed by many Reform Jewish leaders. However, it appealed alike to the religious impulses of the orthodox, to the national aspirations of a persecuted people, and to the humane sentiments of those who sought a haven for victims of inhumanity.

Herzl spent the rest of his life in fruitless negotiations with the governments of Europe. He was succeeded in leadership of the movement by Chaim Weizmann, British chemist, through whose efforts the Balfour Declaration was secured, committing the British government in 1917 to "look with favor" upon the "establishment in Palestine of a national home for the Jewish people." During the 1920s work went forward despite obstacles. Funds were raised, and the Jewish population of Palestine steadily increased. The Jewish Agency, organized in 1929, gave the movement a central organization. The persecutions before and during World War II increased the tempo of immigration to Palestine and with it the opposition of Arab states. In 1939, under pressure from the Arab states and facing the mounting peril of world war, Britain abandoned the Balfour Declaration. However, immigration of Jews to Palestine continued even during the war, and following the war it increased sharply. Tension between Jews and Arabs increased in proportion. Despite severe opposition from all the Arab states, Palestine was partitioned by the United Nations in 1948, and the State of Israel was born. It was successfully defended by its own armies for several months against attacks by Egypt and other neighboring Arab states. Intervention by United Nations mediators brought a cease-fire which was followed by an uneasy peace.

The Zionist movement, as well as the Jewish population of Palestine, shows a wide variety of religious and social beliefs. The religious range is from orthodox Jews who regard the state of Israel as a fulfilment of prophecy, to secular Jews who view the new state in a completely nonreligious light. Socially and politically, the breadth is from types of communal and socialist communities in Palestine, to Zionists who favor unadorned capitalism as the economic basis of society. During 1951 the Ben-Gurion government fell, due to religious differences between orthodox and secular groups. The new nation also faces severe problems of finance due to the continual influx of population. What future the little nation has is hard to say. Surely there is no lack of problems to face. Surely, too, the future of Judaism, whatever it may be, will be crucially influenced by events taking place in Palestine.

Jewish Devotional Practices

Judaism involves, in a sense and degree unparalleled in most other religions, a concrete way of life. This way is delineated in great detail in the Torah and the bodies of interpretation which have accumulated through the centuries. A few of the more important observances which Jews still follow in varying degrees of loyalty and rigor will be sketched.

1. *The observance of the Sabbath,* or seventh day of the week, as a holy day dates from the earliest biblical period. Israel seems to have borrowed this observance from Babylonia, but the meaning was completely transformed. Strictness of observance has varied in different times and places. Today, orthodox Jews follow the ancient rule of the seventh day, extending in time from the appearance of the first stars on Friday to a similar hour on Saturday. On the Sabbath no work can be done; it is a day of holy rest. So far as possible no cooking is done on the Sabbath. Often the house is cleaned on Thursday or Friday in preparation for the day. Sabbath observance begins with the lighting of the Sabbath candles by the mother, accompanied by a traditional prayer. Later the father returns from the synagogue, often bringing a guest with him. At the Sabbath meal, hands are ceremonially cleansed, and the father blesses the wine and pours the *kiddush* cup for the family. Sometimes Scripture is read, espe-

cially the passage in Proverbs in praise of a virtuous woman.
On the Sabbath day orthodox families go together to the
synagogue, though at the synagogue the women must sit apart
in the women's gallery.

2. *The dietary laws* are observed with many varying degrees
of strictness. Rooted in the Bible, especially in the Book of
Leviticus, these laws have been greatly developed by century-
long tradition. In addition to the prohibition against eating
pork, as well as other animals which do not "part the hoof
and chew the cud," the laws require the slaughter of meat by
specially certified Jewish officials. Another law forbids the
mixing of milk and meat dishes; thus in orthodox kitchens,
there must be two sets of pots, pans, and dishes. In some
households there are as many as four sets, including those used
at Passover time. The origin of the dietary laws is seldom
probed by orthodox Jews; it is enough for the faithful Jew to
know that these regulations are part of God's law, and an
age-long force in maintaining the continuing identity of Israel.

3. *Circumcision* is the single "sacrament" of Judaism.
Different strands of biblical tradition attribute its origins to
Abraham, Moses, and Joshua respectively. In any case it signifies God's covenant with Israel, and an individual's membership in the covenant community. The ceremony takes
place when a child is eight days old, either at home or at the
synagogue. Male friends are invited to the ceremony, which
is a festive occasion. A godfather holds the baby, while a
synagogue official performs the operation. Then the father
offers a traditional prayer and announces the name of the
child. There is a parallel ceremony for girls in which the
father offers prayer at the synagogue, imploring divine blessing on the child, and announcing the girl's name.

4. *Bar-Mitzvah*, which means literally "son of the commandment," takes place according to orthodox tradition on
the sabbath following a boy's thirteenth birthday. It is a time
of celebration, and of receiving gifts. Among the gifts are a
talith, or prayer shawl, with which to cover the head during
prayer, and a *tephillin*. The tephillin is a small box containing the words of the "shema,"

"Hear O Israel: the LORD our God is one LORD; and you shall love the LORD your God with all your heart and with all your soul and with all your might." (Deut. 6:4-5.)

In accordance with Deuteronomic teaching, the words are placed within the box and bound on the forehead and left arm. At the Bar-Mitzvah ceremony, after singing and prayer, seven portions of the Torah are read by as many men of the congregation. Then the "Bar-Mitzvah boy" also reads a passage of the Bible. Sometimes this is followed by a speech by the boy himself, and another by the rabbi. The Bar-Mitzvah is considered a celebration of a boy's coming of age in the things of religion. In Reform synagogues there is a parallel ceremony for girls, and the whole celebration more nearly resembles confirmation as celebrated in some Christian churches.

5. *The synagogue* is more than a place of worship. For Judaism it inherits the traditions of church, school, and town hall. A congregation may be constituted by ten men, and the presence of ten male members is necessary for any service of worship at the synagogue. It is organized under the president of the synagogue, and no synagogue has any power over others. The status of the rabbi is, as the term implies, that of a teacher rather than that of priest. The rabbi may preach and lecture upon religious subjects, but he is in no way religiously set apart from laymen. The reading of the Torah, which is the heart of the synagogue service, is done by laymen of the congregation.

The central object in the synagogue is the Ark of the Covenant, behind the curtains of which are the scrolls of the Torah. Above the Ark is the eternal light. On the curtain of the Ark is placed the six-pointed star of David, whose origins are obscure, and beside it are sometimes the protecting figures of two lions, symbols of the tribe of Judah and the house of David, holding stone tablets on which are engraved the Ten Commandments. The daily prayers at the synagogue, as well as those for the Sabbath and for the holy days, vary widely in proportion to the orthodoxy of the congregation.

6. *Holy days and festivals*. The Jewish religious year begins with New Year or *Rosh Hashanah* which comes late in
September, and is a day for both celebration and religious
reflection or stock-taking. Apples dipped in honey are served
in the home to express the hope that the New Year will be
happy. There are special prayers and services of worship at
the synagogue. The first ten days of the year are called the
Ten Days of Penitence, and the tenth day is *Yom Kippur*, or
the Day of Atonement. Often it is a day of fasting, and always it is a time of public and private prayer for forgiveness
of sins.

Following later in the autumn is the *Feast of Succoth*, or
Feast of Booths or Tabernacles. Many Jews make arbors or
huts of leaves and live in them while the festival continues,
recalling the time when their ancestors lived as nomads in
the wilderness. Succoth is also a festival of thanksgiving for
the fruitfulness of nature. Homes and synagogues are deco-
rated with fruits and flowers.

Coinciding with the winter solstice, and coming close to
the Christian Christmas, is the Jewish holiday of *Hanukkah*,
or the Feast of Lights. It celebrates the cleansing and rededi-
cation of the temple at the time of the Maccabean revolt. It
is largely a family festival. For eight days a *Menorah* or can-
delabra with eight candles, is placed in the window. In some
families, one candle is lighted on the first night, two on the
second and so on to eight. Often the youngest child is
granted the privilege of lighting the candle on the first night.
Gifts are exchanged between friends, and there is special
Hanukkah food, with parties and merry-making.

A similar spirit of gaiety pervades the *Feast of Purim*, which
comes in late winter, and traditionally celebrates the deliverance of the Jews from their tormentor Haman, through
the courage and loyalty of Esther. Passages from the Book
of Esther are read in the synagogue at this season of
the year.

The climax of the religious year is the *Passover* or *Pesakh*.
Traditionally, it celebrates the deliverance of the Jews from
Egypt, though some scholars believe that it originated as a

spring agricultural ceremony celebrating the birth of lambs
and the sprouting of grain. There are special prayers and
services at the synagogue, but the central celebration is the
Seder feast which is eaten by the whole family assembled together.

Extensive preparations are made in every Jewish family for
the Passover. The house is cleaned, the Passover dishes and
silver are brought out and cleansed, and new clothes are purchased. During the Passover only unleavened bread may be
eaten, so some families have a ceremony of hunting the
leaven, in which the father hunts through the house to find
pieces of old leaven which the mother has hidden for him to
find. At the Passover table, the father's chair is heaped with
cushions. A pitcher of water and towel are passed around
for the ceremony of washing the hands. The father blesses
the wine, saying a traditional prayer, and then all drink. Next,
the youngest child over six years of age asks the traditional
"four questions," in response to which the story of the Exodus is related. Placed on the Seder table is a large platter on
which are the Seder symbols: a roasted lamb bone, symbolizing the sacrificial lamb; a roasted or hard-boiled egg as the
symbol of hope; radish and parsley, as bitter herbs symbolizing Israel's hard lot; and a mixture of apples, nuts, and wine,
whose red color recalls the bricks which Israel was forced to
make in Egypt. When the Exodus story is finished, fish,
fowl, and other delicacies are served. Matzoth or unleavened
bread is the dessert.

Fifty days after the Passover is the Feast of *Shebuoth* or
Pentecost. Originally a feast of first-fruits or of the barley
harvest in Palestine, it came in the course of time to celebrate
the giving of the Law or Torah on Mount Sinai. The Jewish
religious calendar is also marked by other less important and
less frequently celebrated religious holidays. Taken together
the holy days and festivals constitute an important phase of
Jewish religious life, and remind us again of the practical and
concrete character of Jewish religion. For the Jew, religion
is not so much a matter of contemplation or speculation as it
is a concrete doing or performance of the Law.

SUGGESTIONS FOR FURTHER READING

ARCHER, JOHN C. *Faiths Men Live By.* New York: The Ronald Press Co., 1934, chap. xiv.

BAECK, LEO. *The Essence of Judaism.* New York: Schocken Books, Inc., 1948.

BOUQUET, ARTHUR. *Comparative Religion.* Harmondsworth: Penguin Books, Ltd., 1950, chap. ix.

BUBER, MARTIN. *I and Thou.* Edinburgh: T. & T. Clark, 1942.

———. *Israel and the World.* New York: Schocken Books, Inc., 1948.

BROWNE, LEWIS (ed.). *The Wisdom of Israel.* New York: Random House, Inc., 1947.

CLEMEN, CARL. *Religions of Mankind.* New York: Harcourt, Brace & Co., Inc., 1931, IV, 3.

COHEN, ABRAM. *Everyman's Talmud.* London: J. M. Dent & Sons, Ltd., 1937.

FINKELSTEIN, LOUIS. *The Pharisees.* Philadelphia: Jewish Publication Society, 1938.

——— (ed.). *The Jews, Their History, Culture, and Religion.* Harper & Bros., 1949.

——— (with Ross, J., and Brown, W.). *Religions of Democracy.* Devin-Adair Co., 1941.

FITCH, FLORENCE M. *One God, the Ways We Worship Him.* New York: Lothrop, Lee & Shepard Co., Inc., 1944.

HERBERG, WILL. *Judaism and Modern Man.* New York: Farrar, Straus & Young, 1951.

HERZL, THEODORE. *The Jewish State.* London: Central Zionist Organization, 1936.

ISSERMAN, FERDINAND. *This Is Judaism.* Chicago: Willett, Clark & Co., 1944.

MOORE, GEORGE F. *History of Religions.* New York: Chas. Scribner's Sons, 1946, Vol. II, chap. iv.

———. *Judaism.* Cambridge: Harvard University Press, 1927-1931.

NOSS, JOHN B. *Man's Religions.* New York: The Macmillan Co., 1949, chap. xiii.

SACHAR, ABRAM. *A History of the Jews.* New York: Alfred A. Knopf, Inc., 1930.

STEINBERG, MILTON. *Basic Judaism.* New York: Harcourt, Brace & Co., Inc., 1947.

———. *A Partisan Guide to the Jewish Question.* Indianapolis: Bobbs-Merrill Co., 1945.

The Babylonian Talmud (English trans.). London: Soncino Press, 1935-1945.

Chapter 7

JESUS AND EARLY CHRISTIANITY

CHRISTIANITY was born into the world as a daughter religion of Judaism. Many of the basic ideas of Christianity are essentially Jewish in character. But Christianity has also been the heir of many other influences. Greek and Roman culture made important contributions; during the past nineteen and a half centuries innumerable other influences have made themselves felt. Amid great diversities and differences, perhaps the only single principle on which all Christians would agree is that, in Jesus Christ, God has spoken a decisive and final word to mankind. Yet even this central affirmation has been the subject of a great many widely differing interpretations.

The World into which Christianity Came

By the beginning of the first century A.D., Greek and Roman influences had united to create in the Mediterranean area a single, cosmopolitan Greco-Roman civilization. The creative period of Greek culture was past, but Greek language, literature, and philosophy had been spread thin over the entire Mediterranean world to form a common mind. The Greek city-states had committed political suicide in fratricidal strife during the fourth and third centuries B.C., and political leadership had passed to the Romans. Roman power and administrative genius had joined separate peoples and lands into a single empire ruled from Rome, and netted together by Roman roads. Like ours, it was a large cosmopolitan world.

One trait of this world is of special significance for religion. Gilbert Murray has called it a failure of nerve.[1] By the first century A.D. many in the Greco-Roman world had given up the search for the good life in purely human, this-worldly terms, and had appealed for guidance to magic, mysticism, and dramatic philosophies of life. Into such a world Christianity came, and against such competitors it made its way.

Though Christianity made its way into the Greco-Roman world, Jesus scarcely ventured beyond the bounds of his native Palestine. First-century Palestine was an eastern province of the Roman empire. The order to crucify Jesus came from a Roman official, Pontius Pilate. We have already met in other connections such first-century Palestinian groups as the Pharisees, the Sadducees, the Zealots, and the Herodians, all of whom enter as actors in the drama of Jesus' life. First-century Palestine seethed with revolt which was often interpreted in messianic terms. Such was the background for one who came to be called the Messiah or Christ.

THE LIFE OF JESUS

Sources of Knowledge

Before proceeding to Jesus' life and teaching, it is worthwhile to look briefly at sources of knowledge. A few classical writers allude briefly to Jesus. Pliny and Tacitus speak disparagingly. Josephus has, in addition to interpolations, an allusion which is probably genuine. The Talmud refers a few times to Jesus. The Letters of the New Testament have enough references for us to reconstruct a bare outline of events. But the main sources are the Four Gospels. They are a selection from a larger body of such biographical literature; and we may believe that the fittest survived.

For many centuries tradition accepted the Gospels at face value, without raising questions, making comparisons, or seeking origins. However, during the past two centuries these

[1] See Gilbert Murray, *Five Stages of Greek Religion* (New York: Oxford University Press, 1925), chap. iv.

documents have been as exhaustively analyzed as any writings in the world. The results of this study up to this point may be briefly summarized. The first three Gospels, Matthew, Mark, and Luke, taken together, show a common outline for the life and teachings of Jesus, in contrast to the fourth Gospel which seems to have a radically different outline and orientation. Of the first three (called the Synoptics since they view together the life and teachings of Jesus), the question has been asked, which was first, and what relation does it bear to the other two? Mark is generally conceded to be the earliest, though there is clear evidence that back of Mark lies a period of oral tradition, when the chief facts about the life and teachings of Jesus were handed down by word of mouth. The first precipitate of the oral tradition was a lost document, to which the name, Q (the German word "Quelle" means "source") has been assigned, and which consisted of selections of Jesus' teachings on topics of importance. Scholars differ in the date assigned Mark, but somewhere around 70 A.D. is a good guess. Some two or three decades later, Matthew and Luke sought to combine Mark and Q into an integrated narrative of the life and teachings of Jesus. They differ in style and in viewpoint, but they agree in many specific facts. And they clearly show a dependence upon Mark. The fourth Gospel, attributed to the disciple John, appears to have been written around the turn of the second century. Aside from differing in the order of events of Jesus' life, it is also guided by a quite different viewpoint, the Logos philosophy of the Greeks. In this sketch of Jesus' life and teaching, the order of events suggested by the Synoptics will be followed.

Nativity Stories

Mark, the earliest Gospel, gives no account of Jesus' birth, and before him the Apostle Paul writes of Jesus as born of woman (Gal. 4:4) and of the Davidic line (Rom. 1:3). The nativity stories in Matthew and Luke are the only references to the Virgin-birth in the New Testament; and they differ from each other so radically that it may be concluded that they contain legendary elements. Their value lies not so much in their historical accuracy, as in showing the estimate which Jesus' early followers placed upon his life. Here was one at whose birth the angels sang, kings came from the ends of the earth to bring gifts, shepherds knelt in homage, and Herod trembled on his uneasy throne. And for this unique person there must be a unique mother, around whom the tenderest elements of devotion could cluster.

From the evidence, it may probably be concluded that Jesus was the son of Joseph and Mary, that he was of the Davidic line, and that his home town was Nazareth in Galilee. The date of his birth must be placed somewhere near the end of Herod's reign. The evidence is not unanimous, but 6-4 B.C. is the most probable inference. (When dates came to be reckoned from the birth of Jesus, an error was made in calculating the year 1 A.D., so paradoxically Jesus was born a few years B.C.)

Of Jesus' childhood in Nazareth almost nothing is known except by imaginative reconstruction from the narrative of his later, public life and from our knowledge of first-century Jewish life. Joseph drops out of the picture during Jesus' childhood, from which it is inferred that he died during this time. Jesus followed his father's trade of carpentry. There are references in the New Testament to six other children, four brothers and two sisters.

Baptism and Temptations

According to Luke (3:11, 23) when Jesus was about thirty years old, in the fifteenth year of Tiberius Caesar (i.e., 29 or 30 A.D.), John the Baptist appeared on the scene in Palestine. John was a Hebrew prophet born out of due season, after the period of officially recognized prophecy had ended. He was a striking figure, dressed in hair cloth and a leather belt, and eating locusts and wild honey. His words and bearing attracted a large following as he preached and baptized in the Jordan Valley. In prophetic manner he preached the judgment and redemption by God. Repent, he warned his hearers, for the kingdom of God is at hand. He spoke of the coming of God's Messiah, so that Christians afterward said that he was the forerunner of Jesus. John's rite of baptism was a kind of anticipatory cleansing which prepared one for entrance into the kingdom.

John preached a clear-cut and radical social morality: a man with two coats should give to him who had none; soldiers must not extort money or make false charges; tax collectors should take only their due. He did not hesitate to condemn Herod Antipas for living with his brother's wife—a criticism which cost John, first imprisonment, and then death. John attracted a following, and there is evidence that his followers constituted a group independent of the Christians and other religious groups.

It was natural for Jesus to be attracted and stirred by such a man. Mark tells most simply of Jesus' experience as he was baptized by John. He saw the heavens open and the spirit of God descend like a dove upon him, and he heard the voice of God saying to him, "Thou art my beloved Son; with thee I am well pleased" (Mark 1:11). The later Gospels transform the experience into something objective and external. The important point, however, is its significance in Jesus' life. Like the prophets before him, he felt called by God to a special vocation. The Spirit of God was upon him, giving him his appointed task to do, leading him into his unique destiny.

The Synoptic Gospels (Matt. 4; Luke 4) describe the way in which, immediately following the baptism, Jesus went into the wilderness and was tempted by Satan. Matthew and Luke describe the temptations in detail, telling how Satan asked him to turn stone to bread, to cast himself unharmed from the pinnacle of the temple, and how Satan offered him the whole world in return for his worship. Behind these imaginative details, the real issues are visible. Jesus was pondering the methods by which his vocation was to be accomplished. Should he gather a following by such dramatic miracles as throwing himself unharmed from the pinnacle of the temple? Should he be concerned primarily with economic affairs— turning stone to bread? Should his movement be based upon a political and military messianism, so common in first-century

Palestine? No. His service of God would be of a different sort.

Galilean Ministry

Jesus began his public career not in the Jordan Valley where he was baptized but in his home province of Galilee. Luke places the beginning in his home town of Nazareth, while Mark and Matthew place it in Capernaum on the Sea of Galilee. In all three Gospels these cities, together with other Galilean towns such as Chorazin and Bethsaida, are often mentioned. From the first, Jesus proclaimed the imminent coming of the kingdom of God and called for repentance and obedience to God, as conditions of entrance into the kingdom. He also healed the sick and performed exorcisms. Preaching at first alone, he subsequently gathered a group of followers about himself, of whom twelve, called disciples, occupied a position of peculiar intimacy. Almost from the first there was opposition from the leaders of Judaism. This opposition grew as Jesus' following increased.

How long did the period of public preaching in Galilee last? Estimates range from six months to two years. And why, when it was going most successfully, did Jesus break it off so abruptly? For quite without transition or explanation, we find him wandering to the north to the borders of Tyre and Sidon with his disciples (Mark 7:24). One reason sometimes inferred for the departure from Galilee is that Jesus was fleeing Herod Antipas who had recently imprisoned and killed John the Baptist. Another is that he wished to get away from the Galilean multitudes who so completely misunderstood his message. Still another reason sometimes suggested is that he wanted time alone with the disciples for reflection and discussion in preparation for the climax of his life.

Confession of Messiahship

Whatever the reason for Jesus' abrupt departure from Galilee, it was during this time of wandering in the north that an event of climactic importance took place. All three Synoptic Gospels agree that during this time Jesus first spoke with the disciples directly concerning the Messiahship. (Matt. 16:13 ff.; Mark 8:27 ff.; Luke 9:18 ff.) Jesus asked his followers, "Who do men say that the Son of Man is?" Some thought he was Elijah, according to a popular tradition which held that Elijah would return before the End. Others said he was John the Baptist returned to life. "But who do you say that I am?" Jesus asked. Peter replied, "You are the Christ, the Son of the living God." (Matt. 16:16.)

Several aspects of this simple but important scene call for explanation. In the first place, it must be understood against the background of messianic expectation and agitation which characterized first-century Palestine. Messianic claims were frequent, but they were often regarded as blasphemous by the leaders of Judaism, and as subversive by the Romans. For such reasons Jesus enjoined secrecy upon his followers.

The term "Christ" (or *Christos*) is the Greek translation of the Hebrew word "Messiah," which means "anointed." Its use in Jewish religious thought goes far back in Old Testament times. The kings of Israel, Saul and David, were spoken of as anointed. But during later Old Testament times, the term had taken on more special meaning. The Messiah in some of the apocalyptic documents was the special, divinely-sent agent who would bring to a close the old, evil age, and bring in the New Age. For many first-century Jews the Messiah was a political and military figure.

Many students of the New Testament, looking to such first-century conceptions of the Messiah, doubt that Jesus could have applied such a term to himself. Is this not, they ask, another instance of the Christians reading their own interpretations back into the life of Jesus? However, other scholars reply that Jesus may well have appealed here as he did at other points to the Old Testament prophets, finding there a conception of the Messiah with which he identified himself. He was probably deeply influenced by Deutero-Isaiah's vision of the "suffering servant." His messianic claim thus involved a radical redefinition of the Messiah concept. He did believe himself to be God's Messiah, but in a way very different from that expected by his contemporaries. In any case, he clearly came to think of himself as uniquely involved in the coming of the Kingdom.

The question of Jesus' messianic claim is of crucial religious importance for Christianity. For Jesus' followers were, quite simply, those who believed Jesus to be Messiah or Christ. Later other terms came to be applied, such as "Lord," "Savior," "Word of God," and others. But they were attempts to find equivalents for the original title of Messiah. In a real sense, Christian faith began with the apostolic confession of Jesus as the Messiah.

Following the confession of Messiahship, as a sequel, was the Transfiguration (Matt. 17; Mark 9; Luke 9). The three Synoptic Gospels describe an experience of Peter, James, and John in which they saw Jesus exalted on a mountain top along with Moses and Elijah. Moses and Elijah symbolized the Law and the Prophets, so that Jesus is here depicted as appearing to his disciples as the fulfilment of the Law and the Prophets.

Last Days and Death

Jesus returned privately and incognito to Galilee, following these events in the north, and then set his face toward Jerusalem. Here, Luke (9-18) differs from Matthew and Mark in his description of a leisurely journey through Perea and Samaria. But in all three Gospels Jesus appeared to be going quite deliberately toward the capital city, with full knowledge of the perils of such a visit. He seemed to be timing his arrival to coincide with the Passover festival.

The question may be asked, why did he do it? Traditional Christianity has often invested Jesus with miraculous foreknowledge of the events which awaited him in Jerusalem, though this is belied by his response to them as they happened. His previous references to these events can be read as his natural anticipation of opposition and conflict in Jerusalem and as the hindsight of the disciples who were actually unprepared for them. Others have believed that Jesus expected a miraculous deliverance by God at Jerusalem which would vindicate him and his Kingdom. But it is quite pos-

sible, and quite consistent with Jesus' life, to believe that he
went to Jerusalem in simple trust and obedience to the will of
God as he understood it, knowing nothing in detail of what
awaited him there.

Approaching the city, he entered on the back of a donkey,
amid a popular demonstration that had clear messianic implications. His entrance may be understood as a further attempt
to transform the concept of Messiah. Many expected a Messiah who would enter the city on a war horse; as a man of
peace he entered on the back of a donkey, fulfilling the prophecy of Zechariah (9:9). Once in the city he went to the
temple and threw out the money changers and sellers of sacrificial animals—again an act which clearly implies messianic
claims on Jesus' part. Otherwise how can we understand the
sense of authority with which the act was done? This deed
also crystallized the opposition against him, causing a plot
against his life. During the days in Jerusalem he lodged with
friends in Bethany over the Mount of Olives, east of Jerusalem, coming into the city each day to teach in the temple,
and to argue his case with scribes and Pharisees. The disagreement became sharper and sharper.

On Thursday Jesus' disciples arranged secretly for a room
in which he might eat a last Passover meal with them. The
bread and wine of the traditional Jewish Passover meal were
reinterpreted by Jesus to mean his own body and blood
through which he believed God would make a new covenant
with man. After the celebration, the Master and his disciples
set out for Bethany, pausing for prayer in the Garden of Geth-
semane on the slopes of the Mount of Olives. There a crowd,
sent by the leaders of the Sanhedrin and directed by the
traitor Judas, took him prisoner. He was tried illegally at the
home of Caiaphas before the Sanhedrin on charges of making
messianic claims and of threatening the destruction of the
temple. The climax of the trial was Jesus' own clear avowal
of the messianic role (Matt. 27:11), according to the Synoptics the only public statement on this point during his life,
a statement made in the certainty that it meant death. The
charge of blasphemy carried the death penalty in Judaism.

But for this penalty Roman permission was necessary. Therefore, the next morning Jesus was taken before Pontius Pilate,
where the charge was not blasphemy (which would not have
greatly impressed Pilate) but sedition, a charge to which the
Romans were very attentive. Pilate's motives are not clear,
but he acquiesced in the proposal, and Jesus was led away to
be crucified. So, it was thought, ended the life of one who
claimed to be King of the Jews.

THE TEACHINGS OF JESUS

Attention must now be turned to the content of Jesus'
teaching. What were the main ideas which he proclaimed in
Galilee and in Jerusalem? First and foremost he taught the
reality of God. It is often suggested in our time that we may
take the ethics of Jesus and let the religion go. That is a view
which Jesus would never have allowed. For him, ethics and
religion, faith and works, were two aspects of a single, seam-
less reality: Jesus' God was Jahweh, the God of his fathers,
creator and ruler of all things. From him our lives derive;
to him we belong, Jesus said. God was never, for Jesus, a
philosophic concept. He never argued the existence of God;
assuming it as the basic fact of life, Jesus' thinking sought by
parable and symbol to point to a reality which must be known
firsthand to be appreciated. Though Jesus never argued from
nature to nature's God, nevertheless nature was important for
him as a part of God's creation. But it was in the sphere of
human action that he saw God impinging most directly upon
man's life. For Jesus the proper end of man's action is to do
the will of God. Hence the cardinal importance of ethics in
religion for Jesus, and the emptiness of religion without ethics.

Love of God

Much has been said and written about Jesus' views of the
love of God. Recent Christian liberal writers have spoken of
Jesus' teaching of a loving, heavenly Father as his most unique
and distinctive doctrine. It must, however, be kept in mind
that some of the prophetic writers of Israel, notably Hosea

and Jeremiah, taught the love of God. It must also be kept in mind that the concept of love for Jesus possessed an austerity which it lacks for many moderns. To him love meant justice and judgment as well as mercy and forgiveness. With these qualifications, it is accurate to speak of Jesus' God as sovereign love. In a manner more intimate and more frequent than his Jewish contemporaries, Jesus spoke of God as heavenly Father. For him God was the father of the prodigal son, ever willing to receive back his erring children if only they would come (Luke 15:11-32). Or he was the shepherd who left the ninety-nine sheep in the wilderness while he sought for the wandering hundredth.

God and God's Kingdom

Jesus' teaching about God was closely related to that about the kingdom of God, or as Matthew puts it, the kingdom of heaven. The term had been a part of Jewish religion from the earliest days, and had always signified the kingship of God, —the rule of God over all men. Jesus followed in this tradition, but in his thought the term took on many new shades of meaning. Indeed, the precise meaning of the kingdom of God in Jesus' thought is one of the most difficult and complicated questions of New Testament study. Was the kingdom present or future? Was it this-worldly or other-worldly? Was it a social concept, or was it individual and personal? How did Jesus conceive his own relation to the kingdom? These are only a few of the questions over which scholarly ink is shed.

Such scholarly and often complicated discussion cannot be pursued here further than to suggest that for Jesus the kingdom of God signified the state of the world when God's whole will would be done. "Thy kingdom come," he taught his disciples to pray, "thy will be done on earth as it is in heaven." (Matt. 6:10.) Often the kingdom seems to be a future reality similar to other first-century ideas of the Last Day and the New Age. All three Synoptic Gospels report the content of Jesus' first preaching in Galilee in the words: "Repent, for the kingdom of God is at hand." (Matt. 4:17; Mark 1:15.) Sometimes the inward, spiritual nature of the

kingdom was emphasized. At other times the nature of the
kingdom as a moral imperative was emphasized. "Seek first
his kingdom and his righteousness." (Matt. 6:33.) The
Parables of the Seed and the Sower (Matt. 13; Mark 4; Luke
8), as well as the Parable of the Mustard Seed (Matt. 13;
Mark 4) and the Leaven (Matt. 13) emphasized the similarity of the kingdom to the silent processes of growth, as
well as the fact that growth is a thing not within human power
to control. The Parable of the Tares (Matt. 13:24-30) as
well as those of the Vineyard and Husbandman (Matt. 21:33-
46) and the Marriage Feast (Matt. 22:1-14) pointed to an
eschatological future. In general, Jesus seemed to teach that
the kingdom had actually begun with his teaching, but that
its full realization was still to come in the imminently expected Last Day. In any case it is the proper aim and goal
for all human striving in history, the proper criterion by which
all man's words and works are judged.

The kingdom had for Jesus genuine moral content. It
would be characterized by universal human brotherhood.
But there is no basis in his teachings for identifying the kingdom with any particular type of society or social organization.
When Jesus spoke of the kingdom of God, he was not thinking of democracy, socialism, or any other specific type of social
organization or arrangement. He was dealing with a radically
different sort of problem, namely with man's relation to God
and God's will.

Ethical Teachings

Jesus' ethical or moral teachings were rooted in his conception of the divine will, so that ethics and religion were, for
him, fused together. Moral values were absolute, being rooted
in an unconditional "Thou shalt" which sets them apart from
the various loyalties which claim human allegiance. Jesus
had much to say about this absoluteness and the tensions
which it sets up in human life. Even such basic loyalties as
love for father and mother must have no conflict with the
claims of God and his kingdom (Matt. 10:37). Concerning
such normal goods as food and clothes, Jesus taught his fol-

lowers, "Do not be anxious for your life, what you will eat, or what you will drink, nor about your body, what you shall put on." (Matt. 6:25.) The service of God and his kingdom is the pearl of great price, which when a man sees it, he sells his possessions in order to purchase (Matt. 13:45).

The content of Jesus' ethic is adequately expressed in his own summary of the Law and the Prophets: "You shall love the Lord your God with all your heart and with all your soul and mind, and your neighbor as yourself." (Matt. 22:34-40; Mark 12:28-34; Luke 10:27.) The basic moral attitude for Jesus was respect for personality as something made by God in his image for his service and worship. Thus Jesus' neighbor-love was at once something more inward and more exacting than any precise legal code might demand. It involved perfection, not only of act, but also of inner attitude. For example, in the Sermon on the Mount, Jesus traced such acts as murder and adultery to their source in inner motive and attitude (Matt. 5:27 ff.). Furthermore, Jesus extended the area of this moral ideal beyond any artificial or man-made limits to the borders of humanity. The Parable of the Good Samaritan defines one's neighbor as any needy human being (Luke 10:35-37). The demands of Jesus' ethic are so great that no man can honestly claim to fulfil them. Yet once stated, they are seen as so true that they cannot be ignored. Were it not for the fact that Jesus viewed God as love which forgives as well as judges, his teachings would be more of a judgment than a gospel of optimism.

Evil for Jesus was ever-present and persistent self-centeredness, which sets man against God and divides him from his neighbor. Sometimes it is trust in one's possessions, as with the Rich Fool (Luke 12:16-21), sometimes it is the religious pride of the Pharisees who "trusted in themselves and despised the others."

In all this, Jesus built solidly upon the faith and morality of Moses and the prophets. As he put it, he came "not to destroy but to fulfil" (Matt. 5:17). But what was religiously most important about Jesus' teaching was the unity of precept and practice. He practiced—indeed he was—what he taught.

BEGINNINGS OF CHRISTIANITY

Resurrection

Christianity has been conceived by its adherents as faith or personal trust in Jesus as Messiah. In the origin and spread of this attitude the experiences of the Resurrection of Jesus played an important part. At the Crucifixion, Jesus' disciples forsook him and fled. One of them denied him and another betrayed him. They were, if any group ever was, a completely disillusioned lot of men. It may be surmised that they fled from Jerusalem, returning to their native Galilee to resume the occupations they had left to follow Jesus. But a few weeks later we find these same men with a completely different attitude. They were the intrepid servants of a faith which in the space of a generation burst the bonds of Judaism and made its impact felt from Corinth to Alexandria, from Antioch to Rome. What accounts for this revolutionary change? The answer which Christianity has given is the Resurrection, which served to convince them that Jesus was not dead but alive—more living and more powerful than he had been in the days of his flesh. The Resurrection was thus for the early Christians a very crucial matter, for it certified to them the living spirit of Jesus as a present reality.

Precisely what happened at the Resurrection is another, a more difficult, and a less important question. There were two main testimonies in the early Church. The Gospels tell the story of the empty tomb, the surprised visitors on the first day of the week, the appearances of the risen Christ (some quite vividly physical, others more spiritual), and as a sequel, his ascension on a cloud to heaven. This view of an objective resurrection has been widely held. There are, however, difficulties, among which is the problem of the physical ascension. In the light of twentieth-century astronomy or cosmology, what happened to the physical body of Jesus? On the other hand, what is one to make of the empty tomb?

Paul held a different view. About 51 or 52 A.D., some two decades before the earliest Synoptic account of the Resurrection, he wrote to the Corinthians the story which he had received:

> For I delivered to you as of first importance what I also received, that Christ died for our sins in accordance with the scriptures, that he was buried, that he was raised on the third day in accordance with the scriptures, and that he appeared to Cephas then to the twelve. Then he appeared to more than five hundred brethren at one time, most of whom are still alive, though some have fallen asleep. Then he appeared to James, then to all the apostles. Last of all, as to one untimely born, he appeared also to me. (I Cor. 15:3-8)

Note that emphasis is placed here upon the appearances of the risen Christ and that no mention is made of an empty tomb. No places or times or other details are given for these appearances. Most important of all, Paul includes among the resurrection appearances his own experience on the Damascus road, an experience which occurred after the time of the presumed ascension of Jesus (Acts 9:1-9). This, for Paul, indicates the nature of the resurrection appearances. That he did not regard it as a physical resurrection is further attested by the statement later in the same chapter: "flesh and blood cannot inherit the kingdom of God." (I Cor. 15:50.) Whatever its precise nature, it was the Resurrection which brought the Christian movement into being. The Church which was conceived at Caesarea-Philippi was born with the Resurrection—with the faith that his death was not the end but rather the beginning of Jesus' reign in human hearts.

Pentecost

The early chapters of Acts describe the opening events of the early Christian movement. Among them was an event of great importance which took place in Jerusalem at the Feast of Pentecost or First Fruits in the same year in which Jesus died. As the author of Acts tells the story, the Holy Spirit descended upon the little band of Christians with the supernatural accompaniments of wind, fire, and "speaking with tongues." Peter then made a speech proclaiming Jesus

and the Resurrection, at the conclusion of which three thousand converts were made. Pentecost for Judaism was the festival of the giving of the Law; and according to rabbinic tradition the Law at Mount Sinai had been given in the seventy
languages of mankind. The story, as related in Acts, is thus
a Christian parallel to the symbolic story in Judaism, of the
giving of the new and universal law, with the usual symbols
of supernatural power, fire, and wind.

"Speaking with tongues" was a frequent phenomenon in
the early days of the Christian movement. The author of
Acts (Acts was written more than half a century later) seems
here to be attempting to account for the origin of the practice.
As Paul refers to the practice (I Cor. 12-14, and elsewhere) it
appears to have been a series of ecstatic outbreaks or utterances, unintelligible to the outsider, but regarded by the initi-
ated as the authentic voice of the Holy Spirit. Such ecstatic
phenomena are familiar data in the history of many religions.
Under the stress of strong emotion, religious experience breaks
the bounds of normal experience. As Paul saw the matter
(I Cor. 12:28), speaking with tongues belonged with the
whole series of praeter-normal phenomena, prophecy, visions,
healings, etc., which accompanied the emergence of the
Church, showing the enlargement of human power which
accompanies religious revival. Paul also clearly saw that (I
Cor. 13:1), the value of these things depended upon the spiritual and ethical quality evoked by the experience.

The Jerusalem Church

The earliest group of Christians was composed of men and
women who were good Jews in every respect except one.
They kept the *Torah*, and they went to the temple for worship. But they believed that the Messiah, expected by all
good Jews, had actually come in Jesus of Nazareth. To their
contemporaries they seemed an eccentric sect of Judaism.
What made them even more eccentric was their belief that
Jesus had been raised from the dead, that he was present in
spirit in the community of believers, and that soon he would
return to earth in power to rule over the new kingdom.

The little community celebrated its faith and its hope in the breaking of bread and in prayers, held presumably in private homes. The love-feast or *agape* feast was patterned after the Last Supper, and it celebrated Jesus' memory, his presence in the community, and the expectation of his return. The repetition of the Last Supper itself came to be regarded as a re-enactment of the sacrifice of Jesus on the cross. The leadership of the community was in the hands of the apostles, among whom Peter stood out for his qualities of leadership. They also practiced a community of goods, each person selling his possessions and bringing what he earned and placing it in a common treasury from which the needs of all were supplied (Acts 2:41, 45; 4:32). The practice was related to the belief that Jesus would soon return. It was also an expression of the sense of community which the group had discovered, as well as an expression of awareness of the spiritual perils of possessions. But it lent itself to abuses, as the story of Ananias and Sapphira illustrates (Acts 5:1-11). And it may well have contributed to the impoverishment of the Jerusalem church.

From the first, the Jerusalem church was characterized by intense missionary zeal. From Peter's speech at Pentecost onward, they did not cease to tell their story of Jesus' death and resurrection. This they felt to be in direct obedience to Jesus' expressed will. But it brought them into occasional conflict with the government. The civil authorities of Jerusalem seem to have wavered between the toleration recommended by Gamaliel (Acts 5:33-38), and occasionally severe repression (Acts 4:13-22; 5:17-32; 12:1-11). The latter policy raised an issue which was to be of great importance later. Ordered by Jewish authorities to be silent, Peter and John replied, "We must obey God rather than man." (Acts 5:29.) Such a conclusion followed consistently from the Hebrew-Christian belief in God as an absolute sovereign. It produced in Christian conduct a quality of absoluteness which eventually brought the new religion into head-on conflict with the Roman empire.

But another source of conflict was not slow to emerge. Some members of the Christian community began to take liberties with the Jewish law. Differences of opinion are described over the distribution of food between Hellenists and Hebrews, probably between Christians who were Hellenistic Jews, and those who were Palestinian Jews. To meet this situation the office of deacon was devised (Acts 6), the first deacons being representatives of the Hellenistic party who would oversee the financial affairs of the community. It is significant, however, that their leader, Stephen, was soon actively engaged in preaching and teaching. He was soon in trouble with the civil authorities, the charges against him being that he had taught disloyalty to the Law and the temple. On such charges Stephen was lynched (Acts 7:54-58).

The real significance of this episode, however, is that it shows the emergence in the Christian community of a party not completely committed to the Torah. Other similar events followed: Peter, as a result of a vision, violated kosher food laws and baptized a Gentile into the Christian community (Acts 10). A conservative party, insisting upon the law as a necessary part of the new religion, was not slow to arise. Thus emerged a conflict with the Torah which was to engage Christianity for a generation, and which was of great importance for its whole history.

Paul and Gentile Christianity

The rise of Gentile Christianity was associated above all others with the name of Paul of Tarsus. Paul is second in importance only to Jesus in the history of Christianity. The Book of Acts introduces him first as a persecutor of the Christians, holding the coats of those who stoned Stephen (Acts 7:58). He was a native of Tarsus, the capital of Cilicia and a center of Stoic philosophy and Greek mystery-religions. He was a child of devout, Pharisaic parents. His father was a Roman citizen, an honor bestowed on those in the provinces who performed distinguished service to the Empire, for Paul speaks with pride of being "Roman born." Trained in boyhood to be a tentmaker, he was also destined for a rabbinical career, and was sent to Jerusalem to study under Gamaliel. Apparently he arrived in Jerusalem shortly after the Crucifixion. His attitude at this time was that of a pious Jew, deeply devoted to the Torah. He was thus drawn quite naturally to the group who sought to repress Stephen and his followers. He would regard such men as Stephen as renegade Jews who played fast and loose with holy things.

If Paul's words written later to the Romans may be interpreted autobiographically, he was at this time deeply divided within himself. "I do not understand my actions. For I do what I do not want, but I do the very thing I hate . . . I can will what is right but I cannot do it. For I do not the good I want, but the evil I do not want is what I do." (Rom. 7:15; 18-19.) He wrote also of the helplessness of the Torah to clear him of the consciousness of guilt which held him fast and made him impotent to do good. Many of these problems are similar to those which modern depth psychologists deal with. As is so often the case with a man beset by such problems, Paul sought release in persecuting others. He went on a mission to apprehend Christians who had fled north from Jerusalem to Damascus. But as he approached Damascus he underwent an experience which changed his whole life. He was struck down by a light which he believed to be the resurrected Christ, and he heard a voice, which he believed to be that of Jesus, speaking to him, saying "Paul, Paul, why do you persecute me?" As he put it, he "was not disobedient to the heavenly vision." (Acts 26:19.) He was led blind into the city of Damascus where his conversion became known. (For descriptions of the experience, see Acts 9, 22, 26.)

So radical a change in his life required time to understand, so Paul retired to Arabia for meditation. After missionary work in Damascus and a brief trip to Jerusalem for consultation with and approval from Peter and other leaders of the Church, he settled down to some fourteen years of labor in Tarsus and Antioch. There is no direct knowledge of these years, but they were of great importance, for here in these cities where Jew met and mingled with Gentile, Paul's most fundamental convictions were taking shape.

While by no means alone responsible for it, Paul was the most important figure in the spread of the new faith to non-

Jews. From Antioch he, with Barnabas and John Mark as travel companions, set out for Cyprus and then for the cities of southern Asia Minor (Acts 13-14). The journey possibly was experimental in nature; the results were good, so Paul looked farther afield.

But before setting out, he journeyed to Jerusalem to try to settle the dispute between himself and the Jewish party of the Christian church in what is often called the Council of Jerusalem. He met in 49 or 50 A.D. with the leaders and people of the Jerusalem church and worked out a compromise. Paul was to limit his missionary work to Gentiles, and the Jerusalem church to Jews. But the compromise soon proved futile, and Paul cut himself loose entirely from the Jerusalem church with its insistence on the Torah.

Soon after the Council he set out for Europe, traveling overland to Troad, and crossing by sea to Philippi, visiting successively Berea, Thessalonika, and Athens, preaching and organizing churches. He went on to Corinth where he worked for over two years. After a brief trip to Jerusalem, he worked for three years in Ephesus. During these years the break with Judaism became definite. In Paul's mind Christianity was becoming an independent religion—a fulfilment of Judaism which could embrace Jews and Gentiles alike.

Paul made a last journey to Jerusalem to bring relief funds to the famine-stricken Jerusalem church. Here Roman soldiers saved him from lynching at the hands of angry Jews. He was placed under protective custody, first in Jerusalem, and then in Caesarea. Despairing of a fair hearing for his case, he appealed, after two years' imprisonment, to Caesar. Following the voyage to Rome he spent two years of teaching and preaching there. The New Testament does not tell the outcome of his trial, but a well-established tradition has it that Paul perished as a martyr (ca. 60-64 A.D.), perhaps in the Neronian persecution of Christians.

No less important than his travels and activities were his ideas. More than anyone else, Paul influenced the development of Christian thought. Essentially Paul was a Jew who found the Messiah in Jesus. While his thought shows, at many points, the influence of Greek philosophy and Greek mystery cults, the core of it was Jewish. His God remained the God of his fathers, the sovereign will who created and ruled the universe, who had spoken to man through Moses and the prophets, but who now spoke decisively ·and finally in Jesus Christ.

In his own original interpretation of the new revelation, he introduced new ideas. Jesus was the Messiah of Jewish faith, but Paul frequently used the term "Lord" (the Greek term *Kyrios* meant, originally, a social superior who possessed authority). But going beyond these terms Paul came to think of Jesus as a pre-existent, divine being who had taken human form, and in his death struggled victoriously with the cosmic forces of evil, and now reigned with God in heavenly places (Phil. 2:6-11; Rom. 5:5-14, etc.). By a personal trust in Christ, his followers might win a similar victory over sin and death in their own lives (Rom. 6:1-3).

This gospel of the dying and rising savior bore unmistakable likeness to the mystery cults and their tales of the dying and rising God, in union with whom the participant gained salvation. Paul's conception of the Lord's Supper fortified this likeness. But there were all-important differences as well. Paul's story of the dying and rising God was not fiction but history to which many of his auditors could testify. Furthermore, the mystical union with Christ was never divorced from ethical life. If a man was "in Christ," as Paul put it, his life was expected to show the result in moral renewal.

Paul also gave a prime place in his thought to the freedom of the Spirit. Freedom for Paul meant, in the first place, freedom from the burdens of the Torah, which he had found so intolerable. As he reflected upon it, the Law had both a negative and a positive significance. It held out to men a high standard of action without giving them power to do it, and thus it made them feel completely lost. But the Law was the content of God's first covenant with man, and thus the Christian's tutor or schoolmaster to Christ. The coming of Christ, however, abolished the Law, making it irrelevant and unnecessary. Christ was God's new covenant with man, the bringer of the great New Age which Paul believed to be at hand.

Since Christ made the Torah unnecessary, the dietary laws, circumcision, and the ceremonies of Jewish religious year were null and void. Such views brought Paul into violent conflict with Judaism. Much of his work and writing were polemically concerned with just this issue. (See Galatians.) Paul's fundamental idea was that the Christian had in Christ a source of spiritual and moral power and direction which made the Law unnecessary and irrelevant. The positive aspect of freedom was for Paul the inward spirit of Christ (he used the phrases "spirit of Christ," "spirit of God," and "holy spirit" interchangeably) acting in a man's life to heal the breach with God, giving him unity of mind, and power to do what he wished to do.

Paul's conception of ethics followed logically from this conviction. A good life was not, as Judaism held, the condition for faith in God; it was the spontaneous by-product of this new relation to God in Christ. This view of the matter reflected Paul's own experience. He had tried to earn God's favor in his former zealous practice of the Torah, but he had failed. And the new revelation in Christ had meant to him that what man was powerless to earn, God, in his love, freely gave, if man would only receive the gift. The person who has received so great a gift would seek spontaneously and gratefully to live in love with his fellow-man. Moral qualities are, in Paul's phrase, fruits of the Spirit (Gal. 5:22). The content of morality for Paul, as for Christ, was neighbor-love. In Paul's case he frequently characterized this love simply and eloquently by pointing to the figure of Christ.

Johannine Christianity

Paul's interpretation of the new faith was not the only one in the early Christian community. Significant both for its similarities and contrasts with Paul, and important throughout Christian history, was the anonymous fourth Gospel. Traditionally attributed to the disciple John, modern biblical scholarship has concluded that this is virtually impossible. Written around the turn of the second century, the document shows its author as a man familiar with current Greek philosophy. Jesus appears as the Logos or word of God. The term had been familiar to Greek philosophy from Heraclitus onward. But as we have seen in the previous chapter, it had new and distinctive meaning in the thought of Philo of Alexandria, for whom the Logos was the divine intermediary between God and man, active in all creation. In the first century the Logos-concept became widely current in Gnostic philosophies. Such a concept the fourth Gospel appropriates for the interpretation of Jesus. He was, it says, the embodiment of the divine activity in creation. In his life the basic meaning and structure of the universe becomes visible.

In this use of terms two motives are apparent. The author was undoubtedly adapting himself to the language of the people to whom he was speaking. He has often been referred to as a Christian Gnostic. But in this language he sought to say something quite contrary to Gnostic or Greek teaching, something fundamentally Jewish, namely, that the divine Logos had become flesh.

The author placed primary emphasis upon the life of Jesus, and he took dramatic liberties with the facts. His portrait of Jesus differs strikingly from that of the Synoptics. Here Jesus moves through human life as a mysterious divine figure, discoursing upon his unity with the Father and upon the mystical, divine life which men may have in union with him. Eternal life is an ever-recurrent term in this Gospel; it means the immediately perceived quality of life in union with Christ, the divine Logos.

This book had incalculable influence on later writers and thinkers. When, in the fourth and fifth centuries, the Church sought an official credal formula, it turned back to the fourth Gospel and its divine Logos. Throughout Christian history mystics have found the fourth Gospel a fountain of truth.

Varieties of New Testament Religion

There were still other forms of faith and life than those of Paul and John. The Synoptic Gospels, Matthew, Mark, and Luke, were written between 70-90 A.D. They marked a real development in Christian thinking about Jesus. The earliest Christians had concentrated attention upon the death and Resurrection and expected second coming of Christ. But as the years passed and no second coming took place, more and more Christians concerned themselves with his first coming—with the religious significance of Jesus' life and teachings. It was this motive which impelled the writing of the Gospels.

A radically variant type of thought is expressed in the Book of Revelation. While for some the hope of the second coming faded with the years, for others the passage of time only sharpened this hope. This was particularly true in time of trouble. Revelation was probably written during the persecution of Christians by Domitian in 95 A.D. In its bizarre and vivid pages, evils and tragedies are piled upon one another until, at the climax, Jesus appears as the supernatural Messiah. Despite the years, Christ would return to claim his own. Revelation pictured him as a military commander on a white horse, with a flaming sword.

There were still other trends of thought. The Letter to the Hebrews, for example, shows Platonic influence, as it depicts a duality between the world of spirit and the world of flesh. Hebrews was also greatly concerned with bolstering flagging faith. It has been called the first Christian apologetic. Still another type of religion is represented in the Letter of James, with its polemic against faith which does not issue in works, and in its strongly moral emphases.

THE CHRISTIAN CHURCH, 100-350 A.D.

Church and State

By the end of the first century Christianity had found its way through many parts of the Mediterranean world. It was frequently regarded as an illicit movement, which in the following two centuries often had to maintain itself against hostility and persecution. The alternations of scorn and hostility on the part of the empire were important not only as historical incidents but also for their impact upon the Christian church. Many aspects of the Christian movement were determined by the fact that it lived for its first three centuries in a chiefly hostile environment.

For many Romans the Christian movement was only one more of the Oriental superstitions which in recent times had flooded the empire with their bizarre rites and irrational beliefs. The Romans would have been glad to leave it at that, for they were remarkably tolerant of superstitions. But there were ugly rumors about the Christians. Gossip had it that cannibalistic rites took place in Christian worship. Many Christians refused military service and public offices. It was also said that Christians worshiped a king other than Caesar. It was a known fact that they refused to perform the rites of worship of Caesar, respected by everyone in the empire. It was especially for this last charge that Christians were persecuted.

To the Romans the rites of Caesar, consisting of placing a pinch of incense on the altar or performing sacrifices, were thought of as more patriotic than religious. But to the Christians they constituted an idolatrous form of worship, a violation of the First Commandment. To the Christians it seemed that they were being required to affirm that the whole meaning of life was to be found in the empire. They were ready and willing to call the empire good, and to pray for the empire. But they would not call it God. It was for them an issue very similar to that faced in twentieth-century totalitarianism. Here, too, men are forced to find the whole meaning of life in a given social order. Then as now Christian resistance was based squarely upon the foundation of God's transcendence. The fact that God is, in Christian belief, above the world prevents the identification of any human object or force with God. Nowhere has the power of this belief been more clearly manifested than in the struggle of Christianity with the Roman empire, ending in the shattering

of the power of the pagan state, though it must be granted
that Rome fell partly because of its own internal weaknesses.

The history of Christian conflict with Rome shows both
sporadic, local outbreaks and also systematic empire-wide
campaigns to obliterate the new faith. In 64 A.D. Nero burned
Christians in Rome, though this persecution probably did not
extend beyond the capital city. In 95 A.D., under Domitian,
there was further violence. Trajan (98-117 A.D.) is known
for his letter to Pliny, the Younger, informing the latter on
the proper course to take with Christians. To Trajan the
policy must have seemed mild and tolerant. It is presupposed
that Christianity is criminal, but Pliny was told that Christians are not to be hunted out, and if willing to sacrifice are
to be acquitted. Only if they persist are they to be punished.
The emperors who succeeded Trajan alternated between this
policy and more active hostility. It was, however, not until
Decius' edict of 250 A.D. that a universal and systematic persecution was undertaken. Decius' object was to force worship
of the old gods, and to reassert the unity of the empire
against a subversive force. There were many martyrdoms,
but also many who fell away from the Church under pressure.
Christian assemblies were forbidden, churches and cemeteries
confiscated, Church officials executed or banished. The persecution lasted from 250-259, but the Church came out of
the struggle stronger than before.

The battle against the Church was resumed in earnest by
Diocletian who came to the throne in 284 A.D. Viewing with
alarm the close-knit organization of the Church, Diocletian
acted in 303 with a series of edicts which destroyed churches,
confiscated sacred books, and forced all Christians to sacrifice to the emperor. Again there were many martyrs and
many "lapsed." But again persecution not only failed to
stamp out Christianity, but left it stronger than it had been.

Diocletian's retirement was followed in 311 by an edict
of toleration issued by Constantine and Licinius, granting
Christianity the status of *religio licita*—recognized cult. Se-
curing himself in power, Constantine proceeded with a positive pro-Christian policy. He seems to have believed that

the Christian God had given him military victory. Furthermore, he was sufficiently astute as a politician to join what
he could not defeat. He saw the unifying value for his empire of the new religion. In a series of edicts the Christian
church was given a preferred position, and in 319 heathen
sacrifices were forbidden.

The new position of the Church was a milestone in church
history. Christians could now serve their God openly, without the perpetual fear of persecution. But the new situation
was not without peril. In the days when Christianity was an
obscure and a hunted sect, integrity of conviction might be
assumed. But now when it was legal and fashionable to be
a Christian, all the perils of compromise presented themselves. As the matter has frequently been stated, it is a
question whether the Church conquered the empire or the
empire conquered the Church.

Christian Faith and Thought

The beginnings of Christian faith and thought in Paul and
John and others in the New Testament have been described.
The development continued in the period at which we are
looking. Generally speaking, two problems confronted the
Church: (1) What is the nature of Christian faith? (2) What
is its relation to the faiths and philosophies of the world in
which the Church lives? Varying answers were given to both
questions.

One type of answer was given by the *Apologists*. As the
Christian movement spread over the Gentile world it proved
to be attractive to many intellectuals and philosophers. Many
of them were men who had wandered among many philosophies and faiths in search of a satisfying credo. This they
found in Christianity, and they proceeded to set it forth as
an adequate philosophy. Their writings and teachings thus
took the form of an *apologia* (not an apology) for Christianity as true philosophy. Among this group of Christian
thinkers were such men as Municius Felix, Aristides of Athens,
Melito of Sardis, and most famous of all, Justin Martyr.
Justin lived and taught in Rome during the first half of the

second century. Having searched in vain for an adequate philosophy in Stoicism, Pythagoreanism, and Platonism, he found the answer to his question in Christianity. Justin was also a practical man for whom the moral nature of the He-brew-Christian God was attractive. He regarded as grossly immoral the notion that God should be impartial between good and evil. The new life which Christianity gave to its adherents was, according to Justin, a life of love for God and man. Judaism had much of this spirit, but it was encumbered with a vast legalism. Christianity, having simply the life and teachings of Jesus, was superior. Christ, furthermore, had come in fulfilment of Old Testament prophecy.

Justin also made extensive use of the Logos-idea in his interpretation of Christ. The Logos is, in effect, divine rea-son, an aspect of God, through whom all things were created, and through whom men have been guided to think of God and of human righteousness. By the power of the divine Logos, the philosophers of Greece lived and thought. Indeed, "all who have lived rationally are Christians even if thought to be atheists." But while the Logos is thus universal in scope, divine truth is manifested supremely in Jesus Christ who was the Logos incarnate. Christ's coming was thus able to banish ignorance and sin, giving men a new heart and a new mind. Human freedom, responsibility, and reason were thus clearly articulated in Justin's thought. It was Christianity, he believed, which brought these things to their highest expres-sion.

As Christianity grew, its educational needs greatly ex-panded. The most celebrated educational institution of the ancient Church was the catechetical school in Alexandria. Alexandria had long been famous as an intellectual center, celebrated for its library and university. Under Pantaenus, a converted Stoic philosopher, and his successors, Clement (150-220) and Origen (185-251), the Christian catechetical school gained renown. Clement sought to combine Greek intel-lectualism and Christian faith. He taught that there are two sources of truth, Scripture and reason, with one divine Logos inspiring and guiding both. In Christ this Logos is uniquely active, making Christ supreme as the teacher of men's minds and high priest of their souls. But Clement gave the highest place to intellect. In contrast to the simple Christian who by faith might save his soul, the learned or intellectual Christian might have knowledge or *gnosis*. Clement spoke of such a man as the true or Christian Gnostic. Salvation for Clement meant essentially correct knowledge of God. He felt that if a man had this knowledge, good conduct would naturally follow. Moreover, *gnosis* enabled its possessor to seek out allegorical meanings in Scripture, which Clement did with great avidity.

Origen, who was Clement's pupil, took up where his master left off. Similar in his broad intellectual interests to Clement, he possessed greater powers as a philosopher. In his thought, Christianity took on an ontology (theory of being) and cosmology (theory of the world). However, he never ceased to be interested in the Bible and its truth. He found three levels of meaning in it, beginning with the literal meaning, and proceeding to two levels of spiritual meaning, which enabled him allegorically to find in the Bible practically what he wished to find.

Origen also gave the Logos-idea a distinctive development. The problem of how to understand Christ had been a thorny one from the beginning. If God is one, what is Christ's relation to him? If Christ is the Logos, does that not involve ditheism, or two gods? Origen met such problems by teaching that the Logos was begotten of God eternally and not created. Thus both the Logos and God the Father are divine beings embraced in a single transcendent unity. Worship may thus properly be given the Logos. Origen furthermore had much to say about the Holy Spirit as the Logos operating within the Church and within the hearts of believing Christians. Thus, implicit within Origen's theology were such problems as the divinity of Christ and the nature of the Trinity, over which subsequent generations were to struggle and work.

Origen's cosmology divided the world into two parts, material and spiritual, and he frequently seemed to imply

that spirit is good and matter evil, though he never plainly
said so. The spiritual universe, he taught, is populated by
free rational spirits who have immediate and unceasing communion with God. Man on earth is good in so far as he is
spiritual, but he is imprisoned in matter. The salvation
brought by Christ restores man to the realm of spirit. Heaven
for Origen is a place of pure spirit; he rejected the sensuous
paradise of popular belief. Hell is a necessary implication or
conclusion of wrong choice which cuts a man off from God.
But even in Hell another chance is given, and ultimately all
beings may be saved. At last God will be all in all.

A very different type of Christian thought was represented
by Tertullian (150-222). A lawyer by profession, he carried
many of the terms and concepts of the law court into his
exposition of Christian faith. The first church father to write
in Latin rather than Greek, he commanded a terse epi-
grammatic style. Intense and vigorous in spirit, he thought of
Christ as God's great paradox surpassing and confounding
the highest wisdom of man. Such an attitude led Tertullian
to a dim view of the use of reason and philosophy to expound
and defend Christian faith. "What is there in common between Athens and Jerusalem? What between the Academy
and the Church?" he asked scornfully.[2] Nevertheless, Tertullian's own writings borrowed more than he was aware from
the language of Stoic philosophy. In keeping with his other
beliefs, Tertullian had an intense sense of sin, of the punishment which sin carries with it, and of the grace of God which
is conveyed through the sacraments of the Church. Out of his
lawyer's experience, he suggested that just as three persons
(personae) might share title to property (substantia), so in
the godhead there are three persons and one substance. Later
trinitarian formulations followed his lead. He also defined
the relation of Christ to God in a way which anticipated the
later creeds and councils. Tertullian has justly been called
the father of Latin theology.

[2] H. Bettenson, *Documents of the Christian Church* (New York: Oxford
University Press, 1947), p. 10.

Creeds and Heresies

As ideas proliferated, it was necessary for the Church to formulate standards of belief, or creeds. The modern student is likely to deplore the heresy-hunting attitude of the early Church, with its premium upon conformity and orthodoxy, and its anathemas for heretics. To the twentieth-century Western world this looks like an enterprise in totalitarian thought-control. In many respects it was just that. Also it represented a subtle degeneration from a confessional attitude in which the Christian community celebrated its common affirmations, to a dogmatic attitude where it sought to impose some beliefs and proscribe other beliefs. However, certain extenuating factors may be noted. The enterprise of formulating beliefs was important in a hostile world, and if certain lines had not been drawn, Christianity would probably have perished early in its existence. In any event, the historical fact remains that the creeds came out of controversies as attempts to formulate correct and sound belief. If it was to maintain itself as a distinctive faith, Christianity must have a party line.

The first creed of importance is usually known as the *Apostles' Creed*. From the early Church onward, it has carried apostolic authority. Modern students of church history tend to believe that it came out of the struggle of the Church in the second century with Gnosticism. Gnosticism was a widespread intellectual and religious phenomenon of the later Greco-Roman world. Generally speaking, it was based upon a dualistic cosmology in which the world is bifurcated into realms of good spirit and evil matter. In the former a remote, unknowable, transcendent God reigns supreme. But the realm of spirit is populated with hosts of other beings, (angels, principalities, and powers) who mediate between heaven and earth. For Gnostics man is a good spirit imprisoned in an evil body, and his salvation consists in rescuing the former from its prison. This is done by imparting esoteric knowledge (gnosis) which each Gnostic school presumed to possess.

In addition, Gnosticism also involved an ascetic morality. Since the flesh is evil, it must be mortified or suppressed.

Many Gnostics taught and thought quite outside Christianity, but some of them sought to adapt the new religion to their purposes. For the Christian Gnostics, the chief article of belief was that Christ was the divine Logos, the chief intermediary between God and man. But it was unthinkable that the divine, spiritual Word should take on evil, human flesh. Therefore the Gnostics denied the incarnation. The human life of Christ was apparent and not real, they said. Christ had hovered over mortal life, never really entering into it by birth, suffering, and death.

The most famous Gnostic teacher, Marcion of Rome (ca. 160 A.D.), developed other ideas of his own. The God of the Old Testament he found offensively anthropomorphic. Therefore, he argued, this God was not the supreme deity, but a minor godling. True, the Jewish God had created the material world, but that was a very dubious achievement, for along with other Gnostics Marcion believed the material world to be evil. He sought to eliminate from the Bible the Old Testament and the Jewish sections of the New Testament. Only parts of Luke and the letters of Paul remained.

The early Church set itself against Marcion and other Gnostics. Out of this struggle, and reflecting the issues of it, came the Apostles' Creed. The first affirmation, belief in "God the father Almighty, maker of heaven and earth" was directed against Gnostic dualism which denied that the supreme deity had created heaven and earth. By implication, it affirmed a basic biblical tenet, the goodness of creation. The affirmations concerning Jesus' birth, suffering, and death were directed against the Gnostic denial that Jesus had actually become man. The last article of the Creed, belief in the "resurrection of the body and the life everlasting," affirmed the salvation of the whole man and not simply the spirit. It is interesting to note that the early Church was most concerned to affirm the humanity of Christ and the goodness of material things.

Another type of heretical belief that arose in the second century was *Montanism*. Originated by a man named Montanus who before conversion to Christianity had been a priest of Cybele, it was essentially a reaction against compromising and secularizing tendencies in the Church. Montanus declared himself to be the passive instrument through whom, by ecstatic utterance, the Holy Spirit spoke. He proclaimed that the evil world was soon to end and that the heavenly Jerusalem was soon to be set up in his native town of Pepuza in Phrygia. People relieved themselves of possessions and responsibilities and journeyed to Pepuza to await the return of Christ. Montanism taught an ascetic morality. Food and clothing must be kept at a minimum, and abstention from all worldly amusements was declared essential for true Christians. In a time when Christianity had begun to compromise with the world, such moral rigor had great appeal. Also, in an age when formalism had replaced spontaneous conviction, Montanist ideas of the spirit were attractive to men. Even Tertullian was led into this heresy. Montanism stands in church history as an illustration of the kind of apocalyptic, ecstatic, puritanical religion which has recurrently appeared.

While the Church acted against Montanism, it was more concerned with other problems. The central intellectual problem of early Christianity remained the question of the significance of Jesus Christ. Jesus' first followers, as good Jews, thought of him as the Messiah. But when Christianity came to be largely a Gentile movement this term ceased to have meaning. The Pauline term "Lord" (Kyrios), and the Johannine "Word" (Logos) have been described. In the course of time the new religion came to be more deeply involved in Greek philosophy, and the Church undertook to use later Greek philosophy to express its convictions about Jesus Christ. Many interpretations and opinions arose, and the almost endless details of the christological controversies lie beyond our field of inquiry.

Matters came to a climax at the *Council of Nicaea* (325 A.D.), often regarded as the most important council in Chris-

tian history. The issue at stake was the relation of Christ to
God. Arius, a presbyter of the Church at Alexandria, taught
that Christ, while the "first-born of creatures" was subordinate
to God. He was motivated apparently by a strict monotheism. But to others, including the Bishop of Alexandria,
such views seemed inadequate. A champion for the opposition arose in the figure of the Bishop's secretary, Athanasius,
who argued with great fervor that unless Christ were fully
God and fully man, the gospel of the redemption of mankind
was jeopardized. Arius' views were inadequate religiously, he
said, making Christ a sort of *tertium quid* between God and
man.

The Council was called by Constantine, who was more
interested in achieving harmony than in any theological issue.
There were three parties at the Council, though many of
the members had little interest in and little knowledge of the
issues at stake. After rejecting a formulation of Arius, the
council went on to affirm belief: ". . . in one Lord Jesus
Christ, the only begotten son of God, Begotten of the Father
before all worlds, Light of Light, true God of true God,
begotten not made, of one substance with the Father, through
whom all things were made; who for us men and for our
salvation came down from heaven, and was incarnate of the
Holy Spirit and the Virgin Mary, and was made man." [3] Explicitly condemned by the Council were those who say of
Christ, "There was a time when he was not," or that "He
came into existence from what was not," or who say that
the "son of God is of a different substance from the Father."
Thus Christ was declared to be both God and man.

However, the question remained how this might be. How
could one man combine a human and a divine nature? Again
there were many answers which conflicted with each other.
Apollinarius (d. 392) taught that the divine Logos took the
place in Jesus of a human mind. He sought to avoid the
notion of a dual personality, but to others he did less than
justice to the humanity of Jesus. Theodore of Mopsuesta

[3] Quoted from Philip Schaff, *The Creeds of Christendom* (New York:
Harper & Bros., 1877), Vol. II, p. 59.

held that the union of the two natures in Christ was not one of substance but of moral attitude, like the union of husband and wife in marriage. His student, Nestorius, carried the same idea further, denying that Mary was the Mother of God (*theotokos*) since from her was born only the human nature of Christ. Finally, after interminable controversies and anathemas, the Church, at the *Council of Chalcedon* (451 A.D.), declared for the two-nature conception of Christ, ". . . one and the same Christ, Son, Lord, Only-begotten, to be acknowledged in two natures, unconfusedly, unchangeably, indivisibly, unseparably; (the distinctive natures being by no means taken away by the union), but rather the property of each nature being preserved, and concurring in one Person and one Subsistence, not as parted or separated into two persons, but one and the same Son and Only-begotten God, the Word, Lord Jesus Christ; . . ." [4]

Thus the Church formulated its faith. To many present-day people the Creeds speak a language foreign to their experience, and empty of religious meaning. It may be helpful to distinguish between two elements in creed making. The central conviction of the early Church was, as the New Testament expressed it, "Jesus is lord." In its simplest terms, this was the heart of Christian conviction. What the creed makers undertook to do was to state this conviction in the philosophic and theological language of their time, and to guard this central conviction against interpretations which endangered or imperiled it. It is possible to appreciate the convictions of the creed makers without necessarily using all their phrases, or concurring in their anathemas. Their formulations, subject to reinterpretation with changing times, have remained normative for most of the Christian church to the present.

Church Organization and Life

The Church during the New Testament period was extremely informal both in its organization and in its worship.

[4] Quoted from Henry Bettenson, *Documents of the Christian Church* (London: Oxford University Press, 1943), p. 73.

The disciples and Apostles were leaders in worship and in administration. Authority was determined more by inspiration than by appointment. But with the passage of time new problems arose. Resident bishops claiming apostolic succession supplanted traveling evangelists as the bearers of authority. The writings of Ignatius of Antioch at the beginning of the second century emphasize the virtue of subjection to the authority of bishops.

At first, usage varied concerning the authority and also the selection of bishops in different regions. But again there was a development in the direction of greater formalism, and also greater central authority. A clear line came to be drawn between clergy and laity. The ministry became not only a full-time occupation, but a vocation set apart by special ordination and vows. A hierarchy of Church officers emerged; under the bishops were presbyters, deacons, and various other officers. The ablest exponent of episcopal authority was Cyprian, Bishop of Carthage in the middle of the third century. During the persecution of Decius many Christians had "lapsed" from the faith, performing the imperial Roman rites and renouncing Christianity in order to escape torture and death. When the persecution was over, many of these people, full of remorse, wished to return to the Church. In some cases presbyters received them back into the Church without consultation with the bishop. Cyprian soundly rebuked this practice, maintaining that such power could properly be held only by the bishop. As he dealt with this issue he also developed his conception of the episcopate. Each bishop, he declared, acted independently though his decisions were checked by councils of bishops. And more important, each bishop was united with others by the Holy Spirit. "The episcopate is one," Cyprian argued, "each part of which is held by each one for the whole." This principle implied the equality of all bishops. Subjection to the bishop's authority was the mark of a true Church member. And the Church for Cyprian was the ark of salvation. "He can no longer have God for his father who has not the Church for his mother. If anyone could escape who was outside the ark of Noah, then he may also escape who shall be outside the Church." [5] Heretics thus have no part in the Church or in Christian salvation. Cyprian went so far as to declare that even if heretical martyrs died confessing the name of Christ, they were not genuine martyrs and would have no salvation.

Cyprian held that authority resided equally in all bishops, though he did speak of Rome as "the chief church whence episcopal unity takes its source." [6] Others developed the same theme, carrying the primacy of Rome much further. The authority and prestige of the Church at Rome had always been great. According to tradition, it had been founded by Peter, to whom Christ had given the keys of Heaven and Hell. It was at Rome that Paul had died as a martyr. Moreover, Rome was the capital city of the empire, and its Church naturally had great influence. During the second century the Roman church successfully fought the heresy of Marcionism. Irenaeus declared about 185 that "it is a matter of necessity that every church agree with this church." [7] At the end of the second century Victor, Bishop of Rome, excommunicated protesting churches of Asia Minor in a dispute over the proper date for the celebration of Easter. Thus Roman power grew.

During the fifth century this power was greatly increased by men of great ability and initiative. Innocent I (402-417) not only claimed for Rome the custody of apostolic tradition, but also specifically claimed authority over all churches in Christendom. Under Leo I, 440-461, these claims were reinforced. Leo was a man of great ability who in the time of invasion by the Huns and Vandals took the lead in treating with the invaders. He expounded and believed in the primacy of Peter among the Apostles in both faith and government. And he believed that these prerogatives had been passed on to Peter's successors. Leo's successor Gelasius wrote to the

---

[5] On the unity of the Church, *Ante-Nicene Christian Library*, Vol. VIII, p. 382.

[6] *Ibid.*, p. 173.

[7] J. C. Ayer, *A Source Book for Ancient Church History* (New York: Chas. Scribner's Sons, 1913).

Eastern emperor, "there are . . . two by whom principally this world is ruled: the sacred authority of the pontiffs and the royal power." [8] Thus by the middle of the fifth century the Pope's authority, if not uncontested, was widely recognized and greatly respected.

Christian worship and life as well as Church authority developed toward greater formalism. The love feast or common meal of New Testament times was supplanted by a more formal celebration of the Lord's Supper, or *Eucharist*. It was celebrated only by ordained clergymen, and only full members of the Church were permitted to participate. Participation was preceded by a period of catechetical instruction. The elements were increasingly regarded as the body and blood of Christ, which would impart eternal life. Gradually the ideas of Christ's physical presence in the elements of the Eucharist and of the Eucharist as a sacrifice to God prevailed. The celebration of the Eucharist (Eucharist means "thanksgiving") was the central act of worship of early Christianity.

Worship consisted also of Bible reading, prayers, hymns, and a discourse or sermon. It was customarily held on Sunday, but also at other times during the week. The great event of the year was the Easter season. The days leading up to Easter were a time of fasting to commemorate Christ's sufferings, and Easter was, by contrast, a time of rejoicing. Prayers for the dead and the veneration of martyrs became common, and more gradually the veneration of saints became an established feature of Christian worship.

A further important feature of early Christian worship was baptism. Pre-Christian in origin, it had been taken over by the Church. Originally baptism by immersion was the general practice, but gradually it was supplanted by sprinkling, or pouring. It was administered to converts and to young people when they had reached an age which made free choice possible. Again, with the passage of time, infant baptism became common. It was thought to effect a cleansing from

[8] *Ibid.*, p. 531.

original sin and to symbolize the new soul's entrance into the Church as the body of Christ.

Confession of sins was also widely practiced, confession being made at first to the congregation, which granted absolution. Only later was this power vested in the clergy. In line with the increasing formalization of Christian belief and practice, there were lists of sins. Tertullian listed seven, though not precisely the seven which later gained official status as the seven deadly sins. The practice of penance for sins was general by the beginning of the fourth century.

The increasing popularity of Christianity raised serious ethical problems. First-generation converts could be depended upon to maintain a high standard of conduct, especially when their profession of Christian faith was made in a hostile society. But their children and grandchildren, growing up in the Church, tended to take many things for granted. Their zeal flagged. This problem has been discussed in connection with Christianity's change of status under Constantine. Increasingly, worldliness made inroads into the Church, sapping zeal and leading to ethical compromise. As previously noted, the heresy of Montanism was a violent protest against these tendencies.

These trends in Christian practice were reflected in ethical theory. The Sermon on the Mount with its law of love was more and more regarded as a counsel of perfection. Ambrose, fourth-century Bishop of Milan, suggested that Stoic natural law be accepted as a compromise between Gospel perfection and actual human practice. It is difficult to run an empire, or even a diocese, on the basis of the pure ethics of the Sermon on the Mount.

But some men were loath to accept compromise. The spirit of absolute dedication to God was in them, and they scorned the Church's growing worldliness. Out of this spirit, combined with the general *malaise* and other worldliness of the times, came the monastic movement. Many faiths and philosophies of the Greco-Roman world taught asceticism and renunciation of the world. It was thus no great novelty that during the third century individual Christians left the civilized world and fled to solitary existence in the wilderness. St. Anthony (b. 250), often regarded as the originator of Christian monasticism, lived for some years as an ascetic in his own Egyptian village, before taking up a hermit's existence in the desert. Pachomius (b. 292) made a significant change by gathering groups of monastics together into communities. At his death there were ten of his monasteries in Egypt.

During the fourth century monasteries spread, especially in Syria and throughout the East. It was introduced into the West by Athanasius, but Western monasticism was given unity and organization by Benedict of Nursia (b. 480) whose rule is still the norm of Western monasticism. It was notable for its combination in the monastic life of prayer, manual work, and study. Benedict's monks were among the first men in the Western world to affirm the dignity of labor. They were also important for their intellectual pursuits.

SUGGESTIONS FOR FURTHER READING

ARCHER, JOHN C. Faiths Men Live By. New York: The Ronald Press Co., 1934, chap. xv.

AYER, JOSEPH C. A Source Book for Ancient Church History. New York: Chas. Scribner's Sons, 1913.

BETTENSON, HENRY. Documents of the Christian Church. London: Oxford University Press, 1943.

BOUQUET, ARTHUR. Comparative Religion. Harmondsworth, England: Penguin Books, Ltd., 1950, chap. ix.

CLEMEN, CARL. Religions of the World. New York: Harcourt, Brace & Co., Inc., 1931, IV, 3.

CRAIG, CLARENCE T. The Beginnings of Christianity. Nashville: Abingdon-Cokesbury Press, 1943.

DODD, CHARLES H. The Bible Today. New York: The Macmillan Co., 1948.

————. The Apostolic Preaching. New York: Harper & Bros., 1949.

GOGUEL, MAURICE. The Life of Jesus. New York: The Macmillan Co., 1933.

GOODSPEED, EDGAR J. The Story of the New Testament. Chicago: University of Chicago Press, 1916.

GUIGNEBERT, CHARLES. Jesus. London: Kegan Paul, Trench, Trubner & Co., Ltd., 1935.

KNOX, JOHN. The Man Christ Jesus. Chicago: Willett Clark, 1941.

————. Christ the Lord. Chicago: Willett Clark, 1943.

————. The Meaning of Christ. New York: Chas. Scribner's Sons, 1947.

————. Chapters in the Life of Paul. Nashville: Abingdon-Cokesbury Press, 1950.

LATOURETTE, KENNETH S. *A History of the Expansion of Christianity.* New York: The Macmillan Co., 1937-1945.

LEBRETON, JULES, and ZEILLER, J. *The History of Primitive Christianity.* New York: The Macmillan Co., 1942-1947.

———. *The Life and Teachings of Jesus Christ Our Lord.* New York: The Macmillan Co., 1950.

MAJOR, H., MANSON, T., and WRIGHT, C. *The Mission and Message of Jesus.* New York: E. P. Dutton & Co., Inc., 1938.

MANSON, THOMAS (ed.). *A Companion to the Bible.* Edinburgh: T. & T. Clark, 1947.

MINEAR, PAUL. *Eyes of Faith.* Philadelphia: Westminster Press, 1946.

MOORE, GEORGE F. *History of Religions.* New York: Chas. Scribner's Sons, 1946, chaps. v-viii.

MOULD, ELMER. *Essentials of Bible History.* New York: The Ronald Press Co., 1951.

NOCK, ARTHUR D. *St. Paul.* New York: Harper & Bros., 1937.

NOSS, JOHN B. *Man's Religions.* New York: The Macmillan Co., 1949. Chap. xiv.

SCHAFF, PHILIP. *A History of the Christian Church.* New York: Chas. Scribner's Sons, 1882-1910.

THOMAS, GEORGE (ed.). *The Vitality of the Christian Tradition.* New York: Harper & Bros., 1944.

WALKER, WILLISTON. *A History of the Christian Church.* New York: Chas. Scribner's Sons, 1918.

Chapter 8

CATHOLIC CHRISTIAN WAYS OF FAITH AND REASON

THE CATHOLIC CHRISTIAN HERITAGE

WE HAVE now glimpsed the rapid development of Christianity from its humble origins as an obscure sect of Judaism to its establishment, within four remarkable centuries, as the official religion of the Roman Empire, with an elaborate and carefully developed party line culminating in the theological formulations of Nicaea and Chalcedon. Within a century of the establishment of Christianity, however, the Roman Empire was on the brink of collapse as the result of internal decay and corruption and external pressures from northern barbarians. When the Western Empire thus dissolved, the Church was the only significant remaining source of Western unity, and for a thousand years Western European culture was bound up with the beliefs and practices of the Catholic Christian church. In a sense, the life of the Church was European culture during this post-Roman period. It was imperative, therefore, that the Church face the world with unified doctrine, organization, and practice.

Some steps on the road to unified doctrine have already been presented. We have seen, too, how the Church gradually adopted and adapted the imperial political organization for her own purposes, with the logic of events culminating in the recognition of the supremacy of the Bishop of Rome, the imperial city, over all other bishops. This latter claim was to be challenged by the Eastern churches with the division of the Empire into eastern and western segments. And the political, cultural, and theological differences between East and West were to culminate, in the eleventh century, in a formal separation of the Eastern Orthodox churches from the West. For the West, however, the Bishop of Rome was to become the dominant spiritual and, at times, political power. Until the Protestant Reformation in the sixteenth century the Christian Church of the West was the Holy Catholic Church, and the Holy Catholic Church was the Church of Rome. For a thousand years the Catholic Church, centering in Rome, was the principal seedbed of and framework for Western civilization. Furthermore, the Roman Catholic church remains to this day the spiritual home and political-cultural hope of millions of men. Her doctrine, organization, and practice are therefore of paramount interest to any one seeking an understanding of the great ways of faith to which men have turned.

But the Catholic heritage in the broadest sense of the term "catholic" is the heritage of all Christians. Many of the classical Catholic answers to crucial questions relating to the relation of faith to reason and of the Church to society are accepted by many Christians not identified with the Roman Catholic church. The historic Catholic faith of Christendom as a whole must be differentiated from the particular doctrines and practices which distinguish the Church of Rome from other Christian bodies.

Possible Relations of Faith to Reason

We have already seen how Christianity was forced to move from the first simple and unsophisticated affirmations of faith of the earliest Apostles through an increasingly sophisticated expression of that faith to minds trained in Greek philosophy and Eastern religions. The problem of the relation of faith to reason, of religious belief and commitment to objective rational knowledge, was not settled by the brilliant early Christian Fathers, however. There are at least four logically consistent views of the problem, and each of the four has been espoused at times by Christian thinkers.

1. One may hold, for instance, that *faith excludes reason*
—that all that is needed for salvation is unquestioning acceptance of the dogmas of faith, and that independent rational
criticism of these dogmas is a presumptuous and impious assertion of human pride that can lead to no good end. Such a
view was espoused by thinkers like Tertullian, who sneeringly
asked, "What has Jerusalem to do with Athens?" and pointed
to the evil results of Greek philosophizing which, he said, endlessly raises but never answers basic questions. Indeed, said
he, there is merit in accepting the "foolishness of Christ"
precisely because it is philosophically absurd. Actually, Tertullian borrowed more from the Greek thinkers in his own
formulation of Christian faith than he realized. But down
through the centuries there have been men and groups who
have shared Tertullian's basic feeling on the matter of faith
and reason. Though they have not been in harmony with the
official views of the Roman Catholic church, their number
has been legion in all branches of Christendom, and their
most consistent and vocal spokesmen are to be found in the
ranks of the Protestant Fundamentalists.

2. Another possible view of the matter holds that *faith
includes reason*—that any act of faith has manifold implications for the rational structuring of life and the world and thus
implies, consciously or unconsciously, a rational system; and
that, on the other hand, any rational system rests ultimately
upon certain basic presuppositions or affirmations of faith
which are taken for granted. Therefore, completely irrational
faith and completely faithless reason are equally impossible in
the unified life of man, who is both a believing and a knowing
creature. This view received its classic formulation in the
thought of Augustine. It was to be, with variations, the official view of the Church for a thousand years; and it is a view
which today is attracting the attention of an increasingly
large number of thinkers working in many different areas of
human concern.

3. Again, one may hold that *reason excludes faith*—that
the ability objectively to order and reflect upon human and
natural experience is man's crowning glory, and that intellec-

tual integrity forbids the use of faith either as a short-cut to intellectually questionable conclusions or as a super-rational buttressing of reason in regions where knowledge is impossible. Just as Tertullian and his followers are suspicious of reason, so those holding this view are suspicious of faith. Some of them may concede that faith is necessary for the multitudes of intellectually deficient or immature men and women who, up to now, constitute the majority of the world's population and who must have some sort of "crutch" to fall back upon in the buffeting of life. But faith, they would hold, is at best prerational, and science and philosophy achieve increasingly superior and more precise knowledge of that which faith handles more childishly in the picture-thinking of theology and popular devotional practice. This view is a popular one in some intellectual circles today. It was encountered by the Church both in the early years of doctrinal development, as espoused by certain Greek philosophical schools, and later in the Middle Ages, as espoused by a few daring thinkers within and by a fully-developed Jewish-Mohammedan school outside the Church.

4. The reaction of the Church to this late medieval challenge resulted in the formulation of what is today the official Roman Catholic view of the problem: namely, that faith and reason are each autonomous in spheres which can be clearly marked out, but that when each is clearly understood they are seen to supplement and complement each other in a great harmony of faith and knowledge. A great many truths about nature, man, and God many be known through the use of reason alone; other truths revealed by God may be accepted on faith, because they involve areas in which reason is incompetent to judge either affirmatively or negatively. But the truths of correct knowledge never contradict the truths of revelation; and the truths of revelation, properly understood, never contradict the truths of correct knowledge. This view, given its classic formulation by Thomas Aquinas, is basic to contemporary Roman Catholic thinking on the relation of religion to science or of faith to reason in any area. Let us now consider in more detail the development of views 2 and

4 by Augustine and Thomas Aquinas, since they underlie the most widely-held positions of Christian thinkers, Catholic and Protestant, classical and contemporary.

THE AUGUSTINIAN SYNTHESIS

Augustine's monumental synthesis of faith and reason is not the product of mere dispassionate curiosity. Rather it was forged on the hot anvil of personal and social struggle for meaning and stability. In a sense his philosophy was his life, and his life his philosophy. It is fortunate, therefore, that he has left us a moving and perceptive account of his personal development in his *Confessions*, the first great volume in a long tradition of Western autobiographical or existential literature.

Faith and Reason

The theme of the *Confessions* is the search for and discovery of God. But Augustine learned that as one discovers God he must know himself, must discover and wrestle with the fact of human selfhood in all its complexity. Born the son of a Christian mother and a pagan father who was a minor consular official of Tagaste in North Africa, in 354, his early years were marked by an eager and restless quest for intellectual certainty and emotional stability. In the *Confessions* he describes his intellectual pilgrimage from Stoicism to Scepticism to Neoplatonism. And he also describes his more personal struggle with self-will expressed in lust, and with the threat of meaninglessness posed by the fact of death.

At first he rejected Christianity as childish and stupid, but as he came to a more sophisticated understanding of some of its doctrines he felt that it was not incompatible with the Neoplatonic philosophy to which he was attracted. More important, in the Pauline doctrine of "justification by faith" and absolute self-surrender to the love of God revealed in Christ, he found an answer to his personal problem of sin. Thus, under the tutelage of Bishop Ambrose of Milan, he was baptized a Christian in 381. The remainder of his life he gave to the service of the Church, serving for thirty-five years as Bishop of Hippo in North Africa. When he died in 429 the Vandals were at the gates of Hippo, but Augustine, through his tireless scholarship and able statesmanship, had envisioned and described a "City of God" which was to withstand the attack of pagans for a thousand years and more.

Augustine learned from personal experience that all philosophical and theological systems begin with some primal act of faith or personal decision. His own quest for peace of mind through acceptance of supposedly detached and objective philosophical schemes failed. Only when he turned within himself and recognized the essential unity of personality did he make real progress in his search for salvation. Through his personal struggle with irrational desire he learned that in a sense the seeker after truth can find only what he is looking for or is prepared to accept. In order to make sense of the chaos of life it is necessary for a thinker to adopt some viewpoint and then, using such reasoning power as he possesses, see what the world looks like from that viewpoint. In Augustine's experience the whole of life, including his own life-and-death struggle with lust and the meaninglessness of death, came clear only when he consciously took his stand on Christian premises.

Thus the heart of his view of the relation of faith to reason is contained in the phrase "I believe in order to understand." But the logical acumen of his thought reveals that he accepted also the responsibility to understand intelligently in order to believe effectively. Thus there was for him no divorce of faith from reason. Faith implies reason, and reason rests on faith. Someone has put the point of Augustine's insight in the remark that "many people argue about religion, not because they do not understand it, but because they are afraid they do!" Augustine's personal struggle deepened as he became increasingly aware of the radical personal transformation which acceptance of the Christian faith would mean for a man of his temperament. Finally, by his act of self-surrender he felt that he had found that final freedom from whence springs spontaneously creative thought—thought free from anxiety.

The Nature of God

Belief from which true knowledge flows is rooted in faith in God. "Love God, and do (and think) as you please." From the Neoplatonists Augustine learned to think of God as The One, The Unconditioned, The Timeless Perfection which is the source of all being. From the Christians with their Hebrew heritage he learned to think of God also as the creator of all—not to be identified with that which God sustains and explains, as is the case in Neoplatonism and other forms of pantheism or monism. The Hebrews and Christians thought of God as a personal "Lord of history," not merely as the impersonal or superpersonal "ground of being." Indeed, the Christians affirmed that "God, The Father Almighty, Creator of Heaven and Earth," the Eternal One, had entered time and become incarnate as a man, manifesting his power in the sacrificial love of the Christ. In Augustine's thinking these Greek-Jewish-Christian ideas of God merged, as he tempered Jewish personalism with Neoplatonic absolutism, and Neoplatonic absolutism with a Christian sense of history. Expressing the whole in his version of the Christian doctrine of the Trinity, Augustine thought of God as both the creator and the redeemer of men, whose Holy Spirit of truth and power is an ever-present comfort and guide to new truth.

The Problem of Man

Man, like all other creatures, was created *ex nihilo*, "out of nothing." Like other creatures he is finite and hence tends toward that evil-through-ignorance which is the consequence of finitude. But man is made in the *imago dei*, the "image of God." Through his rational capacities he may increase his knowledge and hence his goodness. *Nonhuman* evil, indeed, is what the Neoplatonists said it is, merely negative, the absence of good: decay, disease, disharmony, and the like. But

human evil, *sin*, is something more. Sin is not merely ignorance or absence of good. Sin is positive rebellion of the
creature against the Creator, the refusal of the creature to
accept the limitations of creatureliness. Its chief manifestations are thus selfishness and pride. The archetype of this
rebellion and pride is the disobedient act of Adam; Adam's
rebellion is the original sin, and all men, as sons of Adam, are
infected by original sin. They are "totally depraved" in that
no one of their faculties, such as reason or will, is free from
the taint of anxious egotism, self-justification, and self-defeat.
Knowledge alone is not virtue, and sin is more than ignorance.
Augustine knew the meaning of St. Paul's lament "the good
which I would I do not, but the evil which I would not that
I practice." (Rom. 7:19.) He also knew the answer to St.
Paul's cry "who shall deliver us from the body of this death?"
because he himself had experienced deliverance by the power
of God's love as revealed in the sacrificial love of Christ. This
deliverance had come, however, not as an achievement of
mind or will, but as a divine gift, freely bestowed when in
true repentance he had opened himself to its riches—when he
had surrendered himself to One higher than himself.

Coupling this conviction with belief in God as sovereign
will, the ultimate cause of all that happens, Augustine was led
to affirm what has been called the doctrine of *predestination*.
If men cannot of themselves save themselves; if some are
saved and some are not; and if all that happens is ultimately
traceable to the will of God; then it seems logically to follow
that God must have predestined some men to the joys of salvation and others to the pain of separation from God. If one
accepts Augustine's major premises, there seems no escaping
the logic of the argument. Yet it seems to do violence to the
Christian sense of the dignity of man, which seems to imply
autonomous freedom. Thus, Augustine's formulation of the
Christian doctrine of freedom was vigorously attacked by
many, including the British monk Pelagius. In the controversy which ensued the logic of Augustine's analysis was reaffirmed, but with modifications for practice which meant less
than an unqualified acceptance of the doctrine in subsequent

Catholic thought. In Augustine's own life and action his doctrine did not have the fatalistic and quietistic consequences
which a purely theoretical consideration of it would seem to
indicate. In this respect it is like other doctrines of apparent
determinism which lead their followers to ever more active
freedom. It was to be revived in its early Augustinian form
by John Calvin in the Protestant Reformation.

As for the ethical consequences of a doctrine which seems
to ascribe cruel and arbitrary behavior to a God who mysteri-
ously condemns helpless men to everlasting torment while
plucking some from the fire for reasons known only to himself, Augustine pointed out, as Calvin was to point out later,
that for the Christian God love is a blend of mercy and justice
and not mere sentimentality. If God were only just, no man
could be saved, because serious appraisal of motive and conduct measured in the light of Christ's perfection can only
reveal the unworthiness of any man to be saved. That God
does save some is an expression of his mercy, and that he condemns some is an expression of his justice. The apparent
ambiguity need concern no one who does not, in his pride,
mistake himself for God.

Salvation, however, does not come to man in a vacuum;
the "good news" is entrusted to and proclaimed by a community, a fellowship—the Christian church. And he who experiences Christian grace becomes a member of that fellowship,
with the attendant duties and privileges of membership. Supposedly, his life, like that of the fellowship, will reflect that
charity and peace which are the fruits of self-surrender to a
God of love. At the same time he and the Church must live
in the world, which is made up of all sorts and conditions of
men. As a statesman of the Church, Augustine was practically concerned with this problem of the nature of the Church
and its witness to the world, and in reflecting upon it he produced one of the great philosophies of history, *The City of
God*. When we turn to the development of Roman Catholic
theories of Church and society we shall see that Augustine's
social philosophy reflects the basic premises of his personal
philosophy.

The Application and Breakdown of the Augustinian Synthesis

Popular Augustinianism

The thousand years of Augustinianism in the West were characterized by an intellectual falling away from the rich and sophisticated philosophical and theological techniques of Augustine himself. Soon after his time, the political and social environment for careful inquiry was destroyed with the destruction of the Roman Empire, and men were concerned with more immediate and mundane problems of survival. With Rome went the heart of Greco-Roman culture, and as the center of Western civilization shifted gradually westward and northward, such scholars as the times produced turned more and more to a simple, dogmatic, and authoritarian type of faith. They understood only the outlines of the Augustinian vision of the drama of salvation, and in the so-called Dark and early Middle Ages the drama was presented to common folk and scholars alike in a crude but comprehensible simplicity. The two *foci* of interest, as for Augustine, were God and the human soul. Nature entered the picture only as the backdrop for the drama. It is not true to say that men in this period were not interested in nature and natural processes. But they viewed those processes and interpreted them from the vantage point of presuppositions quite different from those held in the ancient and modern worlds. For them "this world" and "this life" were, at most, preludes to the world to come and the life to come. What mattered was not so much the material comforts of living here and now, as the promise of spiritual comforts hereafter which awaited men who duly cared for the destiny of their souls. Such care entailed the performance of those duties which the Church prescribed, the acccptance of such beliefs as she underwrote, and the carrying out of those devotional practices which she provided.

Now the Augustinian approach to the problem of faith and reason was in part responsible for this development, which was otherwise an almost inevitable consequence of the social and cultural difficulties of the time. Augustine had shown that all fruitful thinking must begin with some things taken for granted, and his own thinking was most fruitful after he had accepted the Christian faith. It was thus suggested that inquiry conducted outside the framework of the Christian faith is futile if not dangerous, and that the course of wisdom lies in turning at once to the revealed certainties of Christian dogma, and limiting one's reasoning exercises to the deduction of implications of these dogmas for problems of everyday living and thinking. But more and more thinkers of the post-Augustinian period took more and more dogmas for granted and applied less and less critical thought to the statement and implementation of these dogmas. Thus a philosophically subtle authoritarianism was replaced by a crude and dogmatic theological authoritarianism. Eventually such intellectual activity as occurred in Western philosophical and theological circles was limited to the search for and citing of various authorities for those dogmas which individual thinkers wished to take for granted in their deductive demonstrations. It was felt that all truth needed for the most important thing in life —salvation—had already been revealed. Wisdom was to be discovered in the past, and present activity should be limited to the proper understanding of past revelation.

Anselm

By the eleventh century, however, new currents of independent inquiry were beginning to flow through medieval speculation. For centuries men had placed chief emphasis on the belief which produces proper understanding. Now scholars appeared who suggested that a new emphasis should be placed on the understanding which supposedly follows correct belief. Indeed, it was such a thinker, Anselm, Archbishop of Canterbury in the eleventh century, who rephrased Augustine's *credimus ut cognoscamus* to read *credo ut intelligam*— "I believe that I may *know*." [1] Anselm accepted in principle

[1] Anselm, *Proslogion, I*, trans. by S. N. Deane (Chicago: The Open Court Publishing Co., 1910).

most of the common core of Christian belief, but he felt that it was a misuse of God-given reason, the image of God in man, to insist on mere blind faith for most of the issues with which Christians were concerned. Not only must theologians use reason to deduce for believers the consequences of their belief, but they must also use reason to prove to unbelievers the reasonableness of faith. Anselm was convinced that the latter is possible. The most significant example of his thought in this connection is his statement of the so-called ontological proof of the existence of God, a proof which, he was convinced, would show the most intransigent unbelievers the logical inconsistency of their doubt.

The basis for the proof is found in Augustine's emphasis upon the necessity of grounding thought and reality in some common meeting-place which is the source of both—the God of Neoplatonism. All deductive rational thought assumes one basic dogma, namely that the order of knowing and the order of being are one. This presupposition is not something which can be proved by the reasoning which assumes it. Thus Augustine, in his quest for certainty, had been thrown back through consistent doubt, first upon himself, whose existence as a doubter he could not doubt, and then upon a starting-point for doubt and for all other rational inquiry. The assumption of such a starting-point expresses the conviction that the order of thinking and the order of being are one— that the self-consistent truths of mathematics, for instance, are true of the real world and not merely of a mathematical logic-world.

Anselm states the ontological argument in this fashion:

> Even the fool is convinced that there is something, at any rate in the understanding, than which nothing greater can be conceived, for when he hears this he understands it, and whatever is understood is in the understanding. And certainly that than which a greater cannot be conceived cannot exist in the understanding alone. For if it be in the understanding alone, it is possible to conceive it as existing in reality, which is greater. If therefore that than which a greater cannot be conceived is in the understanding alone, that very thing than which a greater

cannot be conceived is one than which a greater *can* be conceived. But this assuredly cannot be. Without any doubt therefore there exists something both in the understanding and in
reality than which a greater cannot be conceived.[2]

Now many readers will respond to a statement of the ontological argument with the bewildered impression that some
sort of logical legerdemain has been practiced upon them.
However, when properly understood it may be recognized as
one of the most important religious and philosophic statements of the Western world. Let us see if analysis will not
clarify it. First of all, let us recognize, as Anselm so clearly
did, that it is not so much proof, in the strict logical sense, as
it is a clear and logical formulation of faith. Proof undertakes to move the mind from a state of uncertainty or doubt
through a chain of logical implications to assent of certain
conclusions; and it is a fact that very many capable and honest
minds are not moved to certain belief by the ontological argument. The significance of Anselm's argument lies in its unusually perceptive formulation of certain assumptions or presuppositions.

Embedded in Anselm's compressed phrases are two sets of
assumptions. (1) First, the assumption that the order of thinking and the order of being are one. As we have seen, this
assumption that reality has a rational structure apprehensible
and expressible by the human mind has underlain Western
thought from the earliest days of Greek philosophy onward.
This ontological principle, as it is sometimes called, assumed
great importance in such later philosophers as Spinoza and
Hegel. (2) But there is a further assumption in Anselm's reference to that being "greater than which nothing can be conceived." The term "God" has meant widely different things
in human history. These words of Anselm's represent his
attempt to state in the language of scholastic philosophy the
transcendent God of biblical and Christian tradition. Greek
thought had generally conceived of God or gods as entities
within the structure of reality, but the biblical Hebrews para-

[2] Anselm, *op. cit.*, II.

22

doxically asserted that God is both within and above the world. Anselm's proof clearly formulated, for the first time, belief in a transcendent, absolute God,—a God who is, in the terms of our definition of religion, ultimate, or may legitimately claim from men a concern which is ultimate or absolute. This sense of the absolute, originating in the Bible and here entering Western philosophy, has haunted the mind of Western man ever since.

Abelard

By suggesting that reason has its autonomous work to do in the defense of faith, Anselm opened the door to more daring and radical speculations. The man who epitomizes this rebirth of critical thought is Abelard, who lived in the latter part of the eleventh and early part of the twelfth centuries. It appears to have been Abelard's intention to make the Christian faith even more intelligible to doubting minds by showing that it could withstand all the criticisms of independent reason and purify itself of irrational extremes in apologetic. It is the Christian's duty, he felt, to be as intelligent in the understanding and defense of his faith as he can be. In effect, he reversed Anselm's dictum to read *intelligo ut credam*—"I know in order to believe." For "he that believes quickly is light-minded," said Abelard, and "it is by doubting that we come to inquiry, by inquiry we discover truth." Actually Abelard was recovering the critical spirit of Augustine in such statements, but to men of his age who had lost sight of that side of the Bishop of Hippo, Abelard's remarks seemed rank heresy. Their suspicions were confirmed when he published his famous *Sic et Non*, a manual of dialectic in which he selects a number of dogmas commonly accepted on authority and then quotes equally revered authorities for (*sic*) and against (*non*) the common interpretations. Though he never subjected the basic authorities of Scripture and Church to such treatment, he was much freer in his understanding of them than were most of his contemporaries. As a result of opposition led by Bernard of Clairvaux, he was condemned as a heretic, though the sentence was not carried out; rather he spent his last years quietly at the famous monastery of Cluny. The critical spirit of Abelard could not be silenced, however, and partly as a result of his work, increasingly large numbers of younger theologians began to examine anew the complacent authoritarianism of their day.

The Mystics

Another type of Christian thinking which appeared again and again in the development of Catholic thought also helped to challenge the increasingly rigid and sterile dogmatism of the pseudo-Augustinian thinkers, or Schoolmen as they came to be called. This type is Christian *mysticism*, traces of which are found in the thought of Augustine himself. The mystics claimed direct knowledge and experience of God, leading to perfect communion or even actual union with him. In this claim they cut through the cumbersome deductive arguments of the Schoolmen by which medieval believers were instructed in religious knowledge. Some of the mystics were not interested in philosophizing about God. Others were excellent philosophers and careful thinkers who subordinated reason to intuition and claimed to gain from the latter a fresh and free treatment of the former.

In the fifth century a collection of mystical-theological treatises ascribed to Dionysius The Areopagite appeared. These, along with mystical passages in Augustine and others, were appealed to by mystics in various generations. The author of the Pseudo-Dionysian treatises had said that there are three forms of knowledge of God: linear, spiral, and circular. Linear knowledge moves from the observation of particular elements of creation to an understanding of the creator. Spiral knowledge moves through question-and-answer speculations to knowledge of the goal of speculation. But circular knowledge, which is the highest, comes when the thinker retires within himself, letting his thoughts go out to God and return to himself, gradually drawing him closer and closer to a direct intuitive union with deity. John Scotus Eriguena, an Irish thinker of the ninth century, though not a mystic, appealed to Dionysius' *negative theology*, which held that man's mind ascends to God by negating all the finite or limiting conditions of man's life. Like mystics in other traditions, the Christian mystics declared that the object of their deepest experience is ineffable—indescribable in any human language. Yet the Schoolmen had developed more and more complex and rigid descriptions of the Christian God. Eriguena, appealing as Abelard had to the obligation to use reason to its limits, tried to show that a rational theology also points to a deity whose ultimate nature can be described only symbolically, and that there should therefore be great flexibility in such descriptions as dogmatic theology puts forth.

Bernard of Clairvaux, Abelard's opponent, wrote extensively of the need for warm and intimate communion of the total person with God—a communion going beyond the reaches of both faith and reason, as these were ordinarily employed in theological discussions. The mystical movement reached its climax, however, in the work of the German Meister Eckhart in the late thirteenth and early fourteenth centuries. Eckhart reaffirmed Dionysius' statement of negative theology, but went beyond Abelard in declaring that the goal of the Christian life is not merely the deepest communion of man with God, but the actual *union* of man and God, in the "rebirth of Christ within the soul." The work of Christ is to unite man and God, which means essentially elevating man to the status of deity. Because of his extreme position, much of Eckhart's work was condemned, but it remained popular, especially in Germany and northern Europe, and influenced such documents as the *Theologia Germanica* which appeared in the fourteenth century. This document, in turn, influenced the thinking of the reformer, Martin Luther, and also helped prepare the way for further orthodox Catholic manuals of devotion like the fifteenth-century *Imitation of Christ.*

Averroes

Even more disturbing to the deductive dogmatic theological enterprise of the Schoolmen was the contact of western European culture with the Jewish-Mohammedan culture of

North Africa and southern Spain in the twelfth and thirteenth centuries, a contact dramatized in such undertakings as the Crusades. The theological consequences of the Crusades sprang from the fact that in this Jewish-Mohammedan culture were found a non-Christian philosophy and theology which, by methods more cogent than the Schoolmen had developed, could establish points of doctrine at variance with those which Christian thinkers had long taken for granted. This intellectual superiority of the Mohammedans, reflected also in their medical schools and other scientific achievements, was due in part to their having preserved and incorporated in their thinking the scientific works of Aristotle. Aristotle was indeed known to the West. But only those parts of Aristotle which were closest to deductive Platonism, such as his logic, had been of much effect in molding typical Western thinking. Gradually those parts of his system which deal in an inductive fashion with matters of scientific interest had been lost to the West, and Plato, through Neoplatonic Augustinianism, had been the West's philosophical master. Aristotle's scientific works, however, had been preserved in Arabic and had furnished the basis for remarkable intellectual activity within the more highly developed Arabian cultural centers. In the twelfth century this culture produced a theological spokesman whose work, when known in western Europe, was profoundly to disturb the thinking of Christian theologians. This scholar was Ibn Rochd, better known in the West by the Latinized form of his name, *Averroes*.

Averroes, like Abelard in the West, insisted that reason is God's chief gift to man, and he attacked Mohammedan theologians for relying too complacently on faith in the development of the Mohammedan scholasticism. Faith, expressed in the picture-thinking of theology, may be needed by the masses who cannot follow more rigorous philosophical analyses, but those who are capable of critical rational thought must not fall back too easily upon it. Rather they must push reason as far as it will go, no matter how difficult the enterprise may be. Indeed, said Averroes, most of the truths which the masses must take on faith can be rationally demonstrated by those capable of following the demonstrations. Thus the existence of God and the freedom and immortality of the soul can be proved by reason alone to be rational implications of Aristotelian science. The God so proved is not a personal God, however, and the immortality is not a personal immortality. But this simply means that those who claim these things are either going beyond or flying in the face of reason. Furthermore, the idea of a creator God who creates a world with a beginning and end in time is also irrational. Reason points to the eternity of nature.

Here, then, was a rationally cogent system which, on the one hand, purported to prove by reason alone truths which most Western theologians had considered matters of faith; and which, on the other hand, used that same rational technique to prove the irrationality of some Western interpretations of those truths. Furthermore, this philosophical system was rooted in a scientific Aristotelianism which seemed at certain basic points to challenge the major premises of that Platonic philosophy which the West had long taken for granted. It is understandable, then, that most Christian thinkers viewed the introduction of such ideas into the West with alarm, and formally condemned Aristotelian philosophy as a framework for understanding the scientific problems of nature to which Western men were already redirecting their attention. But the final answer of the Church was to absorb Aristotelianism in an impressive new philosophical and theological synthesis which, in its major emphases, was to dominate Catholic thought to the present day. The great architect of this synthesis was Thomas Aquinas.

THE THOMISTIC SYNTHESIS

Thomas was born in 1225, the son of a noble family of Aquino in Italy. He received his early education in the Benedictine school on Monte Cassino, but later joined the Dominican order of mendicant teachers and preachers. His master was Albertus Magnus, who had translated many of Aristotle's scientific works into Latin and had begun the development of a new Christian synthesis. In a relatively brief lifetime of forty-nine years Thomas carried to completion the work of his teacher, producing a monumental body of writings covering nearly every aspect of Christian faith and practice. Though his work was suspect at first, it was eventually recognized as normative for subsequent Catholic thought. His two major works are the *Summa Contra Gentiles,* a classic of *natural* theology, showing the extent to which religious truths may be known through reason alone; and the *Summa Theologiae,* a classic of *dogmatic* theology, showing the implications of basic Christian dogma for the whole range of life. Since the views presented by Thomas in these works form the basis for contemporary Catholic thought on most of the matters treated in them, we shall here summarize a few of the major arguments, not precisely in the form in which they appear in the original, but in the form in which they typically appear in contemporary discussion.

Faith and Reason

On the basic issue of the relation of faith to reason, Thomas and later Catholics agree with the Aristotelian Mohammedan scholars, and with many thinkers within previous Christian tradition, in holding that many important truths about nature, man, and God may be known through the use of reason alone. These truths are open to anyone capable of following the canons of correct logic in the analysis of scientifically observable phenomena, whether the observer be a Christian or not. Reason, in other words, has its own autonomous sphere in the knowledge of those things which concern men most deeply. Indeed, for the ordinary affairs of life—for scientific investigation, political wisdom, and the like—there is no need to appeal to revelation; God has made certain universal truths plainly apparent to all rational creatures. There are areas of the deepest human concern, however, which are beyond the scope of scientific reason as such. In these areas reason must remain simply agnostic, without knowledge, unless it is further illuminated by the light of revelation. It is unreasonable to suppose, however, that the God who enables man to know so much about himself and his world through reason should present man with revealed truths which are irrational or contrary to the truths established by reason alone. Catholic thinkers maintain that the basic truths of Christian dogma are not irrational. They may be suprarational, going beyond reason, but they are not and cannot be contradictory to reason. Indeed, reason itself points to the need for truths beyond reason, as we shall note later. But the truths of reason and the truths of revelation are harmoniously supplementary and complementary, forming a unified whole of that knowledge which man needs for his salvation. Some things men may know, other things they may believe. The exact content of knowledge and belief will vary with individual capacities, and some things may be matters of knowledge for technically trained theologians which remain matters of belief for the average layman. In any case, men should not claim to know that which they actually believe; nor should they rest content with belief in areas where knowledge is possible. Knowledge needs belief and belief needs knowledge, but the distinction between the two must be kept clear if truth is not to be distorted.

What, then, are some of the things which may be known through reason alone? They include the knowledge that God exists, and considerable insight into his nature; the knowledge that man is a free, rational, and immortal creature; and extensive knowledge of the ways in which man may most fruitfully live his life both here and now and in preparation for a higher life beyond.

Proofs of the Existence of God

At least half a dozen major arguments may be used to show that reason points to the existence of God. The ontological argument is not one of these, however, because Aquinas, following Aristotle, was convinced that proving the logical necessity of an idea does not prove the existence of a being corresponding to that idea. All knowledge properly so-called must begin with the observation of concrete sense-data, the stuff of existence, and only that existence which is logically

implied in the analysis of scientifically observable phenomena
may rightfully claim rational validation.

FROM MOTION TO AN UNMOVED MOVER. Consider the fact
of motion in the world. Motion as such is a mystery; it does
not explain itself. Science may describe the fact of motion in
various theories and laws of motion, but these theories and
laws point beyond themselves for their own final explanation.
In Aquinas' day motion was conceived, after Aristotle, as
transition—a process of coming-from and going-to—transition
from a state of mere possibility or potentiality to a state of
actual attainment. That which initiates motion in an otherwise static world, it was thought, is the drive or urge of something static to make the transition from a lower to a higher
state, from a state of relative disharmony and lack of equilibrium to a state of relatively more harmony and equilibrium.
Motion, then, was explained as the transition from lower to
higher as a result of the attraction of the higher for the lower.
Each created process and thing has its end or place in the
scheme of things; the drive toward these ends constitutes
motion. However, though any single motion may be thus
explained in terms of transition toward an end, and various
lower transitions may be explained in terms of higher transitions, still how is the fact that there is motion at all—that
there is a universal process of transition and end-seeking—to
be accounted for? Only in terms of a cosmic "unmoved
mover," Aristotle had said, and Aquinas agreed. There must
be, somewhere, something like a divine magnet, not itself in
motion, which is the final source of all motion. And it is
this notion of a final source, among other things, which men
have had in mind when they have used the word "God."

But the reader may object that science no longer conceives
of motion as transition; indeed, since Newton it is not motion
but rest which, if anything, needs to be explained. The contemporary Thomistic thinker would reply that such changes
in scientific theory do not alter the basic problem. Changes
in the description of motion do not lessen the necessity for
a metaphysical ground for the mystery of the fact of motion

as such. It should be made clear, in other words, that metaphysical proofs of the existence of God are not offered as scientific theories. The scientist in his day-to-day activities need have no recourse to the metaphysical foundations of his enterprise—indeed, he may not have even reflected upon them at all and may be unaware of and unconcerned about them. But if the scientist is a whole man and does not simply close his eyes to problems which cannot be handled by scientific techniques alone, or if science is fruitfully to exist within a rationally ordered system of knowledge, such metaphysical questions as that of the final or trans-scientific significance of such facts as motion cannot be ignored.

This suggests that we might consider more critically the whole scientific notion of causality as such. Aristotle said that when we ask for the cause of anything we are really asking four questions: (a) "From what" is it; (b) "Of what" is it; (c) How is it defined; and (d) "For what" is it. The answers to the four questions reveal in turn the (a) Efficient, (b) Material, (c) Formal, and (d) Final causes of the phenomenon in question. Thus, fully to answer the question What is (the total cause of) a book? we say: (a) a book is what it is because certain operations in the past made it what it is; (b) a book is what it is because it is made of certain materials—paper, ink, cloth, etc., put together in a special way in those previous operations; (c) a book is what it is because it has a certain definition—that is, it can be placed in a system of linguistic symbols having a logical structure of its own; and (d) a book is something to be read.

Generally speaking, contemporary science would limit the word "cause" to (a) and (c) above, and would reduce (b) and (d) to terms of (a) and (c). To give a scientific account of a book would be to describe accurately the operations which caused it to come into existence, and then to define it finally in terms of the elements of which it is made, expressing these in mathematical symbols. That is to say, the "of what" is reduced to mathematical definition of chemical elements and physical properties, and the "for what" is either ignored as being of no concern to science or reduced to the "from what" and "what" (definition) explanations. When the Thomistic thinker uses the word "cause," however, he means it in its full Aristotelian sense. And he would maintain that science itself really needs the full sense in order to understand finally the partial senses with which it operates day by day. Not only specific instances of the law of causality, but also the significance of the fact that we do live in a causal world need to be considered.

FROM CAUSALITY TO A FIRST CAUSE. The Catholic thinker would maintain that, though it may be enough for scientific purposes to explain a given phenomenon in terms of that sequence of events which immediately preceded its appearance and which controlled laboratory experiment shows ordinarily to precede or produce the phenomenon in question, it is not enough for all purposes to stop with this sort of explanation. Such explanation simply points to the fact of causality-as-ordered-sequence. But the fact of causality-as-ordered-sequence itself points to a First Cause. In simplest terms this is the familiar chicken-and-egg argument. Chickens may be explained in terms of eggs, and eggs in terms of previous chickens, but somewhere this regress must stop. A particular cause may be explained as the effect of a preceding cause, and the preceding cause may be explained as the effect of a still prior cause, but somewhere in the chain there must be an Uncaused Cause which explains the existence of a causal chain as such. Such an Uncaused Cause, again, is what men have had in mind when they used the word "God."

FROM CONTINGENCY TO A NECESSARY BEING. Nothing exists necessarily in the world. That is to say, anything we know came into existence and either has passed out of existence or is in the process of passing out of existence. Everything in the world, in other words, is in a state of becoming and exists contingently. This obvious fact need not disturb us in our attempt to explain various contingent existences in terms of other contingent existences—various instances of process or becoming in terms of other instances of process or becoming. But we must recognize the fact that it is impossible that all that *is* should exist contingently; if this were true then there could conceivably have been a time when nothing *was*. And this is impossible, because out of nothing, nothing comes. This means, then, that something must always have existed, not contingently—coming into being and passing away—but necessarily, uncreated and eternal. Once again, it is such an eternal necessary being which men have had in mind when they used the word "God."

FROM DEGREES OF PERFECTION TO A PERFECT BEING. Consider now a similar fact about the ordinary world of observable things and events: nothing in it is truly perfect. Everything we know is imperfect to some degree. Except in moments of poetic enthusiasm, we confess that we have never known a perfect tree, a perfect horse, a perfect man or woman, a perfect picture, a perfectly straight line. But how do we know this? How do we know that the stuff of the world is a mixture of degrees of perfection unless these imperfections are also known to point beyond themselves to perfection? How can imperfect being be known to be imperfect unless perfect being is also posited? Now on the surface this would seem to be a form of the ontological argument—an argument which has supposedly been rejected. But the followers of Aquinas point out that they are not arguing from the necessity of the idea of a perfect being to the existence of such a being. Rather they are arguing from the concrete human experience of degrees of perfection in the sensory world to the necessity of positing the existence of a perfect being to make such experience intelligible. And such a perfect being is what men have meant by the word "God."

FROM ORDER TO A COSMIC DESIGNER. Again, consider the facts of order, purpose, and design in the world—the pervasiveness of "for-what" or final causality; the fact that things are made for ends and that the ends fit together in an orderly, purposeful whole. Continued scientific discovery, properly understood, continuously deepens rather than dissipates man's sense of awe in the face of the intricate and meticulous patterns of order which are discovered in all reality from submolecular structures to astronomical galaxies. Everywhere there is symmetry and pattern, a delicate balancing of patterns-within-patterns through the whole range of inorganic and organic nature. What are we to make of this awesome fact of order in the world? Shall we attribute it to chance? Consider what happens in human experience, which is the beginning and end of all inquiry, when we leave things to chance. Is it not more reasonable to assume that, just as in human experience, order is the result of purpose, so in the cosmic whole, order is the result of cosmic purpose? Suppose one agrees with certain contemporary nontheists that "purpose" is a term which is intelligible only as applied to human experience, and that human beings are the only "purposers" we know. Still, is it more reasonable to assume then that out of a purposeless world purposing beings emerged to read purpose into the world; or to assume that the existence of purposing beings in the world implies a purposive ground of things?

Applying the question to the facts of biological experience supposedly explained by the Darwinian theory of the survival of the fittest, the contemporary Thomist points out that, though the theory gives a limited explanation satisfactory in most respects for biological investigation, it does not answer the basic question "Why do the fit arrive?"—why is the world such that the survival of the fittest seems to be a rule of life? What is the significance of the arrival of the fit, and for what purpose have they arrived? In this connection, also, the theologian may point to puzzling gaps in the application of the theory of the survival of the fittest as such. For instance, how does the theory account for the fact that in the evolution of certain species there are in-between stages in which the organism is not fitted to compete either in its old environment, because of the loss of old appendages and the appearance of rudiments of new ones which will benefit it later, or in a potential new environment, because the new adaptive mechanisms have not fully developed and remnants of old ones are encumbrances? Do not these transitional stages point beyond mere competitive survival for their final explanation?

Is there not a more complex purpose at work? And is not such a cosmic purpose, or the cosmic purposer which it implies, the sort of thing men have meant by the word "God?"

FROM MORAL LAW TO A LAWGIVER. A final argument which was to receive special emphasis and development in the later work of the Protestant philosopher Kant, but which is frequently used by Catholic theologians also, begins with the phenomena of *value*-experience as contrasted with the phenomena of *fact*-experience. Men universally experience things and events not only in terms of what they *are*, but also in terms of what they *ought* to be. And despite the attempts of many modern philosophers to do so, it does not seem possible finally to derive "ought" from "is." That is to say, when we have exhaustively and accurately described the way men actually do behave, and have behaved in various cultures at various times, we have not by such description answered the question of how they ought to behave in any culture at any time. In all human experience men confront not only accomplished facts but also ideal possibilities. And this realm of ideals is not finally reducible to and cannot finally be explained in terms of the world of existing fact. As human experience develops, men discover more and more about moral and aesthetic laws as well as more and more about truth-laws, or laws of nature, which are statistical averages of operations in the world of facts. Moral law is as objective as is what is ordinarily called natural law. (Catholic social thinkers also use the term "natural law" for moral law as it affects society.) Men may defy moral law and deny its existence, to be sure, but they may also defy natural law and even at times deny its existence, and the results in both instances are equally ruinous. In any case, universal obedience to a law is not the condition on which its validity rests. But moral law must finally be accounted for, just as natural law, expressed in the various forms of causality, must be accounted for. The same canons of reason which point to an uncaused cause of motion, a First Cause of efficient causality, a necessary being, a perfect being, and a cosmic purposer, thus point also to the existence of a cosmic source of moral law and value. And when men have used the word "God" they have meant also a divine lawgiver and judge—the source of righteousness and beauty as well as the source of truth.

The Nature of God as Known Through Reason

The reflective reader has perhaps wondered by now whether the proofs outlined above, if they are accepted, point to the existence of one God, or to six different concepts of deity emerging from the analysis of six kinds of mystery in human experience. The Catholic theologian would maintain that the question is answered in the fourth of the considerations outlined above. Here it was shown that an analysis of human experience of degrees of perfection points to the existence of a perfect being. Now a perfect being is perfect in goodness, power, truth, and all other forms of perfection. But is not a being perfect in power just what the analyses of the various forms of causality in nature have pointed to? A being perfect in power would be, in relation to the forces of nature, First Cause, Prime Mover, Cosmic Orderer, and so forth. These are only different ways in which perfect power is known. A perfect being would also exist necessarily rather than contingently. And a being perfect in goodness would be the source of moral law, just as a being perfect in beauty would be the source of all aesthetic norms. Furthermore, a perfect being would, by definition, be one, not many—simple, not divisible, as the older theologians put it. That which is divided or divisible is thereby subject to decay, dissolution, and change. A perfect being is by definition eternal, unchanging, and hence unitary. Thus it appears that the six proofs are indeed analyses of six different aspects of the mystery which underlies and transcends human experience, but the perfection to which they all point is the unitary answer to the total mystery. With the thought of such a perfect being analysis may and should find its rational end.

But is not such a being as described above so far beyond human comprehension as to be ineffable or indescribable, as the mystics have claimed? Granted that experience points beyond itself to mystery, can anything more be said than that such mystery exists? Here the Catholic theologian agrees with the major contention of the "negative theology," namely that no *complete* statement of the nature of God is possible. The finite obviously cannot fully comprehend the infinite. Indeed, Thomistic thinkers are so fully aware of this fact that they insist that no experience of God in his actual nature is possible to men as long as they exist under conditions of space and time—thus denying the claims of some mystics to have transcended temporal limitations in their experience of the divine. Nevertheless, the vision of God in his perfection is the goal of all human thought and activity, and men may have here and now closer and closer approximations of that Beatific Vision which is enjoyed by the angels and saints in glory. Furthermore, some significant things may be said about God even from the limited standpoint of finite experience. At least some things are more truly said about him than others. In general, it is possible to state negatively some of his positive attributes, and to state positively other attributes by analogy. From the knowledge that he is perfect in all aspects, for instance, it may be positively stated that God is not temporal, but eternal; not finite, but infinite, and so on. Similarly, from the knowledge that man is among his creatures and appears to occupy a unique position in creation, it may also be said that, whatever else God may be, he is at least like the highest human good we know. As the creator of persons, then, he is at least not impersonal. It is illogical to assume that the higher can be explained in terms of the lower, the personal by the impersonal. Therefore God is at least personal. But when one speaks of God as personal he ought always to have the word figuratively in quotation marks to remind himself that God is not a person in all respects like human persons, though some souls may be capable of thinking of him only in such a fashion. This principle of analogy is basic to classical Christian theology, Catholic and otherwise, and should be carefully noted.

The Rational Knowledge of Man, His Duty and Destiny

Reason shows that man is a child of nature. He is a psychophysical organism, an animal, with all the basic needs of other creatures. The Catholic thinker would object as strongly to any theory which denies man's creatureliness as to any theory which denies his unique relation to the Creator. And because man is a creature, all scientific knowledge aimed at better understanding of his creature-nature and more expedient filling of creature-needs is good and should be encouraged. As implied in the six proofs of God's existence outlined above, there is no intrinsic quarrel between Catholic theology and science. Indeed, theology, properly understood, is an aid to and ally of science. Theology and science part company only when scientists convert the working principles of science into metaphysical absolutes and become covert theologians—as, for instance, when some deny the metaphysical and theological necessity for a First Cause on the grounds that particular types of scientific investigation do not need such a concept for their purposes. Similarly, Catholic thought welcomes all scientific knowledge of man which may be gained through the social sciences, including psychology—as long as the results of findings in these areas are not interpreted in such a fashion as to conflict with the basic premises of theology—which, the Catholic is convinced, are simply the basic principles of right reason.

But if a psychologist or anthropologist, his vision narrowed by his preoccupation with manifestations of man's creatureliness such as physical or biological needs, declares that, since from the standpoint of his interests such needs explain the whole of human behavior, therefore man is merely a creature; then such a scientist is indulging in theological error. It can be shown scientifically that man is a unique creature. He reacts to stimuli in a fashion radically different from that of other animals, though some animal behavior may approximate human behavior. It is perhaps inconsequential whether the difference between man and other creatures is a difference of degree or of kind—it is the fact that there is a difference which is significant and which must be accounted for in any complete system of thought. And the root of human difference is human reason: man is a rational animal. Included in reason are memory and foresight. Man is able to bring past experience and future goals to bear upon present experience in a manner not open to other animals. It is human memory and imagination which make possible, for instance, speech and language. Man is therefore a symbol-manipulating animal as well as a tool-making animal. It is also through reason that man is free. It is fruitless, of course, to maintain that man is absolutely free in the sense of being absolutely disconnected from previous experience and the consequences of previous choices. He lives in a world whose lawfulness is one of the signs of its Creator's glory. But the laws to which man responds are not merely physical laws. He is capable of responding, through imagination and memory, to moral laws and aesthetic ideals as well. Therefore his behavior is incomparably richer and more difficult to understand than is that of the highest nonhuman animals. Man is not free from the influences of heredity and environment, but he responds to these influences in distinctively human ways—ways that attest to his freedom as contrasted with the more rigid responses of other creatures. Another way of putting it is to say that man is determined, indeed; but in the long run he is determined by the rich dynamic unity of his unique self. His freedom is the freedom of self-determination. He is capable of responding in any situation to his apparent good in that situation, and his salvation lies in making his apparent good identical with the real good, which is God, or God's will.

What God's will is may also be known in part through purely rational analysis of historical human experience and its consequences. Without any recourse to special revelation, men everywhere have learned some basic truths about the kind of conduct which leads to the good life. Among other things, they have learned that rationally good conduct is measured by the four classical cardinal virtues: prudence, justice, fortitude, and temperance. One needs no special illumination to see that justice—doing unto others as one would have them do unto one's self—is basic to the good life; or that more than mere sentimental good will is necessary to execute justice—that prudence is called for; or that mere theoretical understanding and emotional resolution will not build the good life or the good society—that courage or fortitude is needed; or that there is universal wisdom in the Confucian-Buddhist-Greek discovery that the good life is characterized by moderation and temperance.

A careful rational analysis of human goods also reveals that it is not unreasonable to assert that man's soul is immortal. By "soul" the contemporary theologian means something like, but more than, that which some non-Christian psychologists and others mean when they speak of "personality" or "the self." There is a unitary and continuing core of individual experience which is not fully explained in terms of physiological or social identity. Physiologically an individual is never the same individual in any two successive moments—the body is constantly changing, decaying, and renewing itself. Psychologically, minds are never the same minds in any two successive moments; stimuli and responses constantly change. Yet there is something which is the same "I" through all "my" experience.

Indeed, if this inner continuity and identity are seriously impaired, "I" am declared to be "not myself," but disoriented socially or insane. But if this inner "I," this soul, persists through all physical and mental change short of death or insanity; if the more truly rational, the more of a personality one is, the more striking are his uniquely individual responses and at times apparent indifference to the passing scene; then is it not reasonable to assume that the person will also persist through the final bodily change, death?

Consider again the purposefulness of all creation. A major premise of the Thomistic understanding of nature, it will be recalled, is that things are to be understood in terms of what they are for, their goals, as well as in terms of what they are of and from, their material constitution and origins. All beings seem to be made with appetites for status and activity which are, at least in principle, achievable under the conditions of space and time. But man is seized by visions of perfection, of "the light that never was on land or sea." He "hungers and thirsts after righteousness" which can be approximated only imperfectly here and now. He seems made, in other words, for a vision of God, and in this life he can see only "as in a glass, darkly." What, then, are we to conclude? That man is the one exception to the otherwise universal law that beings are made for achievable goals; and that he alone is doomed to hunger for food he can never have, even in principle? This is a rationally possible, authentically tragic view of man, and there are those who have held it consistently. Many in modern culture claim to hold it, but their optimism betrays their inconsistency. And their optimism is unconsciously borrowed from the Christian origins of much of modern Western culture. Christian theologians, Catholic and otherwise, have maintained that it is less reasonable to hold that man is the one tragic misfit than it is to hold that man's soul is immortal, capable of enjoying under other dimly envisioned conditions the fullness of that of which earthly goods are a foretaste. On the other hand, if God be just as well as merciful, and if human moral choices are real choices with real eternal consequences, then it must also be affirmed that man is capable of suffering the eternal consequences of his sins.

The Truths of Revelation

Here in brief outline are some of the truths about man and God which man may know through the use of reason alone: that God, the perfect being, exists; that he is known to exist as the source of motion and power, the First Cause, Cosmic Purposer and Sovereign Judge, existing necessarily rather than contingently; that man is a free rational creature subject to moral laws expressed in basic virtues, capable of envisioning, responding to, and yearning for, perfection; and that man's soul is immortal, so that the consequences of human choice for good or ill are eternal and not merely temporal. What more, then, does man need to know for the good life, and how is it possible for him to know more?

For many reasons man needs more than reason can provide in his knowledge of God and human destiny. For one thing, most men have been and many men still are incapable of grasping, through reason, even those basic truths outlined above. If they are to understand even the fundamentals of the good life, the truths of such fundamentals must be made known to them through revelation accepted on the authority of the revealer. And it is unreasonable to assume that the God whose nature reason shows to be perfectly good should withhold saving truth from all but a few intellectuals—though this is the presumption of many non-Christian philosophical faiths. For many, then, the truths of reason themselves must be safeguarded and transmitted through revelation and its agencies.

But beyond this, all men need assurance on many matters which are beyond the scope of reason, and all men actually do take stands on or adopt attitudes toward such matters —such as conflicting but apparently equally reasonable statements issuing from various religious faiths about the deeper nature of God, or, more important perhaps, on such matters as whether the world is created in time or is eternal. Aquinas agreed with the Averroists that reason cannot comprehend a beginning of the world in time. But he insisted, against the Averroists, that it is equally incapable of comprehending an uncreated or eternal world. Nevertheless, it matters greatly where one takes his stand on this apparently irrelevant theological issue. If he believes in the eternity of the universe he is logically led to the cyclical view of history which is espoused in most Eastern faiths and which the Greek philosophers usually maintained. If he believes in creation, however, a beginning and end of things, then time becomes more important, the notion of progress is possible, and present activity takes on life-and-death significance. Furthermore, if one makes a distinction between the world as created and its Creator, there is a basis for prophetic criticism of all this-worldly achievements and denunciation of all forms of

idolatry. If not, the "tolerance born of indifference" typical
of Hinduism is the logical result. Many Western thinkers,
the Thomist would say, are as inconsistent in their thinking
on such matters as on the matter of immortality mentioned
above.

Man, then, needs and actually does live by revelation of
some kind. Furthermore, reason leads him to see that God
exists as a perfect being. And if a perfect being has produced
a creature who needs revelation, then it is reasonable to assume that such revelation is to be found. Furthermore, reason itself may aid man in deciding just where, amid conflicting
revelation-claims of various faiths, true revelation is to be
found. In a sense, of course, general revelation is found
wherever men have discovered those basic rational truths
about man and God outlined above, in whatever cultural or
religious framework they may appear; God "has not left himself without witness" among any people.

But only one group of men have found God uniquely in
history as well as in nature, and these are the fathers of the
Hebrew-Christian tradition. An objective reading of the religious history of the Jews in biblical times shows that they
adopted an attitude toward the affairs of history as reflected
in the life of their nation unparalleled in other peoples' religious traditions. The biblical prophets, furthermore, had
insights into the workings of history which set them apart
from other men and gave to their utterances a note of divine
authenticity. And the Christian also believes that the prophetic view of history and the religious development of the
Jews can be fully appreciated only when seen in the light
of the supreme revelation of God in Jesus Christ. In Jesus,
the Christian finds the predictions of the prophets and the
deepest yearnings of the Jews fulfilled. In the quality of
his teaching, the unity of his life with his teaching, and the
epic of his life as such—in his miraculous birth, astounding
activity, moving passion and death, and glorious resurrection;
here above all, Christians say, unprejudiced men must see
the unique revelation of God. Christ's teachings have about
them an aura of unquestionable authority, and they are sup-

plemented by many miraculous signs of his supernatural power. But especially in his loving passion and sacrificial death upon the cross do men see the full depths of God's love and the full measure of his perfection. To declare that God was uniquely in Christ is, to be sure, a decision of faith. But it is a decision which seems rational and inevitable to those who have made it and, in the light of faith, compare their Lord with others to whom men turn for salvation.

The work of Christ was done in a community, however, and the authority of divine revelation which first expressed itself in the Hebrew community was carried on in its fullness in the community of Christ's apostles. They shared in his truth and in his power, and to them he promised continuing grace to do even greater things than were done in his earthly ministry. To them Jesus gave the power to forgive sins and heal diseases; to them were given "the keys of the Kingdom." Furthermore, Roman Catholics believe that Christ made it explicitly clear that Simon Peter was the chief of the Apostles and the Rock on which the Christian church was to be built: "And I tell you, you are Peter, and on this rock I will build my church; and the powers of death shall not prevail against it." [3] This statement, say Roman Catholics, was no mere figure of speech, but the gift to Peter of leadership of the Apostolic Church. For Roman Catholics this means that the Church which Peter founded in Rome is the divinely-ordained center of the Church of Christ, and that Peter's successors as bishops of that church are the divinely-appointed bishops of all the bishops. And in the history of the Roman Catholic church, they say, there is ample evidence of her favored position as an instrument of divine revelation. Her rise from humble origins to become the spiritual mother of the Western world; her unity and continuous strength through the centuries when all other powers have yielded and fallen; the rational soundness of her doctrine and philosophy; the supernatural quality of the piety of her saints; the innumerable miracles performed in her name; all of this and

[3] Matt. 16:18.

more is, for the Roman Catholic, abundant reason for accepting the Roman Catholic church as the guardian and dispenser of divine revelation.

If one reasonably accepts, then, the special revelation of God in the prophets, Christ, and the Apostolic Church, there is added to those truths which may be known through reason alone all the wealth of sound Christian doctrine. One may then believe, not merely that there is a God, but that the deepest insight into the nature of God comes from the life and teachings of his son, Jesus Christ, and that continuous comfort and illumination are possible through the work of the Holy Spirit—he may believe, in other words, in the Holy Trinity. He may take as his rules of faith the historic creeds, with their concrete additions to the abstract conclusions of reason. He may find in the Bible—as interpreted by those competent to discern spiritual truth—a guide to the affairs of life. In the continuing tradition of the Church, also, he may find additional insight into the application of Christian truth to the changing problems of the present. Above all, he may find in the sacramental ministry of the Church spiritual nurture for every significant occasion and problem of life.

In the realm of conduct, the believer may enrich the cardinal rational virtues with the three theological virtues, faith, hope, and charity. His actions will then be carried out with concern for more than mundane and human consequences. His faith in the God revealed in Jesus Christ will enable him to have a charity for his fellow-men which seems to the purely calculating soul a bit of divine madness; his hope for a better life beyond, and a supernatural solution of the problems of this world will enable him to bear patiently the reverses of life and to persevere in goodness despite external failure. The word "charity" incidentally, is not to be understood in terms of the paternalistic connotations popular usage has given it, but rather as a human imitation of that blend of justice and mercy which constitutes God's love toward man as revealed in Christ. Nor will the believer's hope for a life beyond remain nebulous. From the premise

of God's love as revealed in Christ it is possible for faith-
filled reason to paint in vivid pictures the life of Paradise and
Heaven, as well as the torments of Purgatory and Hell.
Through faith it is also possible for the believer to draw
upon the treasury of merit stored up by the saints who have
gone before, and to enlist their aid in his fight against "the
world, the flesh, and the devil." In all these ways and more,
faith fulfils, completes, and enriches the life of reason.

SUGGESTIONS FOR FURTHER READING

ANSELM, SAINT. *Proslogion, Monologion* and *Cur Deus Homo*. Translated
by S. N. Deane. Chicago: The Open Court Publishing Co., 1910.
AQUINAS, THOMAS. *Introduction to Aquinas*, ed. A. Pegis. New York: Modern
Library, Random House, Inc., 1948.
———. *The Basic Writings of Aquinas*, ed. A. Pegis. New York: Random
House, Inc., 1945.
AUGUSTINE, SAINT. *The Confessions of Augustine*, ed. E. Pusey. London:
Everyman, J. M. Dent & Sons, Ltd., 1907.
———. *The City of God*, ed. Thomas Merton. New York: Modern
Library, Random House, Inc., 1950.
AYER, JOSEPH C. *Source Book for Ancient Church History*. New York:
Chas. Scribner's Sons, 1913.
BETTENSON, HENRY. *Documents of the Christian Church*. London: Oxford
University Press, 1943.
BEVAN, EDWYN. *Christianity*. London: Oxford University Press, 1945.
GILSON, ÉTIENNE. *The Spirit of Medieval Philosophy*. New York: Chas.
Scribner's Sons, 1936.
———. *God and Philosophy*. New Haven: Yale University Press, 1941.
———. *Reason and Revelation in the Middle Ages*. New York: Chas.
Scribner's Sons, 1950.
LATOURETTE, KENNETH S. *A History of the Expansion of Christianity*. New
York: The Macmillan Co., 1937-1945.
MARITAIN, JACQUES. *True Humanism*. London: The Centenary Press, 1938.
———. *The Degrees of Knowledge*. New York: Chas. Scribner's Sons,
1938.
———. *Science and Wisdom*. London: The Centenary Press, 1944.
MCKEON, RICHARD (ed.). *Selections from Medieval Philosophers*. New
York: Chas. Scribner's Sons, 1929-1933.
SCHAFF, PHILIP. *A History of the Christian Church*. New York: Chas.
Scribner's Sons, 1882-1910.
THOMAS, GEORGE (ed.). *The Vitality of the Christian Tradition*. New
York: Harper & Bros., 1944.
WALKER, WILLISTON. *A History of the Christian Church*. New York: Chas.
Scribner's Sons, 1913.
DE WULF, MAURICE. *History of Medieval Philosophy*. New York: Longmans,
Green & Co., Inc., 1935-1938.

Chapter 9

ROMAN CATHOLIC WAYS OF
ORDER AND WORSHIP

The Common Catholic Heritage

IT should be noted again that much of the foregoing statement of the relations of faith to reason would be accepted by millions of non-Roman Catholic Christians as an expression of common Christian belief. The classical Augustinian-Thomistic tradition belongs to all of Christendom, and the only point at which *all* non-Roman Catholic Christians would take issue with this tradition is in connection with the Roman Catholic interpretation of the authority of the Church and the role of Saint Peter and the Bishops of Rome in that authority. The Protestant Reformation was in part a return to the theology of Saint Augustine. Also, many non-Roman Catholic Christians would accept, wholly or in part, the Thomistic synthesis of faith and reason as normative Christian doctrine. Classical Christian theology is Catholic, to be sure, but it is not merely *Roman* Catholic. It is the historic faith of Christendom. When one turns from these philosophical and theological foundations to the doctrine of the Church, her authority, her witness to society, and the nature of her sacramental ministry, however, he moves into areas of disagreement between Roman Catholics and other Christians.

This chapter is devoted to an exposition of distinctively Roman Catholic doctrines regarding Church organization, worship, and social witness.

CHURCH AND SOCIETY

The City of God

Augustine found spiritual peace in the experience of Christian grace; he also found certainty and authority in the impressive organization of the Catholic Church. As a statesman of the Church in times of political chaos he was called upon to utilize his brilliant powers of thought to work out a rational philosophy of the Church as well as a personal Christian apologetic. For instance, there was in his time a continuation of the old controversy about the status of those who deserted the Church in times of persecution. Were the clergy of such groups forever tainted by their weakness, and were sacraments administered by them or by men they ordained valid? What, indeed, is the relation of the personal morality of the clergy in general to the validity of the sacraments they administer in the name of the Church? In the so-called "Donatist controversy" Augustine maintained that sacraments given by duly-ordained priests are valid irrespective of the inward spiritual health of the priests. The Church as the Body of Christ is the bearer of grace, and sacraments given in her name and in the name of Christ by those she has set apart in good faith are valid—provided, of course, they are properly received by the worshiper. If sacraments were valid only when the priest administering them was morally worthy, no worshiper could ever be certain of valid sacraments. Thus, in this debate Augustine was led to stress the objective character of the ministry of the Church.

In doing so he appealed to the geographical catholicity of the Roman Church as compared with the local preponderance of Donatists in North Africa. The Roman Church, he pointed out, was in fact "catholic," reaching into all corners of the empire, yet everywhere the same in her faith and ministry. There are, he said, following Cyprian, four marks of the true Church: unity, apostolicity, catholicity, and sanctity. The Church of Rome alone is unified in faith and order through her organizational system headed by the Bishop of Rome. She alone can claim true descent from that apostolic fellowship whose head after the death of her Lord was St. Peter, the first Bishop of Rome. She alone can claim true geographical and racial catholicity. And, though the Donatists were the puritans in the controversy over sacraments, the sanctity of the Church of Rome is not limited to the behavior of individual priests in a particular period of time; hers is the sanctity of all the saints who have lived and died in her fellowship through the years. Hers is the treasury of merit of the true communion of the saints.

In writing of the sacramental ministry of the Church, Augustine stressed three sacraments as being essential means of grace: Baptism; the Eucharist, or Lord's Supper; and Holy Orders, or the setting apart of men endowed with special spiritual power to administer the sacraments. The work of the sacraments, properly administered, is objectively efficacious, he believed, and they are necessary means of grace for the Christian life. Indeed, it was the splendor of Catholic ritual as much as the geographical sweep, long tradition, and other "marks of the true Church" which attracted Augustine to the Church of Rome. For him, the Church, as the company of the elect of God, the community of the redeemed, is the guardian of the means of salvation, which include the Bible and pure doctrine as well as the true sacraments. In addition, it is she who supplies the aids to grace needed in Christian growth, through her teaching and preaching and through the exemplary merit of her saints.

But what is the relation of the community of the redeemed to the world at large? Augustine was forced to think through this question when Roman critics began to lay the blame for the decay of Rome at the feet of the Church, saying that it was because Rome had abandoned her traditional gods that evil times had come. In order to answer this charge Augustine wrote one of the great Western philosophies of history, the *City of God*.

In the first part of this work he analyzes various facets of the traditional pagan faith of Rome and shows how inferior it was to the Christianity which replaced it; if anything it

was paganism rather than Christianity which led to the down-
fall of the empire, he claims. This leads him to reflect on
the aims and difficulties of historical institutions in general
and the causes of their rise and fall. That which all social
groups, from the home to the empire, are seeking, he says,
is peace, and this peace is possible only where there is order.
But the same rebellious pride and lust for power which
thwarts individuals in their search for peaceful and orderly
lives corrupts the loftiest social aims and institutions. Indeed, all of history seems to be a great warfare—a warfare
between those in all societies who attempt to live by faith
the life of love and those who, dominated by pride in some
form, continually corrupt the order of society—a warfare between the City of God and the City of Man.

This warfare began with the first rebellious act of Adam
and was expressed in the strife between Cain and Abel; it
is a constant feature of human history. Throughout Hebrew
history there was always the prophetic minority, the remnant,
striving to keep alive the vision of the good society. With
the coming of Christ, the City of God saw its leader in the
flesh, and with his victory over the forces of evil it won an
anticipatory victory over the powers of corruption. In the
next world this victory will be complete. The Church triumphant in Heaven is characterized by that perfect peace
for which all men long—a peace based on order flowing from
pure love. But in this world the strife continues. Earthly
societies may indefinitely approximate the universal peace at
which they aim, but as long as men are finite creatures there
will always be elements of pride which will produce social
corruption in some form. It is the privilege of the Holy
Catholic Church, as the City of God on earth, to keep alive
the vision of perfect peace and perfect love and to provide
those within her fellowship with some foretaste of heavenly
communion through the means of grace and aids to spiritual
progress mentioned above. However, not all those within
the social institution calling itself the Christian Church are
in fact members of the City of God. Many enter insincerely,
and many betray her ideals in their daily conduct. But no

one outside the Church can be a member of the City of God, because the Church is by definition the community of grace through which salvation comes. It is thus imperative that the Church strive to keep her doctrine pure and her catholic organization inviolate, as she seeks to leaven with charity the relatively but never perfectly just societies of earth and, through her sacraments, to carry those who are "called" safely through this world's suffering.

Here again it should be noted that many non-Roman Catholic Christians would accept the basic premises of Saint Augustine's philosophy of history even while rejecting what seems to them his uncritical identification of the Kingdom of God with the earthly organization of the Roman Catholic church. In any event, his vision served through the millennium following his death as a guide to Church polity and social witness, just as his philosophical vision was normative in the area of faith and reason.

The Rise of Papal Power

Though most Christians of his era came to agree with Augustine in his analysis of the ideal relation of the Church to the world, the actual implementation of that analysis in political reality underwent many changes with the shifting currents of political and social power. There were those who felt that he spoke with some ambiguity on the exact nature of the power of the Bishop of Rome over other bishops. Heads of the leading churches of the East had traditionally resented Roman claims to leadership, and with the division of the political empire into Eastern and Western areas this resentment increased. At the Council of Chalcedon in 451, therefore, the bishops of the Eastern churches declared that "to the throne of Old Rome, the Fathers gave privileges with good reason, because it was the imperial city. And the 150 bishops, with the same consideration in view, gave equal privileges to the most holy throne of the New Rome (Constantinople)." [1] Thus from the fifth century onward the

[1] Henry S. Bettenson, ed., Documents of the Christian Church (London: Oxford University Press, 1943), p. 117.

Eastern churches tended to assert their independence in many matters of faith and morals.

In the West, however, the Bishop of Rome gained considerable power by default as the empire crumbled. Usually he was the only center of moral authority, and frequently he was also the only center of political stability. Thus in the four hundred years from 400-800 A.D. there was a gradual but steady rise in the power and prestige of the Pope. The word "Pope" is derived from the Italian *papa*, "father," and simply refers to the status of the Bishop of Rome as the Father of Fathers. In addition to the political and moral factors mentioned, there was an increasing emphasis upon the Petrine tradition as the source of Roman authority. From the fifth century on there appeared from time to time lists of Popes tracing the hierarchical descent back to Peter and Paul, and eventually to Peter alone. Finally, in the eighth century there appeared a document called "The Donation of Constantine" which recounted how the Emperor Constantine, in gratitude for healing from leprosy effected by Pope Silvester, whom he had previously persecuted, conveyed to "the oft-mentioned and most blessed Silvester, universal pope, both our palace, as preferment, and likewise all provinces, palaces, and districts of the city of Rome and Italy and of the regions of the West; and, bequeathing them to the power and sway of him and the pontiffs, his successors, we do . . . determine and decree that the same be placed at his disposal, and do lawfully grant it as a permanent possession to the holy Roman Church." [2] The authority of this document was unquestioned for centuries, and its astounding deed of gift played a large role in subsequent controversies between the Popes and political rulers.

At the same time the papacy grew steadily in economic power through gifts of lands and other wealth by the faithful who hoped thereby to add to their store of merit. Thus the "Patrimony of Peter" grew large, especially in Sicily and Italy, and the Church eventually became one of the largest

[2] Bettenson, *op. cit.*, pp. 139-40.

holders of land in the West. Since ownership of land in the feudal system meant control of appropriate military power, the armed might of the Church also increased, and from 900 A.D. on there were independent Papal States.

Papal power also spread with the work of Christian missionaries, most of whom were sent out under papal auspices. Thus, Patrick won Ireland for Rome, Columba won Scotland, and Augustine (not the Bishop of Hippo) won Britain. The Franks were converted to Roman Catholicism through the marriage of Clovis, King of the Franks, to Clotilda, a Burgundian Catholic, in 496. And through the notable missionary activities of Boniface (680-754), Frisia, Hesse, Thuringia, and Bavaria came into the Roman Catholic church's fold. This religious consolidation of the West received added impetus with the threat of Mohammedan conquest in the eighth century, and Charles Martel was battling for Roman Christendom when he stopped the Mohammedans at the battle of Tours in 732.

Christmas day of the year 800 saw the symbolic founding of *The Holy Roman Empire*, when Charlemagne received his crown from Pope Leo III—though Charlemagne had intended to crown himself. In fact, however, the next two centuries were characterized by the practical subordination of the Pope to the Emperor in political matters and frequently in spiritual matters as well, though in theory the Pope was supreme in spiritual, and the Emperor supreme in political affairs. With the increase of political and economic privilege had come corrupting temptation, and during these years the Church sank to a low ebb in moral prestige. Then in 1054 came the final secession of the Eastern churches from communion with Rome.

The Eastern Churches

Causes of the final break between East and West were manifold, but political causes were paramount. We noted that the East claimed the authority of Rome for Constantinople after the division of the Empire. Throughout the early period of the Byzantine Empire the Patriarch of Constantinople enjoyed practical supremacy over the patriarchs of the lesser centers. And with the rise of Islamic power Byzantium was increasingly cut off from Rome, as the Mediterranean fell under Islamic control and many Eastern countries were conquered in the name of Mohammed. Islamic conquest also served to loosen the bonds of Eastern Christian unity, however, and bishops of lesser Byzantine centers were driven to assert and practice more and more autonomy. From time to time the popes of Rome attempted to reassert their supremacy, but they were too much cut off from the centers of Eastern power to make good their claims.

Along with the political divisions there were genuine and deep-seated cultural differences between East and West which expressed themselves in theological controversy. In general, the East placed more emphasis upon the devotional life of the Church, while the West stressed theological and philosophical orthodoxy. Eastern devotion, in turn, centered in the doctrine of the Incarnation. To the Greek mind the heart of the Christian gospel lay in the affirmation that the Word, the Logos of the philosophers, became flesh—the gap between the infinite and the finite was bridged. Thus the consecration of the elements became the highlight of the Eastern eucharist. The Feast of the Epiphany, celebrating the "showing forth" of Christ to the Gentiles, became a chief festival. And, most important, worship was enriched by lavish use of pictures, or icons, designed to make vivid the presence of God in Christian worship. But the theologians of the Eastern churches felt that the use of *statues* by the Western churches smacked of idolatry, and the "iconoclastic controversy" was a major issue in the eventual break between East and West.

The normative theologian of the East was the eighth-century thinker, John of Damascus. John stressed the concrete experience of God in the devotional practices of the Church, and was skeptical of theological and philosophical speculations about those areas of divine mystery which are in principle closed to man and of which, he felt, man needs no knowledge anyway. Though he held to the traditional doctrines of the Trinity, Virgin Birth, Resurrection, and the Second Coming, as well as to the doctrine of the Incarnation, John maintained that the formulation of such doctrines is secondary to the inner experience of which they are supposedly reflections. Therefore such doctrines as the Augustinian interpretation of predestination, or any other that seems to hamper the life of devotion, must be rejected. As a matter of fact, theological speculation and philosophical thinking did become, in the Eastern churches, subordinate to liturgical exercises which retained the ancient creeds intact, and which tended to venerate the past in increasingly colorful but increasingly complex, obscure, and in some instances mechanical ritual exercises.

The theological controversy over which the break came in 1054 concerned the status of the Holy Spirit in the Trinity. Western creeds had maintained that the Holy Spirit proceeds from both the Father and the Son, and is with the Father and Son to be equally glorified. In effect, this meant that continuously new understanding of the truths of revelation and continuously new experiences of Christian comfort and fellowship, which are supposedly the work of the Holy Spirit, were emphasized in the West. The Eastern theologians, on the other hand, maintained that the Holy Spirit proceeds from the Father alone and is not to be glorified equally with the Son, in whom the Incarnation took place. In the eleventh century Pope Leo IX sent legates to Constantinople to rebuke the Eastern church for holding such views. The papal legates were refused an audience, and so they deposited their anathemas on the high altar of Saint Sophia; whereupon the Eastern Church anathematized Rome as holding to the really erroneous side of the controversy. (It may be remarked that, if the reader feels that it was theological quibbling which caused the break between East and West, he might bring to mind and compare the political quibbling which in the present day reveals the complex and deep-seated differences between the modern East and the modern West.)

With the dissolution of the Byzantine Empire through the conquest of the Ottoman Turks in the fifteenth century the Eastern church lost even more of its strained unity. Though the Patriarch of Constantinople today claims and is recognized to have some spiritual supremacy over the Orthodox churches of the East, for the past few centuries the various national and regional churches have been autocephalous, ruled by the patriarchs of the leading cities in each area and reflecting the changing political power-structure of the lands in which they have been established. In Czarist days the Russian church frequently exercised practical supremacy, and the re-established Russian church today is seeking to renew the old appeals for Slavic unity. These appeals have had some effect in Rumania, Bulgaria, the Baltic countries, and Czechoslovakia. The Greek Orthodox church and that branch of the Russian church outside Russia which refuses to recognize the authority of the present Patriarch of Moscow, however, were sufficiently strong to control a recent election of a Patriarch of Constantinople. The chief conflict within the Eastern churches at present is therefore between the representatives of Soviet Russian supremacy and the representatives of the traditional supremacy of Constantinople. Theological activity within the Moscow-controlled Russian church seems to be at a low ebb. Though that Church was re-established during World War II, the official philosophy of the Russian state is still anti-Christian. In expatriate Russian groups and in western European and American Greek Orthodox circles, however, there is considerable intellectual activity, as a group of modernist theological leaders seeks to reinterpret and re-evaluate the traditional Eastern Christian message for modern times. These groups have also furnished significant leadership for the contemporary ecumenical movement culminating in the establishment of The World Council of Churches.

The Monastic Orders

Just when it seemed that political corruption, schism, and external pressures were about to destroy once and for all any hope of implementing the Augustinian vision of the City of God on earth, new life came to the Church. From the earliest days of the Church there had been those who felt that if the Christian Gospel were to be taken literally and its demands seriously obeyed, the life of perfection to which it pointed could be led only in withdrawal from the corrupting powers of this world. This feeling was, of course, particularly strong in periods when either Church or State or both seemed doomed to disintegration. Many of the earliest Christian ascetics were hermits, and hermit-asceticism continued in the Eastern churches for many years. In the West, however, even those who aspired to live a life of Christian perfection felt that such a life was intrinsically communal. The founder of Christian monasticism was Saint Anthony, whose dramatic conversion was later an inspiration to Augustine; and the founder of Cenobite or social monasticism was Pachomius, a converted soldier who established a monastery at Tabennisi in southern Egypt around 315. The Cenobite Rule of Saint Basil became and remains normative for most establishments in the Eastern church, while the West adopted the rules of such monastic leaders as Saint Jerome.

THE BENEDICTINES. During the chaotic times of the fifth century Benedict of Nursia, born of wealthy Roman parents and given a good Roman education, despaired of the laxity and license of his day and retired to a cave in the mountains of Subiaco, east of Rome, there to spend his days in study, prayer, and meditation. Word of his piety spread, and he was asked to become head, or abbot, of a nearby monastery. The monks soon rebelled against his strict rule, however, and he once again went into retirement. In time, wealthy parents of Rome began sending their children to him for instruction, and thus began a long tradition of Benedictine education. Finally in 529 Benedict established atop Monte Cassino the mother-house of the Benedictine Order. To this famous institution were to come the rich and the poor, the great and the obscure of Europe in the coming millennia. Destroyed in wars only to be rebuilt—the last destruction coming at the hands of American airmen attempting to dislodge Nazi soldiers who had made it a bastion—its school and library, its cloisters, and art treasures have symbolized the continuity of Christian culture through periods of chaos and reconstruction. At Monte Cassino, Benedict worked out a "rule" for those who would join his order. It was a rule characterized by relative moderation, which placed equal emphasis upon worship, work, and study. The social life of the order was to be completely communal, with common ownership of property in a self-supporting, self-contained social unit. Through Cassiodorus and others, the Benedictines became the great teaching order of the Middle Ages prior to the thirteenth century, and the agricultural and general cultural activities of Benedictines throughout Europe helped to keep alive memories of an older civilization in a continent slowly emerging from barbarism.

THE DOMINICANS AND FRANCISCANS. The thirteenth century was perhaps as critical a period in the life of the Church as had been the fifth. In addition to the disrupting factors mentioned above, new threats came with the Crusades. These expeditions, aimed at rescuing the Holy Land from the Mohammedans, brought Western Christendom into contact with a vigorous and advanced civilization. Some effects of the contact on the intellectual life of the Church have already been noted. The Crusades also proved to western Europe the value of foreign trade and suggested the possibilities of commerce. The port towns became trading cities, and gradually there emerged over Europe a new class to disrupt the traditional feudal agrarian social unity: the trading or business class. But with economic and intellectual stimulation came also spiritual unrest. Many within the Church felt that her very existence depended on the continuation of the feudal order and set themselves against all forces making for change. Others despaired of reform within the Church and dared to defy her authority as they set up independent sects dedicated to a recovery of what they believed to be the original gospel, simple and austere in its ethical demands. Such were the Cathari and the Waldensians of southern France and northern Italy. The Church's first answer to these groups was the

Inquisition, dedicated to the location and suppression of heresy by violent or peaceful means.

A more positive and constructive answer came in the establishment of two new and vital monastic orders, the Dominican and Franciscan. Dominic, born in Castile in 1170, was, like Benedict, a brilliant and pious young man. Disturbed by the successes of the Cathari, convinced of the partial validity of their protests, and disgusted with some of the techniques employed by the Church to meet the challenge, he sought a better way through the establishment of a convent near Toulouse in 1206 and a monastery in the same city in 1215. The Dominican Order was recognized by Pope Honorius III in 1216. Dominic was convinced that the Christian Gospel must be carried to the people and made relevant to the new currents of thought then sweeping Europe. These centered in the new trading cities, so the Dominicans preached on the street corners and in the market places, rather than remaining in their monasteries. They were mendicants, moving about from place to place and living on the charity of those whom they aided. New currents were sweeping the educational centers, too, so the Dominicans went to these— to Paris, Bologna, Rome, and other cities—there to rethink and reinterpret Christian truth in the intellectual debates of the day. We have already noted the work of such Dominican scholars as Albertus Magnus and Thomas Aquinas. The Dominican rule combined strict authority with a form of representative government, and at Dominic's death in 1221 there were some sixty Dominican houses in Spain, Italy, Germany, and England. Unfortunately, the order later attracted also men of lesser vision and more reactionary techniques for meeting the challenge of the age, but the constructive work of the Dominicans was and is of incalculable value in the witness of the Roman church to society.

Giovanni Francesco Bernadone was another young man who was deeply stirred by the challenging unrest of the thirteenth century. Born in Assisi in Umbria in 1182, he grew up as the impetuously gay son of a prosperous textile merchant. A period of serious illness led him to deep reflection on the ways of God in nature and society, and eventually he announced his marriage to "Lady Poverty." Forsaking his father's house and a promising business career, he wandered out into the highways and byways to help men in whatever ways he could. At times he engaged in simple and cheerful preaching, and eventually an odd assortment of followers whom he called his "Little Flowers" joined him in his radically simple ministry. Francis and his group tried to live by the teachings of Christ literally understood. They adopted a brown cowl and beggar's rope as their garb, and lived on the charity of those they befriended.

Eventually the order was recognized by Pope Innocent III. When women asked permission to join, a women's order was established and called the "Poor Clares," after their first leader. And, more significantly perhaps, Francis of Assisi made provision for those who did not feel called to forsake completely the affairs of the world but wished to approximate as closely as possible the simple Christian life by establishing a "Third Order" of laymen and laywomen. The Tertiaries vowed to respect the ideals of poverty and service and refused to bear arms—a significant factor in breaking down the old feudal military power. Everywhere they went the Franciscans breathed new life into the piety of Christendom. Francis himself joined one of the Crusades—as a missionary rather than as a soldier. When he returned from a sojourn in the Holy Land he found that his order had grown by leaps and bounds, and that more rigid discipline and more complex rules of organization were needed. These went against the grain of the nature of one who lived simply and preached even to the birds and beasts, so Francis gave up leadership of his order that others might carry out the mundane tasks of organization. His latter years he spent in quiet devotional exercises. It was said that so intense was his worship at one time that the Holy Stigmata, the wounds of Christ, appeared on his body. It was said that his nature was so warm and so gentle that even the birds and animals loved him and understood his preaching, and that he died singing his own composition, the famous "Canticle To The Sun," in which God is praised for Brother Sun, Sister Water, and other natural friends of man. The traditions that grew up around his life reflect the impact of a startlingly fresh and devoted soul, open to the wonders of nature that were to stimulate new activity in the arts and sciences, singing his Creator's praises in the vernacular, in a manner which inspired later poets to follow suit. At the time of his death there were some five thousand Franciscan Friars in chapter houses all over Europe.

The Triumph of the Papacy

THE GOLDEN AGE OF THE PAPACY. Thus, between the eleventh and the fourteenth centuries the Roman Catholic church, centering in the Papacy, not only withstood the threatening forces mentioned above, but actually achieved new heights of political power and spiritual prestige. The political power came in part as a result of clever diplomacy in the changing power-patterns of the day; the spiritual prestige came in part from the revitalizing activities of the monastic orders, in part from a deepening sense of the indispensable role of the Church as the guardian of the means of grace through which alone men could hope for eternal salvation. Typical of these blending forces was Hildebrand, Pope Gregory VII (1020-1085). Hildebrand proclaimed the supremacy of the Church, represented by the Pope, in political as well as spiritual matters. The claim was challenged by the Holy Roman Emperor Henry IV, who retaliated by appointing a Bishop of Milan without the Pope's consent, implying thereby the supremacy of the State in Church affairs. After a bitter struggle, however, Henry recanted when Gregory threatened excommunication, which would deprive Henry of the sacraments which were the "medicine of immortality." When Gregory summoned Henry to Augsburg to be deposed as well, the two met at Canossa and Henry was forgiven only after waiting three days in the snow.

The limits of papal and imperial power were further clarified in the Concordat of Worms, 1122, which reaffirmed the supremacy of the Pope in spiritual affairs, including the appointment of Church officials, but recognized the supremacy of the Emperor in temporal affairs, including the disposition of lands. It remained for Pope Innocent III (1198-1216) to realize the Hildebrandian ideal. He was able to force Philippe of France to put away a wife considered unlawful by the Church and to force the hand of John of England in the matter of the appointment of an Archbishop of Canterbury. During his time the Church gained further extensive papal lands in Ireland and England. And throughout the period the Crusades were effective instruments of papal foreign policy, uniting people under the banners of the Church and gaining wealth for some, even while breeding the problems mentioned above.

However, the rising tides of nationalism were too strong for Boniface VIII (1294). Edward I of England and Philippe the Fair of France were able successfully to defy him on tax matters, and Philippe even held him prisoner for three days at Avignon. This was a foretaste of the sixty-six years when the Holy See was located at Avignon and the Pope was politically subordinate to the French state. When Pope Gregory XI returned to Rome the French cardinals dared to elect a rival Pope at Avignon, and when the Council of Pisa in 1409 elected a third as mediator, neither of the others would resign. Thus for a time there were three claimants to the throne of Peter. The Council of Constance settled the matter in 1414 by the election of Pope Martin V. This unfortunate incident resulted in a further loss of papal prestige, and finally the growing pressures of intellectual, economic, political, and religious unrest erupted in revolution and reformation.

FROM THE COUNTER-REFORMATION TO THE PRESENT. The Roman Catholic answer to the Reformation was the Counter-Reformation, sometimes called the Catholic Reformation, which began with attempts on the part of some to recognize and deal with those corruptions against which the Protestants protested. Eventually, reform became involved also in negative reaction and an attempt to reassert the traditional Roman Catholic way by any available means. Of great significance in the Counter-Reformation was the work of a new monastic order, The Society of Jesus. Ignatius Loyola (1491-1556) abandoned military life to give himself in strict military obedience to the work of the Church as commanded by the Pope. The order which he founded revitalized many churches by supplying them with persuasive and popular preachers; reformed and extended the educational work of the Church in new schools and university centers; engaged in extensive missionary activity in the Far East and in the New World of the West; and served also as an agency of papal political action. At the theological level, The Council of Trent, 1545-1563, instituted some reforms in Church polity and issued a statement of doctrine consciously aimed at refuting what was believed to be the error of Protestant theology. At the same time the Inquisition and the Index, a list of proscribed books, were utilized in Spain, Italy, and France.

In part as a result of these movements, and in part as a result of rising French, Spanish, and Portuguese political and military power, considerable reconquest of areas initially lost to Protestantism was possible. Southern Germany, Austria, Poland, southern areas of the Low Countries, and other territories returned to the Roman Catholic fold. Reconquest stopped short of England with the defeat of the Spanish Armada, but significant gains were made in North and especially in South America with the Latin and French conquests there. In France the pressures of French nationalism and Protestant Christianity were successfully resisted until the eighteenth century, but the Revolution of 1789 loosed a tide of anti-clericalism and established the short-lived "Religion of Reason." In 1801 Napoleon signed a Concordat with Pope Pius VII "harnessing the Church to the State," but when the Pope failed to carry out all of Napoleon's wishes he was made prisoner and the papal states were annexed. The period 1814-1870 was a period of resurgence, however, as the Church became the spiritual and diplomatic symbol of stability through conservatism in a Europe continually threatened by revolution. Pope Pius IX, 1846-1878,

was a constructive statesman popular both within and outside the Church, and under his leadership the basic principles
of contemporary Roman Catholic church-state policy were
formulated. Though the "Syllabus of Errors," issued in 1864
and approved by Pope Leo XIII in 1878, formally condemns
naturalistic rationalism and political democracy founded on
rationalistic principles alone, and reaffirms the duty of the
state to afford the Roman church a favored position, there
also appeared in this period constructive statements of Catholic social policy reaffirming the supremacy of moral principles
in economic and social philosophy. Though the Church
condemns atheistic communism in any form, papal social
pronouncements from the nineteenth century onward have
also warned against the excesses of uncontrolled capitalism.
A just wage as well as a fair profit are necessary if capitalism
is to be approved, says the Church, and any economic system
may be Christian which respects the dignity of the individual
and the mutual responsibilities of men as children of God.
Similarly, any political system which implements for its
people the recognition of Catholic moral principles may be
approved. Christian democracy is, of course, included among
these systems, but other systems may be best for various
peoples at various times.

With the rise of an independent Italian state in 1870, the
temporal political power of the Pope was restricted to Vatican
City. The papacy of Leo XIII, 1878-1903, was characterized
by quiet advance. Relations between Church and State in
Germany were on the whole harmonious, the Roman church
being established in those areas traditionally and preponder-
antly Roman Catholic until the rise of the Nazis in 1935-1936.
Since World War II, the pre-Nazi arrangement has been
obtained in Western Germany. There was a formal separation of Church and State in France in 1905, but it is estimated that today about a quarter of the French population
is at least nominally Roman Catholic. The Lateran Treaty
signed by Mussolini in 1929 guaranteed the political sovereignty of Vatican City and placed the Roman church in
charge of Italian education and such civic matters as mar-

ROMAN CATHOLIC ORDER AND WORSHIP 323

riages, and so forth. Since World War II, this arrangement has continued. The Roman church is also established as the state Church of Spain and enjoys similar prestige in many countries of Latin and South America and in French Canada. Since the end of the bitter struggles of the English Reformation, relations between the State and the Roman church in Britain have been peaceful. Church schools and other institutions have in recent times received government aid of various sorts for the performance of their public services, and many Roman Catholics have rendered distinguished service to the cause of British democracy. With the spread of Russian Communist power in eastern Europe the Church has been forced into a life-and-death struggle to maintain her influence in its traditional forms, and it appears that a period of sacrificial witness, including martyrdom, is at hand there.

Roman Catholics came with the first Spanish and French settlements to those parts of the New World which were later to form the United States. The first British Roman Catholic colony was Maryland, and here one of the first state constitutional guarantees of religious freedom was formulated. British Catholics had experienced at first-hand the horrors of religious persecution, and they wanted none of it in the New World. Thus when the British and those of British descent rather than the French or Spanish emerged as the principal powers of the New World, Spanish Catholics in the southwest and French Catholics in Louisiana and elsewhere accepted along with English-American Catholics the principle of separation of Church and State and the guarantees of religious liberty written into the American constitution. Roman Catholic citizens constituted a very small minority of the population of the country as a whole until the latter half of the nineteenth century, when the rapid expansion and industrialization of the nation brought thousands of new Americans from traditionally Roman Catholic countries like Ireland, Italy, and Poland. It is estimated that Roman Catholics constitute approximately twenty percent of the population of the United States at the present time.

Contemporary Roman Catholic Polity

In view of the fact that the place of Roman Catholicism in societies founded on democratic principles is a matter of continuous debate and political concern, it seems appropriate to turn at this point to a statement of the nature of papal authority, Roman Catholic church organization, and Catholic political responsibilities, as presented by a contemporary American Catholic scholar.[3] In dealing with questions relating to church-state relationships Roman Catholic scholars are careful to point out that the practices of some Roman Catholics may fall far short of official Catholic principles. But they would also note that all groups are subject to similar shortcomings, and would maintain that ideals and official principles espoused by various groups must be compared with each other, just as practices may be compared with practices.

THE NATURE OF PAPAL AUTHORITY. It has been noted that the Christian church from the earliest Apostolic times has held that final and absolute authority rests with God as revealed in Christ. Beyond this common conviction, however, controversy has attended each attempt by various Christian groups further to clarify and define the exact nature of such authority in the visible Church. Most Christians accept also the Bible—with the Old Testament as preparatory and the New Testament as witness to the Incarnation—as basically authoritative. The Holy Spirit, it is held, "spake by the prophets," and the books of the New Testament are sanctioned by Apostolic authority. In the course of time, however, further questions have arisen as to the interpretation and application of biblical truth and as to the status of traditions of the apostles not included in biblical writings. The role of the opinions of the great thinkers of the continuing Church had also to be decided. Thus we have noted the rise of ecumenical councils, representing in principle the mind of the world-wide Church, as accepted interpreters of au-

[3] J. Elliott Ross, in Louis Finkelstein, J. Elliott Ross, and William A. Brown, *Religions of Democracy* (New York: Devin-Adair Co., 1941), Part II.

thority. With the rise of papal power the voice of the Bishop of Rome in such councils gained ever-increasing significance, at least in the eyes of the Western Church. Furthermore, statements by Popes made outside conciliar gatherings came gradually to have the practical authority of statements made by councils themselves. Through most of the Middle Ages the word of the Pope on important matters of faith and practice was accepted as the voice of the Church.

It was only in the nineteenth century, however, during the time of Pope Pius IX, that the doctrine of papal infallibility in certain limited areas was formally proclaimed by a council of the Church as such. The Vatican Council of 1870 issued the following statement:

> . . . We (i.e. Pope Pius IX), adhering faithfully to the tradition received from the beginning of the Christian faith—with a view to the glory of our Divine Saviour, the exaltation of the Catholic religion, and the safety of Christian peoples (the Sacred Council approving), teach and define as a dogma divinely revealed: That the Roman Pontiff, when he speaks *ex cathedra* (that is, when—fulfilling the office of Pastor and Teacher of all Christians—on his supreme Apostolical authority, he defines a doctrine concerning faith or morals to be held by the Universal Church), through the divine assistance promised him in blessed Peter, is endowed with that infallibility, with which the Divine Redeemer has willed that His Church—in defining doctrine concerning faith or morals—should be equipped: And therefore, that such definitions of the Roman Pontiff of themselves—and not by virtue of the consent of the Church—are irreformable.[4]

Now it will be noted that this statement of papal infallibility applies only to the Pope's teaching authority, and not to his governing authority, and only to certain carefully defined and prescribed areas of teaching authority having to do with faith and morals. The Pope as head of the organization of the Church has no infallible governing authority over her members. Furthermore, the authority recognized does not mean that the Pope is capable of receiving and transmitting new revelation. All revelation was given once for all in Christ,

[4] Bettenson, *op. cit.*, pp. 381-82.

the Bible, and Apostolic Tradition. The Church may receive new understanding of that which has been revealed,
and new insights into the application of revealed truth to
the affairs of the world. But neither the Church as a whole,
nor the Pope as earthly head of the Church receives new
revelation as such. So carefully circumscribed are the conditions under which the Pope may speak infallibly on matters
of faith or morals that the privilege has been seldom used,
and then with reference to matters which had long been
common belief in the Church. Also it should be noted that
a relatively small number of dogmas are declared to be *de
fide*, absolutely essential to salvation; many others are enjoined with lesser degrees of seriousness.

The work of the Pope as head of the Church is aided and
implemented by a number of Congregations, or bureaus of
experts, in various matters of faith and practice. But the
bulk of day-to-day administration of the government of the
Church is carried out by the bishops of the various dioceses.
Each bishop, it is believed, enjoys the authority granted by
Christ to his apostles. Bishops are appointed by the Pope,
after appropriate consultation with those in a position to
render good judgment in particular instances, and have religious authority over the pastors of congregations within
their dioceses, who in turn exercise religious authority over
the priests assisting them and over the lay people of their
parish. Archbishops govern archdioceses and have some authority over the bishops under them, though in general each
bishop is directly responsible to the Pope. The ruling of a
local pastor may be appealed to a bishop, and from the
bishop to an appropriate Congregation, and finally even to
the Pope himself. All priests must belong either to some
order or to a diocese. A Cardinal, as such, has no territorial
authority. The title is honorary and may be given to a
simple priest like Cardinal Newman or even to a layman.
The College of Cardinals, however, elects the popes. If he
belongs to a monastic order, a priest is responsible both to
the bishop in whose diocese he labors and to the governing
authorities of his order, with varying arrangements of the

division of authority applying to various orders. If he belongs to no order but is a secular priest, he is solely responsible to his bishop, if he is pastor of a parish, and to his pastor also if he is an assistant. All of this means, says Father Ross, that "the Pope has no civil or temporal authority over Catholics in the United States. It is true that the Pope is a temporal sovereign, but his temporal authority is restricted to Vatican City, which has a few acres and a few hundred subjects. Still less have bishops or pastors any temporal authority over Catholics." [5]

CHURCH AND STATE. This does not mean that the Roman Catholic has no special responsibilities as a citizen by virtue of being a Catholic. To quote extensively from Father Ross:

> Catholicism should affect every phase of life. Fortunately the American separation of Church and State does not mean the subjection of the Church, or religion, by the State, its confinement to the sacristy, while political, economic, and social activities are freed from the teachings of religion on all these traditions. . . .
>
> Because an American Catholic lives in a democracy, he has the obligation of voting honestly and intelligently as the occasion arises. He should vote so that there may be a reasonable expression of public opinion. For large numbers of religious minded citizens to refuse this responsibility is to allow professional politicians and venal voters to control elections by default. A Catholic either as leader or as led should never become part of a corrupt political machine. Wherever, as a matter of fact, Catholics have formed such groups, they have to that extent been false to their religion. The ideal is that Catholics should inform themselves on the facts and principles of political issues, and then vote in accordance with their convictions.
>
> Catholics should be wise enough not to be deceived by designing demagogues, too shrewd to become dupes of professional politicians who happen to be nominal Catholics and try to play upon the Catholic sympathies of their fellow religionists. A Catholic's religion should affect his part in politics in the sense that it makes him upright, just, and honest. . . . There is no Catholic party in this country, and no solid Catholic vote. Some Catholics are Democrats in their political affiliations, and some

---

[5] Ross, *op. cit.*, p. 107.

are Republicans. In some places, it is true, most Catholics of Irish extraction are Democrats; but then in other places most Catholics of German extraction are Republicans. That is not due to their religion. . . . Indeed, there are very few political questions on which all good Catholics will have the same political opinion. . . .

Catholics support the American separation of Church and State. . . . It is true that the Vatican has concordats with many countries defining the relations between the Catholic Church and those specific nations. But this treaty-making of the Vatican does not keep American Catholics from giving their strict adherence to the situation in the United States where there is no concordat.

For in America we have a tradition which guarantees much more surely than can a treaty with an autocratic government the rights of the American Catholic. And in America the Church has more freedom without union with the State than she enjoys in some countries where she is united with the State. . . . there is nothing in Catholicism to prevent an American Catholic from being loyal to the American principle of freedom of religion.[6]

On a matter which has recently been the occasion for widespread discussion in the United States, religious education, Father Ross writes:

The teaching of religion is an all-important matter for the devout Catholic parent. . . . Hence Catholics at considerable expense to themselves have built up a system of schools in which Catholicism is taught. This self-sacrifice on the part of Catholics in supporting two school systems implies no opposition to the underlying fact of the state having its own schools. But Catholics do have the conviction that for the best interests of the State religion should play a part in education. And they hope that some day a way will be found by which, without violating the American principle of separation of Church and State, the religion of the parents will be taught the pupils of State schools.[7]

Meanwhile, American Catholics have claimed, and have been granted in some areas, public funds for the transportation of

[6] *Ibid.*, pp. 160-63.
[7] *Ibid.*, pp. 165-66.

children to parochial schools and for various health services provided for children in state schools. Many feel that this aid should be extended to include nonreligious textbooks, and others would go further still. As Father Ross points out, the exact role of religious education in American life is a matter which has yet to be fully worked out.

ROMAN CATHOLIC WORSHIP

The Body of Christ and the Communion of Saints

From Augustine's time and before, Roman Catholics have taken seriously the figure of the Church as the Body of Christ. That is to say, there has been a deep sense of the organic unity and interrelatedness of members of the Church, living and dead. Indeed, it has been customary to speak of the Church on earth as the Church Militant, the Church in Purgatory as the Church Suffering, and the Church in Heaven as the Church Triumphant. But the Church in all these aspects is one and the same Church. Therefore her life on earth is affected by her life in Heaven, and her life in Purgatory is affected by her life on earth. This means that those whose perseverance in the Christian life has brought them the victory of the Beatific Vision are still concerned with loving compassion for those who struggle through earthly existence and those who, in Purgatory, are suffering the temporal consequences of their sins in order to purify themselves for entry into Heaven. Similarly, the prayers and merits of good souls on earth affect the destiny of souls in Purgatory. That which concerns one member of the Body of Christ concerns the whole Body, and the life of the Body as a whole encompasses and sustains the life of each member of the Body.

Life on earth is viewed as essentially a preparation for eternal life beyond. This world is a proving-ground, a testing-place, where those who accept the means of grace and the aids to Christian living which the Church provides may grow into that saintliness without which the Beatific Vision is impossible. But the lives of few souls on earth are of such quality as to merit immediate bliss after the death of the body. Furthermore, many souls who have been saved and delivered from the *eternal* consequences of their sins nevertheless come to the end of earthly existence with the *temporal* consequences of many sins upon them. Therefore the Church believes that there is, between Heaven and Hell, a transitional state of Purgatory, in which souls suffer the temporal consequences of sins which have not been remitted in life by acts of repentance and love.

A *venial* sin is "an offence against the law of God less grievous than mortal sin, not depriving the soul of sanctifying grace. A sin is venial either when the matter is not given or when, given grave matter, either full advertance to its gravity on the part of the intellect or full consent on the part of the will is wanting. Venial sin can be remitted by prayer or other good works." [8] That is to say, relatively evil intentions not carried out, or relatively evil deeds, the gravity of which was not understood or which were done with reluctance, constitute venial sin. *Mortal* sin, on the other hand, is "a transgression of the moral law in a serious matter, committed with clear advertance to the grievous nature of an act and with full deliberation and consent on the part of the will. It is called mortal since it deprives the soul of its supernatural life of sanctifying grace. It deserves eternal punishment, since the offence is a deliberate act of rebellion against the infinite majesty of God." [9] Therefore, those who die in mortal sin go, not to Purgatory, but to Hell. According to Catholic belief, at the Last Day the bodies of all souls will be resurrected, in order that souls may reap eternal reward or punishment as embodied individuals.

As stated above, Roman Catholics believe that there are those already in Heaven whose earthly lives have enabled them to achieve the Beatific Vision which is the end of all striving. These are the saints. While many Protestants hold

[8] Donald Attwater (ed.), *A Catholic Dictionary* (New York: The Macmillan Co., 1945), p. 490.
[9] *Ibid.*, p. 490.

that sanctification in this life is impossible, it is the belief
of Roman Catholics that it is possible for some men and
women—indeed the privilege is in principle open to all—to
live with even more merit than is necessary for their salvation. Since they are members of the living Body of Christ,
their additional merit accrues to the health of the whole
Body. It is laid up in a treasury of merit from which the
Church may draw for the assistance of souls in need.

The lives of the saints also serve as examples of Christian
living in all walks of life. Coming from all sorts of back-
grounds, and reflecting all types of temperament, the saints
offer to average Christians inspiring patterns for their emulation. Since they are closer, as it were, to the throne of God,
they may be prayed to—or rather through—for intercession
with God. Just as souls on earth covet the prayers of devout
parents and friends, so it is appropriate that souls on earth
should request the prayers of those who have gone before
and won their victory. It is believed that various saints have
various special interests and concerns for human welfare, and
that prayers concerning each of these may appropriately be
addressed to an appropriate patron saint. There are also
special feast-days in the calendar of the Church when various saints receive special remembrance and special petitions
are offered to the saint whose day is being celebrated. The
Church, however, does not presume to know and identify all
the saints. Many unknown saints have enriched the life of
the Body of Christ. Furthermore, the Church does not
actually make anyone a saint in the processes of canonization;
saints are what they are because of God's grace and their own
merit. In order to aid and safeguard devotional life, however, the Church has from time to time formally declared
her belief that specific individuals have attained sainthood.
The process of making such a decision and proclamation
is a long and intricate one. Every facet of the life of the soul
in question is examined with great care. A Devil's Advocate is appointed to discover any impediment to sainthood
that may have been manifest in the life of the person whose
canonization is being considered. After appropriate investi-

gation the person may be declared Venerable, and worthy of
certain emulation. Eventually, after further tedious investigation and conclusive evidence of sanctity—including objective evidence of miracles performed by or in the name of the
saint in case—the final step of canonization is taken in a
colorful and joyous ceremony.

The Role of the Virgin Mary

The saint who has most enriched Roman Catholic devotion is Mary, the Mother of Christ. From the earliest days
of the Church the Virgin Mother was of special significance
for Christian piety. It was during the Middle Ages, however, that the Church became increasingly aware of her role
in the divine economy of grace. Her purity, her maternal
care and compassion, and her spiritual beauty appealed to
the universal need for the tender and the maternal in that
which is intimate and ultimate. She became the inspiration
for the most moving Christian art in all its forms, and she
became the center of the piety of many Christians. As the
Mother of God she is believed to be closest to the source
of divine love and aid, and prayers addressed to her carry
with them most fervent hopes of fulfilment. It is believed
that she has appeared from time to time to simple and trusting souls with words of aid and comfort for the faithful, and
many marvelous works are said to have been wrought in her
name.

As the nature of her piety became clearer to the Church,
it was believed by more and more of the faithful that she,
like her Son, must have been without original sin; she must
have been the perfect human source of the perfect life.
Therefore, Pope Pius IX in 1854, in the Bull *Ineffabilis
Deus*, proclaimed the doctrine of the Immaculate Conception: namely, that "the Virgin Mary was, in the first instant
of her conception, preserved untouched by any taint of
original guilt, by a singular grace and privilege of Almighty
God, in consideration of the merits of Jesus Christ the
Saviour of mankind." [10] This doctrine should not be con-

[10] Bettenson, *op. cit.*, p. 379.

fused, as it often is, with the doctrine of the Virgin Birth, which maintains that Christ was born of Mary as a Virgin through the power of the Holy Spirit. The significance of Mary for Roman Catholic devotion continues to increase, and recently an additional belief concerning her was made a formal dogma—namely the belief in her Blessed Assumption. According to this belief, her body at death was preserved from corruption and was shortly afterwards taken into Heaven (assumed) and reunited with her soul.

The Roman Catholic belief in the communion of saints and the treasury of merit in the Body of Christ forms the basis for many popular devotional practices. It has enriched Church music, art, and architecture; and music, art, and architecture in turn have enriched the life of devotion. Pictures and statues of the saints serve to focus the attention of worshipers upon their special merits and graces. Roman Catholics would make clear to non-Catholics that statues and images of the Virgin or other saints are not worshiped as idols in authentic Catholic practice. They serve rather as beautiful reminders of the lives of the saints and of their special intercessory functions. Thus, as a worshiper enters a Church and kneels before a statue he is aided in addressing his prayers to God through the saint imaged therein. When he departs he may leave a candle burning as a token of his continuing prayer rising to God through the saint in question. He may wear around his neck or elsewhere on his person a medal bearing the image or symbol of a patron saint, specially blessed by a priest, for special aid in the various affairs of life. He may have in his home other pictures and images. As he prays at any time he may use a rosary, a set of beads symbolizing cycles of prayer, by the use of which he may be aided to make a more intelligent and complete act of worship.

The Seven Sacraments

The guideposts of Roman Catholic worship, however, are the Seven Sacraments, through which each important stage in life is given religious meaning and continuous grace for daily living is provided. A sacrament, literally a sacred thing or mystery, is "a sacred sensible sign instituted by Christ . . . to signify sanctifying grace and to confer that grace on the soul of the recipient." [11] Augustine expressed the mind of the Roman church when he declared that the efficacy of a sacrament depends on its being performed by the formula agreed upon by the Church, by one duly set apart for such ministry, and on the inner spiritual state of the one who receives it—not upon the moral state of the priest or other accidental circumstances. It is the Church as the Body of Christ who mediates the grace of God through the sacraments divinely instituted in Scripture or Tradition. Nearly all Christians from the earliest times onward have believed that Christ instituted two such sacraments—though some would call them memorial "ordinances" instead—namely, Baptism and the Lord's Supper. We have seen that Augustine spoke frequently of a third, the sacrament of ordination or Holy Orders, by which those are set apart who are commissioned to administer the sacraments. In the course of time the list was extended from three to seven in the popular belief and practice of the Church, and today Roman Catholics believe that these seven were divinely instituted as channels of grace.

Baptism is chronologically and logically the first of the sacraments, and is a prerequisite for any of the others. In the act of baptism, which includes always the causing of water to flow upon the body of the baptized person while the one who administers it states that it is being done in obedience to divine command and in the name of each of the Persons of the Trinity, the stains of original sin are washed away. The person receiving it, usually an infant, is thus formally united with the Body of Christ and made fit to receive further aids to grace. The service of Baptism is usually also a Christening, when the child receives for the first time his Christian name, identifying him as a unique individual in the society of the Church and the world. So

[11] Attwater, *op. cit.*, p. 466.

important is the sacrament of Baptism that it is not absolutely necessary that it be performed by a priest, though it should be if at all possible. If such is not possible—as in the case of imminent death, for instance—some other person may perform the rite. Or, if it is impossible for even this to be done, the Church believes that God accepts the "Baptism of Desire," or the intention of the person or his parents to have the sacrament. Another form of baptism is the "Baptism of Blood," by which unbaptized persons who give their lives for Christ and the Church are received into the Kingdom of God.

The Church also recognizes the validity of non-Roman Catholic Christian baptism which includes the essential elements referred to above. If a person comes to Roman Catholicism from some other Christian group he may be rebaptized in order to remove any unknown impediment that may have hindered previous baptism. But in other cases, for purposes of matrimony and so on, the validity of non-Roman Catholic baptisms is recognized. Indeed, the Church does not presume to pass final judgment on any human soul; the final and inward disposition of a soul is known to God alone. The Church may declare that some souls are saints, but she will not declare that any particular soul is certainly eternally damned. Thus persons outside the earthly organization of the Roman Catholic church are not believed to be eternally lost by virtue of that fact. It may be that they have never been in a position fully to understand the identity of the true Church; they may have lived in pre-Christian times, or in non-Christian lands, or in Christian environments where the nature of Roman Catholicism has been so distorted in their thinking as never to have made its acceptance possible—they may be in what the Church calls a state of invincible ignorance. If so, it is believed that God does not hold men responsible for that which they do not know. If one knows and truly understands the Church wherein lies his salvation and then deliberately turns his back upon her, he has committed mortal sin. Otherwise, he may, in God's good time and in his own way, be saved. Of course he must somehow, some time, enter the true Body of Christ before this is possible. But it cannot be said at any time that a person who has not identified himself with the earthly expression of that Body is certainly damned. If a soul never attains the use of reason, its destiny may be Limbo, a state characterized by neither the sufferings of Hell or Purgatory nor the bliss of Heaven. In any event, St. Cyprian's much-quoted dictum "outside the Church there is no salvation" is simply true by definition, i.e., outside the Body of Christ, through which salvation comes, there is no salvation. It is not to be interpreted as meaning that there is certainly no salvation for a soul not identified with the Roman Catholic church on earth.

Confirmation is not considered necessary for salvation or for the reception of other sacraments, but it should not be neglected. It usually is received between childhood and adulthood. It is ordinarily performed by a bishop, and includes anointing with episcopally-blessed oil. Through this act the person confirmed receives the special power of the Holy Spirit to aid in meeting the problems and temptations of adult life. It is usually preceded by a period of instruction in the fundamentals of the Christian faith, and in many places it is a joyous occasion in the life of a child which calls for special dress and family celebrations.

Penance is based on the recognition of the fact that, though Baptism removes the taint of original sin, and other sacraments are aids to purity, human beings will continue to live in varying degrees of imperfection, accumulating venial or perhaps even mortal sins which must be forgiven if temporal or, in the latter case, eternal punishment, is to be avoided. Catholics believe that the forgiveness of sins is a power which Christ exercised and which he transmitted to his Church as embodied in the Apostles. Therefore, when sins are truly confessed to a properly ordained priest of the Church and other conditions of the sacrament of Penance are met, the priest, in the power of the Church and of Christ, may absolve the penitent from the guilt of his sins according to their gravity.

In the reception of the sacrament four elements are necessary: contrition or attrition, confession, satisfaction, and absolution. The first necessary element is a genuine act of sorrow. The most perfect sorrow, contrition, springs from the consciousness that one has offended a loving God; less perfect sorrow, attrition, springs from fear of the consequences of the offence. Indeed, an act of perfect sorrow is, when other elements are necessarily lacking, sufficient for the forgiveness of sin. In any case, the sacrament of Penance is of no avail unless the penitent is genuinely sorry for his sins and sincerely intends to live a better life. With this disposition, then, he should make oral confession of his sins to a priest. Every word said in the confessional is kept in absolute secrecy. He should hold nothing back, nor should he linger morbidly over all details of his sinful life since his last confession. When the priest has heard the confession he will then prescribe a spiritual act which the penitent is to perform as a token of his resolution not to sin again—a token "satisfaction" for what he has done. In medieval times and earlier, these penances were quite rigorous, but as time went on it became customary to commute these sentences into something less severe. Later these commutations were called "indulgences," and it was criticism of their misuse which touched off the German Reformation. This misuse has been corrected in contemporary Catholicism.

An indulgence is of course not permission to commit sin or a payment in advance for future sins. It is rather the substitution of certain spiritual acts, such as prayers or other devotions, for the temporal consequences of the sins confessed, which would otherwise follow, either in this life or in Purgatory. Thus when it is said that the performance of certain prayers or exercises gains an indulgence of a certain number of days, it means that such acts draw from the treasury of merit sufficient grace to foreshorten punishment in Purgatory by that number of days which correspondingly strenuous acts would have gained in earlier times. On condition of the act for indulgence being performed, then, the priest pronounces absolution.

Matrimony is the sacrament of marriage of two baptized persons. Though it is ordinarily performed before a priest in connection with a Nuptial Mass, the priest is actually a witness to the sacrament; the contracting parties themselves perform it. Thus in certain extreme instances the sacrament may be performed when no priest is present. In Catholic belief, marriage is not only the most beautiful and intimate union of two mortal souls, comparable to the union of Christ with his Church; it is also the means through which new souls are brought into the world and eventually, it is hoped, into Heaven. It is therefore a matter of utmost solemnity, eminently worthy of the sacramental dignity to which, Catholics believe, Christ elevated it. Because of its solemn significance it follows that in the case of valid Christian consummated marriage there can be no dissolution by divorce so long as both parties to the marriage live. If the marriage is not consummated there may be divorce. Or, if because of some impediment—and there are many possible impediments—it proves to be not a valid Christian marriage, the marriage may be annulled. In such a case the parties were never truly married, and hence each is free to marry truly at a later time. Furthermore, the Church does not hold that the civil validity of a marriage is dependent on its having been accompanied by the Sacrament of Matrimony, and in countries where State and Church are separate does not insist on the State's following her views so far as the civil status of marriages is concerned. She recognizes the fact that persons may be validly married in the eyes of the State and not in the eyes of the Church, or in the eyes of the Church and not in the eyes of the State.

Since the religious end of marriage is the bringing of new souls to God, the Church insists that in the case of marriage of Catholics with non-Catholics, the non-Catholic party to the marriage must promise in advance that any children born to the union will be raised in the Roman Catholic faith. Indeed, the Church feels that, other things being equal, it is much better for Catholics to marry within their own faith. If this is not possible or desirable to the Catholic party concerned, however, marriage with a non-Catholic is permitted on the condition stated above. Of course the ceremony must be performed before a priest if possible, and the non-Catholic party is frequently requested to take some instruction in the fundamentals of Catholicism before the marriage, in order that he may fully understand the nature of the obligations to which he is committing himself.

Because the natural as well as the religious end of marriage is the bringing of new life into the world, Roman Catholics believe that any artificial or mechanical obstruction of that end is sinful. In line with the general purposeful or teleological view of the world found in Aristotelian philosophy and used in the Christian philosophy of Aquinas as the basis for one of the proofs of the existence of God, Catholics maintain that all physical functions have a natural end for which they are obviously designed. The natural end of sexual intercourse is procreation, though it also serves other biological, psychological, and even spiritual functions. There is, however, a natural rhythm in the sexual processes, and there is nothing wrong in respecting this rhythm in connubial relations. To thwart the divinely designed natural operations of sex and procreation by artificial, chemical, or mechanical means in order to enjoy sexual intercourse without the possibility of procreation is, however, contrary to basic Roman Catholic belief.

Holy Orders is the sacrament by which priests are ordained to the sacramental ministry of the Church. It includes the laying of a bishop's hands upon the head of the person receiving the sacrament. In this act, Catholics believe, the historic apostolic succession is maintained, with the priest receiving thereby the full apostolic power of the Church. The sacrament is irrevocable—"once a priest, always a priest"—and in cases of emergency even apostate priests may validly administer necessary sacraments. In the Latin rite followed by most Roman Catholic churches in the West, the Sacrament of Holy Orders precludes the Sacrament of Matrimony, and vice-versa. In some Eastern rites recognized by Rome, however, married men may become priests. Priests are under the authority of their ecclesiastical superiors with reference to the administering of various sacraments at specific times.

Extreme Unction is the sacrament by which the Church prepares the faithful soul for the transition from this life to the next. Ordinarily it includes anointing the body of the person facing death with specially blessed oil. Usually it is also accompanied by *viaticum,* or a last Communion, preceded by a last confession. In cases of emergency, however, these accompaniments may be omitted, though the person receiving the sacrament should in any case have made some act of sorrow preceding death and it is presumed that he has done so. The rite may be received more than once, but only once for the same danger. The sacrament may be given even some time after apparent death, because it is not always easy to determine the exact moment of death. Under special conditions, such as warfare, persons other than a priest may offer some of the comforts of this last rite, through hearing the prayers of the dying and reassuring him of the faith of the Church.

The Holy Eucharist or Mass, is in many senses the central sacrament of the Church. The word "Mass" is the English form of the Latin *Missa,* and applies technically to the sacrament as performed in Latin rite churches only. It appears to be derived from *missio,* meaning dismissal, and is associated with the dismissal of various groups from the sacrament at various stages of its enactment during earlier days of the Church. The phrase *Ite, missa est* is still used at the end of the Mass of the Faithful in the Latin rite. The official name of the sacrament, Eucharist, is derived from the Greek word *eucharistia,* "thanksgiving." The sacrament includes more than thanksgiving, however; it embodies virtually every form of worshipful experience: confession, abasement, adoration and exaltation, sacrifice, spiritual communion, and joyous praise.

The sacrament, it is believed, was established by Christ in his Last Supper with his disciples, and the sacrifice which it embodies was fully made on Good Friday. The Catholic church believes that when Christ took bread, broke it, and gave it to his disciples, saying "Take ye and eat, for this is my Body," and when he later took the cup and said "This is the cup (chalice) of my Blood," the elements of bread and wine were miraculously transformed into the Body and Blood of Christ and offered up as the perfect sacrifice for the sins of the world. Therefore, when the priest in a properly performed Mass repeats the sacred words of consecration over the bread and wine on the altar before him, these elements are again transformed into the Body and Blood of Christ. This belief is called the doctrine of transubstantiation. According to Aristotelian metaphysics, all things are made up of substance and accidents. Accidents are, in general, the sense-qualities of things—that about them which can be seen, touched, tasted, smelled, and so on. Standing under (sub-stance) these sense-qualities is that which constitutes the unity and real being of the thing in question. Using this conceptual language to express its faith, then, the Roman Church teaches that in the Sacrament of the Mass, at the climactic moment of the Consecration, the substance, that which "stands under" the sensory qualities, of bread and wine is transformed into the substance of the Body and Blood of Christ. The physical appearances and physical properties are still those of bread and wine; but substantially, in deepest reality, the Body and Blood of Christ are once again present on the altar, as the sacrifice of Calvary is reenacted for the salvation of the world.

Ordinarily the Mass is said by a priest wearing a number of traditional garments or vestments, each of which symbolizes an act of spiritual preparation made by the priest. Colors of some of these vestments change with the changing seasons of the Church year, and certain colors are always worn for special occasions like weddings or funerals.

The Mass begins with certain preparatory prayers and a responsive saying of the *Kyrie* ("Lord, have mercy upon us" . . .), the only Greek phrase in the Latin rite Mass. This is followed by the *Gloria* ("Glory to God in the Highest . . ."), and certain prayers or *Collects* appointed for the

day on which the Mass is said. Next come readings from
the Epistles and the Gospels, perhaps followed by a short
sermon, though the latter is not an essential part of the Mass.
These portions of the Mass are called collectively *The Mass
of The Catechumens.* In earlier days non-Catholics and
those who were taking instruction to become Catholics were
dismissed after this part; today anyone is welcome to remain
through the entire Mass provided he maintains an attitude
of proper reverence. However, only baptized Catholics who
have made proper preparation may receive the Holy Communion.

The Mass of The Faithful begins with the recital of the
Nicene Creed, followed by the Offertory. Next the priest
symbolically cleanses himself in the *lavabo* and offers special
prayers to the Trinity and appointed prayers called the *Secret.*
The language of most of the prayers is taken directly from
the Old and New Testaments. After the *Preface* comes the
Sanctus ("Holy, Holy, Holy . . ."). The Sanctus, Kyrie,
Gloria, Credo, and Agnus Dei which follow later constitute
the *Proper* of the Mass and are sung by the celebrant and
choir in all but "Low" masses. In Low Masses the proper
responses are said by the acolyte assisting the priest. After
the Sanctus comes the *Canon* of the Mass—that part which
is always and everywhere the same. The Canon begins with
a prayer of consecration and the *Pater Noster* or Lord's
Prayer. Then comes the Fraction of the Host and the *Agnus
Dei* ("Lamb of God Who taketh away the sins of the
world . . ."). Finally, the heart of the Mass is reached,
with proper prayers and gestures by the priest signifying the
consecration of the elements. This is followed by the Communion of the priest, who receives both elements, and then
the Communion of the people, who receive the wafer alone.
Roman Catholics believe that, since transubstantiation
unites the Body and the Blood, both the Body and the Blood
are present in each element. Therefore, for aesthetic and
other reasons it has long been the Roman Catholic custom
to offer the people the Body and Blood in the bread, or
wafer, alone.

Before a baptized Catholic receives Holy Communion he should have had the Sacrament of Penance, or made some other act of penitence in special cases, and should have fasted for a stated period of time. He receives the Host upon his tongue from the hands of the priest while kneeling at the altar rail. Every Catholic in good standing must receive Communion at least once a year, at Easter time and is urged to do so on other "Holy days of obligation." He is expected to do so, circumstances permitting, every Sunday; and he may do so as often as he wishes up to once a day. Most priests say Mass every day, but no priest may say more than two masses on any given day except with special dispensation.

After Communion, ablutions are performed by the priest, who then reads a Communion Verse of Scripture. Then come post-Communion prayers, the dismissal, a last blessing, and the last Gospel—verses from the first chapter of the Gospel of St. John. Concluding prayers now include prayers for the conversion of Russia, and the *Ave Maria*. Throughout the Mass its various stages are announced to the people by the gestures of the priest. In the Latin rite the whole, with the exception of the Kyrie—and the sermon, if there is one—is said in Latin. The Church believes that the meaning of the Mass has been precisely stated in the Latin language, and by using it the accidents and difficulties of local languages varying from place to place are overcome. The informed Catholic understands the Mass as said by a priest of any nationality regardless of the languages which the worshiper and the priest may speak in the ordinary affairs of life. Worshipers are encouraged to follow the Mass in specially prepared Missals, which present the Latin and a vernacular translation on facing pages, with pictures and other symbols designed to simplify the process of understanding each stage inserted. During the Mass the worshiper may sit in silent meditation, except at points where kneeling, genuflecting, or crossing one's self are customary. He may reflect upon various phases of spiritual truth. He may offer special prayers for some special intention. He may simply stand or sit respectfully as a spectator. The Mass thus combines colorful expression of corporate unity with opportunity for the expression of individual differences and individual needs.

The simplest or Low Mass is said by a priest assisted by an acolyte; High Mass includes the singing of the Proper of the Mass by priest and choir; Solemn High Mass is celebrated by a priest assisted by other priests and involves somewhat more elaborate ceremony. Pontifical Mass, said with papal sanction and blessing, is the most colorful and elaborate of all. The time required for the Mass varies with its complexity, an ordinary Low Mass requiring about forty minutes.

SUGGESTIONS FOR FURTHER READING

ADAM, KARL. *The Spirit of Catholicism.* New York: The Macmillan Co., 1933.

ATTWATER, DONALD (ed.). *A Catholic Dictionary.* New York: The Macmillan Co., 1949.

BLANSHARD, PAUL. *American Freedom and Catholic Power.* Boston: The Beacon Press, 1949.

BRUNINI, JOHN. *Whereon to Stand.* New York: Harper & Bros., 1946.

———. *A Catechism of Christian Doctrine,* revised edition of the Baltimore Catechism. Paterson, N. J.: St. Anthony Guild Press.

KNOX, RONALD. *The Mass in Slow Motion.* New York: Sheed & Ward, Ltd., 1948.

———. *The Creed in Slow Motion.* New York: Sheed & Ward, Ltd., 1949.

MARTINDALE, CHARLES. *The Faith of the Roman Church.* New York: Sheed & Ward, Ltd., 1950.

O'NEILL, JOHN. *Catholicism and American Freedom.* New York: Harper & Bros., 1952.

ROSS, J. ELLIOTT (with Finkelstein, Louis & Brown, William A.). *Religions of Democracy.* New York: Devin-Adair Co., 1941.

SHEED, FRANK. *Theology and Sanity.* New York: Sheed & Ward, Ltd., 1946.

SHEEN, FULTON J. *Philosophy of Religion.* New York: Appleton-Century-Crofts, Inc., 1948.

STEDMAN, JOSEPH E. *My Sunday Missal.* Brooklyn: Confraternity of the Precious Blood, 1940.

SUGRUE, THOMAS S. *A Catholic Speaks His Mind.* New York: Harper & Bros., 1952.

Chapter 10

THE WAYS OF CLASSICAL PROTESTANTISM

THE Protestant Reformation was a large and complex historical movement that has meant many things to many people. Modern secular historians, emphasizing its individualism, have sometimes regarded it along with the Renaissance as an aspect of the transition from the medieval to the modern world. Others have seen it as a part of the shift from a feudal, agrarian economy to a modern, urban, middle-class society. Still others have emphasized its role in the emergence of the modern national state. Among religious historians, Catholics have frequently regarded the Reformation as a sorry episode of schism and error, while Protestants have seen it as the source of all-important truth.

Socially or culturally, the causes of the Reformation were many. The rising middle class of northern Europe pressed hard upon the feudal bonds with which the medieval Roman Catholic church identified itself. National spirit inspired resentment against papal religious rule. Papal taxation was particularly onerous in Germany. Low clerical morality cried out for reform. The Humanism of the Renaissance undermined the authority of scholastic philosophy. Efforts to reform the Church from within had come to ignominious failure. Nominalism in philosophy eroded the rational basis of authority. Mysticism gave individuals an immediate access to God, thus in effect undermining the Church's elaborate system for attaining the same end.

But the Reformation cannot be understood completely and without remainder in terms of such conditioning and

345

environing factors, important as they are as part-causes. For it possessed its own religious source, called by Paul Tillich "the Protestant principle": the belief that all human life stands under the judgment of God.[1] To the Protestant reformers this meant specifically that no pope or church might legitimately claim an absolute or final allegiance of the sort that man properly gives to God and only to God. The source of this principle was the biblical teaching, "Thou shalt have no other gods before me." To give to any false object the allegiance and trust due only to God was for the Bible and for the Protestant reformers idolatry or blasphemy of the worst sort. It was this deep and intense conviction and not individualism, nationalism, or capitalism which was the religious driving force of the Reformation. Religiously considered, the other factors clustered about this primary conviction as important but incidental aspects.

The Importance of the Bible

This religious principle was found in the Bible, which for this reason assumed primary importance for the Reformation. Protestants frequently err and exaggerate in their statements about the role of the Bible in Roman Catholicism. Nevertheless, it is approximately true to say that the supreme or final religious authority for Protestants is the Bible read by the individual in the light of his own conscience, while for the Roman Catholic that authority is the Church speaking through the clergy, hierarchically organized under the pope. While the Protestant reads his Bible for himself, the Catholic reads it under the authoritative guidance of the Church. To the Roman Catholic charge that the Protestant position has all the perils of anarchy in it, the Protestant replies that he is willing to take this chance for the sake of the freedom he so greatly cherishes.

Since the Bible has such a crucially important place in all the forms of Protestantism, it is not by chance that the Reformation was accompanied by great activity in the translation

[1] Paul Tillich, *The Protestant Era* (Chicago: University of Chicago Press, 1948), chap. xv.

of the Bible into the vernacular speeches of modern Europe, so that it might be directly accessible to common people. It is not too much to say that this provided a great deal of the power of the Reformation.

Translations of the Bible

The activity of translation coincided with the advent of modern printing, Gutenberg having built his first press in 1450. The work of translators might now be spread abroad, despite every effort at suppression by ecclesiastical and royal censors. Translation was also greatly aided by the new linguistic scholarship of the Renaissance, which made more reliable translations possible. Erasmus published the first Greek New Testament in 1516.

It was Luther who translated the Bible into German, an event of great importance not only in the history of Christianity but to the German language and literature. In English the work of translation goes far back into the Middle Ages to such figures as Wycliffe (d. 1384) or even to the Venerable Bede (d. 735). But the sixteenth century brought this work to full flower. William Tyndale published an English New Testament in 1525, but was martyred in 1536 by agents of Henry VIII, before his Old Testament was finished. The years which followed saw other translations, such as those of Coverdale, Rogers, and Taverner, the Great Bible in 1539, the Geneva Bible in 1560, and the Bishops' Bible in 1568. The King James Bible in 1611 brought the process to a climax. As in the case of Luther's Bible, it was an event of greatest importance not only in religion, but in language and literature. Also, the climax was not a conclusion, for the work of providing accurate and clear translations of the Bible continues to the present, as the Revised Standard Version so well proves.

The Influence of the Bible

Making the Bible directly accessible to the people may be compared in its social or cultural effects to a vast irrigation project which provides water for dry land. Men's religious natures were provided with life-giving water; they could read their Bibles and find such truths as the sovereignty of God, salvation by faith, and the vocation of Christian men. But similar effects also took place in social phenomena often closely related to religion. In Germany, Holland, and the Anglo-Saxon countries the Bible gave a strong stimulus to popular education. In Great Britain and America there has been a close relation between the Bible and the origin and development of democratic government. Throughout the Western world the free reading of the Bible has sensitized men's consciences and stimulated their social imagination, thus inspiring social reforms ranging from temperance and abolition to slum clearance. It is hard to exaggerate the effect of the Bible upon the whole social fabric of Western culture.

LUTHER AND LUTHERANISM

Luther's Life

While the modern student can perceive causal factors extending far back into the Middle Ages, the Reformation seemed at the time to burst suddenly upon Europe. On October 31, 1517, Martin Luther nailed his Ninety-Five Theses to the door of the abbey church at Wittenberg, Germany. It was the spark that set off a conflagration which extended over half the world and over a century and a half in time. Large sections of northern and western Europe, and subsequently of North America were torn from Rome to go their own divergent, and often mutually exclusive ways. Christendom was torn to shreds. However, amid the apparently endless and confused variety of Protestantism we may discern four main types or patterns of thought and practice.

The distinctive features of the Lutheran churches cannot be understood apart from Luther's life and character. He was both a profoundly religious and a thoroughly German man. Born of peasant stock in Eisleben in 1483, he had the advantage of a good education, preparing for law at the University of Erfurt. But in 1505 the death of a friend and a narrow escape for himself turned Luther to a monastic life.

He became a member of the German Augustinian order in 1505, and two years later was ordained a priest. He continued to study for a professorship in the years that followed, lecturing and writing on the Psalms, Galatians, Romans, and other books of the Bible. In the years 1510-1511, he made a momentous trip to Rome, seeing at first hand the need for reform in the Church.

However, the deepest problem which concerned him during these years was his own personal religious problem. Luther felt himself desperately and tragically alienated from God; and he sought by all the rigors of monastic discipline, by every means of grace in the Roman Catholic system, to put himself right with God. It was all in vain. The heavy burden of his sin lay hard upon him. But as he studied the writings of the Apostle Paul, light began to come to his troubled mind. Justification—being put right with God—was not a thing to be earned by human effort. It was rather a free gift of God which sinful man cannot in the least earn or deserve. This free grace can be appropriated only by man's trust or faith. Faith was for Luther, as it had been for Paul and Augustine before him, simply and inwardly the act of saying "yes" to God, turning in trust and loyalty to him as the center and source of life. Such a conception of religion, rendering useless and trivial much of the elaborate medieval Catholic system, took shape in Luther's mind as he studied and lectured on the Bible.

Matters reached a climax when the pope's agent, Tetzel, appeared in Germany selling indulgences, the proceeds of which were to be used in the building of St. Peter's in Rome.

An indulgence is a remission of the temporal penalty of sin. As Roman Catholics point out in this connection, it has no direct relation to God's forgiveness, which cannot be purchased in Catholic theory any more than in Protestant theory. But when the priest absolved a person from sin, it had long been customary for him to assign a penance, to make partial amends for the sin. Indulgences were remissions of such penances, which the Church, acting for God, might grant to the sinner. To this had also been added the idea of the treasury of merit. The saints, having accumulated more than their necessary merit, the surplus was deposited in an account, on which, as it were, the pope and his agents might write checks for the assistance of those with insufficient merit. Such benefits had also been extended beyond earth to souls in purgatory. In the sixteenth century the sale of indulgences was employed as a means of raising money for the building of the new St. Peter's in Rome. Salesmen such as Tetzel did not hesitate to use high pressure methods in peddling their wares.

Luther's Ninety-Five Theses were an invitation to debate some of the theological assumptions underlying indulgences. While he did not formally challenge the pope's authority to issue indulgences, he did point to alleged abuses, and he also regarded repentance as an inward attitude rather than any specific outward act. Luther could not have predicted the response to his theses. He was soon deep in debate with Catholic spokesmen, and in argument he was continually pushed toward positions more and more hostile to Roman Catholic authority. In 1519, at Leipzig, in debate with Eck he maintained the Scriptures as an authority above the Church. The following year he was excommunicated; he responded by burning the Bull excommunicating him. In the same year four of his greatest writings were produced: *On Good Works, To the Christian Nobility of the German Nation, The Babylonish Captivity of the Church,* and *On Christian Liberty.* In 1521 he was summoned to appear before the highest authorities of Church and Empire at Worms. Shown his writings and asked to recant, he refused, uttering the famous words "Here I stand. I can do no other. So help me, God."

On the way home from Worms, he was abducted by friendly hands and hidden in the Wartburg Castle where in the following months he produced his translation of the New Testament into German—from Greek rather than the traditional Latin. Two years later he was back in public life, taking an active role in reforming the Church services, and in resisting the efforts of others who sought to push the reforming process to a radical extreme. In 1525 he married an ex-nun, Katherine von Bora, thus evoking Erasmus' jibe that the Reformation which had at first seemed a tragedy, was really a comedy, the end of which was a wedding. Luther's marriage and family life evoked some of the most amiable and winsome aspects of his many-sided personality. He continued his manifold and active life, though his later years were far from happy. Bad health and the incessant quarrels of the reformers distressed him. He died in 1546 on a visit to Eisleben, the town of his birth.

Luther's Thought

Luther's thought was closely related to his life. Never a systematic thinker, his theology was his own intensely auto-biographical commentary on the events in which he played so momentous a part. His struggle with Rome was reflected in sharp contrast with Catholic scholastic thought. His conception of sin was deeper and more extreme than that of Roman Catholicism. The natural state of man, he said, is alienation from God and proud self-worship. By man's own acts he is powerless to save himself. His efforts only mire him deeper in depravity. The Catholic system, he felt, breeds in man a false self-confidence.

Luther also disagreed with Catholic thought in his estimate of reason and philosophy. His own training predisposed him both to the extreme nominalism and skepticism of William of Occam, and to mysticism. Thus it is small wonder that he placed little confidence in the capacity of reason to turn man to God. The reason of fallen man is itself depraved and sinful, and thus leads man away from God. Such reason is, in Luther's phrase, a "devil's harlot." In itself philosophic speculation is trivial, but seized and put into service by man's depraved heart such reason may become actively evil and dangerous.

Not reason but faith was for Luther the way by which man approaches God. By faith Luther means neither simply the assent of the intellect nor so-called mystical experience, but rather a trust of the heart and commitment of the will born

of a sense of man's complete helplessness, and evoked by
God's grace or love. For Luther, the Gospels, the message
of the Word of God, was precisely this deep conviction that,
apart from reason and rite, God has acted in Christ to heal
the alienation between himself and man. Christ is the reconciliation between God and man. Man's part is to turn in
humble but confident faith to God in Christ. The joyous
acknowledgement that man is reconciled to God is what
the Reformation came to know as justification by faith. Justification, which soon became a cardinal doctrine of the
Reformation, meant for Protestants a new God-given, faith-
appropriated unification of life, with a consequent release of
energies for the service of God and man.

The tidings of this reconciliation are born to us in the
Bible, which assumed for Luther a place of supreme authority.
Apart from tradition, and church, and pope, the direct teaching of the Bible is the final authority in all matters of religion.
One has only to read its inspired pages with honest and seek-
ing mind, guided by the inward promptings of the Holy Spirit.
Luther distinguished, in his biblical interpretation, "the
Word" from the "words" of the Bible, saying, for example,
that the words of the Bible are "the cradle of Christ." He
was thus able to resist the temptation to biblical literalism
and to maintain a flexible and critical attitude toward the interpretation of the Bible. The significance of the words of the
Bible is that they bring us tidings of the Word of God in
Christ. But Luther did not find this Word equally in all
parts of the Bible. In fact, he termed the Epistle of James
"a right strawy epistle," and would have liked to exclude it
from the canon.

The riches of faith to be had in the Bible not only make
philosophical speculation unnecessary—the direct accessibility
of the Bible leads straight to the doctrine of the priesthood of
all believers. God's truth in Christ is not the exclusive pre-
rogative of priest or pope; rather each man may and must
guide his own life by scripture and right reason, interpreted
according to his best judgment. Finding this truth, or rather
being found by it, the Christian is a free man; and a part of

the exercise of his freedom consists in bearing witness to the truth to others. The priesthood of believers meant not only every man his own priest, but also every man a priest to every other man.

From the life of faith so conceived springs love as the spontaneous and uncalculated fruit. Few men have described the Christian love of man for man more vividly or persuasively than Luther. But such love as a virtue is severely limited, he thought, to individual or personal relations, to such spheres as family and church. It has, according to Luther, no legitimate application to the wider areas of social life. For the world is an evil and fallen world where group relations are determined by self-will and power. Luther made a clean cut, putting love in heaven and power on earth. Luther was, moreover, socially very conservative. He castigated the Peasants' Revolt of 1524-1525, writing *Against the Murderous and Thieving Rabble of the Peasants*. He denounced unsparingly the radical aberrations of other reformers. The result of these attitudes was to deprive Lutheran churches, unlike both Catholicism and Calvinism, of any religious criticism of society. The Lutheran church has traditionally asked of the state only the right to preach the Gospel and administer the sacraments. In return, the Church would refrain from any criticism of the existing order. Thus deprived from the start of any social gospel, the traditional ethical and social attitude of Lutheran churches has been one of passive acceptance, often termed "quietism." When the basic rights of the Church to preach and minister are threatened, however, Lutherans may react with courageous defiance of the state, as was the case with some Lutheran groups in Nazi Germany and Scandinavia.

Closely related to this tendency was the deep involvement of the German Reformation in German politics. From the start, much of Luther's support was politically motivated. By 1525 there were important leagues of both Protestant and Catholic rulers. Luther's attitude was one of uncritical dependence on existing political power. After nearly two decades of jockeying for position, war between Catholics and Protestants broke out in Germany and continued intermit-

tently until 1552. A settlement was reached at the Peace of
Augsburg in 1555 on the basis of the policy, *cuius regio, eius
religio* (whose the rule, his the religion). This meant the
establishment of both Lutheranism and Catholicism and a
measure of tolerance between them. It also gave peace to a
nation tired of religious strife. And it established the pattern,
characteristic of the Reformation, of territorial churches.
From Germany, Lutheranism spread to Scandinavia where it
became the established Church. From Scandinavia and from
Germany it spread to America, where its influence has been
largely limited to people of German or Scandinavian descent.

Lutheran worship, while greatly simplifying Catholic practices, has maintained a liturgical basis. Luther's position
regarding the Eucharist or Communion was far closer to
Catholicism than that of other reformers. Following Luther,
the Lutheran churches have recognized two sacraments, Baptism and Communion. Luther himself was fond of music
and wrote many hymns; and congregational and choral singing have been important features of colorful Lutheran worship. The joyousness of the Lutheran gospel was reflected in
Luther's own life and has been characteristic of Lutheran
piety.

CALVIN AND CALVINISM

Calvin's Life and Influence

From the beginning the Swiss Reformation took a different direction from that of Germany. The cantons of Switzerland had won and defended a substantial freedom from the
rulers of Austria and Savoy. By the early sixteenth century such cantons as Zurich enjoyed virtual independence.
At Zurich during the 1520's the soldier-humanist-preacher,
Huldrich Zwingli, taught many Protestant ideas with per-
suasiveness and success. Unlike Luther, Zwingli's approach
to Protestantism was largely intellectual. A student of Humanism and a lover of learning, he became persuaded that the
authority of the Bible was a sufficient basis for religion, and
that Roman accretions were unnecessary and unwarranted.

Under Zwingli's leadership, Zurich abolished fasting during Lent, clerical celibacy, worship of the saints, recognition of papal authority, and other Roman Catholic fundamentals.

Other cantons, however, took different courses, many of them ardently defending the Catholic position. Thus, Switzerland became religiously divided, as it has remained to this day. The case of Geneva was noteworthy. It had long maintained its freedom against the dukes of Savoy. During the late 1520's and early 1530's the city had been torn by internal conflict between Catholic and Protestant parties, the activities of the ardent Protestant, William Farel, serving only to heighten the conflict. In 1534-1535 the argument broke out into open rioting and the forcible seizure of churches by the Protestant party. Finally the city council voted to accept officially the Protestant position. In 1536 there came to the city a traveler whom Farel persuaded to stay and help with the work of reformation. His name was John Calvin, and for the rest of his life he was identified with Geneva and the cause of the Protestant Reformation.

Born in 1509 in Noyon, Picardy, of middle-class parents, he was destined first for a clerical and then for a legal career. He was a student at the university of Orleans and later at Paris, where he came under the influence of humanist and Protestant teaching. But he was at this time simply an earnest and learned humanist with religious inclinations. A sudden religious experience, the details of which little is known, deepened and sharpened his religious outlook, and pushed him definitely into the Protestant camp. At this time his friend Nicholas Cop, newly elected rector of the University of Paris, made an inaugural address so Protestant in tone that both he and Calvin, who was suspected of writing it, were forced first into hiding and then beyond the bounds of France. Calvin sought asylum in Basel, Switzerland, there writing the first edition of the famous *Institutes of the Christian Religion* in 1536. From Basel he traveled to Geneva, where Farel persuaded him to stay.

Once in Geneva, Calvin's strong personality began to make itself felt. Except for a brief interval, 1538-1541, when oppo-

sition forced both Calvin and Farel into exile, Calvin spent
the rest of his life in Geneva, where he died in 1564. Never
holding any office other than preacher and lecturer on the
Bible, he came in time to wield a well-nigh absolute power
over the city. Beginning at first with the proposal to exclude
from the monthly administration of the Lord's Supper all
unworthy people, Calvin came in the course of time, through
the consistory, to dominate both the religious and the political
life of the city. His rule was austere. Individual conduct was
severely regulated, down to matters of clothes and manners.
But Calvin sought to establish in Geneva an ideal Christian
city according to his own severe pattern. He stood for no
opposition, as is illustrated by the trial and death of Michael
Servetus. Servetus, a radical thinker who denied the Trinity
and made insolent fun of Calvin's theology, came to Geneva
in 1553, and allied himself with Calvin's opponents. Calvin
accepted the challenge by demanding his death as a heretic.
After a long trial, Servetus was burned alive at the stake in
1553.

Under Calvin's militant teaching and leadership, Geneva
soon became a center for Reformed (Calvinist) activity.
Refugees came from every nation of Europe, returning home
inspired and instructed in Calvinist teaching. Calvin did
many good things for the city of Geneva. He founded the
Genevan Academy which subsequently became the University of Geneva. While no democrat in the modern sense, he
did sanction the choice of pastors by popular vote of the
congregation, thus providing an opening wedge for democracy. From Geneva, Calvinism spread to other lands. In
Holland it provided the backbone of resistance to Spanish
tyranny, and, under William of Orange, nerved the Dutch to
successful revolt. After rumblings of conflict, the war broke
out in 1572 and lasted for more than a decade. The first national synod of the Reformed church of the Netherlands was
held in 1571. It was Calvinist in theology and polity. Many
factors, including the spirit of the mercantile class, combined
to produce in Holland a larger degree of religious toleration
than elsewhere obtained at the time.

In France, Reformed fortunes fluctuated with politics. By the middle of the sixteenth century it is estimated that there were four hundred thousand Protestants or Huguenots in France, among their leaders being the highminded and devoted Admiral Coligny. After several successful defenses, the Huguenots fell victim to the massacre of St. Bartholomew's Day in 1572. Largely through the instrumentality of Henry IV, they gained toleration by the Edict of Nantes in 1598. A century later, Louis XIV was powerful enough to revoke the Edict. As a result, the Huguenots were a martyr Church until the French revolution, and Protestant influence on French life has never been as strong or pervasive as it has been in other lands.

Calvinism was taken to Scotland by John Knox. Knox had been captured by French forces besieging the castle of St. Andrews in Scotland, and had served for nineteen months as a galley slave. Released, he made his way first to England, and then to Geneva, where he worked on the Geneva Bible and was pastor to British refugees. He returned to Scotland in 1559 to lead the cause of Protestantism, which was closely allied to the cause of Scottish independence from France. With the help of English soldiers, the French were driven from the land. In 1560 a Presbyterian church was organized, and plans for national education and poor relief were sketched. Knox and his followers defended their system against Catholic Mary, Queen of Scots. Mary's marital imprudence as well as Knox's convictions and leadership helped to bring her undoing, and to establish Presbyterianism as the national Church of Scotland.

Calvinism came early to England. Thomas Cranmer, Archbishop of Canterbury under Henry VIII, was sympathetic. Under Edward VI, Calvinism flourished, only to be violently checked under Edward's successor, Mary. Under Elizabeth and her Stuart successors, that form of Calvinism known as Puritanism became an extremely important factor in national life. From England, Scotland, and Holland, Reformed Christianity made its way to America where it became a powerful factor in national as well as religious life.

Calvin's Thought

Calvin's interpretation of Christianity differed notably from Luther's. In the first place, he made a much more thoroughgoing reform of Church worship and organization than did Luther. The pulpit with the open Bible became the center of worship, and the service centered in preaching, prayer, and congregational singing. Like Luther, Calvin recognized two sacraments, Baptism, and the Lord's Supper, but Calvin went much further than Luther in changing the sacraments' Roman Catholic meaning. Far from having substantial significance, as in the Catholic doctrine of transubstantiation, Calvin taught that Christ was spiritually present in the Eucharist. The sacraments, Baptism, and Lord's Supper, were signs of God's promises. The Calvinist church was ruled by elders elected by the people. Calvin and his followers agreed that elders and bishops were identical in authority and rank. The popular election of elders and pastors became an increasingly important feature of Calvinism in Holland, Scotland, and America.

Like Luther, Calvin took a dim view of human nature,—much dimmer in fact than Catholicism. Since the fall of Adam, man's nature, according to Calvin, has been one of enmity to God, or depravity. Depravity is total, according to Calvin, in the precise sense that no aspect of man's life is free of it. Its effect is to paralyze any attempt of man to turn to God. Calvin's conception of sin and depravity did not deprive him of a high estimate of man's abilities and achievements; it simply prevents man, he thought, from his most crucially important decision,—his effective turning to God. This sense of sin produced a somber cast of character in both Calvin and his followers.

God for Calvin is absolutely sovereign *will*, who called the world and all things in it into being, and who maintains them in every moment of their existence. The emphasis upon will in both God and man is altogether characteristic of Calvin. God has disclosed his will to man in nature and in human reason, but because of his sin, man is no longer able of his own power to read what is written there. So, taking cognizance of man's predicament, God has resorted to special revelation through the Bible. For Calvin as for Luther the direct reading of the Bible is the final authority in religion, its truth being attested to the reader by the inner witness of the Holy Spirit in his heart. Calvin's use of the Bible, however, differed from Luther's. For him the actual words of the Bible constitute the revealed will of God. In some of Calvin's followers this doctrine went to the length of contending that the vowel points of the Hebrew text of the Bible were divinely inspired. In the struggles of Catholics and Protestants, it was perhaps inevitable that the authority of the pope should be countered by holding up the Bible as a sort of infallible "paper pope." But this biblical literalism was destined to create many problems for Reformed Christianity in days to come.

Following the lead of Augustine, Calvin inferred from God's sovereignty the doctrines of election and predestination. Salvation is not man's achievement, but God's gift. By nature all men deserve nothing but eternal damnation; therefore, the damned can raise no cry of injustice against God. But beyond God's justice lies mercy, and in his mysterious good pleasure God elects some men to salvation. It is, of course, beyond the knowledge of men to discern who is saved and who is damned, but Calvin exhorted his followers to lives of strenuous and purposeful activity in order to show forth their election. Calvin was always careful to point out that election and predestination are not doctrines of speculative philosophy, but inferences from the glory and sovereignty of God. In the religious experience of Calvin and his followers they signified the absolute dependability of God.

Reformed Christianity, as Calvinism came to be called, produced a morality of great vigor and rigor. The Calvinist has justly been pictured as an austere person, a moral athlete. Sternly, he sought to make all of human life conform to the sovereign will of a holy and majestic God. Max Weber has spoken of a this-worldly asceticism as a trait of Calvinist morality.[2] Humor for such a person was levity. Religiously, the Calvinist was not immune to self-righteousness, and in matters of ethics he was legalistic. Since he considered all parts of the Bible equally inspired, he could turn to the minute details of Old Testament laws for moral and social legislation. Drawing his ethics more from Moses than Jesus, and seeking to impose a code upon the whole of human life, he was apt to insist upon every jot and title of the law. Nevertheless, evaluations which picture Calvinists simply as kill-joys are caricatures rather than historical facts. Calvinism was an interpretation of Christianity based upon humane learning and education, forged in intense personal experience and applied to problems of individual and group living. Present-day Protestantism has not produced anything as comprehensive or as sturdy.

Social Teachings

Calvinism early made an economic alliance with the rising middle classes of Europe. Calvin himself had opposed Catholic teaching by permitting his followers to accept payment of interest in business, a momentously significant act for modern society in which interest is the very life-blood of business. He and his followers greatly emphasized the virtues of thrift, hard work, and industry as signs of election. Conversely, sloth, laziness, and improvidence were considered the worst of vices. It has been pointed out by many students of ethical history that these virtues and vices bear a closer relation to rising middle-class society than to historical Christianity. The tie between Calvinism and early capitalism was a close one.

Politically, Calvin argued for a mixture of aristocracy and democracy, though his own practices were often far from democratic. Nevertheless, Calvinism was a seedbed of modern democracy. For one thing, the democratic election of elders and pastors was an opening wedge for democracy. Furthermore, Calvin's followers in Holland, Scotland, and England found strong biblical reasons for opposing absolute

[2] See Max Weber, *The Protestant Ethic* (New York: Chas. Scribner's Sons, 1920), chap. iv.

rulers and states. If, as Calvinism claimed, "God alone is Lord of the conscience," no ruler or no state could properly claim such a role. The Calvinist sense of "original sin" led to a deep suspicion of the inevitable aims and powers of pressure groups in government, and to the idea of safeguarding checks and balances in a democracy. Thus, Calvinists were in the vanguard of resistance to political absolutism. More generally, the Calvinist conscience was good soil in which to grow many of the virtues essential to democracy.

THE ENGLISH REFORMATION

Henry VIII

National factors, including especially political factors, played a larger role in the English Reformation than in either Germany or Switzerland. In England, the Reformation was powerfully influenced by a strong and deeply rooted national tradition embracing not only politics but all aspects of culture.

The occasion of the English break with Rome was Henry VIII's desire for legal separation from his wife, Catherine of Aragon, in order that he might marry another woman and have a male heir to the Tudor throne, and the pope's refusal of his request. But behind this occasion lay many deeper causes. England had had a tradition of dissent from papal rule, going at least as far back as Wycliffe (d. 1384) who first translated the Scriptures into English. Nationalism had come early to England, and it expressed itself religiously as well as in other ways. In the time of Henry VIII this nationalism had reached a new high. Furthermore, the teachings of Renaissance humanists such as Colet, Erasmus, and More were making headway in England, especially in the universities. The writings of Luther and Calvin found receptive readers, though in the case of Luther, Henry VIII wrote a refutation for which he gained the title *Defender of the Faith* from the grateful pope.

Henry was a strong-willed monarch, and when he found the path to legal separation from Catherine of Aragon closed by Rome, he resolved to break with Rome. In a series of legal enactments culminating in the Act of Supremacy in 1534, Parliament dutifully followed the King's wishes. In 1533 Henry was married to Ann Boleyn, with the strongly Protestant Archbishop of Canterbury, Thomas Cranmer, performing the marriage ceremony. Henry proceeded, in the years 1536-1539, to confiscate the monasteries of his realm, dividing their extensive lands among a newly created and subservient nobility. His Reformation thus assumed an economic and political caste. In theology and Church government Henry was no Protestant, as Calvinists or Lutherans used the term. Having displaced the pope and made himself supreme ruler of the Church, he wanted no more changes. His opposition to Luther's ideas has already been noted; and he was even less tolerant of the followers of Calvin who wished both to simplify, or, as they put it, purify the Church service and Church government, and to introduce Calvinistic theology. The closing years of Henry's reign were marked by severe persecution of Protestant heretics and repression of Protestant ideas and practices.

Nevertheless, the Protestant party in England grew in strength. Henry was followed on the throne by Edward VI, who was a child, and whose Protestant advisors made the most of this fact. A new Book of Common Prayer, adapted from traditional liturgies, was issued in 1549, and a revised edition, more Protestant in outlook, in 1552. Some feel that, more than any other single factor, the Book of Common Prayer has been the unifying center of Anglican Christianity. Forty-Two Articles of Religion, reversing Henry's articles in the direction of Protestantism, were passed by Parliament in 1552. They made the direction of the Church by bishops, presbyters, and deacons the norm for Anglicanism, and insistence on an apostolic episcopate has remained as another Anglican emphasis.

Following Edward's brief reign, his sister Mary, an ardent Catholic, ruled from 1553-1558, and sought with great zeal to undo some of the mischief the Protestants had done. Protestants, who under Edward had persecuted Catholics, were now burned and harried from the land. After such extremes, the commonsense and inclusive nationalism of Elizabeth, who succeeded to the throne in 1558, came as a great relief. For many good reasons, political and religious, Elizabeth was led to chart a Protestant middle-course. The Act of Supremacy in 1559 declared the Church of England to be under the crown, the Book of Common Prayer of Edward VI to be the standard for public worship, and the episcopal (rule by bishops) form of government and a revised Thirty-Nine Articles to be the norm of the English church. Though there were some subsequent changes, the basic features of the Anglican tradition of Christianity had now taken shape.

Richard Hooker

In both theology and policy, the spirit of Anglicanism was admirably summed up in Richard Hooker's *Of the Laws of Ecclesiastical Polity*, published in 1594. Deliberately seeking a middle way amid the extremes of Roman Catholicism and Puritanism, Hooker argued for episcopacy on the basis of biblical precedent, honored and ancient tradition, and also, significantly, on the basis of reason. Not all Catholic Christian practices are bad just because the Church of Rome approves of them, he argued. His approach to all the basic ideas of religion showed the same spirit. The notion of the Anglican church as a bridge between Rome and Geneva, as both Catholic and Protestant, was born. This idea found very fertile soil in Great Britain, appealing to the distinctively British combination of traditionalism and commonsense. The notion of a state church, of a church as the nation at worship, also proved appropriate to the highly unified society and national tradition of England.

While Anglican or Episcopalian Christianity assumed its distinctive form in the sixteenth century, much of importance has happened since then. From England, it made its way to Scotland, forming the Scottish Episcopal church, and to America, forming the Protestant Episcopal church in the United States of America. Through the missionary movement it spread to many lands in Africa and Asia.

The balance of Protestant and Catholic elements in Anglicanism has frequently resulted in uneasy tensions which have been expressed in many of the subsequent historical developments. The eighteenth century saw a dampening of the fires of religious zeal, together with the spread of "low" and "broad" church tendencies under the influence of the Enlightenment. But the Oxford Revival of the nineteenth century under Newman, Keble, and Pusey, produced a new and partisan interest in the whole conception of the Church. There had been high and low parties in the Anglican church from the Reformation onward, but the Oxford movement made the high Church or Catholic party an articulate and militant group. Anglican high churchmen regard themselves as genuine Catholics—and do not recognize the validity of the clergy and sacraments of many Protestant groups. They have shown great interest in liturgy and also in social problems. Low and broad churchmen tend to regard Anglicanism as a form of Protestantism.

Anglicans and Puritans

Many of her subjects were dissatisfied with Elizabeth's policies, and wished to push religious change much further in a more radically Protestant direction. They wished to simplify or purify religious observances, as well as church government, thus gaining the name Puritans. They opposed the episcopal form of church government, and they vigorously advocated Calvinistic theology. Despite recurrent and severe repression, they carried on unceasing activity throughout the reign of Elizabeth. In the century that followed they played a dominant role in English history.

Under James I they formed the spearhead of opposition to the King, and under Charles I they led the rebellion which cost the king his throne and his head, and made England a commonwealth under Oliver Cromwell. Cromwell, the soldier-statesman of the Commonwealth, was a Puritan with inclinations toward the more radical position of the Independents. He wished a national church which would exclude Papists, and intransigent Anglicans. During the Commonwealth, which lasted from 1648 to 1660, the Presbyterians of the Parliamentary majority dominated the national Church, though there was a large measure of toleration for Baptists, Congregationalists, and other sects.

The Westminster Assembly, a group of one hundred twenty-one clergymen and thirty laymen called by Parliament in 1643 for counsel on religious questions, despite the objection of some few Episcopal and Congregational members, soon showed a dominant Presbyterian majority and cast of thought. It formulated the Westminster Confession of Faith and a longer and shorter Catechism, as well as a Directory of Worship, all strongly Calvinistic in outlook. In these documents and events English Presbyterianism assumed definite form.

Its course was closely related to events to the north, in Scotland. As we have seen, John Knox took Calvinism from Geneva to Scotland, where in conflict with the famous Mary, Queen of Scots, Calvinism became the national Church, and in a very real sense, the national faith, of Scotland. From Scotland its influence was strongly felt in England throughout the seventeenth century, and from both Scotland and England it spread to the British colonies in America. Emphasizing the Bible as the sole and supreme norm of religion, it proclaimed the sovereignty of God, the sin of man, and man's salvation through Christ. Severe and strenuous in their ethical life, the Puritans sought, as they put it, to make their election sure.

The Commonwealth broke down in 1600, and with Charles II's reign the Stuart kings returned to the throne. The aggressive Roman Catholicism of Charles' successor, James II, helped to precipitate the Bloodless Revolution of 1688 which drove him from the throne, and brought the Protestant monarchs, William and Mary, to power. The events of 1689 brought also the Toleration Act and the Bill of Rights which have characterized English Christianity to this day, and which also became models for other nations. Toleration was at first not extended to Roman Catholics or atheists, but the free churches of Britain, extending from Presbyterians to Quakers, gained the right to worship and carry on their activities. The Church of England remained, however, the established Church.

RADICAL SECTARIANISM

The Reformation assumed still a fourth different form. Throughout Christian history there have been small protesting groups which have drawn apart from existing church and society to organize their own forms of worship and thought. The difference of outlook between sect and church has frequently become a focus of interest in studying religious history and religious ethics. A church tends to be an organization embracing a whole society—as it were, the society or culture at worship. It tends, therefore, to become closely allied with the life of the society, thus necessitating ethical compromises and adjustments, but offering to all men within the society some religious orientation. In sharp contrast, sects scorn compromise, standing for the ethics of Jesus, as they understand it, in pristine purity. They are smaller groups of people voluntarily joined together, often drawn apart from society and rigorously disciplined for the practice of their faith. Sects take a dim view of the world and its compromises. Many of them have been pacifists, regarding war as an intolerable violation of Christian ethics. Some of them have renounced private property as evil, and some have renounced the family as evil.

The Christian movement, itself, during the first three centuries of its existence may fairly be termed a sect. Only after Constantine did it assume the role of a church. During the Middle Ages the all-embracing unity of the Catholic church never completely succeeded in obliterating sectarian activity. In the late twelfth century, Peter Waldo, a Lyonese merchant, gave up wealth and family to undertake the propagation of his faith, based upon the example of Jesus. The Waldensians, who are sometimes spoken of as the first Protestants, still persist in parts of Italy. The early Franciscan movement showed some sectarian traits. The Albigensian Cathari of the early thirteenth century exhibited the sectarian pattern in the period of medieval Catholicism's greatest power; and they paid the penalty by being mercilessly exterminated by Pope Innocent III.

Anabaptists

Sectarian groups flowered in great profusion at the time of the Reformation. They shared a common conviction that Luther and Calvin were only half-way reformers. Furthermore, they believed that churches should be voluntary groups made up of men committed to Christ. This conviction lay behind the widespread rejection of infant baptism and the insistence upon believers' baptism. Sectarians who insisted upon rebaptism of adults who had received only infant baptism were called "anabaptists" or rebaptizers.

Groups of such Anabaptists sprang up in many parts of Europe, especially Switzerland and Germany. A notable community existed for some years in Waldshut, Switzerland under the leadership of Balthazar Hubmaier. Forced at length to flee, Hubmaier went successively to Zurich, Moravia, and Vienna, where he was put to death. In Zurich, Felix Manz and other Anabaptists were put to death by drowning, in grim parody of their convictions. Anabaptist leaders in other parts of Europe were persecuted alike by Catholic and Protestant authorities. But as so often happens, persecution only spread what it sought to destroy.

In addition to their criticism of other forms of Christianity, Anabaptists were united by their belief in believers' baptism, and a self-governing congregation independent of state control. They sought to order both their beliefs and their conduct by a close study of the Bible. They were devout, god-fearing people. In many cases the Bible led them to socially radical views.

Such ideas lay behind the so-called Münster rebellion. In 1534, a group of sectarians under the leadership of Jan Mathys, a baker of Harlem, and Jan Beukelssen, a tailor of Leyden, seized control of the city of Münster and set up a new order based largely upon the biblical Book of Revelation. Beukelssen was proclaimed messianic king. Polygamy was established, community of goods enforced, and all opponents bloodily put down or driven from the city. The Catholic Bishop of Münster, backed by Lutheran as well as Catholic soldiers, gained military victory over the rebels after a year of the new order, putting the leaders to death with great torture. The same pattern of social revolution in biblical terms is illustrated by the radical "fifth monarchy men" of Cromwell's army in England.

The Münster rebellion was a tragedy which completely discredited the policies of its leaders, with the result that European Anabaptism took a different and more peaceful direction. The leader of this new movement was a former priest, Menno Simons, whose peace-loving, diligent leadership extended from his native Netherlands into Germany and other lands. He believed in, and worked for, small communities of devoted people marked by close-knit fellowship, devotion to exclusive and rigorous ethical ideals, and a complete abstention from violence—all based upon Scripture. His followers were called Mennonites after him. Similar groups are the Hutterian brethren and the Schwenkfeldians.

Congregationalists and Baptists

In England, Puritan criticism of the established Church proved to be a seedbed for more radical views. In 1581, Robert Browne, who had moved leftward from Puritanism, founded a Congregational church in Norwich, England. His preaching landed him speedily in prison. Seeking asylum in the Netherlands, he continued to write, expounding the basis of Congregationalism. The local congregation is self-governing and free of outside control. Infant baptism was retained by Browne, as was a generally Calvinist theological outlook.

Puritans who advocated complete separation from the established Church came to be called Separatists. One such group fled from England and settled in Amsterdam about 1607 under the leadership of John Smyth, formerly a Church of England priest. Introduced to a new interpretation of New Testament teaching by Mennonites, he rebaptized himself and his flock. They returned to London in 1612 to form the first Baptist church in England. During the seventeenth century the Baptist movement grew greatly despite severe repression. In America, Roger Williams founded Rhode Island on Baptist principles in 1629. United by the acceptance of adult baptism, autonomy of the local congregation, and a generally Calvinistic theology, the Baptists have displayed in other respects great variety.

Another Separatist congregation which fled from Scrooby, England, in 1609, under John Robinson, William Brewster, and William Bradford, settled for a time in Leyden, Holland. But their eyes turned westward. Returning home in 1620, they sent their more adventurous and able-bodied members across the Atlantic on the Mayflower to found the Plymouth colony.

Quakers

Other sectarians were less rigorously biblical in their outlook, and more mystical. They looked for religious and moral guidance, less to the letter of the Bible than to the inner illumination of God or the Holy Spirit, though they all undertook some combination of these elements. They were characterized by humane ethical ideals, a belief in the autonomy of each group or congregation, little or no ritual, and separation of church and state. The most important example of this type of organization were the Quakers or Society of Friends. The founder, George Fox (1624-1681) underwent a mystical conversion in 1646, and thereupon set out upon a lifelong career of missionary teaching. True religion, he fervently believed, is not acceptance of a traditional creed, or attendance at church, but inner illumination by the Holy Spirit, which may come to any man regardless of outward circumstances. Fox and his followers rejected the notion of a professional clergy as well as sacramental worship. True worship as they have practiced it consists in sitting together in silence until God moves someone to speak. Fox and his followers rejected oath-taking, titles, war, and slavery, as well as established religion. Among the important early leaders of

Quakerism was William Penn (1644-1718), under whom the Pennsylvania colony was founded as a refuge in America for Fox's harried followers. Pennsylvania is notable as an experiment, under Quaker leadership, in complete religious freedom. Among American Quakers John Woolman (1720-1772), and in the twentieth century, Rufus Jones, have been noteworthy. In both America and England the Quakers have exerted an influence on social morality far out of proportion to their numbers.

Pietists

Another group similar to the Quakers in emphasis upon individual religious experience, though more passive ethically, and theologically more traditional, were groups generally known as Pietists. Orthodox Lutheran and Calvinist theology became in many quarters, as the seventeenth century proceeded, extremely rigid. Correct intellectual belief came, in fact, to be regarded as true religion. To such extreme intellectualism Pietism was an emotional reaction. For Pietism, true religion was a matter of personal, individual, and usually emotional experience. In Germany, Philipp Spener (1635-1705), and later, Herman Francke (1663-1727) were leaders in the movement. They emphasized small groups of devoted people, Bible study, and high personal ethics. For Pietists, doctrines such as man's sin, and God's salvation through Christ, became intense and living experiences.

Influenced by Pietist education was the German nobleman, Count Zinzendorf. He permitted groups of Moravian Hussites, displaced by the Thirty Years' War, to establish a community on his Saxon estate. Entering into their fellowship, he led in 1727 in founding the Moravian church. Inspired by Zinzendorf's leadership, the Moravians became leaders in sending out missionaries, especially to the New World.

Methodists

Pietist ideas and attitudes also found expression in England, in part as the result of contact with continental Europe, in part as the result of conditions at home, and in part as an expression of personal religious experience. Leaders in the movement were John Wesley (1703-1791) and his brother Charles Wesley (1707-1788). The sons of an Anglican minister, they attended Oxford where they were members of a student group devoted to religious worship and the visitation of prisoners in the local jail. They were derided as the Holy Club until someone satirized their methodical habits of study and devotion with the name "Methodists." John Wesley's religion, however, despite his great personal piety, was destined to be worked out through ten years or more of personal search and agony which came to a climax in 1738, when, as he attended a meeting of an Anglican Society in Aldersgate Street, London, he felt his heart "strangely warmed" and was given assurance of his salvation. This experience left its stamp indelibly upon all of Wesley's subsequent life, and upon the movement he founded.

Beginning to preach to the unchurched multitudes in England's new industrial cities, Wesley soon found himself organizing religious societies. But this movement found little sympathy in the Church of England. By degrees Methodism was forced into the role of a new sect. The decisive act of separation from the Church of England was Wesley's act of ordaining presbyters to carry on the work of Methodism in America. Once the process had begun, Wesley ordained clergymen for Scotland, Newfoundland, and finally England.

The Wesleyan movement emphasized a personal acquaintance with the realities of religion combined with a lively interest in the new industrial masses gathered in Britain's cities. For them Methodism offered a world of hope and salvation.

Unitarians

Still another type of sect is illustrated by the intellectual radicals such as the Socinians, Unitarians, and the like. Driven largely by an intellectual criticism of tradition and orthodoxy, these groups have tended to question or reject the Trinity, regarding Jesus as a great ethical teacher. They have also proclaimed the goodness and dignity of man in a way very different from the theology of such men as Luther and Calvin. An illustration of such sectarian teaching was Michael Servetus, burned at the stake in Geneva. Faustus Socinus (1539-1604), member of a distinguished Italian family, came to doubt many aspects of traditional Christianity, and was led to remove himself first to Switzerland, then to Transylvania, and finally to Poland. Largely as a result of his labors, the Polish Brethren church was founded, with a Unitarian creed and a famous college at the city of Rakow. But the return of Catholics to power made Unitarians unwelcome there. They fled to western Europe. Despite discrimination and repression they persisted in England and later in New England. In the nineteenth century, under the leadership of such men as William Ellery Channing, Ralph Waldo Emerson, and Theodore Parker, their influence spread far beyond official ranks of Unitarians.

THE DEVELOPMENT OF PROTESTANTISM

The Absence of Authority

The creative source of Protestantism in the outburst of biblically-based religious conviction which swept over Europe in the sixteenth and seventeenth centuries, and some of the various forms which Protestantism took, have been described. However, the student, in reading this account, is likely to ask what has become of the Reformation, for many present Protestant groups bear small resemblance to their ancestors of two or three centuries ago. We may here briefly glance at a few of the other important influences in the history of Protestantism since its origin.

In the first place, note that since it possesses no central and unifying authority, as does Roman Catholicism, and places great importance upon the liberty of the individual human soul, Protestantism has been particularly open to the multiplication of sects and ideas. There is truth in the Roman Catholic charge that Protestant liberty has the seeds of chaos in it. It is also an important fact that European and American history, from the Renaissance and Reformation onward, has been dominated by forces other than religion. The seventeenth century was the great age of scientific discovery; and from that time onward, science in both its theoretical and practical aspects has bulked ever larger among history-making forces. With science came the Age of Reason and its increasing secularism, as well as industrialism with its vast new social problems. The result of such forces has been to crowd traditional religion to one side, giving it only a small part in human affairs. From the time of its origin, Protestantism has thus been in danger of being crowded off the stage altogether.

Again, after its first ringing proclamation during the Reformation, Protestantism became intellectually ossified. The Reformation was followed by the Age of Protestant scholasticism. Intellectual dogmas and arguments concerning correct belief took the place of genuine religious conviction. Such a religion had small appeal for an age whose mind was being increasingly attracted to the new science. Also, as we have already seen, this intellectualism produced within Protestantism itself the emotional reaction of Pietism. Pietism and its English relative, Methodism, left a permanent mark upon all of Protestantism, in their insistence upon warm, personal religious experience, and upon an austere individual and liberal social morality.

Possessing no authoritative criterion for the evaluation of new ideas, Protestantism was blown about by still other winds of doctrine. The characteristic rationalism of the eighteenth century produced in religious circles a tepid deism, with emphasis upon such matters as natural religion, toleration, and the like. But eighteenth century rationalism in its turn, produced a reaction in the romanticism of early nineteenth century. Many of the romantic poets and philosophers, emphasizing feeling as well as intellect, and looking to the past with more kindly eyes than the previous age had done, found a larger place for religion in their scheme of things. The German philosophers, Kant, Hegel, Fichte, and Schelling; the theologian, Schleiermacher; and the poets Goethe, Coleridge, and Wordsworth all show this trend. But the religion which emerged from their interpretations often differed widely from that of the Protestant Reformers. Thus Protestantism, like an unstable chemical element, has combined successively with different intellectual and religious forces to produce many novel religious and intellectual compounds.

Protestantism in America

Especially in America have new ideas and new conditions radically altered Protestantism. America was opened for European colonization at a time when persecution of dissident groups was still standard religious policy. As a consequence, the new continent afforded a haven for many harried groups. English Separatists settled, as we have seen, at Plymouth in Massachusetts, and Quakers, in Pennsylvania. Under Quaker leadership Pennsylvania freely opened her arms to oppressed groups from both England and Germany, including Mennonites, Moravians, Schwenkfeldians, and others. Lord Baltimore founded in Maryland in 1632 a similar haven for Roman Catholics, insisting upon full religious toleration for all people. With such colonization the stamp of religious diversity was early placed upon the new land. Eighteenth-century rationalism, with its antipathy to religious irrationalism and sectarianism, was added to American thought, and produced strong pressure in the new land toward religious toleration and the separation of church and state. American Protestantism has also inspired social idealism which has manifested itself in ways ranging from the founding of schools and colleges, to abolition, temperance, and other social crusades.

As America pushed westward from the Colony states, the frontier also left its mark upon Protestant Christianity. Life on the frontier tended to be primitive, violent, and meager; and religion was soon adapted to the circumstances. Methodist and Baptist circuit-riders preached sermons, saved souls, baptized, married, and buried the dead on the outposts of American civilization. The frontier also, more than any other single factor, served to fix the pattern of *revivalism* in American Protestantism. In vast camp meetings people from large areas were urged in vivid emotional addresses to make their own acquaintance with the realities of religion, and to conduct their lives accordingly. In this movement, traditional Protestant pietism was charged with a higher emotional voltage, and behavior frequently became ecstatic. Such religious patterns still continue in some regions of America.

The industrializing of America and the consequent large immigration from Catholic sections of Europe opened up still other new problems. Protestantism in the United States, as elsewhere, had always maintained a close alliance with the middle class. Roman Catholicism, as its numbers increased with immigration from Catholic countries of Europe, became largely, though never exclusively, the faith of the urban working classes. Even within Protestantism, class differences as well as regional differences opened up between Episcopalians, Presbyterians, and Congregationalists on the one hand, who tended to identify themselves with middle and upper classes, and Methodists and Baptists on the other, many of whose people originally came from the lower classes.

Recent Developments

During the nineteenth century still another important new influence came to be felt in Protestantism. The centrifugal forces, always so strong in Protestantism, began to be challenged by other forces moving toward a new unity. Interdenominational work in missions and education came increasingly to be the pattern. Groups of Protestant churches and individuals joined forces locally to produce church federations in many cities and towns. Men began to look with bad consciences upon the spectacle of a sadly divided Protestantism. As a consequence of these and other motives, the Federal Council of Churches of Christ in America came into existence in 1908. The Federal Council combined an interest in church unity with the new interest of many Protestants in social ethics. The latter, often called the social gospel, was actively fostered by the Federal Council. The Federal Council was supplanted by the more comprehensive National Council of Churches in 1950.

However, the influence of such ideas was not limited to America. A series of conferences in later nineteenth- and early twentieth-century Europe, coupled with much inter-denominational work on an international scale, produced the so-called ecumenical movement which culminated in 1948 in the founding of the World Council of Churches. This organization, while by no means a reunion of Protestant Churches, is a move in that direction, providing for cooperative work in many fields, for the study of problems on which there are differences, and for continued efforts at closer unity and more effective religious work. Within its ranks are representatives of all major Protestant groups except American southern Baptists. Eastern Orthodox groups have also actively participated in the World Council. The Roman Catholic church has often been invited to participate, but has refused on the basis of its traditional belief that true unity can be restored to Christianity only by a return of all Christian groups to Roman Catholicism. Despite the lack of Roman Catholic participation, the work of the World Council of Churches and the ecumenical movement may be termed one of the most creative religious forces within Christianity in many centuries.

Intellectually, Protestantism, and American Protestantism especially, felt during the nineteenth and early twentieth centuries the full force of new currents of thought. Many Protestants were moved to bitter-end resistance to science and its implications. If science taught ideas contrary to evangelical Christianity, so much the worse for science. Such groups called themselves Fundamentalists. The term "Fundamentalist" was derived from a series of pamphlets widely distributed during the early years of the present century among many American Protestant groups. They contended militantly for such ideas as a verbal or literal conception of the Bible's inspiration, and a literal acceptance of biblical miracles such as the Virgin Birth and the bodily resurrection of Christ. Fundamentalists were outspoken in their rejection of evolution as an account of human origins. But other Protestants sought a compromise with science. Looking for a middle way, they sought to reconcile Christianity to the new ways of thought and life. Variously called Liberals and Modernists, they sought to compromise the differences between traditional faith and new knowledge.

A striking feature of more recent Protestantism has been a revival of traditional Christian theology. This has taken place within the context of the renewed interest in religion which has marked western Europe and America in recent decades. And the theological revival, in turn, has focused attention more sharply upon the ideas expressed by Luther and Calvin. Often sharply repudiating the spirit and many of the specific teachings of liberalism, the new theology has sought once more to proclaim the sovereignty of God, justification by faith, human sin, and salvation through Christ. In Europe, Karl Barth and Emil Brunner, in America, men like Reinhold Niebuhr and others, have become leaders in the movement. Beyond a limited group of followers their influence has been felt in a general revival of theological thought. To date, this revival has been largely limited to intellectuals, to theological seminaries, and to universities. Whether it will make a lasting impression upon churches remains to be seen; until now its influence has been greater in Europe than in the United States.

SUGGESTIONS FOR FURTHER READING

BAINTON, ROLAND. *Here I Stand, a Life of Martin Luther.* New York: Abingdon-Cokesbury Press, 1950.

BETTENSON, HENRY. *Documents of the Christian Church.* London: Oxford University Press, 1943.

BOEHMER, H. *Road to Reformation.* Philadelphia: Muhlenberg Press, 1946.

BROWN, WILLIAM A. *Religions of Democracy.* New York: Devin-Adair Co., 1941.

FITCH, FLORENCE M. *One God, the Ways We Worship Him.* New York: Lathrop Lee, and Shepard Co., 1944.

FOSDICK, HARRY E. (ed.). *Great Voices of the Reformation.* New York: Random House, Inc., 1952.

HALLER, W. *The Rise of Puritanism.* New York: Columbia University Press, 1938.

KERR, HUGH T. *A Compend of Calvin's Institutes.* Philadelphia: Westminster Press, 1939.

KERR, HUGH T. *A Compend of Luther's Theology*. Philadelphia: Westminster Press, 1943.

LATOURETTE, KENNETH S. *A History of the Expansion of Christianity*. New York: The Macmillan Co., 1937-1945.

LINDSAY, T. *A History of the Reformation*. Edinburgh: T. & T. Clark, 1907.

MILLER, PERRY. *The New England Mind*. New York: The Macmillan Co., 1939.

NICHOLS, JAMES. *Primer for Protestants*. New York: Association Press, 1947.

PIKE, JAMES, and PITTINGER, NORMAN. *The Faith of the Church*. New York: National Council of the Protestant Episcopal Church, 1951.

SMITH, PRESERVED. *The Age of the Reformation*. New York: Henry Holt & Co., Inc., 1920.

SWEET, WILLIAM W. *The Story of Religion in America*. New York: Harper & Bros., 1950.

THOMAS, GEORGE (ed.). *The Vitality of the Christian Tradition*. New York: Harper & Bros., 1944.

WAKEMAN, H. *An Introduction to the History of the Church of England*. London: Rivingtons, 1893.

WALKER, WILLISTON. *A History of the Christian Church*. New York: Chas. Scribner's Sons, 1913.

Chapter 11

THE CHALLENGE OF
THE MODERN MIND

THE Protestant Reformation, we have noted, was actually a revolution within a series of revolutions which produced the modern world. Even as the Reformers brought the medieval Church under the judgment of the "Protestant principle," other men were carrying a new spirit of adventurous questioning into other areas of medieval culture. The Reformers themselves clung to medieval views on many matters. Even though Luther stressed the primacy of faith over reason, and Calvin asserted that the unregenerate soul cannot appreciate the evidences of God in nature, both of these men accepted many of the principles of scholastic philosophy and assumed that sciences and letters are ultimately aspects of a purposeful world best understood through theology. For both of them, science was simply the Aristotelian science which the Church had at first resisted, then baptized into Christianity through the work of Thomas Aquinas. Furthermore, the fresh contributions of the Reformers were soon squeezed into the rigid limits of a Protestant scholasticism.

Similarly, most Roman Catholic theologians insisted on following the *letter* as well as the *spirit* of the Thomistic synthesis. Aristotle became known simply as the Philosopher. If more daring men saw weaknesses in the Aristotelian system or in its medieval Platonic counterpart as the result of fresh investigations of nature and man, they were denounced. They were threatening the science with which Christianity had come to terms, and therefore, in the eyes of many they were threatening the Christian faith itself. Both the classical Protestant theologies and the Catholic syntheses were formulated in the very dawn of the modern era. But there were, from the beginning, Catholic and Protestant thinkers who resisted any change in the content of the accepted syntheses, even though such conservative reaction was actually false to the spirit of Augustine, Thomas, and the Reformers.

THE HUMANIST RENAISSANCE

However, there were within the Church men who dared to go ahead with the new spirit of fresh inquiry. Luther was first encouraged, then denounced as extremist, by a brilliant Catholic scholar named Desiderius Erasmus (1466-1536). Erasmus epitomized a growing movement which came to be called *Humanism*. We have noted that Calvin also came under Humanist influences in Paris, and the English Reformation attempted to embrace Humanist insights in its liberalized synthesis of biblical authority, Christian tradition, and "right reason." What, then, is Humanism?

The classical Humanism of the Renaissance was a many-sided affair. It was fundamentally Christian, but it sought to recover for Christian culture the lost glories of pagan Greco-Roman culture. It was stimulated in part by a re-awakened interest in the classics of Greek and Roman literature, many of which lay forgotten in medieval libraries. But the interest in the classics was itself merely a facet of the new spirit of independent inquiry stimulated by the total complex of social and cultural forces which formed the background of the Reformation. Men moved by this new spirit were no longer content to restrict their study to the Christian fathers of the Church and scholastic philosophies. Aquinas himself had insisted on the dignity and independence of rational inquiry as a guide to divine truth, and his views on many matters were simply adaptations of Aristotelian philosophy. Why, then, should rational investigation be limited to those portions of Aristotle and Plato which Christendom had accepted and assimilated? Why should men not read any and all Greek philosophers? Indeed, why should they not read and recover for a richer culture Greek and Roman poets and other writers as well?

The return to the classics necessitated, however, more intensive and accurate study of the Greek and Latin languages. No longer would hoary Latin translations do; even Luther had to have the Greek New Testament for his German translation. Thus, the Humanist interest in the classics gave rise to significant developments in philology and other aspects of language-study. Eventually, many scholars became more interested in the tools and techniques of such scholarship than in the content of the documents themselves, and this interest in turn led to a period of sterile pedantry in Humanistic studies.

But the early Humanists themselves were challenged and excited by the Greek and Roman ways of life which unfolded before them in the pages of the classics. Here were men of earlier centuries who had reflected wisely and deeply on the basic issues of life, and had developed rich and meaningful answers without recourse to supernatural revelation, Christian or otherwise. Here were men who learned to live the good life while thinking of themselves as rational animals, citizens of a world of nature who admitted no radical discontinuities between the human and the nonhuman, the mundane and the divine. Here were men who were at least as much interested in beauty as in righteousness; as much interested in the rational life as a good in itself as in revelation which could save their souls. And so the Christian Humanist scholars began, consciously and unconsciously, to revive in their own lives and for their own culture the classical pagan emphasis on man as "the measure of all things" and on nature as the final scene of human affairs.

To this new adventure the Humanists brought all the pent-up discipline of the long Christian centuries, all the patient scholarship of the monastic schools. The Christian sense of the significance of the individual self, lyrically celebrated in the New Testament and profoundly explored in Augustine's *Confessions*; the Christian sense of the essential

goodness and meaningfulness of nature viewed as the creation of a God of love; and, above all, the Christian sense
of history made meaningful in the mighty acts of God culminating in the entry of God himself into history—all these
and more were distinctive Christian contributions to the
Humanist revival.

But Christians themselves had forgotten or minimized
many of these insights which had enriched earlier Christian
philosophies of the Hellenistic period. Though they believed
in the doctrine of Creation, they had come more and more
to think of the world of nature as an insignificant backdrop
for the great drama of human salvation. Though they believed in the dignity of man made in the image of God, they
had come to stress man's fallen state and to view the individual as merely a part of the complex feudal pattern, born
to a proper station in life and enjoined to keep it. Though
they believed in the possibilities of historical progress, they
tended to think that history had reached its earthly goal in
the medieval society of the City of Man which Mother
Church, as the earthly witness of the City of God, had sanctioned and ordained.

So Erasmus was moved by his Humanist scholarship to
attack the evils of a static Christian philosophy and a stagnant
if not rotten Christian ecclesiastical and social order. In his
works, In Praise of Folly and Enchiridion, he satirized the
empty formality of much current worship and the ignorance
and immorality of many church dignitaries. The Church
must return, he said, to the simple moral teachings of Christ,
and must embrace in a more generous Christian philosophy
the appreciation of the ancients for the ordered goods of this
life. Erasmus, like most other Humanists, believed the flexibility of the Catholic church would make it possible for all
necessary reforms to take place within the historic framework
of Christian faith and institutions. As mentioned before, he
gradually came to oppose the more radical—and, from his
point of view, less cultured—views of Luther. If Calvin could
assert that man's chief end is "to glorify God and enjoy
Him forever," the Humanists could reasonably assert that

God may be glorified most excellently through understanding and enjoying the gifts of his creation.

Thus a great wave of creative activity swept over those parts of Christendom most hospitable to Humanist teaching. The names of Michelangelo and Leonardo da Vinci, Petrarch and Pompanazzi, Chaucer and Shakespeare, are enough to recall the brilliance of the period. A new intoxication with life, with all aspects of man and nature in all of their fascinating variety and wonder, took hold of scholars and artists alike. Experimentation with new forms and new ideas was rampant in all fields from the fine arts to politics (Machiavelli, for instance). In the main, however, the Humanists were concerned to discover, celebrate, express, and enjoy the rich goods of life. With the exception of a few men like Leonardo da Vinci, few were interested also in the investigation of nature for the sheer joy of factual understanding, or for the more practical purpose of controlling natural forces for human ends. Celebration and expression are goals of the artist; understanding and control are goals of the scientist. New understanding and control came with the birth of modern scientific inquiry. The Humanists prepared the way for it, however, by their daring challenge of old ideas and accepted forms, and by their insistence on the independent, nontheological significance of nature and man—particularly of man as a concrete, free, existing individual.

The Origins and Nature of the Scientific Spirit

The essential structure of modern scientific method did not emerge *ex nihilo* from the Renaissance, as many modern scholars have implied. Rather science, like Humanism, was the product of centuries of Greek, Roman, and Christian culture. The Platonic philosophy which Augustine employed and which afforded a basis for acute philosophical thought in the Middle Ages rested on a fundamental premise: namely, that the universe is a rationally intelligible whole which can be understood and expressed by the human mind. Furthermore, Plato himself was influenced by the Pythagorean numbers school, which held that number is the key to the rational understanding of reality—that mathematics is the norm for all rational knowledge. Plato himself exalted mathematics as the most perfect form of knowledge and finally envisioned the whole of reality as an ordered hierarchy of "forms" or "ideas" similar to mathematical concepts. For Platonic philosophy the goal of knowledge is the beatific vision of that form ("The Idea of The Good," for Plato; "The One," for Plotinus), in terms of which all other forms and relations become intelligible. The good life, accordingly, is the life which is rationally ordered by ideals of perfection.

The Aristotelian philosophy, which Aquinas finally integrated with Christian faith, also assumed that reality is an intelligible whole, and deemed contemplation the highest form of human activity. Indeed, the only activity of the "Prime Mover," said Aristotle, is "thinking on thinking"— pure actuality is pure thought. But Aristotle was also interested in observing facts in what Plato called "the world of opinion," as well as in contemplating relations between facts in the "world of truth." It is said that Aristotle commissioned his pupil, Alexander the Great, to collect biological and botanical specimens for him during his far-flung expeditions. Aristotle was convinced that mathematical structures or forms have no existence apart from the material (Plato's "matter") which they structure. So he insisted on *inductive* (leading up) observational knowledge of that which can be grasped through the senses as well as on *deductive* (leading down) knowledge of logical relations. He maintained that the cause of anything has been explained only when four questions have been answered: (1) *What* is it? (Definition or Formal Cause); (2) *Of* what is it? (Material Cause); (3) *From* what is it? (Efficient Cause); and (4) *For* what is it? (Final Cause).

Now the Platonic emphasis on intuitive, mathematical, rational, deductive vision or understanding; and the Aristotelian emphasis on empirical (experiential), observational, inductive, experimental inquiry are two basic aspects of what we today call scientific method. The scientist is concerned to know or understand, through mathematical analysis and expression of reality; he is equally concerned to investigate and experiment with the ever-fresh and ever-changing materials of sensory observation. The deductive side of modern scientific methods springs from the Platonic tradition; the empirical side roots in the Aristotelian tradition.

But the Greek scientists never synthesized the two emphases. Why? The answer to this question is complex, and only a few suggestions may be listed here. For one thing, Greek society was so organized that only people of substance and leisure could engage in philosophic speculation and scientific investigation. The practical tasks of the workaday world were left to serfs, slaves, and artisans. It was undignified and plebeian to concern oneself with the mundane questions of ends and means of physical existence. Higher knowledge was speculative and ordered, like "useless" mathematics; knowledge of techniques for controlling nature was a matter of "opinion," the commonsense of the masses.

Again, underlying most Greek thought was a deep sense of *Moira*, or impersonal fate. Time was thought of as essentially cyclical, and history was conceived as essentially an endless repetition of ordered social changes. If this is the case, the best one can do is bravely to make the most of the situation by living as intelligently as one can and getting out of life such pleasures as one can—or to search for a way of escape from time in the manner of the mystery-religions, and the Hindu philosophy of India. In such a view the Pauline injunction to "redeem the times" is meaningless. Equally meaningless is the patient scientific research which may bear no fruits at all, or may bear fruits to be enjoyed only by some future generation. There was in Greek culture little basis for a view of science as a means of controlling nature and society in the interest of unending human progress.

But the Hebrew-Christian tradition brought to Western civilization the biblical sense of the meaningfulness of creation and history. And a sense of the meaningfulness of time is as essential to modern scientific inquiry as are the Greek emphases on rational understanding and empirical investigation mentioned previously. Furthermore, the rediscovered Hebrew-Christian sense of the inexhaustible riches of creation and of the dignity and power of man made in the image of God, gave new depth and new impetus to the work of discovery in the interest of human good. The early modern scientists brought to their work the enthusiasm of religious vocation. It seemed to them that in investigating the wonders of nature and man, they were thinking their Creator's thoughts after him. Many of them were theologians as well as scientists, and most of them still thought of theology as the queen of sciences.

But classical Catholic and Protestant theologies were based on classical Platonic and Aristotelian science. Indeed, the concept of Final Cause in Aristotelian science came to be the dominant notion of causality employed by medieval scientists. Explanation in terms of *purpose* superseded explanation in terms of mathematical structure, material content, or preceding events. Thus it was generally assumed that all things and events are made and happen for specific purposes and ends. It was natural, then, to explain nonhuman phenomena in terms of human purposes, and human purposes in terms of divine providence.

This type of explanation seemed all the more reasonable in a universe which was believed to be a snug and tidy habitation made for man. The world beyond the earth must be observed from the earth by earth-bound men; so it was natural that the point of observation should be considered the center of the universe. It seemed, then, that the universe revolved around the earth, and the earth was made for man, and man was made "to glorify God and enjoy him forever." Man's response to the purposes for which he was made, as these purposes were revealed by right reason and Christian dogma, determined man's final place in the scheme of things: Heaven, Hell, and Purgatory were as real as the earth, sun, moon, and stars.

Now the new spirit of inquiry manifested in the Humanist Renaissance and in the birth of scientific method burst the bonds of the snug and tidy universe of Greek science and classical Christian theology. Soon men began to observe facts about the world which Greek science could not explain or accepted theological dogma interpret. So much the worse, then, for the old framework, said a few intellectual pioneers. The four greatest barriers to intelligent understanding, said Roger Bacon (1214-1294), are dubious authority, ancient custom, the pooled ignorance of the masses, and the reluctance of men to admit ignorance and error. The commands of God as well as the dictates of reason demand an openness to and humility before facts—any and all facts— and only knowledge verifiable in experience is pleasing to God or profitable for man. In the fifteenth and sixteenth centuries a few intellectual heroes heeded the warnings of this thirteenth-century prophet.

Thus, Nicholas Copernicus (1473-1543) dared finally to challenge the Ptolemaic theory of an earth-centered universe. Interestingly enough, Copernicus was led to his theory, not by observing stars, but by reading Greek. Aristarchus, in the third century before Christ, had suggested that the earth rotates on its axis and revolves around the sun. By combining this suggestion with the accepted Platonic notion that celestial phenomena are to be finally understood in terms of mathematical relations, Copernicus worked out a new "geometry of the heavens"—geometry then being the most advanced form of mathematics available. By using the sun rather than the earth as his fixed point of reference, Copernicus was able to explain simply many phenomena which the older Ptolemaic astronomy could explain only complexly and ambiguously if at all. Copernicus was thus one of the first in the distinguished line of theoretical mathematical scientists. The revolution in men's thinking about the world which resulted from the application of his theory was incidental and secondary. One continuing emphasis of science, we have said, is the dispassionate vision of truth for its own sake.

But the Copernican revolution could not long remain dispassionate. Stimulated by Copernicus' theories, such men as Tycho Brahe (1546-1601) and Johann Kepler (1571-1630) carried forward the work of refining and correcting them to account more readily for observed phenomena. Kepler pointed out that the movement of the planets around the sun is elliptical rather than circular, as Copernicus had thought, and also discovered that the velocity of their movement can be expressed geometrically. Thus, theory led to more accurate observation, and new observations led to refinement of theory, in the leap-frog pattern now normative for science. As the inquiry went forward, men were leaving behind the last outlines of the tidy universe in which they had once lived. Now infinite spaces stretched out in all directions and the earth dwindled to an insignificant satellite of the sun. But the wondrous order of mathematical harmony ruled throughout.

Where, then, was the necessity for the Prime Mover of the Thomistic-Aristotelian system? Why, indeed, raise the question of purpose or Final Cause at all? Is it not enough simply to state mathematically how things happen and let it go at that, without indulging in speculations concerning why they happen? And if the final truth about things can be expressed mathematically, that is, in terms of the quantitative aspects of things—what happens to all the rich world of colors, sounds, ideas, emotions, and "such stuff as dreams are made of?" From now on there would be men who could declare, in the name of science, that such questions are ultimately either meaningless or irrelevant or both, because for science the "real" world is the world of mathematical order.

It was natural, then, that Church and society should strike out blindly at the new knowledge and its proponents. Thus, when Galileo Galilei (1564-1642) devised a telescope and observed phenomena for which the old Aristotelian-Ptolemaic system had no explanation, he was forced to disavow his findings and forbidden to publish anything in the field of astronomy. But Galileo simply turned to the study of terrestrial motion and proceeded to discover equally revolutionary laws in that field. Whether or not he actually dropped his steel balls from the leaning tower of Pisa, he was able to express the law of falling bodies in terms of mathematical ratios and thus to challenge the whole Aristotelian concept of motion. By thus explaining the relation of motion to velocity in terms of Formal Cause rather than Final Cause he set the pattern for modern physics as contrasted with Aristotelian physics.

Furthermore, Galileo emphasized another foundational concept of modern physics by turning to atomic theory as the basic framework in terms of which physical laws may be most handily expressed. Here again the Greeks had a word for it, in the writings of Democritus (460-362 B.C.?), poetically celebrated by the Roman Lucretius (96 B.C.-55 A.D.). Democritus had sought to banish superstition and fear by affirming that all reality is ultimately reducible to the motion of molecules in the void. Galileo found that in terms of such a theory he could neatly express the laws of changes of solids into gases, and many others.

When René Descartes (1596-1650) perfected analytical geometry, and Gottfried Wilhelm Leibniz (1664-1716) and Sir Isaac Newton (1642-1727) discovered the calculus, the basic mathematical tools of modern physics were at hand. Accordingly, the Newtonian view of the world as a mechanically-ordered balance of mathematically describable forces reducible to atoms gradually took shape, and was accepted as the true picture of the real world. Even Newton, however, wrote more books on theology than on physics, and Descartes was driven to postulate an omniscient and benevolent God to hold his system together. But the old world view in terms of which Christian theology had once been comfortable and secure was gone forever. The Aristotelian science on which Aquinas had built his system was discredited; the Ptolemaic world of the Reformers was lost. Men of western Europe found themselves in a vast, coldly impersonal, but harmoniously ordered universe.

For a while they could take comfort in the marvels of the human spirit which could comprehend the universe. If man was a thing, at least he was a "thinking thing" (res cogitans), said Descartes. And the world of thought could not be reduced to the world of matter. Perhaps mind and spirit lay at the heart of things, after all. At least there was an unassailable dignity in man so made in the image of God that he could think God's thoughts after him. Perhaps the real world is, after all, the world of values and ideals which transcends the physical world studied by science. If theology was no longer needed to explain nature, it was all the more needed to explain man.

But the appearance of Charles Darwin's *Origin of Species* in 1859 seemed to many to breach the last citadel of human dignity and transcendence. Man, said the evolutionists, is also merely a child of nature—the end-product of a long struggle for survival among living things, a struggle determined by impersonal laws of natural selection. The creator of nature had long been superfluous; now the creator of man seemed to become superfluous too. Encouraged by the insights of the biologists, men turned hopefully to the development of the sciences of man, the social sciences. Eventually, it was believed, the mysteries of human creativity would be comprehended and expressed as neatly and scientifically as the mysteries of the nonhuman universe had been. Man emerged from the scientific revolution thinking of himself as an animal among animals, with animals and all other phenomena of nature to be understood finally, really, or truly in terms of physical-chemical-biological complexes of a basic energy expressible in mathematical symbols.

But the loss of man's dignity and perhaps of his God were compensated in part by a revolutionary increase in his powers of control and direction of nature and society. Using science as a new and wonderful weapon, he proceeded to transform the face of the earth: to build factories and touch off thereby the social forces of the industrial revolution; to conquer space through new means of communication and transportation; to make significant progress in the conquest of disease; in brief, to make of the world a more comfortable if not a more meaningful place in which to live. "Social Darwinism" pointed to endless progress in the development of more complex and successful survival-mechanisms. The Hebrew-Christian tradition had always pointed to some fulfilment of human life in a glorious future. Perhaps science was the key to that fulfilment; perhaps, when the last experiments were done, the last graphs plotted, and the last statistics gathered, the Kingdom of God (or Man?) would really be at hand. In the light of all that "they" had done, there was simply no telling what "they" would do next, said the man on the street. For many, the laboratory scientist in his white coat replaced the priest in his vestments as a symbol of hope and authority. If science had dethroned God, perhaps science herself (or itself?) should be hailed as the new Messiah in the excitement of the dawning messianic era. Such, in extreme terms, was the more positive and optimistic side of man's reaction to his new method of inquiry and control.

How, then, were men nurtured in the classical Hebrew-Christian tradition to meet the challenge of the new world view in its classical-modern forms? There were, in general, at least three courses open.

1. One could accept the new world view without qualification, transfer his religious devotion to the new truth there embodied and model his life accordingly. This way is epitomized in the religious philosophy of Benedict Spinoza (1632-1677).

2. One could cling to the traditional formulations of faith, confront them with an uncritically accepted scientific view of the world, and emerge an agnostic—convinced that the affirmations of faith and the conclusions of science are irreconcilable and can be jointly believed by one person only if he keeps them in two tightly-sealed compartments of his mind. This way is epitomized in the religious philosophy of David Hume (1711-1776).

3. One could take a second look at both the assumptions of science and the assumptions of traditional theology and perhaps emerge with a more critical view of each which would render them compatible on a deeper and more fruitful basis. This way is epitomized in the religious philosophy of Immanuel Kant (1724-1804).

THE WAY OF RELIGIOUS DEVOTION TO SCIENCE:
BENEDICT SPINOZA

Spinoza's Career

Spinoza began life with the Hebrew name Baruch. He was born in a Jewish family of Amsterdam which had been driven there by the Spanish Inquisition. The Hebrew community in which he grew up was therefore anxiously conservative, uncertain of its future, and adamant in clinging to the old doctrines in their old forms. At the age of fifteen he began studying for the Rabbinate and learned Latin as well as Hebrew. In the process he was greatly influenced by the radical scientific world views of his Dutch teacher, Van den Ende. Eventually he was driven to deny the traditional theory of the Mosaic authorship of the first five books of the Bible, and for this view as well as others he was forced to leave the Hebrew community at the age of twenty-four. It was at this point that he adopted the Latin form of his Hebrew name Baruch—"Benedict." In either tongue the name means blessed, and Spinoza was to know the blessedness of a deep and highly intellectual piety during the remainder of his life as a citizen of the world. He took up the quiet and exacting occupation of lens-grinding, which left him much time for patient study and writing. His trade aggravated a tubercular condition, however, and he died at the age of forty-five as quietly and gently as he had lived. But he left behind the outlines of a philosophical system, breathtaking in its scope and dazzling in its clarity. The Spinozistic vision is one of the great ideas by which men have attempted to understand and live in their world.

Knowledge and Reality

The science which Spinoza knew was the mathematical-rational science of the Platonic-Copernican-Cartesian tradition. His occupation as a lens-grinder was itself a reflection of his interest in the science of optics, one of the earliest sciences to yield exciting results in man's quest for complete mathematical expression of physical phenomena. The reduc-

tion of the mysteries of light to clear mathematical formulae
gave promise of the achievement of similar clarity in all
other areas of human concern. To Descartes and others it
seemed that the basic structure of the universe itself must
ultimately be as rationally consistent and precisely ordered
as geometrical systems. Thus, their intimate and ultimate
concern was to discover the geometry of reality.

But Descartes was finally baffled by the mystery of man,
the "thinking thing." Is thought itself reducible to the
mathematical patterns of things? And how can man be sure
that the structure of his thought reflects truly the structures
of the things thought about? As we have previously noted,
Descartes was finally driven to prove the existence of a most
perfect being after the manner of Anselm and Augustine in
order to secure a divine guarantee that the world of thought
and the world of things thought about are the same world.

To Spinoza, the Cartesian solution of the mind-body problem seemed unnecessarily laborious. It is true, said Spinoza,
that reality is basically rational, ordered, and mathematically
structured: this the science of his day had "proved" con-
clusively. And just as a geometrical system must begin with
certain accepted definitions and axioms, so there is at the
heart of the system of reality a basic reality, the premise in
terms of which all the rest of reality is comprehended. Aristotelian philosophy had used the word substance for that
which stands under all observed phenomena to render them
intelligible as wholes, holding together their "accidents"
(sense qualities) in definable and enduring identities. Spinoza saw no need to discard the traditional metaphysical term,
so he redefined it to make it compatible with the new mathe-
matical-scientific world view. There is at the heart of reality,
he said, "substance." And substance is simply that "essence,"
or definition, the meaning of which necessitates existence:
that which exists necessarily, by definition. Substance is that
which is taken for granted.

But substance, that which exists necessarily by definition,
manifests itself in an infinite number of modes or modifications. Human beings know only two of these modes—mind

and body. But since mind and body are simply two modes of the same infinite substance, that which obtains in the realm of mind also obtains in the realm of body. In the light of the concept of an underlying infinite substance, Descartes' problem of getting mind and body together in a reliably consistent system becomes meaningless. Mind and body are never separated in infinite substance; rather they are two dimensions of the same reality, two aspects of the same world.

God

Spinoza used the word "God" to designate that infinite substance which constitutes the heart of reality. Many interpreters of Spinoza have maintained that his use of theological terms is a sentimental anachronism which only misleads the reader. He no more means by the word "God" what the traditional theologians meant than he means by the word "substance" what Aristotle meant, they say. In a sense this is true, and the student must beware of reading traditional meanings into Spinoza's terms. But in a deeper sense Spinoza appears quite justified in calling the ultimate concept of his philosophy, God. The function of God in his philosophical faith is the historic function of God in the faith of his fathers. God was for Spinoza as for the Hebrew sages who preceded him Alpha and Omega, the first and the last, he who endures through all change and gives final meaning to all things and all events—the object of intimate and ultimate concern. God is the trustworthy structure of reality—the way of things, or the way things are.

Some have said that this means Spinoza is a pantheist, that he affirms the ultimate identity of God with all that is, and thus forsakes the transcendent God of his fathers who is the creator and sustainer of all, but who is not to be identified with any creature. Careful reflection on Spinoza's definition of God and on the function of God in his system as a whole, however, reveals that this is not quite the case. God is, for him, the reason for all that is and the basis of all that is; thus God is, in a sense, *in* all that is. But he is not therefore identical with all that is. He is the infinite and eternal ground of reality whose inexhaustible mystery is manifest in the fact that the mental and physical realities which finite men know are but two of an infinite number of his modes.

But is it correct to speak of the rational structure of reality, that which necessarily exists by definition, as "he?" Is Spinoza's God of philosophical intelligibility actually the warm personal God of traditional religious faith? Well, of course, God as defined by Spinoza is not a person; such an idea is, in his system, ridiculous. And men should not be misled by the personal language used in theology into thinking that God is literally personal. But it is in terms of God that persons are to be finally understood. In the long run it is no more accurate to speak of that which necessarily exists by definition as impersonal than it is to speak of it (or him) as personal. Spinoza was attempting, in his all-inclusive system, to give an intelligible account of all things human as well as of the nonhuman universe. Perhaps he was justified, then, in using the more humane language of personal devotion in referring to that which for him was intimately ultimate.

Salvation

What are the practical implications of Spinoza's ideas of God and the world for the specifically religious problems which have concerned men most deeply? Fundamentally, said Spinoza, religion has been concerned to discover and show to men the way of salvation, or, literally, "health"—to show them how to live the good life and to save them from the consequences of error or sin: to save them from despair. And the root of most sorrow or despair is disappointment, or disappointed desire. Men want those things which they cannot obtain; or, obtaining them, they no longer want them. Herein lies the tragedy of life. Now we have seen that Buddha also tracked down the problem of salvation to the problem of desire. Buddha's solution to the problem was the eventual elimination of all desires. But Spinoza was a man of the West, a child of the life-affirming, history-redeeming Hebrew-

Christian tradition. Therefore he could not counsel men to master and eventually eliminate all their desires in a quest for an indescribable desireless state beyond time and space.

No, said Spinoza, the way to salvation does not lie through the suppression and elimination of all desire. Rather, men must learn to discriminate between those desires which can be fulfilled and those which cannot. And though they must learn to live without the illusory comforts of irrational desires and wishful thinking, they may live all the more fruitfully in the patient, rational pursuit of those goods which a scientific understanding of man and the world permits. There are laws of human nature and human activity just as there are laws of nonhuman nature and nonhuman activity. As the ancient Hebrews proclaimed, God himself is the Lawgiver, the source of that lawful structure of life which man must learn to know and obey if he is to live happily. If the new scientific understanding of the laws of nature makes many of the hopes and affirmations of traditional theology seem impossible or ridiculous, that same understanding applied to the rational direction of human conduct may lead to saner and happier living. If the way of life it enjoins is sober, it is also ultimately more godly and righteous—"a godly, righteous, and sober life," as a familiar Christian prayer puts it.

But what of man's freedom if the ultimate nature of things is simply that inflexibly rational order which scientific investigation discloses? Well, said Spinoza, there is no freedom if one means by freedom exception to the reign of law. Everything that happens, happens because of some law, some logical pattern which reason may disclose. Man himself is no exception to the lawfulness of reality, and human acts are not free in the sense of being lawless. But belief in freedom as completely spontaneous and unpredictable—lawless—activity is inherently contradictory, anyway. If there were any exceptions to the reign of law in nature there would be natural chaos; if there were any exceptions to the reign of law in human affairs there would be social chaos. There would be no moral responsibility for acts completely discontinuous from other acts performed by the same person; there could be no growth of character as a stable whole. And there is a deeper and more meaningful freedom which comes from recognizing all this. In so far as man knows that by which he is determined he is, in a sense, its master. To know what is and what is not possible is the basic requirement for freedom of mind and spirit.

And what of immortality, that other member of the triad God, Freedom, and Immortality with which Western religion has traditionally been concerned? Well, said Spinoza, in the light of the scientific view of the world and the philosophy it suggests there is no basis for believing in the indefinite or eternal existence of particular human beings beyond death. On the contrary, all the evidence points to the end of the individual with the end of his body. But this does not mean that man has no dealings with and no eternally significant relations to that which is above the vicissitudes of time and change. It is given to man to know eternal truth, to comprehend at least some aspects of that which was and is and ever shall be. Though the individual may be mortal, he may know and enjoy in his mortal lifetime that which is immortal. Though he may disappear, there is that which abides. And historic Israel was content for centuries to leave the matter there. The individual may die, it was said, but the community lives. The community may die, but the God of Abraham and Jacob, the God of the living, lives eternally. "I know," said Job as he faced a meaningless death, "that my Redeemer liveth." For Job that was enough; for Spinoza, cosmopolitan child of a later Israel confronting a new scientific view of the world, that was still enough. God, the truth about things which redeems men from false choices and disappointed desires, is eternal.

But what, finally, are we to make of the fact that men live in a world in which the problem of disappointed desire arises? *Why* are there frustrations, why is there pain, why is there evil? What are we to say about the goodness of God in the face of the problem of evil and the ever-present fact of tragedy? Is Job's problem really solved? Well, said Spinoza, let us remember that evil is ultimately tracked down to disappointed

desire. And desires are disappointed because men do not
know what they can, and cannot do, or have. Evil, in other
words, is the result of ignorance. And ignorance is not final;
ignorance is conquerable. This means that evil is not final,
not something to be accepted as the will of God or borne in
the hope of some life of bliss beyond death. Evil and ignorance constitute a challenge, not a problem. And, "under the
aspect of eternity" there is no ignorance. Only truth is eternal; the eternal God is the truth about things. The temporal
appearance of evil is due to man's finitude, his inability to see
things as they really are. As things really are, from the point
of view of God, as it were, there is no evil. Of course, some
thinkers might go on to raise the question, why the appearance of evil? Pursuit of this question might lead to the prior
questions, why time?, or why finitude and history? But Spinoza was content to let the matter rest there.

One more question remains to be asked of Spinoza's system as a religious faith: is it, or can it be, a faith for the masses
of men? Does it not say, finally, that only he who knows can
be saved, that happiness is proportionate to intellectual ability? Does it imply a hierarchy of men based on degrees of
intellectual acumen? Is it ultimately a religion for intellectuals only—and a pale and dispassionate faith at that? In a
sense this is the case, the follower of Spinoza would say. But
the kind of wisdom Spinoza speaks of is not to be identified
uncritically with formal education or book learning. The poor
and the simple may be more profoundly learned in the rational
understanding of the problem of disappointed desire than the
rich and foolish who never really face it. Furthermore, the
saving wisdom of which Spinoza speaks is in principle open
to all men. It is the duty of those who know to know more,
and to share that which they know with those who do not.
There is no limit to the scope and possibilities of scientific
investigation and education based thereon. Certainly Spinoza's own life was characterized by deep humility and quiet
kindliness. And if his way seems harder and less glamorous
than some others, it is Spinoza who reminds us that "all things
excellent are as difficult as they are rare."

THE WAY OF PHILOSOPHICAL AGNOSTICISM: DAVID HUME

The British Empiricists

We have noted that modern scientific method embraces a dual emphasis on logical mathematical deduction, on the one hand, and on experimental sensory induction on the other. Ordinarily, the two go hand in hand; observation leads to theory, and theory leads to observation. Historically, however, the rationalistic-mathematical side of science was advanced significantly before the full impact of the necessity for cautious, accurate observation of facts was felt. Thus we have seen that for Spinoza science was primarily the attempt to express the laws of reality in rationally ordered terms. The Cartesian school with which he was acquainted had little interest in the observation of facts.

In Britain, however, there had been an increasing emphasis on the inductive, observational, empirical side of science. Newton and others there retained the rationalistic ideal of a complete mathematical description of reality in terms of atomic theory. But Newton's own work was greatly influenced by his careful attention to facts hitherto overlooked by scientific theorists. Whether he was stimulated to reflect on the fact of the force of gravity by the fall of the apple is dubious; but certainly he insisted on an openness to new experience and a careful attention to data of sensory observation in his work. And this new emphasis on sense-experience as the final court of appeal in questions of truth and error resulted in a revolution in English philosophy.

John Locke (1632-1704) was so impressed by the success of Newtonian science that he decided it was time for some one to review the whole problem of how men come to know anything. The purpose of his epoch-making *Essay Concerning Human Understanding,* he said, was to "clear the ground before the incomparable Mr. Newton." And this meant clearing philosophical theory of all the assumptions of Cartesian rationalism. The basic assumption of this rationalism, we have seen, is that the human mind is so structured that what

Descartes called "clear and distinct ideas" are grasped by it as intuitively true. And these true ideas of the mind, basically mathematical-logical in character, give clear and certain knowledge of the true structure of reality. To answer the question how we know that this is the case, Descartes was forced to appeal to a most perfect being and Spinoza was forced to ground the mental and physical orders in a divine substance.

But is it true, asked Locke, that there are any ideas intuitively given to the mind, "innate," as it were, in the mind? Actually, the mind at birth is a *tabula rasa,* a blank wax tablet. All knowledge that comes to the mind must come through the five senses—through the medium of sensory experience. Only what we experience is written on the tablet of the mind, and all ideas are built up out of fundamental sensory data. Of course there is still the problem of how the subjective mind makes contact with the objective world in order to prove the accuracy of its sensory impressions. But truth must be defined as the correspondence of mental impressions with the objective world which gives rise to the impressions. One way of checking on the truth or falsity of impressions is to act in the real world on the basis of the impressions and see whether the action conforms to the true pattern of reality. Is this not what the scientists do when they check their theories by experimentation?

But what is the basic character of the "real" world outside the mind? The Newtonian scientists agreed with the Cartesian scientists that the real world is finally that which can be described mathematically. Now mathematics deals with quantity, not quality—with position in space and time, with weight and density, not with colors and sounds as they are apparently experienced in the mind. The physical world which gives rise to sense-experience on which all knowledge rests is, in other words, the measurable world of quantities and nothing more. How, then, does the physical world of quantities give rise to the rich qualitative world of human experience? Well, said Locke, that is where the mind comes into the picture. The experience of qualities is the result of the interaction of mind and physical world. But all experience of qualities is secondary to the primary experience of quantities, and is based, as it were, on the quantitative aspects of reality. Colors, sounds, and all the rest in their richer qualitative nature he called "secondary qualities." And so Locke moved from the eternally-structured world grasped by intuitive ideas of the rationalists to a world divided into a physical world of primary, measurable quantitative units and a mental world created by physical sense-impressions but capable of experiencing secondary qualities.

George Berkeley (1685-1753) felt that Locke had stopped short of consistency. If all knowledge of the world is rooted in sense-experience, or "perception," and such perceptions constitute the basic stuff of the only world man knows anything about, why not say so and let it go at that? Why divide the world into primary and secondary phenomena? Actually the experience of quantities is just as much perceptual as is the experience of qualities. And splitting the world into a quantitative world "out there" and a qualitative world of experience "in the mind" is a carry-over from abandoned rationalistic assumptions. Actually the experienced world is the real world, and the real world is the experienced world. Or, more accurately, the world of perceptions is the world of reality and the world of reality is the world of perceptions and nothing more: *esse est percipi.*

Hume's Theories of Knowledge and Causality

It was with this view that David Hume (1711-1776) began his reflection about man and the world and the relevance of the God of traditional theology to such a world. Born in Edinburgh, he studied law, served as secretary to various statesmen, became librarian of the Faculty of Law in Edinburgh and, finally, Under-Secretary of State (1767-1769). He was, in other words, a man of affairs, and his interest in philosophical matters sprang from his desire to work out a science of human nature. The first edition of his monumental *Treatise Upon Human Nature*, written during a stay in France (1734-1737), was largely unnoticed. A revised and popularized edition attracted some attention, but his chief literary fame during his lifetime came from his history of England.

In the *Treatise* Hume carried forward the insights of Locke and Berkeley concerning the way by which men come to know anything. The basic stuff of experience, he said, consists of impressions and ideas. Impressions are the original perceptions which the mind has of anything—external object or internal mental activity, including those mental activities involved in the working out of mathematical laws. Ideas are later copies, memory-images, of impressions. Truth consists of the agreement of ideas with impressions. Reality, then, is simply the sum-total of multitudinous, discrete, atomistic impressions appearing in temporal sequence: sense-data appearing in time. Time itself is simply the successive moments in which impressions appear. All things, including human selves, are finally reducible to, and most accurately described in terms of, bundles of perceptions. The whole Aristotelian notion of substance thus becomes superfluous.

More significantly for traditional theology, three of Aristotle's types of causality also become superfluous if reality is ultimately nothing but a sequence of sense-data strung along like beads on a string—or like a stream of shot. The string is time; but time is nothing but the discrete moments in which sensations appear, so the stream-of-shot image is perhaps more accurate. In the world of science known through sense-experience as understood by Hume there is no need to raise any questions about purpose, material cause, or formal definition. Final, Material, and Formal Causality are reducible to what Aristotle called Efficient Causality. Our whole idea that the universe is made of causal relations, said Hume, is traceable to the fact that we habitually experience things in certain temporal sequences. Event A is followed by event B, and B by C, and so on. If this sequence is experienced often enough we come to *expect* B when we experience A, and to expect C when we experience B, and so we say A is the cause of B, and B the cause of C. "Causes" are simply the ways in which we usually experience things. Someone has suggested that if "habit is second-nature," "nature," for Hume, is "first-habit."

This means, of course, that we can never have absolutely certain knowledge about anything, even about the apparently well-established laws of nature. Laws of nature are ultimately statistical averages of the way things usually happen. By extending and refining our observations we can indefinitely increase our knowledge of the way things probably will happen, on the basis of the way they have happened in the past in varying circumstances. But our more accurate knowledge must be expressed in terms of degrees of probability, not certainty, if by certainty we mean the kind of eternal validity the rationalists ascribe to mathematical principles.

Miracles

Consider what this view of causality and probability means for one of the traditional bulwarks of belief in a supernatural being, namely the occurrence of miracles. Now a miracle is by definition an exception to the laws of nature—a supernatural as contrasted with a natural happening: an event not explainable in terms of natural law. Actually, according to Hume's understanding of natural law miracles so defined are rendered impossible by definition. There can be no real exceptions to natural law if one subscribes to the Humean understanding of what natural law is—namely, the sequence in which things usually happen. There can be apparent exceptions, to be sure; that is, things may happen which are contrary to that which men have come to expect in a given situation. But this does not mean that the law of causality is thereby abrogated —it merely means that the supposed law in that particular instance must be revised to take account of the unexpected event. What usually happens did not happen in the case of the supposed miracle. This means merely that the causal law in such a case must be restated to take account of the rare exception to what is usually the case. But this means a restatement of probability—inflexible and inexorable certainty is ruled out to begin with.

Actually, however, Hume was interested in examining the supposed evidences of unusual occurrences contained in reports of miracles. Such reports or claims must be examined, said Hume, with a number of basic principles clearly and firmly in mind. One such principle derived from his view of truth and causality is that the true is the usual. The highest degree of probability occurs in statements about what usually is the case. Now miracles are by definition highly unusual occurrences, if they can be said to occur at all. The probability of truth in statements which affirm their occurrence must then be judged accordingly. Statements about the occurrence of miracles must necessarily have a very low degree of probability.

This means that it is all the more imperative that one weigh very carefully the evidence put forth in support of miracles. And in weighing the evidence traditionally offered by orthodox theologians one must note at once the remoteness in time of most of the alleged miraculous occurrences. Much can happen to accounts of events as time elapses between the time of the accounts and the time of the events themselves. Furthermore, one must take into account the interests of those who report the events. What have they to gain by establishing the truth of their claims? To what extent would their desires be likely to color their observations and reports? Again, one must examine carefully the documents through which written reports of miracles are passed on. What guarantee is there that the texts of such documents are accurate, particularly if generations have passed since the original documents were written, no originals are available, and both the original writers and those transmitting later copies would have a personal interest in establishing the truth of miracle-claims? And finally, what is the significance of the fact that different religions make the same miraculous claims in support of the supernatural origin of their beliefs? This fact at least suggests that no one religion can rest its case on such miracles alone.

In general, then, Hume concluded, belief in the occurrence of miracles is reasonable only if all other possible accounts of the events concerned appear to be clearly less reasonable. The presumption in any case is against the occurrence of the miracle. One is justified in revising that presumption only if no other course seems reasonable. This means, then, that in the

matter of miracles and related phenomena traditionally associated with supernatural faiths, it is the course of wisdom to
remain agnostic,—without claims to knowledge.

The Existence of God

Hume's view of causality is devastating for much of traditional theology's arguments for the existence of God. The
only kind of causality which Hume found meaningful, let us
recall, is what Aristotle termed efficient causality. And Hume
believed that he was supported in this view by the actual operations and implications of the scientific theory of his day. Indeed, there are many scientists today who would agree with
the fundamental premises of Hume's view of causality, at
least so far as the specific purposes of scientific investigation
are concerned. Scientific truth, say such scientists, rests on
the statement of natural laws understood as the statistical
average of probabilities in the sequence of selected events. If
one holds to this view as normative for all areas of inquiry,
what becomes of the traditional case for the existence of God?

It is apparent at once that the only one of Aquinas' five
proofs which has any relevance at all is his argument from the
fact of efficient causality to the necessity for belief in a First
Cause in which the chain of such causality is grounded. The
only relevant argument, in other words, is the "chicken-and-
egg" argument, which holds that if all events are effects of
preceding causes, then there must be a First Cause to start the
chain of events going: an uncaused cause which is not itself
an effect. Otherwise, the argument goes, the causal sequence
stretches out to infinity, and then no cause is finally explained.

In reply to this, one who follows Hume argues that such a
First Cause is actually not necessary for purposes of scientific
investigation. The only thing science is concerned with is
the explanation of given events in terms of other events—the
relating of specific effects to specific causes. This process is
not vitiated if one believes that there is an infinite series of
causes and effects rather than a finite series rooted in some
First Cause. The results for science are the same in either
case,—and it is to science that we must turn for trustworthy

knowledge. If particular causes of particular effects are known, what is gained by raising the question of the cause of the whole cause-effect sequence?

Anyway, the concept of an uncaused cause is empirically meaningless. The only causes that we actually experience— and all knowledge must begin and end with experience—are also effects. And all effects we know anything about are also causes of other effects. We simply have and can have no experience of a cause which is not itself an effect.

Furthermore, even if it were intelligible to speak of a First Cause, men could know nothing positive of its (or his?) nature. This point Hume labors brilliantly and at some length in his *Dialogues Concerning Natural Religion*. It is a thrust at a crucial doctrine of traditional theology—the doctrine of analogy, which, it will be recalled, maintains that meaningful statements may be made about God, or the Infinite, in terms of its (or his?) likeness to selected finite realities. But what reason have we for saying that the whole of reality is any more like one of its parts than it is like others—or that the infinite is more like given finites than like other given finites, asks Hume? In the first place, we have no experiences of the whole of reality. We can know only a very little about an infinitesimal part of the whole, if for no other reason than that all the evidence is never in. If one takes time seriously, he can make no final statements about what reality as a whole is like, for new experience might revise the estimate.

Furthermore, what is gained by affirming that the cause of the whole is more like intelligence, for instance, than it is like anything else? One can still ask what caused the intelligent cause? If one is thus driven into an infinite regress, is it not better to rest content with what we actually do observe about the world and not go flying off into speculations about what caused it and what the cause is like? Again, if it were asserted that the cause of the whole world is like intelligence, the intelligence of the cause would be so much greater than and so different from the intelligence of finite beings as to be unintelligible to them. Divine intelligence might well appear to finite intelligence to be divine ignorance, so great is the difference between the divine and the human, the infinite and the finite.

Or again, it is nonsensical to turn to the argument from degrees of perfection to establish belief in a most perfect being as the cause of perfection and the absolute standard by which relative perfection is known to be relative. Causes need to be adequate only to their effects; the assumption that the lower must be explained in terms of a higher is unwarranted. If we experience only relative perfections, then only a cause of relative perfections is demanded—if any cause is demanded at all. And when one is pointing to the relative goods of the world to establish the existence of a most perfect cause of them, let him not overlook the equally numerous and equally significant evils of the world. Evil needs to be explained just as much as good does. Thus, if one feels compelled to relate all goods to a most perfect good, he had better also relate all evils to a most perfect evil. Put into theistic language, this means that at least two Gods rather than one are needed. Actually, the course of wisdom lies in accepting the goods and evils as they are actually experienced and in doing what one can to increase the goods and decrease the evils, without leaping off into useless and time-consuming speculations about the ultimate causes of good and evil.

Freedom and Immortality

Denial of the necessity for a most perfect being undermines the basis for the traditional argument for the immortality of the soul. It is not necessary to point out that there is no sensory experience of immortality to appeal to. Even so-called spiritualist phenomena could prove no more than the indefinite existence of some sort of consciousness beyond the death of the body. It could not prove the eternal existence of anything. Man simply has no experience of eternity or timelessness. All his experience is limited to time and space; to speculate about timeless conditions is nonsensical.

But actually, the traditional arguments for the immortality of the soul rest not so much on these empirical considerations as on the belief in a most perfect being. It is on the goodness of God rather than on the constitution of man that the case for immortality finally rests. God being what he is, Aquinas said, it is unreasonable to suppose that he would make man the glaring exception to the rule that all longings in the world are fulfilled—that he would put into man's soul a thirst for eternity which can never be quenched. But according to Hume's views it is impossible to know, philosophically, what God is, or if he is. If the existence of a most perfect being cannot be proved, then the immortality of the soul cannot be proved either.

Turning finally to the other member of the theological triad, God, Freedom, and Immortality, it remains to be shown that there is no meaningful sense in which it may be said that man is free. This should be apparent from the basic premises of Hume's views of man and causality. The human self, he said, is ultimately a bundle of perceptions and nothing more. But all perceptions are part of the vast world of perceptions constituted and held together by causal law which is simply the way things usually happen. For every event is an effect of some cause, and every cause is also the effect of some other cause. A spontaneous, free act in the sense of something which originates itself is therefore impossible. All that men are and do is the result of some lawful cause. Men are merely constellations of events strictly determined by heredity, or environment, or both. Hume's view of freedom, let us note, is simply a reflection of his views of selfhood and of time; and these, in turn, are reflections of his basic assumption that reality is merely the sum-total of atomistic impressions.

Agnosticism and Faith

Science, as Hume and those who follow him understand it, cuts the ground from under many of the affirmations of traditional theology. Does this mean that religious faith becomes irrelevant for one who accepts the basic principles of Humean analysis? In answering this question let us recall a fundamental premise of the whole Humean outlook: *it is impossible for men to have certainty about anything.* This means that men can no more be certain that God does not exist, that there is no freedom or immortality, etc., than they can be certain that such traditional beliefs are true. Nothing more than probability holds in either case. Therefore, one would be untrue to the Humean outlook if he arrogantly and finally denied any of the affirmations of faith. He must be as humble and cautious in his denials as in his affirmations. In other words, the most he can be is agnostic—without knowledge, reserving judgment on dubious theological assertions. The most he can say is, "while it may be the case that miracles happen, that man is free and immortal, and that a First Cause like Intelligence or Perfection exists, because nothing is certainly impossible; nevertheless, the most reliable evidence available to me, interpreted according to the principles of that science which I trust in all other areas of life, makes it extremely doubtful that these things are true; and I will therefore order my life accordingly."

Other thinkers, in turn, would underscore the significance of the phrases "evidence available . . . interpreted according to the principles of . . . science." At most this means that a philosophy based on science as Hume understood it can offer no proofs for the existence of God, immortality of the soul, and so on. In other words, the case for natural theology, or the approach to God through unaided reason may be seriously damaged if not destroyed by this type of philosophical analysis. But is the case for revealed theology also destroyed? Does the discrediting of reason in these matters also discredit faith? If man cannot establish a God by reason, is he then prevented from believing in a God who reveals himself to man when reason breaks down? Indeed, is not the whole attempt to prove the existence of God ultimately a form of proud blasphemy from the standpoint of religious faith? Perhaps man is made to know only that about God which God freely reveals and which man accepts in trusting faith. Perhaps the whole enterprise of natural theology is really an attempt to make God into man's image, and perhaps Hume, the agnostic, is motivated in his criticism by a profound religious instinct.

It is interesting to note that the spokesman for philosophical skepticism in Hume's *Dialogue* is encouraged and usually supported by the spokesman for theological orthodoxy as against the spokesman for rational theology. Demea, the believing Christian, applauds the efforts of Philo, the skeptic, to destroy the complacent rational arguments of Cleanthes, the natural theologian. There are those who maintain that Hume is thereby ridiculing orthodoxy as well, and that the skepticism is ultimately more devastating for Demea than it is for Cleanthes. Indeed, there are points at which Philo wistfully entertains the possibility of at least part of Cleanthes' argument's being sound. But the difficulty of knowing just where Hume's tongue is in relation to his cheek makes it very difficult to say which, if any, of the views argued in the dialogue he himself is espousing most heartily. At other times he spoke like an orthodox Christian; but perhaps he was then paying a cynical lip-service to a view with which he had to get along in his public career. In any case, there are among contemporary theologians a number who would hold that philosophical skepticism or agnosticism are actually implied as prerequisites to profound faith. We turn now to one who, roused by Hume's criticisms, went on to criticize the basis of the criticisms themselves and emerged from the venture with a suggestive and significant view of the relation of religious faith to scientific knowledge.

THE WAY OF CRITICAL KNOWLEDGE AND MORAL FAITH: IMMANUEL KANT

Kant spent nearly his entire life (1724-1804) within the bounds of his native city, Koenigsberg. He was reared there in a Pietist Protestant family, attended the university there, and later became a tutor, librarian, and professor of a wide range of subjects in the university. He developed an early interest in mathematical science and worked out some astronomical hypotheses which still receive attention. But his interest in astronomy led him into the broader field of philosophy, and he eventually decided that the problem of knowledge

is basic to all fields of human concern. He was at first a follower of the rationalistic tradition espoused by Descartes and
Spinoza; his masters in the tradition were Leibniz and Wolfe.
But the writings of the English Empiricists convinced him
that the basic assumptions of Rationalism must be re-exam-
ined in the light of the development of the empirical, observational side of the new scientific method. "The writings of
David Hume," he said, "roused me from my dogmatic slum-
bers." Yet he could not go all the way with Hume in his
Empiricism; he still felt that there are valid insights in the
rationalistic tradition for which the Humean philosophy could
not account. What was needed, then, was a bold new critique
of Rationalism and Empiricism alike: a critique of scientific
method.

Kant's Critique of Science

THE NATURE OF SCIENTIFIC KNOWLEDGE. In his *Critique
of Pure Reason* Kant accepted the Empiricist premise that all
knowledge is rooted in sense-experience. Yet, he said, the
mind's role in cognition is not simply the passive role of
Locke's "wax tablet." Closer analysis of what men actually
know reveals that there are certain truths which seem valid
apart from the sense-experience which may bring them to
mind—truths to which experience itself must conform if it is
to be intelligible. How can this be, if the Empiricists are
right? Kant phrased the question technically as "How are
synthetic judgments *a priori* possible?" A synthetic judgment
is a statement which includes truth in the predicate not already implied in the subject; *a priori* means prior to experience. Such mathematical statements as "two plus two equals
four," and such metaphysical statements as "every event must
have a cause" are examples of synthetic *a priori* judgments,
said Kant. From a deductive analysis of the concept "two"
and the concept "plus" we cannot arrive at the concept "four";
yet we know that two and two are four whether or not there
are four items there to be counted. Such a statement would
be true even if there were no items to be counted. Similarly,
the causal character of experience is not given in the bare

sensory processes of perception. Rather it seems as if we knew prior to any possible experience that any and every item of experience must be understood in terms of cause and effect.

Now later logicians would take serious exception to these examples of what Kant thought to be "synthetic judgments *a priori*." Nevertheless, they may serve to point to the basic fact which Kant had in mind—namely, that the mind brings something to experience as well as receives something from it. There are limits to the way in which the world can be intelligibly experienced, and these limits are constituted by the nature of mind itself. Experience is not merely the unfolding of *a priori*, innate ideas, as the Rationalists assumed; nor is it merely the building up in the mind of concepts derived entirely from sensory impressions, as Hume and the British Empiricists assumed. Rather, experience is a two-termed affair to which mind and world both contribute. "Concepts without percepts are empty," said Kant, but "percepts without concepts are blind." Science demands for its full operation both the *a prioris* of the Rationalists and the sense-data of the Empiricists. Neither is reducible to the other, and scientific method is impoverished if it stresses the one to the exclusion of the other.

How, then, do mind and world interact to produce knowledge? Well, said Kant, all knowledge begins, as Hume said, with the physical fact of sensation. Things impress themselves on the mind as the result of physical contact with sense-organs. We can know things only as they appear to human sense-organs under specific conditions. We cannot know things as they are "in themselves," we can know them only as they appear to us. Kant expressed this by saying we can know only "phenomena," not "noumena"—only what reality is like from the point of view of human minds, not what it is like apart from the distortions of such relativity. But phenomena are all we need for scientific purposes, and the whole of scientific knowledge consists of the careful structuring and testing of the experience of phenomena.

What, then, does the mind bring, as it were, to the encounter with reality which originates in sensation? In the first place, there are two necessary "forms of sensibility" in terms of which all sensation must occur: time and space. We can have no sensations which are not located in space and time. And location in space and time is a function of the interaction of mind with things-in-themselves; it is not a fact of the world apart from mind. Again, sensations located in space and time must be understood in terms of certain basic "categories of the understanding" if they are to become intelligible materials for knowledge. The previously-mentioned, cause-effect character of all perceptions is an example; all knowledge must be related to the category of causality, and the category of causality is a function of the encounter of mind with reality—it is not given in things-in-themselves. In this vein Kant proceeded to deduce twelve such categories, including existence and relation.

But finally—and more significantly, for our purposes—it seems necessary for men to relate all empirical knowledge, structured by the forms of sensibility and the categories of understanding, to three broader and more fundamental ideas, if the actual operations of scientific method are to be intelligible. In the first place, it is necessary to hold all the multifarious data of experience together in terms of some universe, some whole of experience. There must be some principle of unity for all external experience. This principle of unity of external experience Kant called "the world." Similarly, there must be some principle of unity of all internal experience. Man is not, as Hume claimed, simply a bundle of perceptions with no integrating center, no *I* which persists through all the changes of perceptual life. The changes of internal experience themselves would be unintelligible if it were not possible to refer them at all times to the immediately given sense of *ego*, personal identity persisting through all sensory change. This principle of unity of internal experience Kant called "soul." And, finally, the world of internal experience and the world of external experience are somehow always understood to be ultimately aspects of one world. Descartes, Spinoza, and the other Rationalists were correct in saying that there must be some fundamental assumption of identity between the subjective world and the objective world in true knowledge. Though the ontological argument employed by Descartes in this connection is unsound from the standpoint of scientific method, nevertheless there must be some principle of unity in terms of which the unified objective world and the unified subjective world are immediately known to be one and the same world. There must be some common ground for soul and world. This principle of unity of internal and external experience Kant called "God."

SCIENCE AND THE THEISTIC PROOFS. Does a correct analysis of scientific method lead to a proof of the existence of God? Not at all, said Kant. As a matter of fact, he took great pains to expose what he believed to be the fallacy involved in all the historic proofs of God's existence. All of them, he said, are really forms of the ontological argument. That is, the most that any of them does is prove the necessity of a certain idea in terms of which certain operations of the mind in the world are rendered intelligible. For instance, the argument from causality in the world to the necessity for a First Cause proves nothing more than the necessity for some idea in terms of which causality becames intelligible. Similarly, the teleological argument at most proves the relevance of the idea of purpose to certain human concerns. But to prove the relevance of an idea is not to prove the existence of a being corresponding to that idea. The assumption that logical necessity means necessary existence is the root-fallacy of all Rationalism, which the Empiricist critique must banish once and for all. Its classic expression, we have said, is the ontological argument. In this argument the relevance of the idea of a most perfect being is taken to be proof of the existence of a most perfect being. But no idea in itself implies existence, said Kant. One can have a perfectly clear idea of a hundred dollars in his pocket. For all rational purposes, the mentally-existing hundred dollars have all the characteristics of actually existing money. But the only way in which it can be proved that such money actually exists is to put one's hand in the pocket to see. That is, judgments about the existence of anything and everything are subject to the test of sense-experience.

Now it is obviously impossible for men to have any sensory experience of a most perfect being as an existent in space and time; in this Hume is clearly right. Similarly, it is impossible for men to have any experience of the world as a whole, the soul, or God defined as the principle of unity for world and soul. The world as a whole is never experienced because all the evidence is never in. And reason cannot determine whether the evidence will ever be in—whether the world is eternal, with no beginning in space and time, or whether it is finite, with beginning in space and time. Pursuit of either notion leads to insoluble difficulties, as Kant showed in his famous "antinomies of pure reason." In dealing with the notion of world, reason is dealing with its own limits—and with one of its own basic presuppositions. Man cannot experience the world as a whole; yet none of his experience of parts of the world is intelligible without reference to the idea of world-as-a-whole. How, indeed, can he be aware of the partial, finite, relative character of his knowledge without some reference to an unlimited, infinite absolute?

Similarly, we can have no sensory experience of the soul. As Hume said, we can experience only states of consciousness, perceptions; from the standpoint of experience we are merely bundles of perceptions. But what is the "I" which holds the bundles together? We cannot experience the soul, but we can make no sense of any experience without reference to the soul, or ego. Indeed, men who lose all sense of ego-identity are insane and incapable of any rational judgment.

It follows, then, that we can have no experience of God as *a* being among other beings, existing in space and time. If we can have no sensory experience of world or soul, then we can obviously have no sensory experience of that which is the ground of world and soul. And it is ludicrous to speak of God as "*a* being," if he is that in terms of which all beings are understood. Hume is right; there is no scientific experience of God. But on the other hand, no scientific experience of anything is intelligible without reference to the idea of God. Scientific knowledge cannot establish the existence of, but at the same time cannot do without, God. The ideas of world, soul, and God are "transcendental ideas" or regulative ideals of all possible knowledge. They do not point to concrete beings accessible to empirical observation. They point rather to the limits and presuppositions of all possible observation and knowledge. In brief, careful analysis of pure reason, or scientific method as Kant understood it, suggests that pure reason points beyond itself for its own justification. The operations of reason themselves are rooted in some primal acts of faith. The demands of practical experience are prior to the demands of theoretical considerations. The critique of pure reason leads to an awareness of the primacy of practical reason—the primacy of *praxis*, human existence in the full rich range of its manifold concerns, over *theoria*, the purely intellectual aspect of existence. Scientific method itself is but one expression of the practical or existential concerns of man. Therefore, it is finally to be understood in terms of a broader analysis of the full dimensions of human life. And this means an analysis of man's experience of values as well as analysis of man's experience of facts. "Two things I would determine," said Kant, "what can I *know*, and what ought I to *do*?" His critique of science, or the answer to the question "what can I *know*?" led him to recognize the priority of the question "what ought I to *do*?" Thus, one result of *The Critique of Pure Reason*, he said, was the "clearing of the ground to make room for faith." And faith has to do with *praxis*, not *theoria*.

The Practical Basis of Faith

VALUE-EXPERIENCE AND THE MORAL LAW. A fundamental assumption of Kant in *The Critique of Practical Reason* is the assumption that values are not reducible to facts. Values are values, and facts are facts; value-experience is one thing, fact-experience is something else. "Ought" does not mean the same thing as "is." And no amount of accurate factual knowledge of what is the case is sufficient in and of itself to determine what ought to be the case in any human situation. The confusion of "ought" and "is," or the determination of their exact relationship, are basic problems of contemporary social and ethical theory. Kant, at any rate, was convinced that the answers to questions about "ought" rest on a critical analysis of man's experience of moral values conceived as a ·distinctive and irreducible kind of experience.

Are there, then, any laws of the moral life comparable to the laws of nature discovered in scientific inquiry? Does the practical reason have its own necessary structures comparable to the structures of pure reason revealed in the first *Critique?* Well, said Kant, if man's experience of values is reduced to that which is open to sense-experience and judgments derived therefrom, there are no laws of moral experience. The only facts to which we can point in our experience of values are the facts of desire and satisfaction. One wants this, does that, and experiences specifiable pleasure or pain. That, in effect, is all that can be said about value experience from a strictly scientific point of view. Scientific investigations of value-experience may reveal accurately an amazingly complex pattern of needs or desires, techniques for fulfilling needs or desires, and states of pleasure or pain resulting from the employment of such techniques. But the only laws which can emerge from such investigation are hypothetical maxims phrased in terms of "if . . . then." "Scientific investigation discloses," it may be said, "that *if* men want *these* satisfactions, *then* this course of action is most likely to bring them about." But concerning *what* satisfactions men *should* want, science can say nothing.

Yet practical reason needs law, not maxims, said Kant. Law is characterized by universality and necessity; it applies always and everywhere, not just some time at some place; and it applies necessarily as "must," not contingently as "might." A law of practical reason would have to be stated in terms of "ought . . . always," not in terms of "might . . . if." Is there, then, any such law? Yes, said Kant, there is—but only one such. He expressed it in different words at different times, but one of the most significant expressions is this: One ought always to "act only on that maxim whereby thou canst at the same time will that it should be a universal law." That is, one ought never to adopt as a maxim for his own actions a rule

which he would deny to others. He must judge his own acts
by the same law he employs in judging others'. He cannot
make an exception of himself in justifying moral judgments
and moral acts. Fundamentally, this is the law of recognizing
the essential *equality* of all persons in moral matters. Thus a
more suggestive expression of the moral law is "persons should
be treated as ends, never as means." In matters of morality,
all men are equal under the law. As a matter of fact, it is only
in terms of such moral law that the equality of men can be
plausibly affirmed. Men are not equal in physical gifts or
mental endowments. They are not born to equal stations in
life. The only sense in which it may be said that they are
equal is a moral sense: equality before the law, the moral law.

As a matter of fact, the moral law as Kant understood it,
is simply the Golden Rule of Jesus and the Silver Rule of Confucius. Indeed, it seems to emerge in all cultures where men
have thought profoundly about the bases of moral action.
But its universality is not dependent on its justification by a
sort of cosmic Gallup-poll, Kant would say. It is a "categorical imperative." This means that its validity is universally
prior to any specific applications or discoveries of it. It would
be valid even if no man had ever defined it. The laws of
nature do not depend on their discovery by scientists for their
validity, and they do not become true when their truth is first
recognized by men. Indeed, men's understanding of natural
law changes—but natural law does not thereby change too.
So it is with moral law; it has always been true, is always true,
and always will be true everywhere that men should do unto
others only that which they would have others do unto them.
How men come to recognize this; whether they come to recognize it; how they apply it to specific moral choices; indeed,
whether they apply it to moral choices at all—all these matters
are irrelevant to the law's validity. In other words, the moral
law is not itself a *maxim*. It gives no universal sanction to
any particular *mores*, that is, particular applications of the
law to changing social situations. It has to do with morals as
distinct from mores; it has to do with the principle by which
the moral validity of mores is judged. The moral law, the

categorical imperative, is the supreme principle of moral action.

FREEDOM. The analysis of practical reason, issuing in the statement of the categorical imperative, reveals that those matters of religious faith which pure reason, or science, must leave in abeyance even in its dependence on them, emerge as necessary postulates of practical reason. The "regulative ideals" of pure reason become the necessary implications of practical reason. Where pure reason must remain wistfully agnostic, practical reason speaks with the authoritative voice of practical experience—that is, the experience of human existence in its full dimensions as an ongoing, committed, involved concern. Moral faith must affirm that which science can neither affirm nor deny, but which science needs in the presuppositions of its own life.

For instance, from the standpoint of pure, or scientific reason, there is no such thing as human freedom. Hume is right; the only data accessible to scientific knowledge are facts—deposits of action in the causally-determined world of nature. An uncaused act is, for scientific understanding, impossible by definition; the very purpose of science is to reduce apparently spontaneous and chaotic events to the neat pattern of causal law. Furthermore, science always investigates the past —what *has* happened, and thus its determinism is retrospective as well as definitional. But practical reason demands precisely that freedom which pure reason denies. "Ought," said Kant, means "can"—and "can" means "may, or may not." There could be no sense of "ought" in a completely determined world. Automatons could never experience moral necessity! If there were no freedom, there could be no choice; and if there were no choice, there could be no sense of "oughtness." But a sense of oughtness is a given fact of practical experience. Therefore, practical reason affirms as logically necessary that which for pure reason is logically impossible, namely, human freedom. Furthermore, if there were no freedom, the very pursuit of pure reason would itself be meaningless. In the name of freedom the scientist pursues his free inquiry, and the world is constantly transformed by the results of the inquiry. But a fundamental assumption of the inquiry is that there is no freedom. Clearly, then, we must trust the affirmations of moral faith—the logical postulates of practical reason—if we are to make sense of our scientific inquiries themselves, not to speak of the social causes of freedom and democracy to which even cynics feel that they must at least pay lip-service. The freedom on which democracy is based rests ultimately on moral faith.

God. While pure reason denies any literal existence of God it needs the ideal of God to make intelligible its own operations. But practical reason affirms the practical necessity of God as an implicate of its very being. Why? In simplest terms, merely because the presence of moral law implies a lawgiver. We experience the moral law in all our moral actions, for good or for ill. But how are we to account for it? Where did it come from? What guarantees it? Pure reason cannot account for it; practical reason demands it. Therefore it is more reasonable to believe that there is a divine source of moral law than to believe the contrary. And the Hebrew-Christian tradition as well as others has always thought of God as, among other things, the lawgiver. Belief in God as the only intelligible ground for righteousness is logically demanded by practical reason.

God is necessary, not only as the ground of internal and external experience for pure reason and as the source of moral law for practical reason, but he is necessary as the harmonizer of what is and what ought to be. Consider the fact that the moral law demands obedience, regardless of the consequences in terms of pleasure and pain. Indeed, Kant was so eager to divorce questions of right and wrong from questions of pleasure and pain that he seems at times to say that anything pleasant is likely to be wrong. But even if one does not carry the point to the rigorous and puritanical extremes reached by Kant, a Kantian would say that questions of pleasure or pain for one's self or others do not exhaust the obligation implied in the categorical imperative. A good act is, finally, good for nothing beyond itself. Virtue is—or should be—its own reward. So thought Confucius, with his principle of Yi; and so thought Kant.

At the same time, pleasure and pain are to be reckoned with, and the enjoyment of pleasure is a good. In one sense it could be said that the supreme good would be the achievement of maximum happiness. But in the strictly moral sense implied in obedience to the categorical imperative, the supreme good is *worthiness to be happy*. Happiness is not always proportional to moral worth, or vice versa. And yet rationally there can be only one supreme good. If happiness is a good, and moral worthiness is a prior good, then it is more rational to assume that moral worthiness and happiness are somewhere and somehow balanced in the ultimate scheme of things than it is to assume the contrary. Logically, worthiness implies happiness, and happiness implies worthiness in a single *summum bonum* for man. Once again, then, it is more reasonable to believe in a God who ultimately proportions happiness to worthiness than not to believe. Moral reason demands moral faith in a God who is both lawgiver and judge, working out his law in terms of reward and punishment. Not that hope of reward or fear of punishment are morally justifiable motives for good conduct—good conduct must be an end in itself or it is not good. But if men obey the moral law as an end in itself, and happiness is also a good, then it is more reasonable to suppose that such altruistic conduct will issue in happiness than not to believe this. Moral action is possible, to be sure, without belief in God as judge. But moral action is then simply blind obedience to an irrational law. With belief in God as lawgiver and judge, moral action becomes rationally intelligible.

IMMORTALITY. Rational understanding of the moral law demands an ultimate proportioning of happiness to worth. Now it is obvious that there is no such universal balancing in this world. The problem of Job remains. Is it not more reasonable, then, to believe that there is another world beyond this in which the consequences of rational moral judgment are worked out, than not to believe this, asks Kant? Critical analysis of the implications of the moral life here and now points logically to a life beyond. Thus, while Hume is correct in affirming that there are no grounds in scientific knowledge for affirming immortality, once again there are grounds in practical reason for affirming that which pure reason cannot establish.

Or, perhaps more profoundly, Kant suggested that man is led by the categorical imperative to recognize the validity of moral goals for human society which may never be realized in human society. He is seized by visions of righteousness which is beyond his achievement here and now. Yet his awareness of the "impossibility" of these moral "possibilities" does not vitiate their validity. He may let it go at that, and admit that his ideals are ultimately irrational in the sense of being unattainable. But is it not more reasonable, asks Kant, to believe that there is a life beyond this life in which man can continue his progress toward moral perfection? The very impossibility of achieving in this life the moral ideals derived from the categorical imperative establishes the logical necessity for moral faith in immortality.

A New Basis for Natural Theology

As was the case in the treatment of Spinoza and Hume, we have obviously oversimplified and condensed almost to the point of distortion the religious philosophy of Kant. There is not space here to go into the further reflections on basic religious themes contained in his *Religion Within The Limits of Reason Alone,* and other works. In some of these, he attempts to relate his philosophical conclusions more definitely to the insights of Christianity as a historic faith. Because of his emphasis on such moral categories as sin, judgment, justification, and redemption, he has been called the Thomas Aquinas of Protestantism. In a sense, he did for his age, in terms of pietistic Protestant Christianity and Newtonian science, what Thomas Aquinas did for his in terms of Catholic Christianity and Aristotelian science. While Spinoza transferred his religious devotion to the new mathematical science and redefined traditional religious concepts accordingly, and Hume emerged a philosophical agnostic from his criticism of traditional theology in the light of Newtonian science, Kant went ahead with a critique of both science and faith in quest of a new *modus vivendi* between the two.

Many aspects of his system are of course open to serious criticism, and Western philosophy since his time has in a sense been a continuous debate on the meaning and implications of Kant's "Copernican revolution of the mind." Certainly, religious philosophy since his time has been greatly affected by the new point of departure suggested by him. In many circles all interest in the old metaphysical proofs of the existence of God and other phases of theology as a demonstrative science has disappeared. For many men the question is no longer that of the superior rational validity of theism as a system of metaphysics. Rather the roots of religious faith are sought in man's value-experience—in his moral, aesthetic, and perhaps distinctively and uniquely religious experience.

SUGGESTIONS FOR FURTHER READING

BURTT, EDWIN A. *The Metaphysical Foundations of Modern Physical Science.* New York: Harcourt, Brace & Co., Inc., 1925.
———. *Types of Religious Philosophy.* New York: Harper & Bros., 1951.
BUTTERFIELD, HERBERT. *The Origins of Modern Science.* New York: The Macmillan Co., 1951.
DAMPIER, WILLIAM C. *A History of Science.* New York: The Macmillan Co., 1931.
DESCARTES, RENÉ. *Selections,* ed. R. Eaton. New York: Chas. Scribner's Sons, 1928.
FRANK, PHILIPP. *Modern Science and Its Philosophy.* Cambridge: Harvard University Press, 1949.
HUME, DAVID. *Selections,* ed. C. Hendel. New York: Chas. Scribner's Sons, 1927.
KANT, IMMANUEL. *Selections,* ed. T. Greene. New York: Chas. Scribner's Sons, 1929.
LOCKE, JOHN. *Selections,* ed. S. Lamprecht. New York: Chas. Scribner's Sons, 1928.
RAND, BENJAMIN. *The Classical Moralists.* Boston: Houghton Mifflin Co., 1909.
———. *Modern Classical Philosophers.* Boston: Houghton Mifflin Co., 1924.

RANDALL, JOHN H. *The Making of the Modern Mind.* Boston: Houghton Mifflin Co., 1940.

SPINOZA, BENEDICT. *Selections,* ed. J. Wild. New York: Chas. Scribner's Sons, 1930.

TAYLOR, F. SHERWOOD. *A Short History of Science.* New York: W. W. Norton Co., Inc., 1949.

WHITE, ANDREW D. *A History of the Warfare of Science and Theology.* New York: Appleton-Century-Crofts, Inc., 1897.

WINDELBAND, WILHELM. *A History of Philosophy.* New York: The Macmillan Co., 1901.

Chapter 12

MODERNISM AND HUMANISM

THE orthodox faiths of Judaism, Roman Catholicism, and Protestantism were formulated before the emergence of modern science. What answer has traditional religion given to these questions which science has raised for modern man? One possible answer is a big, resounding no to science at all points where science is thought to encroach upon traditional religion. This attitude of stubborn resistance to science and its religious and philosophical implications has characterized Protestant Fundamentalism. Other thinkers and groups, taking science more seriously, have wrestled with its implications for religion. In this chapter the main tenets of two such groups, the Modernists and the Humanists will be set forth. They are similar in that they attempt to come to terms with science in a positive and constructive manner. But beyond this fact, they are uneasy bed-fellows. Modernists have retained much more traditional religion than have Humanists. Thus Modernists charge Humanists with throwing the baby out with the bath, while the Humanists reply by accusing Modernists of half-hearted compromise with outmoded tradition.

Modernism

In the nineteenth and twentieth centuries, many Jews sought to bring their faith into line with changing times and conditions; however the vital center of Judaism is not philosophy or theology but a way of worship and conduct. Therefore, while many Jews would agree with the tenets of Modernism, it has not assumed the proportions of a definite movement in Judaism. In the case of Catholicism, the closely integrated authority of the pope has prevented the rise of Modernism. In the first years of the present century a group of French and German Roman Catholic scholars adopted many Modernist ideas, and their views were proscribed in a papal encyclical entitled *Pascendi* issued in 1905. More recently the encyclical letter *Humani Generis* of 1950 dispelled any renascent tendency to Modernism in Catholic circles.

Modernism is thus largely a Protestant phenomenon. The absence of any central authority in Protestantism, and the Protestant emphasis upon individual freedom have contributed to making it a varied, protean tendency. It must be kept clearly in mind that Modernism is by no means a unified type of religion or religious thought. Nor is it simply identified with specific Protestant denominations, though its influence has been greater in some than in others. It is at best a tendency or direction of thought, embracing a wide variety of men and ideas. What has unified it is a spirit of accommodation and constructive compromise with new, changing modes of thought. Modernists have sought in many ways to reconcile the new science and traditional religion, resisting alike antireligious attitudes on the part of scientists and antiscientific attitudes on the part of religious Fundamentalists.

Does Science Imply Materialism or Positivism?

Some thinkers in the modern era would answer this question with a yes. Some have argued that the methods and results of science make it plain that matter is the ultimate or final reality, and that therefore belief in God, the human soul, immortality, and other traditional religious tenets is no longer possible for reasonable men. Others have argued that, from the viewpoint of scientific knowledge, these articles of traditional religious belief are past human understanding, since man can truly know only such things as science successfully deals with. The latter answer, in contrast to the former, defines the attitude of Agnosticism or Positivism.

Modernist replies to such attacks upon traditional religion have taken many forms. Often they have taken the form of showing that scientific knowledge, while true and useful in its proper place, cannot be generalized or converted into a total philosophy of life. Often the reply has been an attempt to prove rationally and philosophically what the Materialists and Agnostics deny—an attempt to show that science implies or entails not Materialism or Agnosticism but Theism. Often new developments in scientific theory have been taken to show that science is really not hostile to religion. Thus, new developments in physical theory such as the quantum theory, relativity theory, or the Heisenberg principle of indeterminacy have been taken as evidence that Materialism is false, that God exists, or that man is free. In a similar vein, excursions into philosophy and religion by eminent scientists have been widely used for the same end. The writings of Eddington, Jeans, Arthur Compton, Lecomte DeNouy, and many others have been used to show that science and religion are compatible. Not infrequently religious people have found themselves in the embarrassing position of advocating one side of a controversial scientific question, or at times of espousing a scientific idea that turns out to be mistaken, or even of getting God back into the universe through the holes or gaps in present scientific knowledge.

But despite such pitfalls, Modernism has proven to be a great stimulus to both philosophic and religious thought. The task of relating science to religion in such a way as to do full justice to both—the search for a philosophy adequate to these as well as other forms or modes of experience—has stimulated creative thought in the contemporary world as it has in other times and places. The relation of science to religion emerges as an important theme of such philosophers as A. N. Whitehead, W. E. Hocking, and S. Alexander, as well as occupying the attention of such philosophical theologians as F. R. Tennant, D. C. Macintosh, and others. It is a restatement of the faith-reason problem.

What Are the Religious Implications of the Theory of Evolution?

As we have seen, the developing cosmology of modern science necessarily had great influence upon religious thinking. Thus the scientific conclusions of Copernicus, Galileo, and Newton raised questions and gradually forced revision of previous ideas. But for many reasons their influence on the popular mind was neither immediate nor extensive. The case was otherwise with Darwin and the publication in 1859 of his *Origin of Species*. Reaction was immediate, vigorous, and widespread.

It is true that long before Darwin and Wallace men had believed in the mutability of species. But it had been a speculative belief without scientific, factual foundation. What Darwin did was to amass, carefully and patiently, factual support for evolution from paleontology, from embryology, from comparative anatomy, and from genetics. Also, in the mid-nineteenth century the prestige of science had grown to a point where no major result could be hidden from the general public. As a consequence, men in the street were concerned about Darwin as they had not been concerned about Copernicus or Galileo.

The first religious reaction to Darwin came significantly from Archbishop Wilberforce at the British Association for the Advancement of Science in 1860. The Archbishop had taken honors in mathematics at Oxford, but he had little understanding of science. He had been crammed by scientific friends for the purpose of ridiculing Darwin (note that opposition to Darwin came not only from theologians but from scientists as well). But Thomas Huxley rose to defend Darwin and to administer a severe rebuke to Wilberforce. In the years that followed, Huxley earned the title of "Darwin's bull dog" by his vigorous defense of the idea of evolution.

Further religious reactions to Darwin were mixed. A group of liberal churchmen published in 1860 a book of essays pointing out the compatibility of evolution and the true essentials of Christian belief. But others in Europe and America followed the lead of Archbishop Wilberforce in resisting evolution, denouncing it as a denial of the biblical story of creation, or as an atheistic denial of God. The resistance movement gained such prominent adherents as Prime Minister Gladstone of Great Britain, who crossed swords with Huxley, and later William Jennings Bryan in the United States.

The struggle went on at the level of popular religion and also at the level of serious thought. In the former respect, a crisis was reached in the Fundamentalist movement in the United States in the first two decades of the present century. The Fundamentalists were an interdenominational group which sponsored a series of pamphlets entitled "The Fundamentals." Among the fundamentals of the Christian faith, they maintained, was belief in verbal biblical inspiration and consequently a flat rejection of evolution. Believing Modernism to be a betrayal of precious Christian truth, they fought the enemy wherever they found him. They gained considerable strength in several Protestant denominations. In the state of Tennessee they sponsored a law which forbade the teaching of evolution in any state-supported educational institutions. Issues came to a climax in 1923 in the trial at Dayton, Tennessee, of a high school biology teacher named Scopes for violation of the law. William Jennings Bryan, lawyer, prominent Presbyterian layman and Fundamentalist, offered his services to the prosecution, and Clarence Darrow made a similar offer to the defense. Scopes was subsequently convicted, and it was not until almost three decades later that Tennessee's law against the teaching of evolution was repealed.

But while such proceedings occupied popular attention, the controversy concerning evolution also went on at the level of serious scientific, philosophic, and religious discussion. Some men took the attitude of simple opposition to evolution. (It is to be noted that for many years this was the attitude of some scientists, for instance, Louis Agassiz.) Others took the polar opposite view, arguing that evolution was plainly true, and that it made any theistic account of human origins impossible. But between these extreme positions many men sought in one way or another to reconcile evolution and Christianity.

They presented various lines of thought. In the first place, they were quite willing to surrender the literal, historical truth of the Genesis account of creation. This passage, they said, was myth or poetry whose real purpose was to celebrate God's activity in the creation of man. In a similar vein such men sought to limit science to what they conceived its proper sphere. Science, they argued, made no claim to be total or complete knowledge. Therefore, evolution is to be understood and accepted as a specific theory concerning human origin and development, but not as an all-embracing philosophic view. Some men argued that while evolution might explain man's body, it could not explain his soul. Others understood it as a genetic account of facts, and sought to exempt values or mind from evolutionary explanation.

So understood, evolution was held to be consistent with theism. Science and religion were thought to refer to different aspects of man's life. Evolution gives the *how* of human development and religion the great *why*. Religion goes beyond science, but at no essential point conflicts with it. After all, no scientific explanation touched the concept of an absolute beginning, and that is what the Hebrew-Christian doctrine of creation deals with.

Such ideas received some support from scientific writings. As the scientific examination and development of the theory of evolution proceeded, the concepts of mutation and emergence became more important. Some religious thinkers were quick to lay hold of these ideas and put them into service. Was not emergence a scientific way of saying miracle? God was seen at work not only in mutations but in the whole flow of evolutionary change. Lloyd Morgan's *Emergent Evolution* was thought to provide an adequate foundation for a theistic interpretation of evolution. Bergson's *élan vital*, described in *Creative Evolution*, was seen as the hand of God. The pages of Alexander's *Space, Time and Deity* were likewise studied for apologetic purposes.

Such modernist compromises were by no means unanimous. Many religious thinkers rejected them outright as untenable mixtures of science and outmoded tradition. Nevertheless, however understood or interpreted, the theory of evolution has proven itself a great stimulus over all the range of human thought. In the biological sciences it has turned out to be the integrating and directing theory, which organizes previously gained knowledge and suggests ever-new lines of research. Taken up by the philosophers and written with a capital E, it has been used as an inclusive frame of reference emphasizing the dynamic, moving character of reality. Doctrines of cosmic evolution have been proclaimed from the days of Herbert Spencer to the present. Belief in evolution has been mixed with value judgments to produce conceptions of social progress. In all this there is doubtless much that future generations may discard as uncritical and foolish. But within such a context modern man has lived and thought.

To many religious people, the problem of evolution has in more recent years lost much of its sharpness and urgency. They believe that the Fundamentalists had a false position. Honesty of mind and openness to new truths are great goods and indeed are virtues demanded by the Judeo-Christian tradition itself, they feel. Thus evolution is surely to be accepted and understood for what it is, a well-established and highly useful scientific theory. To them it seems compatible with theism, although it does not positively require theistic explanation. Furthermore, evidence of biological nature, while significant, does not seem to them the most crucial evidence for (or against) religion.

Is the Bible Obsolete?

Another problem for modern religious belief has centered in the Bible. For many centuries, the Bible was clothed in a supernatural sanctity. Regarded not only as the Word of

God but also as the literal "Words" of God, no questions were asked. Scholars allegorized what seemed irrelevant, or trivial, or contradictory, and investigation proceeded no further. But with the coming of modern skepticism and modern methods of historical and literary study the situation has been radically changed. Among the pioneers in modern biblical study was Spinoza, who was excommunicated from the synagogue for his heretical views. The great German author and critic, Lessing (1729-1781), contributed much to applying the methods of literary and historical scholarship to the Bible. Such work gained both in extent and intensity, so that the nineteenth century saw the emergence of a movement called "higher criticism." "Lower criticism," which meant the comparison of different biblical texts with each other, in the search for the most reliable texts, had always been regarded by the Church as a legitimate enterprise. The higher critics, however went much further, drawing upon all relevant evidence from archeology, linguistics, and other sources, seeking to discover the true and original meaning of the biblical text. The methods of the higher critics represented simply an application to biblical study of prevailing methods of literary and historical analysis and these, in turn, were an application of the evolution or development of ideas to these areas. In the case of both the Pentateuch in the Old Testament and the Synoptic Gospels in the New Testament, the problem of authorship seemed crucial. Who wrote these documents, and when, and where, and under what circumstances, asked the higher critics? They refused to accept the voice of tradition as authoritative when it seemed to them to conflict with factual evidence. They might thus be compared to detectives who set persistently to work to solve the question of biblical authorship.

In the case of the Pentateuch, J. Wellhausen (1844-1918) and others amassed a great deal of evidence to show the impossibility of Mosaic authorship. Conservative scholars in Jewish, Roman Catholic, and Protestant circles resisted the hypothesis with great vigor. For Fundamentalists the Mosaic authorship of the Pentateuch was a truth to be defended at all costs against skeptical and unbelieving scholars who sought to undermine the authority of God's word. However, from the first there were students of the Bible (among whom Samuel Driver may be cited) who accepted the new tools of scholarship as valuable instruments for gathering and testing facts, without ceasing to regard the Bible as divinely inspired.

In the case of New Testament studies, Bruno Bauer (1809-1882) and his student, David Strauss (1808-1874) shocked the faithful and drew bitter criticism for their unorthodox conclusions. But as in the case of Old Testament criticism, the movement was seen in the course of time to be less hostile to religion than was at first imagined.

As the movement for biblical criticism proceeded, and Fundamentalist opposition grew ever more intense, Modernists sought again to reconcile traditional faith with new knowledge. Fundamentalists tended to believe in the verbal interpretation of biblical inspiration, arguing that the whole Bible had been miraculously dictated by God. Its inerrancy was a necessary testimony of its divine authorship. Modernists on the other hand were more apt to see discrepancies and conflicts in the Bible. But since they did not hold to biblical inerrancy, such admissions had no religious significance for them. The Bible, they said, presents abiding religious truth in transient categories. The men who wrote the Bible were surely children of their own time and place, but at times the spirit of God spoke through them. An *inspired* book, in the minds of many Modernists, is essentially an *inspiring* book. Their case for biblical inspiration became thus, in the fashion of Schleiermacher, a doctrine about human experience. Some Modernists, seeing the variety of ideas about God and human goodness in the Bible, spoke of the Bible as the record of man's thought about God and human goodness. Other Modernists or Modernist readers saw in its changing categories the double search of man for God and God for man.

It was only a step from ideas of variety and development in the Bible to the application of the concept of evolutionary progress to it. Modernists, ever alert to contemporary modes of thought, made the step by looking at the primitive conceptions of God in the earliest biblical stories and at Jesus' conception of the Heavenly Father. They then proceeded to argue that the Bible illustrates the evolution of religious ideas. (For a popular and comprehensive exposition of this view, see H. E. Fosdick's A *Guide to the Understanding of the Bible.*) Thus, confident Modernism argued that it could preserve in good intellectual conscience all that is religiously necessary or significant in the Bible.

In biblical studies recent decades have tended to bring this judgment into serious question. Biblical students have tended to distinguish more sharply than previously, problems of textual study and of biblical theology. In the former they have continued to accept and to use modern methods of biblical study, though even here they have been able to point out a great many places at which previous Modernist students of the Bible were misled by the assumptions with which they approached the facts. The notion of an evolutionary development in the religious ideas of the Bible has been subjected to a withering fire. The facts of the biblical record must be approached and studied in their own terms, and when they are, they reveal no such neat evolutionary development.

Recent study has also turned its attention from textual matters to the religious content of the Bible, or biblical theology. While it is still a controversial topic among students of the Bible, it is a not unnatural step to proceed from the text to its content. Such post-Modernist attitudes have in recent years become increasingly prevalent and popular. From this viewpoint, Modernism is soon to have fought a good fight in saving biblical studies from the dead hand of literalism and Fundamentalism. But Modernism was too preoccupied with textual questions to ask seriously what the Bible says, and too enamored of modern man to hear anything sharply discordant with his views and ideals.

How Can We Know Which Religion Is Best?

The traditional formulations of Judaism and Christianity antedated West-European man's knowledge of the rest of the earth. Therefore they took no cognizance of the religions of Asia, or of the religions of primitive man. The age of discovery and exploration which opened Europe's eyes to the rest of the world coincided with, and was interrelated with the age of the liberal and radical question of tradition that was sketched in Chapter 11. Travelers from Asia, America, and the islands of the seas brought back accounts of religion and ethics differing significantly from traditional Judaism and Christianity. At first, such tales could be shrugged off as stories of noble savages or benighted heathens, according to one's prejudices in such matters. But gradually they became the material for serious and extensive study. We have already touched upon the development of anthropology and the light it has shed on religion in Chapter 1. Concurrently, an equally important discovery and investigation of the great religions of Asia was taking place. Under the editorship of Max Mueller (1823-1900) fifty-one volumes of the Sacred Books of the East were translated into English. Other contributors to the enterprise of the comparative study of religion included E. Burnouf, C. P. Tiele, C. de la Saussaye, S. Reinach, and G. F. Moore. They sought to broaden the religious perspective of Christian Europe by a look at the Orient. As Mueller put it, "he who knows only one religion knows none." By a study of all religions, some felt, one may select the best which each has to offer, sifting out the errors and mistakes in the rest. Some early students of comparative religion also had a more ambitious aim. By the careful gathering of facts from all parts of the world and an inductive study of the facts, they hoped to produce generalizations which would constitute a science of religion, which would supplant previous methods of studying religion as science had supplanted other methods in other fields of study.

Such an enterprise made a forcible impact upon traditional belief at several points. First and most urgently, the new knowledge of other religions brought into question the finality of the Christian religion. In view of what is now known about the oriental religions, can one believe that Christianity is God's final and only path to salvation? Or are there many ways of faith or paths of salvation? And if so, what of their relative efficacy or validity? Faced with this situation, Fundamentalists were content to retreat to a statement of the exclusiveness and finality of Christianity. Others, surveying the data of the world's religions, concluded that all religions are equally false. Again Modernism sought the middle way of compromise and readjustment. Christianity as a historic tradition and community has, they held, many precious and distinctive elements of truth. But there are other less worthy elements which might be sloughed off. In confronting people of other religions, Christians should seek to share their faith with them, seeking not the destruction of the other religion, but the reconception of both faiths in the light of the new truth discovered through neutral communication.

Such a view was espoused by the report of the Laymen's Foreign Missions Inquiry,[1] by Professor W. E. Hocking. It was bitterly attacked by conservatives as being sub-Christian or unchristian, and by Humanists as compromising with outmoded traditions.

RELIGIOUS EMPIRICISM

Now all of these developments listed above—the emergence of physical science, of the theory of evolution, of the higher criticism of the Bible, and of the comparative study of religion —were actually facets of one scientific revolution. We noted in the last chapter some of the ways in which philosophers tried to come to grips with the rise of the scientific method as the normative form of all inquiry. And we saw that one effect was the increasing prestige of Empiricism in philosophy as contrasted with Rationalism and Idealism. It was natural,

[1] *Rethinking Missions: A Laymen's Inquiry After One Hundred Years* (New York: Harper & Bros., 1932). See also William Ernest Hocking, *Living Religions and a World Faith* (London: George Allen & Unwin, Ltd., 1940).

then, that those religious philosophers who sought to make a constructive liaison with the new scientific spirit should turn to the possibility of developing empirical religious philosophies. But the meaning of the terms "Empiricism" or "empirical" is by no means self-evident; we have noted that the Empiricism of Hume led him to religious conclusions quite different from those reached by Kant on an empirical basis. In general, it seems that philosophers of the recent past who have claimed to be empirical have meant one or more of three things when they used the term.

Religious Realism and the Problem of Evil

The word "empirical" is frequently used to denote a certain temperament, a certain way of approaching problems. William James called the empirical temperament "tough-mindedness." By this he meant an uncompromising acceptance of facts as the beginning and end of all significant philosophizing, and the subordination of all neat theories to the hard facts of experience. Sometimes the word "realistic" is used to denote this attitude—though it may be remarked that the meaning of realistic depends on what is actually real. In any event, we have seen in Hume a rigorous empirical realism which led him to confess a frank Agnosticism rather than try to explain away such stubborn facts as those of human finitude and evil.

Even so, a great many Modernist religious philosophers have committed themselves to an uncompromisingly realistic, empirical approach to the more stubborn and puzzling facts of human experience which religious philosophies purport to explain. No religious dogma and no rationalistic, philosophical assumption may be excluded from the necessity of squaring with the facts of human experience, they have said. And if the facts of experience seem to call in question some of the neat assumptions of traditional religious philosophy, then those assumptions must be either discarded or radically revised. Such an attitude demands courage in the face of opposition by traditionalists, and it demands an ability to live with unsolved problems rather than attempt too-easy solutions.

Now, one of the most puzzling facts of human experience with which any religious philosophy must come to terms is the fact of evil in the world. We have seen that traditional philosophies have usually found ways of explaining evil without apparently explaining it away. But many contemporary religious Empiricists feel that traditional explanations of evil must be discarded in the light of the new devotion to Scientific Empiricism understood as a realistic attitude of mind. Thus, Edgar S. Brightman,[2] for many years a teacher in Boston University and a versatile scholar whose writings have greatly influenced hundreds of Modernist ministers and others, has maintained for a number of years that the fact of irrational evil in the world renders empirically untenable the traditional Christian belief in both the omnipotence and the pure goodness of God. Careful empirical analysis of the facts, he says, suggests that the only coherent interpretation points to a God who is indeed pure goodness in the sense that he wills the best for man in love, but who is finite in power. Like man, God faces a given fund of irrationality and evil. He is continuously overcoming such evil, and man's highest calling is to participate in the work of divine redemption. Man may do this in the confidence that evil will never overcome good, though good is continuously overcoming evil. This is indeed the Gospel of Christianity, says Brightman: the message of a loving God who suffers with and for man in the continuous triumph of good over evil through suffering love.

Other Modernist religious philosophers disagree with the precise formulation of the problem of evil in terms of a finite God put forward by Brightman, but most of them agree that evil in the world is finally something to be grappled with and overcome rather than something to be explained in terms of speculative theory.[3] Many are content to leave the origin of evil a mystery, and maintain that man is called to overcome evil rather than to explain it. Others would explain evil in

---

[2] Edgar S. Brightman, A *Philosophy of Religion* (New York: Prentice-Hall, Inc., 1946), chaps. viii, ix, x.

[3] Thomas S. Kepler (ed.), *Contemporary Religious Thought* (New York: Abingdon-Cokesbury Press, 1941), *passim*.

terms of evolution and progress; the evil man does, they say, is the result of vestiges of bestiality or cultural lag, the price man pays for progress through struggle. Implicit in this view, of course, is the faith that time itself will ultimately redeem man from evil as he extends his knowledge and intelligence. Many who hold this latter view feel that science, in one form or another, is the final weapon put into man's hands for the conquest of evil. In any event, traditional theological-mythical and philosophical explanations of evil are discarded in an effort to be as empirical as possible in approaching the most baffling of all problems in religious philosophy.

The Appeal to Religious Experience

But Empiricism has frequently meant, not only a tough-minded attitude toward problems, but an appeal to experience as the final basis for all philosophizing. We have noted Hume's emphasis on sense-experience as the beginning and end of all fruitful theorizing and the conclusions to which this type of appeal to such experience may lead. Today, certain philosophers in the Logical Positivist or Logical Empiricist tradition are carrying on the Humean form of Empiricism.

However, we have also noted that the results of an appeal to experience as the touchstone of all philosophizing largely depend on one's initial understanding of what experience is. Given Hume's assumptions about the bare facts of pure experience, many of his conclusions follow. It is often the case that the plausibility of such empirical philosophies consists in moving back and forth between at least two different conceptions of experience. Experience is conceived as rigorously limited to sense-experience in attacking other nonempirical philosophies, but it takes on a broader and more inclusive meaning as the Empiricist begins to build his own philosophy.[4] But, if one expressly broadens one's understanding of what bare experience is, to include the experience of self-consciousness and of moral and aesthetic values, as Kant did, then rather

[4] See Y. V. Krikorian, *Naturalism and the Human Spirit* (New York: Columbia University Press, 1944), for numerous examples.

different conclusions emerge. Even so, since the time of Schleiermacher, whose famous *Addresses on Religion* appeared in 1799, many religious philosophers have maintained that any empirical philosophy worth its salt must deal with religious experience as an irreducibly significant form of experience which must be included in any truly empirical philosophical view of the world. Religious Empiricism has also meant, then, an appeal to religious experience as the basis for religious theory.

Schleiermacher himself defined religious experience in terms of feelings of absolute dependence. Such feelings, he said, are universally had by all men, and they are not finally to be explained away in terms of other types of experience. In thinking about God, then, one begins with man's experience of God and works from man to God, rather than vice versa, as was frequently the case in traditional Christian theology. And if some of the traditional dogmas about God are not borne out by an analysis of man's actual experience of God, then such dogmas must be abandoned or redefined. God is the progressively understood object of human religious experience.

From this rather radical reorientation of theological thinking, however, Schleiermacher eventually arrived at some amazingly orthodox Christian conclusions. Further analysis of man's experience of absolute dependence, he said, reveals those more specialized forms of experience dealt with in the traditional Christian doctrines of sin, repentance, and grace. Indeed, said he, the traditional Christian creeds are empirically derived from the basic religious experiences of those who formulated them. And Schleiermacher was sufficiently immersed in an essentially Christian culture to assume that such experiences are universal to all men, and that the Christian formulations are thus universally and experientially verifiable.

While Schleiermacher did not call himself an Empiricist, because the word Empiricism had a somewhat narrow connotation in his day, later Modernists have based their religious Empiricism on the type of appeal to religious experience exemplified in his writings. Thus the late Douglas Clyde

Macintosh, for many years a teacher in the Yale Divinity
School and one of the most influential Protestant religious
philosophers of his day, maintained that theology, based on
religious experience, is as truly an empirical science as are the
natural and social sciences based on more selective appeals
to other types of laboratory experience. In one of his most
influential works,[5] he addressed himself to an exhaustive
analysis of a type of religious experience which he called right
religious adjustment. This experience is basically the Christian experience of sin, repentance, and grace described by
Schleiermacher. More than a thousand years of Christian
history, Macintosh said, have produced a vast store of laboratory examples of what happens when men adopt a certain
attitude toward God and themselves and open themselves
experimentally to the operations of his love. All sorts and
conditions of men and women who have submitted to the
experiment of God's grace have produced abundant testimony
of the results. Furthermore, the essential elements of the
experience and the joyous fruits of its results alike are described in essentially similar terms by men and women of all
cultures and all stations of life. Here, then, are the laboratory
experiments upon which empirical theology may build. Furthermore, as a result of the analysis and interpretation of such
experiences, empirical theology may make confident predictions in the approved manner of hypotheses-for-testing common to all sciences. The empirical theologian can say to anyone willing to fulfil the conditions of the experiment, "if you
will sincerely adopt these attitudes towards yourself and God,
commit yourself to these values and to this creative possibility,
I predict the following results for your life . . ." And no man
who is unwilling to undertake the experiment of Christian
living is in a position to speak significantly of its possibilities
or results. Like all other empirical sciences, Christian theology rests its case finally on a "come . . . and see."

Now, other Modernist religious philosophers have proceeded from somewhat different understandings of what basic

[5] Douglas C. Macintosh, *Theology as an Empirical Science* (New York:
The Macmillan Co., 1919).

religious experience or right religious adjustment is and have thus arrived at somewhat different conclusions. For instance, Henry Nelson Wieman, for many years teacher in the Divinity School of the University of Chicago and also greatly influential in the Protestant Modernist movement, stressed in his early writings a form of experience he called problem-solving mysticism. Such experience involves a quiet and sincere opening of one's self to the vast range of unachieved good; a frank facing of one's immediate problems and shortcomings in the light of this immediately felt infinite creativity; a conscious and determined formulation of specific plans of action to bring one's life into closer accord with the actual creative possibilities of one's immediate situation; and venturing forth in the faith that creative factors in the world are available to sustain one in the venture of creating human good.[6] Through such experimental religious experience men may come to know progressively more about the cosmic source of human good. Incidentally, Wieman feels that God, understood simply as the source of human good, should not be described in terms of the language of the supernatural as contrasted with the natural, common to traditional Christian theism. A metaphysic compatible with modern science, he says, suggests that nature is the most inclusive category of reality. God, as that structure of processes on which human good depends for its existence and increase, is ultimately within rather than outside nature.

Scientific Method in Theology

The foregoing suggests a third meaning for the word empirical in recent philosophical discussion. Empiricism, some philosophers hold, is finally not so much a philosophic attitude or an appeal to experience as the basis for valid theory as it is an insistence on the centrality of a particular method of verifying all truth-claims in all areas of human inquiry. The distinctive thing about science, such philosophers say, is not so much its careful attention to the facts of experience,

[6] See Kepler, op. cit., pp. 290-96; and James A. Martin, Jr., Empirical Philosophies of Religion (New York: King's Crown Press, 1944), passim.

reflected in the patient integrity of the scientist, as it is the highly refined and powerful method of investigation and verification implicit in the scientific enterprise. The essential ingredients of this method are observation, hypothesis, experiment, and formulation of theory designed to lead to further observation, and so on. Science, such men say, is first and foremost a way of doing things—the most successful way yet devised by man to discover truth about himself and his world.

Such an understanding of science has had an effect on the empirical philosophies of such men as John Dewey. The religious Empiricists identified with Protestant Modernism have also made use of such an understanding of the scientific empirical method. Some of them, like Brightman, feel that the emphasis on observation and induction—the appeal to experience, and operations based on such an appeal—must be balanced by a further concern for rational coherence in the interpretation of the data. But Brightman insists that his religious philosophy is faithful to this broader understanding of the empirical method, and he is careful to state again and again that absolute certainty in religious matters is rendered forever impossible by a sensitive appreciation of the hypothetical and unfinished character of empirical verification. The old certainties of traditional theology, he says, must be replaced by faith-hypotheses based on the best available evidence and the most rigorous use of the "method of coherence."

Similarly, Macintosh insisted that his appeal to right religious adjustment as the basis for empirical theology also resulted in religious hypotheses subject to verification by an empirical method in all essentials like that employed in other empirical sciences. And Wieman's "problem-solving mysticism," he says, is actually the more inclusive and more personal experience out of which devotion to scientific method itself flows. In so far as Wieman conceives of God as a form of process, following the lead of Whitehead, it may be said that for him devotion to God and devotion to scientific method are two dimensions of the same basic human commitment. In general, all Modernist thinkers, like the three we have chosen for illustrative purposes here, have felt that their religious faith is in all essentials not only compatible with but actually necessary for the critical, broad characteristic of the scientific empirical method. For rationalistic deductions from theological dogmas they would substitute religious hypotheses derived from an analysis of religious experience through the use of broadly scientific empirical method.

Criticisms of Religious Empiricism

Now many questions have undoubtedly occurred to the careful reader in the course of this brief exposition of some typical emphases of religious Empiricism. In general, these questions probably fall into two categories:

1. There are those who, from the standpoint of theological concern, ask whether the eagerness of the religious Empiricists to come to terms with science has not resulted in unnecessary distortion of the traditional message of the Judeo-Christian tradition in the interest of a curiously ambiguous apologetic.

2. In addition, there are those who, from the standpoint of philosophical concern and intellectual integrity, have asked whether the religious Empiricists and other Modernists are not finally, consciously or unconsciously, half-hearted in their acceptance of scientific Empiricism and its implications for traditional theology. For instance, are the tough-minded religious Empiricists sufficiently realistic in their appraisal of the problem of evil? Is not the logical outcome of their analysis honest philosophical Agnosticism rather than belief in a finite God—a concept which raises as many problems as it solves? Or again, what actually is proved by the appeal to religious experience? By what norms is one form of religious adjustment declared right, and to what extent are the results of religious experiments predetermined by the cultural conditioning and personal bias of the individuals undergoing them? Does not a truly empirical analysis of the religious life of mankind lead to a religious pluralism rather than to the assertion of the superiority of one religion over others? And how actually scientific are the religious Empiricists in their

philosophic method? Do they not finally appeal to unwarranted metaphysical assumptions in order to make sense of data which, in terms of a more rigorously applied empirical-scientific method, must remain unexplained? If one reduces God to a complex of factors in the environment to which man must adjust for human good, and if all significant thinking about God must begin and end, not with God, but with man, then why not make a clean break with traditional theology and frankly adopt as one's basic categories man and nature? Such are the questions raised by naturalistic Humanists, and to a more detailed consideration of their critique and programme we now turn.

THE HUMANIST FAITH TODAY

The Nature of Humanism

The term "Humanism" has been used in a wide variety of ways. The emphasis of the ancient Greeks upon a full and balanced life is often called Humanism. In the same tradition, the Renaissance affirmed in literature and philosophy the distinctive excellence of man's life on earth. Supernatural religion tended to derive all human value from God, and to regard this life as only a preface to eternity. No, replied Renaissance Humanists, man's life here and now has intrinsic worth and dignity. More recently writers such as Paul Elmer More and Irving Babbitt have sought in the name of Humanism to defend man's intrinsic worth against attacks by an often cynical and reductive Naturalism or Realism in literature. Still a different meaning is attached to the term by the French Catholic philosopher Jacques Maritain, who speaks of a Christian or integral Humanism, arguing that the Christian tradition has been the bearer or carrier of human worth and dignity in Western history. In a sense broad enough to embrace all of these uses, Humanism means the affirmation of what is distinctively valuable or excellent in man, whether in art, philosophy, or religion.

In the previous chapter we have looked at some of the factors in modern thought which worked against traditional religious belief. These factors have been largely, though by no means entirely, connected with science. As far back as Democritus and Lucretius men expressed views similar to the Humanism with which we are here concerned. In modern times men like Spinoza and Hume questioned belief in God, immortality, and other aspects of religion. In the nineteenth and twentieth centuries, these questions increased apace. Unable intelligently to believe in God, many men resolved to believe in man and human righteousness. Unable to believe in theological explanations of the major concerns of man, many turned to scientific method and scientific explanation as normative for belief and conduct. This complex of beliefs and disbeliefs may be called "Humanism." It constitutes an attitude widespread in its explicit, articulate form, and even more so in its inarticulate or tacit form.

It may be questioned whether one ought to use the term, religion, for Humanism. Is it properly a way of faith? Many Humanists as well as many traditionally religious people would stoutly argue that it is not. Such questions turn upon the definition of religion. If religion is limited to belief in the supernatural, then obviously Humanism is not religious. But if religion is defined by the role it plays in human life, then surely Humanism functions as a religion in the lives of many of our contemporaries. Many Humanists, for example, Julian Huxley,[7] seeing this function, do not hesitate to call Humanism a religion. Also, it will be noted that Humanism has at times been organized as a religious, or quasi-religious, movement. Since Humanism appears as a genuinely living option for many people, especially among students, teachers, and intellectuals generally, it may be appropriately studied as a religion. Indeed, it is not unfair to call it the fourth main religious option, along with Judaism, Roman Catholicism, and Protestantism, for thoughtful men in the contemporary Western world.

[7] See Julian Huxley, *Religion Without Revelation* (London: Ernest Benn, Ltd., 1927).

Humanist Beliefs

BELIEF IN SCIENCE. Most Humanists would decry anything like a creed. The term, and the idea for which it
stands, have too often been used to perpetuate outworn ideas
and to enforce standards of belief by methods of intolerance
and persecution. Nevertheless, any faith or philosophy has
certain distinctive tenets that may be set forth in systematic
form. What, then, are the basic and distinctive beliefs of
contemporary Humanism?

Humanists show first and perhaps most basically a profound belief in science. The key to Humanism is the impact
of science upon the modern mind, and upon modern life.
The Humanist attitude toward science is one of confidence,
trust, and deep gratitude for past achievements and future
promise. Through science, says the Humanist, man can effectively work out a satisfactory life for himself upon this
earth. This belief has many facets and many implications.

For many Humanists the essence of science is not any conclusion or body of results but its method. Therefore, devotion to the method of scientific knowing is the first article in
the Humanist credo. The enormous success of scientific
method in many fields since its beginnings, a brief three or
four centuries ago, warrants the boldest confidence in the
method, and the greatest hope for its future. Many Humanists are bold to declare that the political and social problems
which now beset mankind will be solved only if outmoded
methods of study and knowledge are supplanted by scientific
knowing.

Often the point is made that, as compared with other
methods of knowing, the method of science is eminently successful. "See the impressive mass of results in verified, tested
knowledge which science has amassed in the fields where it
has been tried," says the Humanist, "and compare these results with other purported ways of knowing." Taking their
stand upon science, Humanists have been highly critical of
other purported methods of knowing as unscientific or prescientific. Corliss Lamont, a forceful exponent of Humanism

today, lists as other ways of knowing "revelation, authority, intuition, and rationalism" arguing that none of them can begin to claim the successful results of science.[8]

Concerning the nature of scientific method there is a variety of views among Humanists. Sometimes no very strict definition is offered; scientific method, it is said, is simply the method of inquiry employed by scientists. Others are content to regard it as commonsense sharpened, made rigorous, and equipped with modern tools or instruments. However, one group of contemporary philosophers, the Positivists, have devoted much effort to a careful and painstaking analysis of scientific method. The term "Positivism" was given currency by the French philosopher, Auguste Comte (1798-1857), who traced three main periods in the history of human thought. In the first or theological period, men explained events by reference to supernatural beings; in the second or metaphysical period, by reference to abstract speculative concepts like Being, Mind, Matter, etc. Only in the third or positive period did men learn to seek specific or positive causes for all happenings. Positivists thus take their stand upon the reliability of scientific method. Taking his stand upon positive or scientific knowing, Comte rejected traditional belief in God, but suggested as a substitute the worship of humanity. He actually organized a positivist "church" and planned its worship and symbolism.

More recently the logical analysis of scientific language has been carried to great refinement among a group called "Logical Positivists." Reliable or verifiable knowledge is obtainable only by scientific method, they say. Metaphysical or theological statements present no possibility of verification or disproving, and are consequently pseudo-knowledge. Other forms of statement possess only an emotive meaning. The support in such a doctrine for Humanism appears dubious, but it is a fact that many Logical Positivists are Humanists.

While Positivism is antimetaphysical, some thinkers who

[8] Corliss Lamont, *Humanism as a Philosophy* (New York: Philosophical Library, Inc., 1949).

stress dependence on the scientific method of knowing are not averse to a metaphysical statement of their position. The object of scientific knowing, they say, is, in one or another of its aspects, nature. Naturalism is the philosophy which holds that nature is all the reality there is. Many Humanists are Naturalists. The term carries many meanings, and is not without ambiguity. Nature as a neutral system of cause-effect relations, which goes its way indifferent to human hopes or fears, is the essential reality according to most Humanists. There is, they say, no God, no "friend behind the phenomena."

But the Humanist does not limit himself to the method of scientific knowing and its object, nature. He takes his stand squarely on the proven results of science. Prescientific ages in all cultures had cosmologies which have been proven by science to be false. For example, medieval Christendom believed in a divinely created universe with the earth at the center and man as a special object of the Creator's attention. Modern science, beginning with Copernicus, has shown how false this picture is. First the sun supplanted the earth as the center of the universe, the earth turning out to be a minor planet of the sun, and the sun itself turning out to be a third rate star in the vast interstellar spaces. Then Galileo and Newton succeeded in stating the physical laws by which all things in heaven and earth move. Chemistry added its bit to the emerging picture by showing the uniform composition of all bodies in heaven and earth. As the finishing touch, Darwin and others provided a theory impressively grounded in widely gathered and carefully checked facts for the development of life and the origin of man in such a world. And now in such fields as psychology and the social sciences, science continues to fill out its account of man and his world. Compared with such a carefully worked out conception, the biblical story of the Garden of Eden and its divinely created inhabitants and its anthropomorphic creator are childish fantasy which any intelligent person of the twentieth century must plainly reject. Man is plainly a biosocial animal who has emerged in the evolutionary process and who shows a certain capacity for intelligence and social idealism. Such, claims the Humanist, is the conclusion which emerges from a study of the sciences.

CRITIQUE OF TRADITIONAL THEOLOGY. In the rejection of a literal belief in creation and other aspects of traditional theism the Humanist finds much agreement among liberal churchmen. However, he pushes his case further to the heart of traditional religion and holds belief in God to be scientifically untenable. Taking his stand on the method and results of science, he regards such a belief as groundless. He rejects belief in God, as Sidney Hook has remarked, for the same reason that he rejects beliefs in fairies and leprechauns.[9] The factual evidence simply does not warrant belief in God's existence. The traditional proofs offered by traditional theology do not stand in the light of scientific scrutiny. If the Theist argues the necessity for a first cause, the Humanist replies that modern conceptions of causation do not require or admit such an idea, asking perhaps in return what caused the first cause? The closely related notion of prime mover has been rendered completely obsolete by modern conceptions of physics. If the theologian turns to the teleological argument, asserting that design in nature presupposes a designer, the naturalist counters with the question of evil. What about earthquakes, tidal waves, and cancers? Or he argues that a quite neutral coincidence of a great many factors offers a more adequate explanation. Or he may simply say that such matters are past human finding out. If the theologian turns from reason to revelation, the Naturalist asks why he should accept revelation, and why the Christian rather than the Jewish, or Mohammedan, or some other revelation. Why should he accept any revelation, when revelation has so often been used as a means of forcing upon men's minds ideas which their better judgment would reject? Thus a fair-minded appraisal of the evidence leads to a rejection of belief in the traditional God.

[9] Y. V. Krikorian (ed.), *Naturalism and the Human Spirit, op. cit.*, p. 45.

The Humanist often supplements this argument with his own theory of how the idea of a God or gods got started and has maintained itself in the human mind. Religion, he says, is essentially a projection upon the neutral screen of reality of man's hopes, wishes, and fears. Thus, while God has no objective existence, the idea of God is a projection of the wishes and values of the men who express this belief. This thesis was first elaborated by L. Feuerbach (1804-1872) in his *Essence of Christianity*. It has been developed psychoanalytically by Freud and his followers. Karl Marx added a sociological interpretation of the wishes involved, calling religion the "opium of the people." Supernatural religion has universally operated as a compensatory device, giving expression to wishes and hopes that are frustrated by reality, according to John Dewey. In one form or another the view that supernatural religion is essentially wishful thinking has attained widespread currency in the contemporary world, and is at the heart of very frequent Humanist criticism of traditional religion as well as argument against belief in God.

But the Humanist does not rest his case here. Basing his life upon scientific reason, he is the enemy of all unreason. And he believes that he can see much irrationality and obscurantism in the past and present of religion. Much religious thought, he says, is the sheerest prejudice and provincialism. Much of it is obscurantism, or double-talk—as one plain-spoken Humanist advocate has put it, "intellectual rubbish." Addiction to such backward habits of mind does not make for clarity, reason, or intellectual progress. Nor is this a merely academic or theoretical matter. Such attitudes are the favorite resting place for social backwardness and reaction. Religion counsels obedience and acquiescence in present ills, whereas the part of reason is to change unsatisfactory conditions. In such passivity religion plays into the hands of vested interests. Humanists have thus been sworn enemies of all that seems to them backward or narrow or unreasonable in traditional religion and have thus stood for such principles as toleration, and separation of church and state, and against special privileges for any sectarian group or interest.

SOCIAL CONCERNS. What remains of religion when the Humanist criticism has completed its work? The Humanist replies that devotion to human and social values emerges as the essence of religion. As Lamont has written, the Humanist postulates that "the chief end of thought and action is to further earthly human interests in behalf of the greater happiness and glory of man." [10] Such ideals have always been the real kernel of the religious traditions of mankind. It now remains to extract the kernel from the husk of outworn and untenable philosophy and theology and to give it concrete and positive expression in this world. Humanists also emphasize the role of intelligence in sifting these ideals and giving them effectiveness in the world. Such sciences as psychology, economics, and political science can aid in guiding their application. John Dewey's writings especially have called attention to the role of education in applying and realizing the social ideals to which Humanism is committed.

The specific values or ideals to which Humanists have devoted themselves have varied widely, though Humanists have generally been on the liberal side in debate about public policies. There has been a vigorous opposition to favoritism to any religious group, to anything which looks like the entering wedge of clericalism, and a corresponding advocacy of the separation of church and state in all its aspects. In economic matters, Humanists have frequently been sharply critical of capitalism, pointing out alleged abuses to laborers and consumers, and pointing to the greater human possibilities of other more cooperative systems of economic production. Such a position has at times taken the form of advocating specific reforms, such as the Child Labor amendment, and at other times it has suggested a wholesale rejection of capitalism and an espousal of socialism.

Politically, Humanists have been enemies of tyranny in all its forms and vigorous advocates of freedom. They have thus been in the forefront of the struggle against modern forms of tyranny such as nazism and more recently Russian communism. But they have also been quick to point out dangerous

[10] Corliss Lamont, *Humanism as a Philosophy, op. cit.*, p. 273.

trends toward tyranny in domestic policy. And they have stood for a widening and deepening of democratic processes in all of social life. Indeed, for many Humanists, such as John Dewey, democracy viewed as a cooperative and rational way of life virtually assumes the place of the God of traditional religion.

Humanists have also often been concerned with sex ethics, often opposing accepted practices and advocating new ethical standards. They have generally criticized the negative view of sex which has at times characterized traditional religion, laboring against puritanical and victorian ideas. Such ideas as male supremacy and very restrictive divorce laws, they say, need to be changed. If a marriage does not produce happiness and satisfaction for the partners, it should be terminated. Laws should be drawn in the light of modern knowledge of psychology and sociology. Modern science has also made possible the control of conception and methods of contraception hitherto impossible. Such methods should be used both to limit families according to the circumstances and desires of the partners, and also to make sexual intercourse an expression of mutual affection. Some Humanists, such as Bertrand Russell, have aroused intense opposition to their ideas concerning sex. Nowhere, claim such Humanists, do entrenched and outmoded ideas take a greater toll in human misery, and nowhere do the ideals of intelligence and devotion to human values have more relevance, than in matters of sex relations.

Humanist Organizations

Humanism has been the unexpressed creed of many people of the past and present. But it has also been organized as a religious movement. We have already noted the founding of a Positivist church by Auguste Comte in nineteenth-century Paris. Similar organizations were undertaken in the United States and elsewhere. One such organization is the Ethical Culture Society of New York City, originated in 1876 by Felix Adler. Adler was a German immigrant who became a professor of philosophy at Columbia University. He studied to be a rabbi, but rebelled against the theology and ceremonialism of Judaism, and withdrew from the synagogue to form a religious organization which would express, as he put it, "the supreme importance of the ethical factor in all relations of life." Adler's philosophy stemmed from Kant. He accepted Kant's conception of ethical norms as postulates, as well as Kant's supreme valuation of personality, though rejecting Kant's theism. But he gave Kant's moral philosophy a liberal and social direction. Society, he said, is the field of interpersonal relations where morality is expressed. Thus a formal conception of duty receives its content from concrete social relations. The fundamental social group is the family, so Adler emphasized intelligent morality in family relations. But school and education also possess an undeniable moral significance. Likewise, economic society and its vocational units are ethically significant and require rethinking and reconstructing in order to express humane and personal values. Adler saw political society with all its problems in terms of ethical significance. Though he was not a pacifist, he still saw war as a very great moral evil. And he believed that the copestone of the various organizations of society should be a religious society or church. Entirely voluntary in its nature, its leaders should be ethical teachers rather than clergy, and its purpose should be to inspire and illuminate members with ethical ideals.

Adler's New York Ethical Culture grew subsequently to more than a thousand members. Societies also grew up in Chicago, St. Louis, and other cities. A national organization, the American Ethical Union, exists. Similar societies sprang up in European nations, though only in England have they survived Nazism and World War II.

The Ethical Culture movement, wherever it exists, engages in educational, philanthropic, and social reform activities. The Ethical Culture Schools of New York, begun as a Workingman's School, have maintained a policy of complete equality of all races, creeds, and economic classes in their classrooms. Membership in Ethical Culture societies is open to people of any philosophic or theological belief whatever, who subscribe to the supremacy of ethical values in all areas of life. Religious services are simple, usually combining readings from inspirational literature of all sorts, including biblical addresses on topics of ethical significance, and silent meditation.

Closely akin to the Ethical Culture movement in many respects, but specifically rejecting traditional theism as a religious belief is the American Humanist Association. Recruited mainly from leftwing Unitarians, its members are held together by common purposes and ideas more than by an organizational tie. Affiliated individuals and groups are found in all parts of the country. A World Humanist Conference was held during the summer of 1952. A bi-monthly magazine, *The Humanist*, is published. In 1933 a statement called *A Humanist Manifesto*, setting forth many of the ideas we have already discussed, was published. Edwin H. Wilson, executive director of the American Humanist Association, in a radio address entitled "Humanism: The Fourth Faith," summarized the Humanist credo as follows:

1. The Humanist lives here and now.
2. He is more concerned for people than anything else.
3. He believes in the equality of man; discovers no master race.
4. Freedom is necessary to his way of life.
5. He accepts the findings, the method, and the authority of science.
6. He has faith that together men possess the intelligence, the skill, and the will to end war and build security in a free and just world. Research in the hands of men of goodwill can meet the challenge of hunger, disease, and hate.[11]

SUGGESTIONS FOR FURTHER READING

ADLER, FELIX. *An Ethical Philosophy of Life*. New York: Appleton-Century-Crofts, Inc., 1918.
AUER, JOHANNES, A.C.F. *Humanism States Its Case*. Boston: The Beacon Press, 1933.
—— with HARTT, JULIAN. *Humanism Versus Theism*. Yellow Springs, Ohio: Antioch Press, 1951.

11 *The Humanist*, IX, 3, June, 1951, p. 108.

AYER, ALFRED. *Language, Truth, and Logic.* London: Oxford University Press, 1936.

BRIGHTMAN, EDGAR S. *A Philosophy of Religion.* New York: Prentice-Hall, Inc., 1946.

DARWIN, CHARLES. *On the Origin of Species.* New York: Appleton-Century-Crofts, Inc., 1877.

DEWEY, JOHN. *The Quest for Certainty.* New York: Minton, Balch (G. P. Putnam's Sons), 1929.

————. *A Common Faith.* New Haven: Yale University Press, 1934.

FOSDICK, HARRY E. *As I See Religion.* New York: Harper & Bros., 1938.

————. *The Modern Use of the Bible.* New York: The Macmillan Co., 1941.

HUXLEY, JULIAN. *Evolution, the Modern Synthesis.* London: George Allen & Unwin, Ltd., 1942.

————. *Man Stands Alone.* New York: Harper & Bros., 1941.

KEPLER, THOMAS S. (ed.). *Contemporary Religious Thought.* Nashville: Abingdon-Cokesbury Press, 1941.

KRIKORIAN, YERVAN H. (ed.). *Naturalism and the Human Spirit.* New York: Columbia University Press, 1944.

LAMONT, CORLISS. *Humanism as a Philosophy.* New York: Philosophical Library, Inc., 1949.

LYMAN, EUGENE W. *The Meaning and Truth of Religion.* New York: Chas. Scribner's Sons, 1933.

MACINTOSH, DOUGLAS C. *The Reasonableness of Christianity.* New York: Chas. Scribner's Sons, 1925.

MACKINTOSH, HUGH R. *Types of Modern Theology.* London: James Nisbet & Co., Ltd., 1937.

MARTIN, JAMES A., JR. *Empirical Philosophies of Religion.* New York: King's Crown Press, 1944.

RUSSELL, BERTRAND. *Mysticism and Logic.* New York: Longmans, Green & Co., Inc., 1918.

————. *Religion and Science.* New York: Henry Holt & Co., Inc., 1935.

SANTAYANA, GEORGE. *Reason in Religion.* New York: Chas. Scribner's Sons, 1915.

WHITE, ANDREW D. *A History of the Warfare of Science and Theology.* New York: Appleton-Century-Crofts, Inc., 1897.

WIEMAN, HENRY N., with MACINTOSH, DOUGLAS C., and OTTO, MAX. *Is There a God?* Chicago: Willett, Clark & Co., 1932.

Chapter 13

OLD WAYS AND NEW DIRECTIONS

The Revival of Interest in Religion

AS THIS study is brought to a conclusion with the present chapter, an attempt will be made to describe the present situation in religion and religious thought. What will be undertaken here is a characterization of religion in our age, with its signs of mingled promise and futility. The description will be limited to religion in the Western world, and thus to the four main strands of Western tradition, namely Judaism, Catholicism, Protestantism, and Humanism, because the serious choices of most readers of this book lie within this range.

Certainly there are stirrings of life in religions elsewhere in the world. Within the past century and a half traditional Indian faith and thought have been revived by such organizations as the *Arya Samaj*, with its nationalism and its slogan "Back to the Vedas" and by such religious figures as Ramakrishna and Rabindranath Tagore, scholars like Rhadakrishnan, and social reformers like the political saint Mohandas Gandhi. Especially as the result of Gandhi's life and thought, new vitality has come into long dormant ideas. In China and Japan recent political events have seriously challenged the traditional faiths, but in both countries there are those who believe that the old faiths may yet adapt themselves to new situations in a constructive manner. There have also been numerous attempts to bring Oriental religions to the attention of the West, particularly in the writings of Gerald Heard and Aldous Huxley, though to date these efforts have had only a peripheral importance.

457

Furthermore, no survey of the present religious situation of the world is complete without at least passing reference to the religious significance of Communism and Fascism. Both have functioned in the lives of countless adherents as religions, or at least as religious substitutes, providing working conceptions of an intimate and ultimate concern. Such an interpretation of Communism is, of course, repugnant to Communists, who regard religion as a prescientific superstition used as a social opiate, and who regard their own views as wholly scientific. However, it is relevant to point out that Communism gives its followers an absolute or total commitment by which to live and die, and also that it has evolved creeds, cults, dogmas, and codes of ethics in the fashion of other religions.

It has often been suggested that Communism is a Hebrew-Christian heresy. The truth contained in this remark is most readily indicated by pointing to its dramatic conception of history. Paralleling the Garden of Eden story is the myth of primitive Communism from which man fell with the introduction of private property. Sin in the Marxist drama of history is acquisitiveness or desire for property. Karl Marx is its Messiah, and as is the case with other apocalyptic groups there is fervent hope and expectation of the violent coming of a great new age. Here is a drama of history to rival that portrayed in Augustine's *City of God* or the biblical Books of Daniel or Revelation.

Religiously speaking, Fascism also functions as a faith to live by, but it is to be understood as a synthetic revival of primitive tribalism rather than as a Hebrew-Christian heresy. In the case of Japanese state-Shinto, there is a direct and continuous line back to primitive Japanese religion, though it must be carefully noted that Japanese militarists deliberately exploited this primitivism for their own purposes. In the case of German Nazism, the religious quality was more veiled and more synthetic. But the appeals of Hitler and his followers to blood and soil, as well as to primitive Teutonic deities and myths, are religiously significant. It is no exaggeration to say that all extreme nationalism is a recrudescence of primitive religion. Thus no survey of contemporary religious phenomena is complete without reference to what has been termed "man's other religion"—namely, extreme or totalitarian nationalism, in all its guises.

But the analysis here will be limited to the fourfold historical tradition of the West, as it bears upon our lives today. At this point attention is called to the data of Chapter 11 describing the Renaissance and the rise of modern science, with their attendant skepticism and questioning of traditional religious attitudes and beliefs. To think significantly about religion at the present time is to think with this background. Contemporary man's approach to religion must be post-modern and thus post-skeptical.

Now while the main direction of the modern age has been away from traditional religion, there has been during the past few decades a fundamental change in many quarters, amounting to a return to religion. This renewed interest in religion is a complex phenomenon which is very difficult to evaluate. In some of its aspects it appears to be nothing more than a wishful projection or escape from the frustrations and vicissitudes of contemporary history. It may be suggested in passing, however, that to indicate the "wishful" origin of an idea or belief does not necessarily invalidate it. Whether or not reality corresponds to our wishes is a question which must be settled on logical and factual grounds and not alone on psychological grounds. Nevertheless, it seems clear that recent events have led to much irrational and antirational religion. But they have also led to much which is religiously creative and highly rational. In any case, recent events have brought about such a change in the religious and intellectual situation of the Western world that many of the books about religion written during the opening decades of this century now seem irrelevant.

Another aspect of the renewed interest in religion is the rebirth of creative religious thought. In the Catholic tradition, Jacques Maritain, Etienne Gilson, and others have made Thomism a live option for contemporary philosophy. A similar revival of distinctively Protestant thought is taking place under the stimulus of such men as Karl Barth, Emil Brunner, Richard and Reinhold Niebuhr, and Paul Tillich. The Eastern Orthodox tradition has been revitalized by such thinkers as Berdyaev, Bulgakov, and Florovsky. Judaism has continued to be notably less philosophic in its outlook, but the attention given to the thought of such men as Martin Buber and Franz Rosenzweig is evidence of vitality of thought and faith.

There is further evidence of a revival of interest in religious problems and viewpoints in the arts. Many see in some schools of contemporary music and painting an essentially prophetic protest against the smug assumptions of recent liberal culture. In the poetry of men like T. S. Eliot and W. H. Auden, and in the novels of men like Werfel, Kafka, and Graham Greene, traditional theological viewpoints are once again utilized in the attempt accurately to portray the present human situation. There are those who feel that the real religious vitality of our age is best seen in prophetically creative art.

A closely related, though distinct phenomenon, is the rise of Existentialism in philosophy and literature. Existentialism defies easy description, but in general its adherents have concerned themselves with the root questions: "What is man, and what does it mean to exist as a human individual?" The "existence" referred to in the term "Existentialism" is the existence of man as an actual, concrete being, irreducible to nonhuman, scientific categories. In their description of man the Existentialists have emphasized such matters as human freedom and responsibility, as well as man's despair and anxiety, and thus have made significant contact with religious thought about human nature and destiny.

The Post-Modern Mind: Beyond Humanism

In Chapter 12 the rise of Humanism as a faith was described, and some of its main tenets were indicated. While certainly not a unanimous credo of modern man, it has nevertheless commanded the allegiance of some of the most sensitive and intelligent men in the modern world. But in the recent years, largely though by no means entirely as a result of the new interest in traditional religions, an increasing volume of criticism has been directed at the Humanist faith. This debate between Humanism and theism is one of the important issues of contemporary thought. What follows is a critical evaluation of Humanism.

Humanist Criticisms of Religion

Humanist criticisms of many aspects of traditional religious creeds and institutions have received consideration from and been accepted by many people who are not themselves Humanists. Creeds and churches are sometimes unreasonable, reactionary, and inhuman; and it is to the credit of Humanism to have pointed this out and to have kept it forcibly before men's minds. Indeed, the underlying moral significance of this criticism seems religiously more significant than the Humanist *credo* itself allows. Many of these Humanist criticisms are analagous to those of the Hebrew prophets in their time and place.

Humanist Ambiguities

Granting these contributions and acknowledging their value, non-Humanists point to what seem to them shortcomings in the Humanist *credo*. There seems to be real ambiguity in some of the Humanists' fundamental concepts. Perhaps the best instances are the concepts of science and nature. From a faith and philosophy based so largely upon science one might fairly expect rigorous and careful analysis at this point. But often it is not forthcoming. What precisely is scientific method? Are the social sciences scientific in the same sense as the natural sciences, or are there important discontinuities? How does the scientific method of knowing differ from other methods? Are there any areas of human concern which science cannot adequately explore and evaluate? Indeed, is evaluation a proper function of science? These are important issues which need to be argued rather than assumed.

"Nature" is an even more ambiguous concept than is science in many Humanist documents. Sometimes nature is equated with matter-in-motion, so that Naturalism is identified with Materialism. Other Naturalists reject such an interpretation and include within the realm of Nature, mind and its values as important and irreducible entities. But in this case what does the term "Nature" mean? Often Nature is identified by Humanistic Naturalists simply as that which science studies. At other times Nature is conceived more broadly as the object of any kind of human inquiry. Sometimes it is given a polemical interpretation, meaning in effect that which is not supernatural. In any case, Naturalists argue against any fundamental dualism in reality. Nature is reality, and all reality can be known by scientific method, they say. It is enough at this point simply to lay bare this ambiguity, and to point to the dogmas which it covers.

The Overvaluation of Science

Non-Humanists often detect in Humanist thought a great overvaluation of science. It has been noted that many Humanists and Naturalists tend to argue that science alone offers valid or *bona fide* knowledge. But theists and other non-Humanists reply that, while science provides a useful and successful method for knowing certain aspects of reality, there is nothing in science which asks its adherents to accept the conclusions of science alone as valid knowledge. The assumption of the omnicompetence of scientific method, asserted as a dogma, is surely not a very scientific assumption. Furthermore, the non-Humanists argue, there are some fields of inquiry in which science seems eminently more successful than in others. In the understanding, prediction, and control of facts, science seems far more successful than it does in any present undertaking to apply scientific method to the realm of value. While this may indicate simply that the physical sciences got under way before the sciences of man, it may also indicate a limitation inherent in scientific method itself. At least, recent attempts to understand scientifically many forms of value, aesthetic, moral, and religious, are not impressive.

The Status of Values

Another closely related argument is often urged against Humanism and Naturalism. What status is given in the Humanist credo to the human values or ideals which Humanism so genuinely cherishes? In what order of reality do they stand? What authority do they possess over man and why? Why these values rather than some others? The reply which is usually made by Humanists is that their values are established through intelligent inquiry, and that the sole authority any value can have is that bestowed by human reason. But non-Humanists persist in maintaining that such an answer begs the real question. It is no mere coincidence, some of them say, that the values cherished by Humanists bear a great resemblance to those of their theistic grandparents. The Humanist, they say, has not really created his own values, but rather has borrowed the values of a religious tradition which he has disowned. Humanism bears, therefore, the same relation to traditional religion as the afterglow does to the sunset. The crucial question is whether, having borrowed values from a religious faith, the Humanist can give them fresh and vital expression within the context of his faith; whether he can reproduce them and pass them on to his children. The theist has his doubts. The values of Humanism, he says, are like cut-flowers,—beautiful while they last, but soon to wither and die for lack of rootage—possessing no reproductive powers. The widespread adherence in contemporary western culture to Humanism as "a faith without God" is a laboratory experiment in religion which students of religious history should observe with careful interest.

The non-Humanist can point to a deeper, more mordant skepticism which applies the same testing acids to the espousal of human values or ideals as those which the Humanist applies to belief in God. Is not allegiance to such values as "truth," "democracy," and "human brotherhood" as arbitrary as is faith in the Hebrew-Christian God? The desire for truth may be, as some skeptics have suspected, a species of power-impulse; and brotherhood may be either bourgeois morality, as Marx suggested, or slave morality, as Nietzsche claimed. Stated more philosophically, the problem is that of the relation between value and reality. What ontological status have human values? One of the cardinal assumptions of many schools of

Humanism and Naturalism is that no values are cosmically grounded. Values are simply and solely human aims or postulates,—that and no more. But it is very difficult to avoid the conclusion that such a view deprives values of the authority necessary for their functioning, and leaves them dangling as arbitrary choices of certain human beings. There is, indeed, no final sanction for the very values which impel the Humanist to proclaim the ethical superiority of ethical relativism. Opponents of Humanism point to the instability of entirely man-centered faiths or philosophies in history. There are few, if any, instances in history of such faiths capturing and holding the allegiance of any large numbers of people. Rather, such faiths or philosophies have been, as a matter of intellectual history, points of transition between the service of one god and the service of another.

Intellectualism

It may be noted that Humanism is a highly intellectual religion, or rather is in fact a philosophy with religious overtones or suggestions. Its appeal is thus largely intellectual, with a consequent undervaluation of the emotive aspects of religion. If this study of religion has proven anything, surely it is the fact that inspiration and celebration, as well as rational analysis, are basic functions of dynamic faiths.

The power of pseudo-religions like communism and fascism to sweep millions of men of good will into their richly emotional movements attests the poverty of a merely intellectual faith in the traditional liberal values. It does not seem possible for men to be religious in a vacuum—for their religious allegiances to be thinly spread over culture in general, in some common faith. Religion is by its very nature institutionally specific, and it must be nurtured in specific historic traditions which celebrate as well as teach, live as well as proclaim their ideals.

Optimism

Another criticism which is often made of Humanism is that it holds an uncritically optimistic view of human nature.

If we are to be guided by actual facts, can we believe quite so innocently and easily in man and in human progress as a simple possibility as many Humanists do? In many quarters, reflection upon human evil and tragedy has been a major stimulus for a fresh evaluation of traditional ways of faith.

Such then, in summary fashion, are some of the arguments now leveled against Humanism as a modern way of faith. If they are carefully and critically stated, many of them seem cogent. In this respect it seems to be true that the modern mind is being outrun by contemporary events. However, any significant return to traditional ways of faith must follow a route through Humanism and not around it, and must lead beyond and not behind it. It will be post-modern and post-Humanist and not pre-Humanist, and it must seek to incorporate the values of Humanism in a new and richer synthesis.

New Light from Old Ideas: A Re-evaluation of Biblical Faith

What follows from here to the end of the chapter is a reformulation of some of the important themes of religious thought in the context of contemporary questions and issues. The questions, Where do we stand? and Where do we go from here? will be answered in the light of the new understanding of biblical faith which has emerged from recent study of the Bible and of the whole Hebrew-Christian tradition. Perhaps the reader will agree; perhaps he will disagree. What is more probable is that he will agree at some points and disagree at others. But what is more important for the study and understanding of religion is that he should reflect upon the issues and attempt to formulate conclusions satisfactory to himself. Seven questions about belief and practice, emerging from the foregoing study and having urgent contemporary relevance, will be raised, and some answers will be outlined.

What Is the Relation of Faith to Reason?

This was the crucial question for the scholastic philosophy of the Middle Ages of Europe. It may be that insights gained

in study of that period will be of use in the widely different
religious and intellectual situation of the present. Despite important discontinuities between the Middle Ages and the present time, there are also some significant continuities. It is in
fact such continuity which gives point and relevance to the
philosophic work of Jacques Maritain and other neo-Scho-
lastic philosophers.

First it is necessary to be clear about what is meant and
what is not meant by faith. Faith does not mean primarily
the acceptance of the truth of a proposition without or against
logical or factual evidence, though it is a fact that many people
assume just such a conception of faith. Faith is, they say,
"believing what one knows is not so." Nor is an experience of
faith, as some religious philosophies suggest, to be equated
with mystical experience understood in some nonrational and
highly emotional sense.

By faith is meant rather that form of trust or confidence
which leads to action. This at least is what faith usually
means in the Bible. William James was content to conceive
of faith simply as a tendency to action; and surely the emphasis
on the primacy of action is the truest and most fruitful aspect
of Pragmatism as a philosophy. In a widely different philosophic and religious context, Kierkegaard placed a similar emphasis upon the primacy of action, arguing that at the beginning of any philosophy lies a leap of faith. Faith may thus be
regarded as an attitude of trust or attachment which has its
proper expression in action.

So defined, faith is universally human. To act is to have
faith in the assumptions on which one acts. There is thus,
as Canon Alan Richardson remarks, [1] a "faith-principle" in
every philosophy, in the precise sense that there are embedded
in its foundations some significant principles which the philosophy assumes rather than proves. Modern logic has taught
us that one cannot prove everything. Every proof or argument
begins with some assumptions or "primitive propositions." At
times a thinker may not be aware of the assumptions which

---

[1] Alan Richardson, *Christian Apologetics* (New York: Harper & Bros.,
1947), p. 35.

lie at the foundation of his system and which give decisive
guidance to his thinking. But his lack of awareness does not
prevent the assumptions from operating. This is the case
with many prominent philosophers who would deny the role
of faith in their thought. Indeed, it is significant to see what
any philosophy believes can be assumed or taken axiomatically,
without proof, and what is held to need proof or establishment
by rational argument. Often in the history of philosophy the
unconscious assumptions of one philosopher become objects
of critical study on the part of others. Furthermore, some
philosophies and faiths give their faith-principles more explicit
expression than others. Some try to suppress them entirely,
but this really forces them underground. What is needed is
a philosophy which will give its faith-principle adequate and
critical expression, since faith is universal.

This assumption of a faith-principle lying at the foundation
of every man's philosophy amounts to the traditional assumption of the primacy of faith over reason. It is in agreement
with Augustine's and Anselm's principle, *credo ut intelligam*.
Just as any structure of thought has its postulates, so all philosophies begin with an act of faith. Just as any process of human reasoning takes the form of assuming *a* in order to prove
b, so there are always primal assumptions which constitute a
man's faith, or his credo.

Attention is called to the similarity of this view with Immanuel Kant's emphasis on the primacy of practical reason.
Reasoning concerning practice or action rather than theory
was for Kant the more basic category for the understanding of
man's total life. Theorizing is, in other words, one of the
things men do. Thinking or reasoning is a form of doing, and
not vice-versa. Thus doing, and its category of decision, underlies the whole life of the mind. The best mind in the world
must be "made up" in order that it may serve its proper function of guiding action.

Now an emphasis on the primacy of action is characteristic
of Hebrew-Christian thought. This becomes clear when Hebrew-Christian thought is compared with Greek and Oriental
thought. For Aristotle, for example, the highest good is in-

tellectual contemplation, in comparison with which action is a poor second-best. Thus the best life possible for man, he concludes at the end of the *Nichomachean Ethics*, is that of the contemplative philosopher, compared with whom the statesman or man of practical affairs is inferior. Oriental thought, especially in Hinduism, Buddhism, and Taoism, frequently expresses a similar judgment. The modern West, under the influence of the biblical view of life, has reversed this judgment. Indeed, at no point is the influence of the Bible on Western life shown more plainly than in the assumption of the primacy of action.

Of course the contemporary West is in danger of making action an end in itself; the contemplative values of aesthetic and poetic pursuits are frequently ignored. The biblical and historic Judeo-Christian emphasis on doing, however, does not minimize the significance of appreciation and enjoyment of God's creation as an appropriate *form* of *doing*. The Catholic Christian tradition has long maintained that the goal of human striving is the Beatific Vision of God. But even here the vision is the active adoration of God by the society of the redeemed and not the passive absorption into God of the isolated individual. Similarly, Jewish mystical movements have never subordinated communal service to individual salvation in their understanding of the final relation of man to God. Judaism and Christianity, following the biblical view of faith and action, have sought perfect *communion* of men with God, rather than the *union* of man and God which many Eastern religious seek. Unlike some Humanists in the West, however, Christians and Jews have treasured contemplation as a necessary ingredient in the full active adoration of God which is man's chief end.

But if faith which leads to action is primary in all human life, it is not autonomous.[2] Rather, faith must always be subject to rational criticism and check. The task of reason is thus to formulate, analyze, and criticize faith. In its most gen-

[2] We are indebted for this formulation to Roger Hazelton, *Renewing the Mind* (New York: The Macmillan Co., 1949).

eral sense, reason may be defined as the capacity to behave in terms of facts. In relation to faith, it is the task of reason to make the assumptions of faith articulate, and to relate them critically to all the various aspects of man's experience of the world. This role of critical formulation, analysis, generalization, and evaluation is one which rational philosophy has often played in the past and is well-qualified to play in the present situation.

Such a view of the relation of faith to reason is likely to be misunderstood and attacked from two sides. Barthian or neo-orthodox Christian theologians may well regard it as a betrayal of faith—as holding up human reason in arrogant and blasphemous judgment upon God. It is the role of true faith, say such critics, simply to believe. The reply of many Christians is that such a course is a curious way of honoring the Creator of the human intellect. Uncritical, irrational faith constitutes a dubious offering to the divine source of all truth.

From a polar opposite view, Rationalists [By Rationalism is meant an *a priori* belief in the omnicompetence of detached human reason, an attitude which in effect deifies human reason, placing in it a faith which is absolute or ultimate.] will probably regard the position suggested here as a lame compromise with irrationalism. To them the answer may be made: "you have your faith-principle, and others have theirs." The one here suggested seems more adequate because it is explicit, and also because it does better justice to the many-dimensioned facts of life. An important part of reason's task is to trace reason's own limits. To assume *a priori* the omnicompetence of human reason is not a very reasonable course. The life of reason, which is an important part of man's service of God, consists of facing facts as they are encountered in action, living in the presence of them, seeking them out, and organizing them into coherent patterns. One such fact is that human reason seems to have its limits. The work of Freud and Marx, while based on extreme views, should make contemporary thinkers keenly aware of the role of rationalization and ideology in human reasoning. The weakness of Freud and Marx is that neither recognized a transcendent principle in terms of which his own basic assumptions could be brought under critical judgment.

Certainly the conception of the role of reason offered here utilizes coherence as one rational criterion. However, unlike some religious philosophies that which is here being sketched rejects the coherence-theory as a wholly adequate theory of truth, because philosophical systems are forever encountering new, brute facts, being shattered upon them, and rebuilt in the light of them. The daily encounter with new facts which invade human life is one of the things which may well convince human beings that they are men and not God. It is for this reason that the philosophy outlined here is realist and not idealist in orientation.

The relation between faith and reason here developed entails a further consequence concerning the relation of religion to philosophy: There is a religious dimension expressed or unexpressed, in every philosophy; and there are philosophical implications for every religion. Paul Tillich, among others, has argued often and eloquently that the existential foundations of every philosophy are religious, and conversely that as a religion articulates its relation to the general processes and structures of the world, it entails philosophical conclusions.

But, while philosophy and religion deal with the same subject-matter, namely reality as a whole, or the scheme of things entire, they involve important differences of attitude. The characteristic attitude of religion is one of attachment, faith, and worship; the characteristic attitude of philosophy is one of detachment and inquiry. Philosophy emphasizes the question-asking attitude, while religion emphasizes the question-answering attitude. As William Temple put it, "the primary assurances of Religion are the ultimate questions of Philosophy." [3]

There has been a great deal of tension between philosophy and religion in the Western tradition. Philosophy from the time of the Sophists of ancient Greece to the present has fre-

---

[3] William Temple, *Nature, Man, and God* (London: Macmillan & Co., Ltd., 1940), p. 35.

quently charged religion with uncritical, arbitrary belief; and religion has answered by charging philosophy with laying profane hands on holy things. Both charges have frequently been justified. The tension is a basic one between the question-asking attitude and the question-answering attitude, and it will doubtless continue as long as human nature includes both. Nevertheless the tension can be genuinely creative. Philosophy is richer and better for the inspiration and imagination contributed by religious faith and religious vision. Religion is better for having the testing acid of critical reason applied to it. Thus the possibility of creative and mutually helpful relations between religion and philosophy is also underscored in Western intellectual history. Many of the great philosophical systems have been deeply concerned with the philosophy of religion, as such names as Plato, Augustine, Aquinas, Spinoza, Kant, Berkeley, Hegel, and Whitehead, to mention only a few, testify. In the light of such chapters in philosophic and religious history, it would seem to be a major tragedy of the present time that philosophers and theologians are intellectually so far apart. Each has much to learn from the other. Divorced from the discipline of philosophical analysis, religious thinking too frequently degenerates into arbitrary fideism and ecclesiasticism. And in such contemporary movements as some forms of Logical Positivism, philosophy fades out into something like the grin of the Cheshire cat.

But, which philosophy can best express religious faith for our day? Whitehead once remarked that Buddhism is a philosophy in search of a religion, while Christianity is a religion in search of a philosophy. And it may be added, in the latter case, "never quite finding one." In its most elemental and fundamental sense, philosophy is a critical search for adequacy. The philosophically-minded student of religion ought therefore to be forever asking himself the question, "What philosophy or philosophies most adequately express religious faith and religious truth?"

As a matter of fact, this question is being raised and discussed afresh by philosophers of religion at the present moment. Here it is possible only to indicate in a very general way a few of the issues and lines of thought. A generation ago it was widely assumed that idealist philosophies were the most appropriate vehicles for expressing religious truth. Recent work in both philosophy and religion has seriously questioned that judgment and has reappraised the religious values of such other philosophies as Naturalism, Realism, and Materialism. These latter schools of contemporary thought have taught us much about the irreducible reality and significance of time and matter, at precisely the same moment when a new reading of the Bible and its view of life have underscored the same themes.

Biblical religion in both its Jewish and Christian forms is distinguished from other religions by its relative materialism, its emphasis upon the reality and importance of all aspects of creation. Many religious thinkers thus agree with the affirmations of Naturalism and Materialism, and disagree only with the negations of these philosophies. And even in the negations it is sometimes possible to discern behind the metaphysical statements the expression of an antiecclesiasticism which has found a significant place in biblical religion ever since the days of the Hebrew prophets.

Idealism has lately come in for much severe criticism at the hands of Western religious thinkers. Its distinction between appearance and reality is closer to the views of Oriental religions than to biblical religion, which is metaphysically realist in its outlook. Nevertheless, one finds in many systems of idealistic philosophy an account of man's freedom and responsibility which seems to do better justice to the facts of human life than the frequently naive views of some Naturalists and Materialists.

Is the attitude toward the current schools of philosophy suggested here eclectic? Many would say so. But there is a unity of *attitude* in the search for a philosophy which can most adequately express the truths of biblical religion. Such a search not only entails an underlying unity; in the present situation of philosophy it constitutes a new and useful task which ought not to be longer delayed.

What Is Man?

The basic questions of religion may be given the formulation "who am I? why am I here? where am I going?" Religion is in essence man's effort to answer such questions. Present philosophy, especially Existentialist philosophy, also raises similar questions. Thus religious thought at the present time can be formulated in terms of answers to such questions about man's nature and destiny.

As a matter of fact, many contemporary religious thinkers have undertaken to provide such answers. John Baillie has characterized the present age in Christian thought as the anthropological age. In his book, *Nature, Man, and God,* [4] William Temple's thought moves dialectically from nature to man to God. In the thought of Paul Tillich, man's existence raises questions,—indeed man's existence *is* the question to which God is the answer. Reinhold Niebuhr has formulated his philosophy of religion most comprehensively and systematically under the title, *The Nature and Destiny of Man.*[5]

Looking back over the pages of this book, it would be possible for the reader to classify the various religions which have been studied in terms of their answers to the question, what is man? That being the case, the attempt to indicate a biblical answer to the question will illustrate the biblical religious orientation. Briefly stated, the two most important traits of man in the biblical view are (1) his freedom and (2) his finitude. Man is irreducibly free, but his freedom is limited.

What does this mean? Freedom in its most fundamental meaning is man's capacity in imagination to stand clear of himself and his world. This capacity of the human mind is implied in the very asking of the religious question "what is the meaning of existence?" Therefore it is not surprising to find this capacity for freedom expressed in most of the great religions of the world. The common wisdom of these religions is expressed in the assumption that man is not simply a

[4] William Temple, *op. cit.*
[5] Reinhold Niebuhr, *The Nature and Destiny of Man* (New York: Chas. Scribner's Sons, 1941-1943).

rational animal, but is also a creature of transcendent freedom, or spirit.

From the freedom of self-transcendence stem the various other aspects of human freedom. From this capacity to stand clear of himself and his world, stems man's ability to discriminate between means and ends, and to choose the ends he will serve; from the freedom of self-transcendence follows the freedom of self-determination. In this freedom most of the traits which distinguish man from his animal cousins are rooted. It is, in short, freedom which makes man human.

But human freedom is not unlimited. Man is a creature of limits as well as of freedom. These limits become apparent as one looks from man's freedom to his dependence. In a previous chapter Schleiermacher's definition of religion as a "feeling of absolute dependence" was noted. Other writers have emphasized the same idea from varying vantage points. According to Erich Frank [6] man is taught by such experiences as remorse and death the hard fact of his absolute dependence on a reality beyond himself. Thus man learns that he lives what Frank aptly calls a "derived existence." He chooses neither when nor where nor under what circumstances he will be born. He is thrust into the world and pulled out of it by a power not his own. Throughout the course of his life much of his behavior reflects not his freedom, but his creaturely, finite, mortal existence. Reinhold Niebuhr summarizes this aspect of the human dilemma in these words:

> While these paradoxes of human self-knowledge are not easily reduced to simpler formulae, they all point to two facts about man: one of them obvious and the other not quite so obvious. The two are not usually appreciated with equal sympathy. The obvious fact is that man is a child of nature, subject to its vicissitudes, compelled by its necessities, driven by its impulses, and confined within the brevity of the years which nature permits its varied organic forms, allowing them some but not too much latitude. The other less obvious fact is that man is a spirit who stands outside of nature, life, himself, his reason and the world.

[6] Erich Frank, *Philosophical Understanding and Religious Truth* (New York: Oxford University Press, 1945), chap. i.

This latter fact is appreciated in one or another of its aspects by various philosophies. But it is not frequently appreciated in its total import. That man stands outside of nature in some sense is admitted even by naturalists who are intent upon keeping him as close to nature as possible. They must at least admit that he is *homo faber*, a tool making animal. That man stands outside the world is admitted by rationalists who, with Aristotle, define man as a rational animal. But rationalists do not always understand that man's rational capacity involves a further ability to stand outside himself, a capacity for self-transcendence, the ability to make himself his own object, a quality of spirit which is not fully comprehended or connoted in "ratio" or "nous" or "reason" or any of the concepts which philosophers usually use to describe the uniqueness of man.

How difficult it is to do justice to both the uniqueness of man and his affinities with the world of nature below him is proved by the almost unvarying tendency of those philosophies which describe and emphasize the rational faculties of man or his capacity for self-transcendence to forget his relation to nature and to identify him prematurely and unqualifiedly with the divine and the eternal; and of naturalistic philosophies to obscure the uniqueness of man.[7]

It is significant to note the different ways in which various religions have construed the relation of body to spirit in man. We have seen that for most schools of Hindu thought, the body is a part of *maya*. For Buddhism also, the body is of secondary importance. Many religions seem to involve a body-spirit dualism in which man's soul is saved when it is rescued from an evil or unreal body. Such views often carry the moral corollary that physical desires are inherently evil. This is often applied with particular force to the impulses of hunger and sex, and often involves an ascetic, life-denying morality. At times, under the influence of later Greek thought, Christianity has tended toward this belief that the body is an impediment to the soul.

The Bible has a radically different view of the relation between body and soul. Man, it says, composed of body and

[7] Reinhold Niebuhr, *The Nature and Destiny of Man*, *op. cit.*, Vol. I, pp. 3-4.

spirit in the closest unity, is as a whole part of God's good creation. For Hebrew thought man is not so much a soul inhabiting a body as he is an active, functioning unity of body and spirit. Thus Judaism has produced a rigorous but never an ascetic or otherworldly morality. And when Christianity has been true to its biblical origins, the same can be said of it. The Bible sees man's proper destiny not as an escape from physical or temporal reality, but as the active service of God within these limits. It sees man's limits as aspects of God's creation, and therefore as good and not evil in themselves.

But man shows his dependent nature in the fact that his vital center is outside himself. With a deep and perennial hunger of spirit, he must worship something beyond himself. All the ways of faith which have been studied (with the possible exception of Humanism) testify to this fact. And the rise of religious substitutes for traditional faiths, such as Communism and Fascism in the contemporary secular scene, only serves to underscore this lesson. Often this tendency of human nature to worship something beyond itself is taken as evidence of the weak and wishful character of the masses of men who are not strong enough to stand alone. "See," it is said, "the way in which men like Buddha and Confucius who had little or no religion in the popular sense of the word, became in time venerated as gods." There is some truth in this contention, but the facts can be interpreted as evidence for the ontological structure in man which has been characterized as "finite freedom." Since man is both free and dependent upon some principle of ultimate meaning, human nature takes vengeance upon faiths and philosophies which do not understand this dual fact. It is not simply a matter of psychology but of ontology that man seeks a center of allegiance beyond himself. Upon this reality he is dependent; from it he draws guidance and strength for daily life. To it he freely commits himself; in its service his freedom is fulfilled.

As has been seen in the course of this survey, different faiths and cultures have widely different views of man in his relation to society. Among these the modern Western conception of personality-in-community is only one. Indeed this Western view of personality as an active, psycho-physical unity in society is itself a very complex concept, which may be traced to many historical sources. Greek and Latin thought, as well as modern science, to mention only a few, have conditioned the way in which modern, Western man regards himself. But important among these sources is the Hebrew-Christian view of man as a creature of the living God, made in the divine image from the dust of the earth, created for the high destiny of serving his Maker through service of the common good. This faith has created in the West a way of life which Maritain and others call Christian Humanism. Christian Humanism, in turn, has been a seedbed of philosophy, art, science, and morality in the Western world.

Does God Exist?

The reader may well say to himself "This may all be true, but where does God come into the picture?" Does not religion necessarily involve God? And what factual evidence is there for the existence of God? Does not the continuance of religion as an active force in human life depend upon continued belief in the existence of God? These and similar questions are raised wherever religion is seriously discussed. What reply can be made to them?

First of all, to ask "does God exist?" seems a very inadequate way in which to pose the essential religious question. For there are religions such as original Buddhism as well as many primitive religions which seem to have little or no idea of deity. There are also ways of faith like Confucianism where God or gods are surely not the central object of religious interest. Furthermore, there are ideas of God, as for instance in the speculative systems of some philosophers, which have little or no religious meaning. It has often been questioned whether A. N. Whitehead prayed to his "principle of concretion," or Samuel Alexander to his "emergent deity;" indeed, the religious status of Aristotle's "First Cause" and "Prime Mover" may be seriously questioned. The idea of God, in short, is of religious interest only when it is raised in a religious context, as an object—or subject—of intimate and ultimate concern.

However, if this survey of man's important religions has shown anything at all, it has demonstrated how persistently the idea of God does emerge in man's religious history. The most important single exception to this rule is the secular Humanism of the contemporary West, which, as previously noted, constitutes a laboratory experiment in godless religion. Disregarding this exception, important as it is, for the moment, the question may be put: Is there anything significant to be concluded from the widespread and persistent belief in God or gods? Catholic thinkers understand it to be the result of the natural light of human reason, which is able to see from creation to Creator. Jewish and Protestant thinkers find in it evidence of a similar, though not identical, general revelation given in the structure of creation. In any event, the universality of belief in deity offers impressive evidence of both the persistence and the variety of man's attempts to conceive a meaningful existence in theistic terms.

But is existence meaningful? Have we any rational or factual basis for believing that anything in reality responds to and answers man's agelong and worldwide quest for meaningful existence? In the Hebrew-Christian tradition this question has often taken the form of undertaking to prove, or to disprove, the existence of God. It is interesting to note, in passing, that the question concerning the existence of God does not emerge with the same insistent force in many other religious traditions, as for example in Hinduism, Confucianism, and Buddhism. Apparently, the way in which God and the relation of God to the world are conceived in biblical religion gives this question special point and relevance. What estimate may be made of the efforts to prove the existence of God, either in their classical scholastic forms, or in their more contemporary forms?

It is an observable fact that the theistic arguments or proofs do not seem to carry conviction for many people of great intellectual acumen and integrity. Some orthodox religionists would answer that this lack of conviction is sin, all doubt being the intellectual form of sin. This seems an unduly narrow and biased view of the matter. While some doubt in religious matters may well be a rationalization of the doubter's evil desires, some of it is incontestably honest and sincere. Why then do the proofs not prove the existence of God to such minds?

A careful inspection of the proofs shows them to be circular. They assume what they ought to prove. To put it more subjectively, the minds of believer and unbeliever alike are guided, as they study the proofs, not merely by a logically coercive chain of reasoning, but by assumptions lying prior to the argument. The beliefs which the religious person regards as the conclusion of argument are in reality the intellectual formulation of his faith. And this view is in accord with the emphasis upon the primacy of faith in biblical religion.

But it leaves open some important questions. Does this mean that all philosophies and faiths have at their foundations nonrational assumptions? Does it mean further that the theistic proofs are simply the rationalizations of the will-to-believe, or to make-believe? Does it mean that belief in God is of an arbitrary, nonrational character? One need not assent to such suggestions. Assumption there always is, but it need be arbitrary. Rather the arguments for (and against) belief in God take their place along with the rest of what traditionally has been called natural or rational theology as the systematic attempt of reason to analyze and express critically the assumptions of faith.

The relation of faith to reason here suggested is not unlike that between hypothesis and experimental verification in scientific inquiry. To be sure, the use of the term "hypothesis" as an analogy to religious faith may be misleading, for faith is inherently categorical and not hypothetical in nature. That is, it involves a life-commitment which is total in its quality and extent, in contrast to the detached, hypothetical character of scientific theory and experiment. Furthermore, belief in God is the result of experiences which are more conclusive than argument. It is a plain fact of human experience that few people are argued into or out of belief or faith in God. But, once it has been created by faith, belief in God, like any other belief, must be analyzed and tested rationally. It is at this point that the analogy to scientific hypothesis and laboratory experiment becomes pertinent. Just as the scientist takes his hypothesis into a laboratory to test and verify it, so rational theology or philosophy of religion must take the hypothesis of faith in God into the arena of rational analysis and criticism for verification and checking. Faith and not reason creates the hypothesis; but, once created, it must be rationally tested.

The arguments for the existence of God thus take their place as important aspects of the program of natural or rational theology. Such a view of their function carries important implications. For one thing, the proofs assume an important ancillary position, but not a fundamental position, in the actual practice of religion. The life of religion is better expressed in prayer than in argument. Furthermore the arguments themselves assume the force, not of demonstrative proof, but of probable reasoning. It is a commonplace of modern logical and epistemological thought that no verificatory reasoning concerning matters of fact is ever more than probable. Again, there can be no one, final proof or set of proofs of God's existence, for the reason that men face the task of formulating and defending their faith in widely different times and places. There is no *philosophia perennis*, as Thomists argue; indeed Thomism seems seriously limited as a philosophy by its involvement in the outmoded science of fourth-century B.C. Greece and thirteenth-century A.D. Europe. No single system of philosophy is perennial, but the enterprise of philosophizing is. That being the case, faith must be prepared to express itself and to relate itself critically to changing systems of thought. The ever-present danger, from which philosophical or natural theology is never free, is that faith should be distorted by the philosophical categories in which it seeks to express itself. But this danger should not lead to abandonment of the attempt, for the alternative to rational expression is silence.

It is important to both religion and philosophy that discussion of the theistic hypothesis should continue. But rational or philosophical theology will be more fruitful when it begins with a recognition of the fact that faith in God, the actual, first-hand "having" of religion, is a matter not of argument but of revelation or faith. By "revelation" is meant the believer's first-hand experience of the reality he discovers in faith. Any statement of revelation takes on the character of confession or witness.

But what conclusions about God emerge from a process of philosophical criticism or evaluation? Since all men must live and act, they must in fact believe in some ultimate. For the question "Does God exist?", one may therefore substitute another question which does better justice to the actual experience of religion, namely "Which God shall I serve?" In part, any man's answer will be, as living religion always is, a matter of personal experience and testimony. But men will test the options of faith in terms of what conforms most adequately to the facts of life as they encounter those facts in daily experience. Many men today are finding that the historic faith of the Bible in God as Sovereign Love: Creator, Judge, and Redeemer of men, meets this test.

What Meaning Does History Have?

In the course of this book frequent allusion has been made to the views of time and history held by the different religions, because it is a subject of intrinsic importance, and also because it is a subject to which great emphasis is being given at the present time. It is possible to make a very significant classification of various religions on the basis of their philosophies of time and history. In such a classification primitive religions may be regarded as prehistoric, for in them man's life is still conceived largely in terms of the cyclical time of nature. The important events of primitive religion are the seasonal festivals of the year and the rites which celebrate the cycle of birth, puberty, marriage, and death in individual life. History as the unique time of man's life seems seldom if ever to be conceived by primitive people or primitive religions.

The religions of the East present different attitudes toward the meaning of time and of historical events. Confucianism is most like Western religions in this regard, in that it strives for ethical and social reform through historical action. But

classical Confucianism looked to a past Golden Age for the
model society toward which reform should move; and Taoist
and Buddhist influences have been sufficiently strong to introduce a note of skepticism—or realism—into Confucian hopes
for significant social improvement. The long view of things,
producing a patience which is at times attractive and at times
irritating to the Westerner, has been a very significant part
of traditional Chinese culture. And this long view derives not
only from longer experience in human affairs, but also from
a deeper sense of the recurrent cycles of time manifested in
nonhuman nature.

Natural as contrasted with historical time (the time of
our life) has dominated most Hindu and Buddhist thought.
The reader will recall the concept of *samsara* in these religions;
and one should never forget that the orthodox Hindu or
Buddhist literally believes that there is for him and for all
men an infinity of time in which to achieve that escape from
time which is *moksha* or salvation. In Buddhism time is
actually the source of evil; it is the temporality of apparent
goods that makes them ultimately *dukka*. Many contemporary Buddhist and Hindu scholars, however, are insisting
on the relative importance of time as the scene of salvation,
and are finding within the historic faiths compelling reasons
for modern social and cultural reform. Granting these qualifications however, Paul Tillich appears justified in his judgment that from the typical Western viewpoint, most oriental
faiths are nonhistorical.[8] In them time is interpreted through
the static concepts of nature and supernature.

In sharp contrast are the so-called theistic religions (Zoroastrianism, Judaism, Christianity, and Islam) where, as Tillich
puts it, history is interpreted not through nature but through
itself. While a beginning in this way of understanding history was made in Zoroastrianism, it was the biblical Hebrews
who may be said to have created the notion of history as the
unique human time. Here the cycle of nature and natural
religion is broken through, and the long thin line of destiny

[8] Paul Tillich, *The Protestant Era* (Chicago: University of Chicago Press,
1948), pp. 16 ff.

stretches from the past into the future. Not nature or super-nature but history is seen to be the primary sphere of God's revelation. In sharpest contrast to otherworldly religions, the biblical Hebrews took man's life in history altogether seriously. For them, history was not just appearance or *maya*; it had serious reality in the sight of God.

The problem of history's meaning has been complicated in the Western world by the fact that the Greeks, so original and so creative in other respects, seem to have had little to say about this problem, and were at some points, as in Plato, Plotinus, and the Gnostics, as otherworldly as the Orientals. Early Christianity achieved a synthesis of Jewish and Greek elements of great importance to the Western world. In this synthesis the Hebraic sense of an active history, while never completely obliterated, was greatly submerged, and medieval religion was in respect to its notions of time and eternity frequently more Greek than Hebraic.

In modern times, in an expanding material world with its new opportunities and ever new and more desperate problems, men have asked more urgently, What is the meaning of history? and have formulated new answers. From the Enlightenment to the present time, many men have answered this question by saying that history means progress. Variously defined and conceived, the notion of progress has generally involved belief in some increment of value through the mere movement of the historical process as such. Sometimes progress has been regarded as inevitable, man being viewed as a passenger on a kind of cosmic escalator which will carry him forever upward and onward. At other times it is only the possibility of progress which is offered to man in modern faiths. Sometimes progress has been conceived to embrace every aspect of man's life; at other times it has been thought of as more limited, involving only certain specified aspects of life. But in all its manifold forms, the idea of progress shows its debt to the biblical consciousness of history as a unique and meaningful process. In Augustinian terms, the idea of progress for moderns is equivalent to "grace,—prevenient, immanent, and irresistible." As Reinhold Niebuhr has frequently commented, the modern faith in progress is an adulterated and sentimentalized version of the biblical conception of history. It is history without any transcendent God, and without any divine judgment on human sin and evil. According to most conceptions of progress, the root of human evil is ignorance, which will presently be cured by education. History is thus made to provide through its own resources for man's redemption, without outside interference. Thus Utopia, the ideal age, can be looked for at some future time in history,[9] and the content of many moderns' faith is simply "a better deal for the kids."

As we have previously noted, Marxism involves a philosophy of history which constitutes a live option to millions of our contemporaries. The Marxist philosophy of history bears significant kinship to both the progress-theory and the biblical view. As in both of them, history is viewed in Marxism as a unique and meaningful process. Like progress-theories, Marxism claims to be scientific. It has provisionally a deeper sense of human evil and catastrophe in its awareness of the perils of acquisitiveness and the desire for property, and the tragic consequences to which these lead. But this restraint is only provisional and superficial, for once private property has been abolished, the Marxist says, Utopia will dawn. Despite its professed atheism, the Communist faith is actually the worship of a false god. For testimony of those who have worshiped this god only to be disillusioned, the reader is referred to *The God That Failed*.[10]

The biblical conception of history in relation to its current secular alternatives of progress and Marxism constitutes a genuine point of relevance for religious thought in our time.

[9] For a historian's sober estimate of the practical miscalculations to which this idea leads not only in philosophy but in practical statesmanship, see Herbert Butterfield, *Christianity and History* (New York: Chas. Scribner's Sons, 1950).

[10] R. H. S. Crossman (ed.), *The God That Failed* (New York: Harper and Bros., 1949). For a closely reasoned account of Communist idolatry, see John C. Bennett, *Christianity and Communism* (New York: Association Press, 1948).

For in the biblical view of man's life in history, meaning can be affirmed with neither illusion nor despair. In terms of the biblical view, one does not give up history with its burdens and responsibilities, fleeing away to some mystical conception of salvation above history. On the other hand, one does not sentimentally invest some specific historical object or movement with absolute or divine significance. Seen from the biblical perspective, the life of modern man has been an alternation between illusion and despair, between sentimentality and cynicism. The life which emerges from the service of the living God of the biblical tradition avoids both of these errors. God as Creator endows history with meaning; as Judge he destroys all false idolatries of specific historical processes and institutions; as Redeemer he saves history from chaos and men from despair.

The conception of history has a further significance for the understanding of religion. Reference has been made to revelation, both Judaism and Christianity often being classified as religions of revelation. In both of them there is the basic belief that God has spoken to man, communicating to him the meaning of life, which man in his own power and knowledge does not understand. In both the Jewish and Christian traditions, this has led some people to think of revelation as the divine communication of information, above and beyond rational knowledge. Thus has arisen the idea of a verbally inerrant scripture and divinely guaranteed dogma, which has created so much havoc in both Judaism and Christianity. This conception of revelation is the root-error of Fundamentalism and all unreflective orthodoxy.

However, current reflection on the biblical understanding of historical revelation has gone a long way toward correcting this mistake. In the Bible, revelation is not the miraculous communication of information, but rather a way of understanding and interpreting history, arising from the reflections of sensitive souls in their encounter with historical events. Revelation involves both event and response, the totality of the appreciative response determining its status as revelation.

Richard Niebuhr [11] has compared the understanding of history to the reading of a new and difficult book, many of whose sentences make little or no sense. Then the reader comes upon a sentence whose meaning is clear, and which in turn throws light on all the rest of the book. By analogy, revelation is an event whose meaning is clear, and which has the power of illuminating the whole course of history. Or, if history may be compared to a drama, revelation constitutes the climax of the drama. For Christianity, this climax is the coming of Christ. For Judaism it is the Exodus and the Covenant, pointing to the still-future coming of the Messiah. For Communist faith, it is the life of Marx (or is it the Russian revolution?); for those who believe in modern progress-theories, the climax is the historical emergence of modern science and education. In each case, revelation and faith correspond to event and appreciation. Appreciative understanding of revealing events constitutes the primary mode of revelation. After men have lived through the events, interpreting them and proclaiming their interpretation, they or other men write a record of the events. It is such a record one finds in the Jewish and Christian Bibles, which thus are not themselves revelation strictly speaking, but rather are human records of revelation. So considered, one may appreciate the unique value of the Bible for Judaism and Christianity, without falling into the pit of Fundamentalism.

What Is the Relation of Religion to Ethics?

In the course of this book much has been said about the relation of religion to ethics. In the first chapter it was noted that ethics (construed in the broad sense as rules of human action in society) is a fundamental component of religion, along with myth and rite. This judgment has been confirmed by the historical evidence presented in subsequent sections. The ways of faith all seem to include ethics as one of their essential elements. And conversely, most if not all the great systems of ethics have been parts or aspects of a religion.

[11] Richard Niebuhr, *The Meaning of Revelation* (New York: The Macmillan Co., 1952), chap. ii.

This statement is often questioned or rejected by students of religion and culture, who argue that religion and ethics vary independently of each other. Such a conclusion usually derives from an awareness of the very great amount of variety in the ethical and religious customs of different cultures, and especially of the differences between other cultures and one's own. Thus the judgment often comes to mean simply that other cultures construe ethics and the relation of ethics to religion in ways which are different from one's own ways. But seen from within by a member of a given culture rather than from the outside, there is an always significant tie between the religious quest for ultimate meaning and the basic rules for human action in any society.

It is significant in this connection to think back over the ways of faith examined in this book and to ask if there are any norms of action common to all of them. Amid the unquestioned variety and diversity, are there any ethical rules which are regarded as true everywhere and always? If the search is limited to specific patterns of action, the answer must clearly be "No." Customs and mores appear to vary infinitely. But if one looks inwardly to human attitudes rather than to acts, to character rather than to conduct, to morals or principles rather than to mores, some similarity is observable. The taproot of all ethics is respect for personality. This attitude is variously expressed in the Golden Rule of Jesus and the Jewish Torah, in the Silver Rule of Confucius, and in many of the highly moral passages of the *Baghavad-Gita*, the *Tao Te Ching*, and Buddha's teachings. In general terms it amounts to something like a universal human insight; in all times and places sensitive men have perceived the momentous truth that human life is a common, mutual life. But the perceptions of this truth are conditioned, limited, and sometimes distorted by historical and cultural circumstances. For example, in most primitive societies only personality within the tribal group is respected. For those outside one's group there are few if any rights. Even within the group, this basic moral attitude is hedged about and limited in innumerable ways. Often women are subordinated to men; slavery and class structures sometimes distort or destroy all sense of personal worth. In some cultures religion becomes so deeply involved in systems of custom that the moral judgments of sensitive men conflict with popular religion; at such times religion and ethics seem utterly opposed. But in any case, with or without institutional religious sanction, moral criticism operates to clear men's minds as to the essential meaning of respect for personality in human relations, and also to extend ever more widely the circle of its operation. Thus for instance in the course of time, slavery and infanticide have been seen to violate personality. And in the course of time the circle of moral obligation has widened until men of sensitive conscience may be troubled about the fate of persons anywhere in the world. But the driving force in all this development is the fundamental, moral sentiment of respect for personality.

This principle may be observed in some form, dimly or clearly, in most of the religions of mankind. But it must also be added that its clearest and most adequate expression is in the Hebrew-Christian rule of neighbor-love. The first explicit enunciation of this rule is in Lev. 19:18: "Thou shalt love thy neighbor as thyself. I am the Lord." It was this command, along with the *Shema* (Deut. 6:4, 5), which Jesus quoted when asked for the greatest commandment of the Torah (Matt. 22:34). It is this teaching which is expressed so clearly in such parables of Jesus as that of the Good Samaritan (Luke 10:25 ff.). The rule of neighbor-love may fairly be regarded as the best and clearest expression of the more general notion of righteousness which underlies all of Hebrew religion. Righteousness, or justice, conceived as an active affirmation of the rights of God-given personality, in direct obedience to the will of God, and employed as a criterion for the judgment of all aspects of life, is the underlying ethical ideal of biblical religion, whether Jewish or Christian.

This ideal has been formulated in many ways in the long course of Jewish and Christian history. It has been expressed in and combined with mores and customs of many different cultures. Throughout Western history it has served as a stimulant and quickener for men's thinking about their social relations.

Furthermore, it can be stated or formulated in relation to current moral theory in such a way that it will satisfy the elements of genuine truth in both moral absolutism and moral relativism. The former may be characterized as the belief that there are moral rules which are true everywhere and always; the latter denies this, maintaining that these rules vary according to society, temperament, and other factors. This argument may be given summary form in what might be termed a moral syllogism, followed by some explanatory comments.

1. I ought to love my neighbor as myself.
2. In the circumstances in which I stand, act x represents or constitutes neighbor-love.
3. Therefore, I ought to do act x.

The first or major premise is the attempt to formulate the truth in moral absolutism. It is a true statement wherever and whenever there are moral agents. Neighbor-love is, in other words, a valid and binding moral ideal for all men. The same norm or principle can be expressed somewhat more philosophically as follows: "I *ought* to respect personality." However, if the principle is expressed in this way it is important to keep in mind the tacit assumption that personality and interpersonal relations are here conceived in Hebrew-Christian terms. The clearest philosophic expression of this truth in Western philosophy is Kant's categorical imperative:

> Act so as to use humanity, whether in your own person or in the person of another, always as an end, never as merely a means.[12]

But whether we take Kant's formulation, or that of Jesus, or of Leviticus, the religious background of the fundamental moral premise is plain enough. Furthermore, the form "I

[12] Quoted in B. Rand, *Classical Moralists* (New York: Houghton Mifflin Co., 1937), p. 555.

ought" in the major premise is an expression of the absolute
claim of duty; it is similar to the absolute "Thou shalt" of the
Ten Commandments. Duty is a religious concept; to be
obligated or responsible means to be obligated or responsible
to someone. To the religious person, this someone is God.

The absoluteness and universality of the major premise
however are purchased at the price of subjectivity. This
premise has to do properly not with any specific act but with
an attitude, not with conduct but with character. The call
of conscience is not so much to any specific pattern of behavior as to conscientiousness in all of one's dealings. The
genuine inwardness of this attitude is one of the great contributions of the Hebrew-Christian tradition to Western man.
Furthermore it is here, at this point of inner attitude, that the
link between ethics and religion takes place; it is here, in man's
heart, that ultimate meaning is effectively related to the
sources of action.

But the inward attitude must receive factual, objective
content from the second premise. In a sense, the relation between the first and second premises is the same as that between any general or universal concept and its concrete instances. The general concept in this case is neighbor-love,
and what the individual moral agent must find are the concrete applications of this concept in his experience. The second premise has the logical form of a factual or empirical
proposition; and it is therefore at best a probable truth. It
is an attempt to state the truth in moral relativism, for it seems
unquestionably true that anyone's perception of general concepts varies with all the innumerable circumstances in which
individual men stand. Geographical, political, economic, tem-
peramental, and many other factors color one's perception of
general truth. The content of duty is not the same for a
Jew of the eighth century B.C. as for an American of the
twentieth century A.D.; for a young man as for an old man;
for an industrial worker as for a farmer, a business man, or
a college professor. It is the virtue of relativistic moral philosophies to grasp and understand such facts as these. Moreover, not only do perceptions of duty vary with changing

circumstances; duties may actually be widely different in different historical and cultural situations. Respect for personality, or neighbor-love, may lead to very different types of action in different social and historical situations. There is no easy solution to the problems which these facts present to moral thinking; there is no way by which the human mind can achieve absolute certainty in areas embodied in the second premise of the moral syllogism. Rather each person, standing under the absolute ideal, and being guided, but not dominated, by tradition, must apply it as wisely as he can to his own life and society. Commitment to the absolute duty of love is also commitment to intelligence in its concrete expression.

Concerning the conclusion of the syllogism, one notes that it has the form "I ought," which it receives from the first premise, this form of "oughtness" or obligation being the distinguishing trait of moral reasoning and experience. However, since the second proposition is logically probable and not certain, the conclusion is likewise probable and not certain. What this means is that moral conclusions are always something of a venture or a gamble. No one knows them to be true with the certainty of mathematics. Rather the moral life is in effect a "betting of one's life" on certain fundamental values amid ever-changing circumstances. In this wager there are both absolute and relative factors, but rightly understood they do not conflict with each other.

Recent religious thought has emphasized a further contribution of the Hebrew-Christian tradition to moral reasoning. Biblical faith in both its Jewish and its Christian forms has included the affirmation of a righteousness of God which forever escapes precise embodiment in specific historical mores and institutions, and keeps all mores and institutions under the judgment of God. From such a viewpoint, some forms of moral absolutism are seen as an expression of man's arrogant tendency to self-deification. It is just as wrong to worship one's own moral code as it is to worship any other idol. On the other hand, to hold one's morality under God induces humility and tolerance. Such a religious perspective tempers

justice with mercy and moral passion with humility and tolerance. The prophetic warning "You are man and not God,"
is thus a resource for checking the human egotism which often
finds expression in the moral behavior of the good man.

Are the Historic Institutions and Symbols of Religion Out-moded?

The current revival of religion and religious thought has
emphasized the concrete, particular character of religion. Religion lives in specific groups or communities and in their
historic traditions. No man is religious in general; he is
Catholic, Protestant, Jewish, Buddhist, Humanist, or something else. But this "scandal of particularity," as it has been
called, raises questions for any philosophically-minded student
of religion, because philosophical reason deals with general or
universal things. How then can the philosophically minded
person consciously or deliberately involve himself in the par-
ticularities of this or that religion? Must he not rather maintain an attitude of aloof and lofty detachment? Do not particular creeds and commitments, with their frequent claims
to exclusive and absolute truth, ill befit the life of reason?

In the opinion of many thoughtful observers there is a solution to these vexing problems—a solution which lies at the
growing-point of contemporary religious thought. Within
present limits of space, it is possible only to indicate a few
lines of thought which may be fruitful leads for further reflection on this theme.

Such current tendencies in philosophic thought as Existentialism and Logical Positivism, while including unsatisfactory
aspects, have provided contemporaries with valuable insights,
as well as with many highly specialized tools of analysis. This
book has shown indebtedness to Existentialism by its formulation of religion as an answer to man's agelong and persistent
question "what is the meaning of existence?" Now the existence alluded to in the term "Existentialism" is the actual,
concrete existence of human individuals. Existentialism has
put the question "what does it mean to be or to exist as a
human self?" Approached from such a vantage point man is

seen to be more than simply a rational animal; he is a creature of feeling, volition, and history. This basic aspect of Existentialist thought may be clarified by a figure of speech: men in actual existence do not sit in the grandstands of speculative thought but rather stand on the playing field of active historic life. Men are not, in actual experience, spectators of the game of life; they are participants. The reader will correctly perceive here another formulation of the distinction repeatedly made in the course of this chapter and throughout the book—the distinction between theoretical and practical reason, between theory and action, between reason and faith. The point which may now be made is that *religions are attempts to state at first hand, from the viewpoint of the playing-field rather than the grandstand, the meaning of existence as it is lived out by actual, existing men and communities at specific times.*

Thus, what a religion says in effect is this: "Standing here, from this vantage point, this is what existence means to us; this is what we believe life is all about." The hearer is invited to stand with the speaker and see if, standing thus, life makes sense to him. A religious community is thus a community drawn together by a common meaning of existence; and a tradition is simply a channel through which such a meaning is transmitted from one generation to the next. The language which expresses this meaning is what previous generations of religious people called witness or testimony. Current religious thought has employed the term "confession" in this connection, meaning by it a first-hand statement of the meaning of existence as that meaning is perceived from the viewpoint of the playing-field. Specific historical religions may thus be studied most fruitfully as existential confessions.

The confessional attitude, so conceived, is to be sharply contrasted with what may be called the dogmatic attitude. To be sure, the term "dogma" has meant many things, its original meaning being simply "that which is thought or decreed." But to many contemporary people it carries the connotation of arbitrary or arrogant belief. To return to the metaphor of the previous paragraph, the dogmatist takes his position in the grandstand and asserts with absolute finality "This is the way things are." The confessionalist, on the other hand, takes his stand on the playing-field, saying rather "From where I stand, this is what things mean to me. In these terms I will play out the game of life. Come and see for yourself." A crucial difference emerges in the respective attitudes toward other, differing beliefs. The dogmatist asserts in complete and intolerant finality the absolute truth of his position and the falsehood of other, differing positions. The confessionalist, while finding his views absolutely authoritative for his own life, is seriously interested in hearing the views of others, in comparing confessions with those who disagree with him. He is concerned with what Karl Jaspers [13] has called "boundless communication" with those whose existential confessions differ from his own.

But to call religions existential confessions is to imply a significant conception of religious language. Current work in the philosophy of language has not yet taken sufficient account of the problems and issues of religious language and symbolism. Among contemporary workers in this field, the Logical Positivists have insisted upon a basic distinction between empirical or scientific propositions, on the one hand, and emotive or poetic propositions on the other—between what is often termed "communication," and what is called "expression." According to some Logical Positivists, scientific or empirical propositions are identified by the fact that they can be publicly verified by any normal human observer. "This patch of color is blue" will serve as an example of such propositions. Emotive statements, while they have the grammatical form of empirical propositions, are not susceptible to such verification. "I like ice cream," "This picture is beautiful," or "This act is good" would be examples of emotive propositions. They are inherently unverifiable because they are the expressions not of outward fact but of inward, subjective attitude. This distinction is variously developed by various positivists, and sometimes it is taken to absurd and

[13] Karl Jaspers, *The Perennial Scope of Philosophy* (New York: Philosophical Library, Inc., 1949), chap. ii.

self-contradictory extremes. At times the Logical Positivists seem to say out of one side of their mouths that metaphysics is impossible double-talk, and out of the other side to assert their own views as valid metaphysics. Nevertheless, their distinction between empirical or scientific meaning and emotive meaning is highly useful for the understanding of religion. One can accept this distinction on the simple but extremely important condition that emotive meaning must be taken seriously. Perhaps a meeting of extremes in contemporary thought may be effected when emotive meaning is taken existentially.

When this is done, religious language and symbolism will be seen to express emotive meaning. Religious language is in fact more like poetry than like the prose of science. Religious communication is frequently the communication through imaginative poetry of that which is of ultimate significance. By "ultimate" is meant here, as throughout this study, the final frame of significance for human life. In the description of such factors, a radically metaphorical dimension is necessarily added to human language, for words created and used within the body of men's experience are here employed to point to the boundaries of experience. It is for this reason that the language of metaphysics, and even more the language of theology, always borders on myth and poetry. While some poetry aims at pure enjoyment, much poetry is a serious attempt to characterize ultimate aspects of the human situation. As such it has religious significance.

In this connection the importance of the religious use of nonverbal symbols must also be indicated. Religions communicate through such symbols as the Cross, the Star of David, the Rising Sun, and innumerable other such objects. They also communicate through what may be called symbolic behavior, such as ceremonial ablutions, eating, bowing, dancing, and innumerable other acts. The purely verbal symbols by which religions are communicated are thus surrounded and supported by other, nonverbal symbols. This fact points at once to the unity of personality in all its many facets, and to the vast importance in human existence of the deeper emotive levels of life which are expressed in such nonverbal symbols. Cult and myth are thus expressions of man's perennial need for nonverbal as well as verbal symbols for the expression of ultimate meaning.

The life of a religion, then, clusters around just such a set of vivid and compelling symbols, which express ultimate meaning as apprehended by a specific faith. Much is written today concerning the present state of these traditional religious symbols. Some writers argue that the old symbols and the language they imply are empty and dead, and that therefore mankind must now wait for the emergence of a new set of symbols for the expression of ultimate meaning. It must wait for a new faith. Others argue that, despite time and change, the old words and symbols of traditional ways still have power and truth. They therefore believe that new directions may yet come from the old ways, and that the future of religion lies with those who work from within the historic traditions to make the old institutions and symbols vividly relevant to the post-modern world. The weight of evidence from the history and philosophy of the world's major faiths seems definitely to support the latter view.

SUGGESTIONS FOR FURTHER READING

For general reference books on religion, see the list following Chapter 1.

AYER, ALFRED J. *Language Truth and Logic.* New York: Oxford University Press, 1936.

BAILLIE, JOHN. *Our Knowledge of God.* New York: Chas. Scribner's Sons, 1939.

————. *The Belief in Progress.* New York: Chas. Scribner's Sons, 1951.

BARTH, KARL. *Credo.* London: Hodder & Stoughton, Ltd., 1937.

————. *Dogmatics in Outline.* New York: Philosophical Library, Inc., 1949.

BENNETT, JOHN C. *Christianity and Communism.* New York: Association Press, 1948.

BERDYAEV, NICHOLAS. *Freedom and the Spirit.* London: Centenary Press, 1935.

BRUNNER, H. EMIL. *The Divine Human Encounter.* Philadelphia: Westminster Press, 1943.

————. *Revelation and Reason.* Philadelphia: Westminster Press, 1946.

BUBER, MARTIN. *I and Thou.* Edinburgh: T. &. T. Clark, 1942.

BUBER, MARTIN. *Between Man and Man*. London: Kegan Paul, Trench, Trubner & Co., 1947.

BUTTERFIELD, HERBERT. *Christianity and History*. New York: Chas. Scribner's Sons, 1950.

CASSERLEY, J. V. LANGMEAD. *The Christian in Philosophy*. London: Faber & Faber, Ltd., 1949.

CASSIRER, ERNST. *An Essay on Man*. New Haven: Yale University Press, 1944.

COLLINGWOOD, ROBIN G. *An Essay on Philosophic Method*. New York: Oxford University Press, 1933.

CROSSMAN, ROBERT H. S. (ed.). *The God that Failed*. New York: Harper & Bros., 1949.

EMMET, DOROTHY. *The Nature of Metaphysical Thinking*. New York: The Macmillan Co., 1945.

FARRER, AUSTIN. *Finite and Infinite*. London: The Dacre Press, 1943.

FRANK, ERICH. *Philosophical Understanding and Religious Truth*. New York: Oxford University Press, 1945.

HAZELTON, ROGER. *Renewing the Mind*. New York: The Macmillan Co., 1949.

HERBERG, WILL. *Judaism and Modern Man*. New York: Farrar, Strauss & Young, 1951.

JASPERS, KARL. *The Perennial Scope of Philosophy*. New York: Philosophical Library, Inc., 1949.

MARITAIN, JACQUES. *True Humanism*. London: Oxford University Press, 1938.

MURPHY, ARTHUR. *The Uses of Reason*. New York: The Macmillan Co., 1943.

NIEBUHR, H. RICHARD. *The Meaning of Revelation*. New York: The Macmillan Co., 1941.

NIEBUHR, REINHOLD. *The Nature and Destiny of Man*. New York: Chas. Scribner's Sons, 1941-1943.

———. *Faith and History*. New York: Chas. Scribner's Sons, 1949.

RICHARDSON, ALAN. *Christian Apologetics*. New York: Harper & Bros., 1947.

TEMPLE, WILLIAM. *Nature, Man, and God*. New York: Macmillan & Co., Ltd., 1935.

TENNANT, F. R. *Philosophical Theology*. Cambridge: Cambridge University Press, 1928-1930.

TILLICH, PAUL. *The Protestant Era*. Chicago: University of Chicago Press, 1948.

———. *Systematic Theology I*. Chicago: University of Chicago Press, 1951.

INDEX

Aaron, 162
Abelard, 281-82
Abraham, 158, 159-60, 205
Absalom, 167
Acts, Book of, 240-42
Adam and Eve, 158
Adler, Alfred
  theory of religion, 42
Adler, Felix, 453-54
Adonijah, 167
Agassiz, Louis, 429
Agni, Hindu god, 109-10
Agnosticism, 426 ff.
  and faith, 408 ff.
  Hume's, 402 ff.
Ahab, 168
Ahimsa
  in Buddhism, 133
  in Hinduism, 97-99
Ai, battle of, 164
Aijalon, battle of, 164
Akiba, Rabbi, 199
Albertus Magnus, 285
Albigensian Cathari, 366
Al Ghazzali, 206
Alexander the Great, 192
Alexander, Samuel, 427, 477
Alexandria, 199, 254-55
Ali, 206
Allah, 205
Amaziah, 171-73
Ambrose, Bishop of Milan, 265, 272
Amida Buddha, 151 ff.
Ammonites, 159, 166-67
Amnon, 167
Amos, 171-73
Anabaptists, 367
Analogy, principle of
  in Aquinas, 295
  Hume's critique, 406-7
Anan ben David, 207

Ananias, 243
Anglican church, 361 ff.
  Anglo-Catholicism, 364
  Oxford Revival, 364
  Reformation, 361-62
  Thirty-nine Articles, 363
Animism, 24-26, 71, 146
Anselm, 278-81, 467
  faith and reason, 278-79
  ontological argument, 279-81
Anthony, St., 315
Anthropology, 17-30
  nature of, 17-18
  significance for religion, 29-30
Antioch, 246
Antiochus IV, 192, 195
Anti-Semitism
  contemporary, 218-19
  medieval, 212
  Moslem, 206
Apocalypse, 186, 191-92
Apollinarius, 260
Apologists, 253
Apostles' Creed, 257
Aquinas, Thomas
  concepts of revelation, 300-4
  contemporary revival of, 471
  doctrine of man, 296-99
    freedom, 297
    cardinal virtues, 297-98
    immortality, 298-99
  life, 285-86
  nature of God in, 294-96
  proofs of the existence of God,
    287-93
    from causality, 290
    from contingency, 290
    from degrees of perfection, 291
    Hume's critique, 405 ff.
    from moral law, 293
    from motion, 288

499